A Commentary

ON

Acts of the Apostles

BY

H. Leo Boles

Author of

"*Unfulfilled Prophecy*," "*Is Instrumental Music in Christian Worship*
Scriptural?" "*Biographical Sketches of Gospel Preachers*,"
"*Commentary on the Gospel According to Matthew*,"
"*Commentary on the Gospel According*
to Luke," *etc.*

GOSPEL ADVOCATE COMPANY
NASHVILLE, TENN.
1987

Complete Set ISBN 0-89225-000-3
This Volume ISBN 0-89225-005-4

PREFACE

The book of Acts occupies a very unique and important position in the divine plan of man's redemption. The first four books of the New Testament—Matthew, Mark, Luke, and John—give the miraculous conception, birth, life, teachings, miracles, betrayal, trial, crucifixion, burial, resurrection, and ascension of Christ. In these the final and world-wide commission of Christ is recorded: "Go ye into all the world, and preach the gospel to the whole creation." In the Acts we have a record of the execution of this commission and the establishment and growth of the church; the terms of admission into the church are recorded in the many cases of conversion. The question, "What must I do to be saved?" is frequently asked and clearly answered. The Acts records the answer as given by inspired men. This makes the Acts a very important book.

J. W. McGarvey wrote a commentary on Acts, published in 1863. Twenty-nine years later, 1892, this commentary was revised and enlarged. In 1896, David Lipscomb wrote the comments on the Uniform Sunday School Lesson for 1897, which were taken from the book of Acts and epistles. He later modified and enlarged upon his comments and put them in a volume, "Commentary on Acts of the Apostles." It was not his original purpose or plan to put them in the permanent form of a "commentary." However the book has proved to be helpful for nearly fifty years. It has been thought that now is an opportune time to publish another commentary on the Acts.

Many questions of great theological import arise in the study of Acts; the ablest and most conscientious commentators have differed and always will differ on them. It has been the aim of the author of this commentary to handle these questions in the light of divine truth without being dogmatic; he has attempted to leave the reader or student free to exercise unfettered and unbiased judgment on these controverted points and passages; he has not attempted to interfere with the liberty of conscience, but has earnestly and prayerfully sought to set forth the mind of the Holy Spirit on all of these passages of scripture. More than two years of special study and thought have been given to the preparation of this volume. In many instances the Greek word has been given, but always with an English spelling so that one with the aid of a Greek lexicon can study and make such research as he may desire. However, in the main, the ordinary English reader can understand the thoughts that are expressed. The author has kept in mind the average church member and has written in a clear and simple way, constantly keeping before him those students of the Bible who only have an ordinary degree of education. This commentary is intended to help all come to a fuller knowledge of the truth of God.

The author is indebted to many writers and commentators. The use of quotation marks has been omitted, but due recognition is made in the bibliography at the close of the volume. The introduction will be found helpful in understanding some things which are essential to a thorough knowledge of the contents of the book. The outline, chronological table, and index will aid the student.

H. LEO BOLES.

April 1, 1940.

OUTLINE OF THE ACTS

PART ONE

HISTORY OF THE CHURCH: PETER AS THE CHIEF ACTOR

SECTION ONE
INSTRUCTION TO APOSTLES; ASCENSION OF
CHRIST; DESCENT OF HOLY SPIRIT
1:1 to 2:13

SECTION TWO
THE CHURCH AT JERUSALEM
2:14 to 6:7

SECTION THREE
GOSPEL PREACHED IN JUDEA AND SAMARIA
6:8 to 8:25

SECTION FOUR
CONVERSION OF THE EUNUCH, SAUL, AND
CORNELIUS
8:26 to 12:25

PART TWO

HISTORY OF THE CHURCH: PAUL AS THE CHIEF ACTOR

SECTION ONE
PAUL'S FIRST MISSIONARY JOURNEY
13:1 to 14:28

SECTION TWO
DISPUTE ABOUT CIRCUMCISION SETTLED
15:1-35

SECTION THREE
PAUL'S SECOND MISSIONARY JOURNEY
15:36 to 18:22

SECTION FOUR
PAUL'S THIRD MISSIONARY JOURNEY
18 : 23 to 21 : 16

SECTION FIVE
PAUL AT JERUSALEM
21 : 17 to 23 : 35

SECTION SIX
PAUL AT CAESAREA
24 : 1 to 26 : 32

SECTION SEVEN
PAUL'S VOYAGE TO ROME
27 : 1 to 28 : 10

SECTION EIGHT
PAUL AT ROME
28 : 11-31

CONTENTS

PART TWO

History of the Church: Paul as the Chief Actor

Section One

Paul's First Missionary Journey (13: 1 to 14: 28)

Section Two

Dispute About Circumcision Settled (15: 1-35.)

CONTENTS 9

INTRODUCTION

Biblical history consists of two great parts—the Old Testament and the New Testament. The New Testament is also divided into two divisions—the life of Christ from his birth to his ascension, and the apostolic history from the ascension to the close of the New Testament. The apostolic history may again be subdivided into two parts—a connected narrative extending from the ascension of Christ to the second year of Paul's captivity at Rome, and a group of detached and incidental statements scattered through the other books of the New Testament. The first part of this subdivision is designated as the Acts.

I. THE AUTHOR

It is generally conceded that Luke is the author of this book; it is his second volume of the great library. The Gospel according to Luke was the first volume and the Acts is a continuation of his narrative of events connected with the Christ and his work in the redemption of man. Luke identifies himself with the first words of this book; he addresses the same person and makes reference to his "former treatise" (Acts 1: 1) in such a way as to identify himself as its author. The connection and unity of the Acts with the Gospel according to Luke emphasizes the authorship of the Acts. He was a companion of Paul; the "we" sections prove Luke to be both a companion of Paul and the author of the Acts. (Acts 16: 10-17; 20: 6-16; 21; 27; 28.) These sections are full of details and very vivid in description; they are conclusive evidence that the writer was an eyewitness of what is recorded. The same style of writing appears in both the Gospel according to Luke and the Acts; there is also the same interest in medical matters by using the same terms which were familiar to physicians at that time.

Finally, the testimony of the early Christian fathers to Luke as the author is unanimous and conclusive. Irenaeus, who lived about A.D. 178, himself intimate with some associates of the apostles, knew the book of Acts and regarded it as the work of Luke; Clement of Alexandria, who lived about A.D. 190, regarded Luke as its author; Tertullian, who lived about A.D. 200, bore accumulated evidence to this fact; Eusebius, who lived about A.D. 325, says, "Luke, a native of Antioch, by profession a physician, was mostly Paul's companion, though he associated not a little with the apostles. He has left us examples of the art of healing souls, which he acquired from the apostles, in two divinely inspired books; first in the gospel, which he testifies to have written according to what eyewitnesses and ministers of the word delivered to him from the beginning, all of which also he says that he investigated from the first; and secondly, in the Acts of the Apostles, which he composed not from report, as in the other case, but according to his own personal observation."

II. THE TITLE

It is very probable that Luke gave no title to this volume of his contribution to the New Testament. We do not have his manuscript, and the manuscripts that we do have give the title in various forms. In some of the important manuscripts of the New Testament, the title is not "The Acts of the Apostles," but "Acts of Apostles," and in one very important manuscript, the Sinaitic, the book is simply called "Acts"; this was written in the fourth century, and has at the beginning the title, "Acts," or strictly "Doings," but at its close reads "Acts of Apostles." The Vatican manuscript, also written in the fourth century, has at the beginning of the work, "Acts of Apostles," but in its margins calls it only "Acts." The Alexandrian manuscript, of the fourth or fifth century, and several smaller and later manuscripts give the title, "Acts of the Holy Apostles." The modern critical Greek editions of the New Testament by Lachmann, Alford, and Westcott and Hort give the title "Acts of the Apostles"; but Tischendorf follows the Sinaitic manuscript and reads simply "Acts." The Revised Greek Testament, however, gives "Acts of the Holy Apostles."

Nearly all of the English versions, from Tyndale's to the Revised Version of 1881, give the title as "The Acts of the Apostles." This title is too broad for the contents of the book, since they chiefly relate to the "acts" or teaching and work of Peter and Paul, and not "the acts" of all the apostles. The book records *some* of the acts of *some* of the apostles, but it is not the works of "The Acts of the Apostles." It contains no detailed account of the work of any of the apostles except Peter and Paul; John is mentioned on three occasions, but he appears rather as the companion of Peter than as the doer of any special act by himself. We have no notice of James the son of Zebedee except of his execution by Herod; more space is devoted to Stephen and Philip, who were not apostles, than to James; more space is given to Timothy and Silas than to some of the apostles.

It is very likely that the book was called simply "Acts," and for some time this designation was sufficient to distinguish it from other books. But after some time, before this book came into circulation, other books were written by uninspired writers with such titles as "The Acts of Peter and Paul," "The Acts of Timothy," "The Acts of Barnabas," and several others of like title; hence, it became necessary, as such literature increased and was circulated, to enlarge the title of this original volume of "Acts," and from such exigency we find in various manuscripts different titles given to it, such as "Acts of the Apostles," "Acting of Apostles," "Acts of All the Apostles," "Acts of the Holy Apostles," with still longer additions in manuscripts of later date.

III. THE DATE

The date of the writing of the Acts is uncertain. The common opinion is that the book was written between the years A.D. 64 and A.D. 70. Some have extended the time as late as A.D. 80; the majority of modern critics place it between A.D. 70 and A.D. 80. This date rests mainly on the idea that the Gospel according to Luke was written after the destruction of Jerusalem in A.D. 70. It is claimed that Luke 21: 10 shows that this tragedy had already occurred, as compared with Mark 13: 14 and Matt. 24: 15. Attention is called to the absence of the warning in the Gospel according to Luke. However, some have placed the date before A.D. 70; this date is supported by some modern critics who claim that there are "very weighty" arguments in favor of the early date. It seems reasonable that the author continued his history fully up to the time when he wrote, so that the last recorded event may be assumed to give approximately at least the time of his writing. On this assumption, the date would be two years after Paul's first imprisonment at Rome (Acts 28: 30), which may be assumed to be the date that Paul was released from prison. This line of argument would fix the date at about A.D. 63.

It seems evident that Luke wrote the Acts before A.D. 70. He mentions Felix, Festus, and Agrippa in exact harmony with what we learn of their history and character from other sources. The mention of the speech of Tertullus before Felix, both by what it says and what it omits, is evidence that we are dealing with the writings of one who lived through the events of which he has given us the history. The frequent notices given of Jerusalem furnish evidence of the date of the writing. Jerusalem was destroyed by the Romans in A.D. 70, and yet in the entire book of Acts there is not a single word to indicate that the author of this book knew anything of that event or even of the causes which brought about its destruction. Jerusalem is always mentioned as still in its grandeur; the temple service and sacrifices continued to be observed; at the great feasts crowds of strangers assembled as the law enjoined, and among its population the scribes and Pharisees and Sadducees act the same parts which they do in the history found in the Gospel according to Luke. Hence, we conclude that it was written and completed very soon after A.D. 63, and not later than A.D. 66.

Paul was brought a prisoner to Rome in the year A.D. 61 or A.D. 62, and was kept in prison at least two years. In the year A.D. 64 occurred the great fire at Rome, kindled by the emperor, Nero, who, in order to avert suspicion from himself, placed the blame on the Christians, and began the persecution of Christians. If Paul was set at liberty after his imprisonment of two years, he must have come out of prison in the end of A.D. 63, or in the beginning of A.D. 64. If he was kept in prison, he probably was one of the first to be executed. In any case Paul was liberated or put to death about A.D. 64, and the manner in which Luke speaks of that imprisonment seems to imply that at the time in which he wrote the apostle's condition had changed. Again we conclude that the book was written about the end of Paul's captivity at Rome, or about A.D. 63 or 64.

IV. THE HISTORICAL VALUE

Every book in the New Testament has its place, or else it would not have been written. The Acts has a very important place in the New Testament. Jesus had given his commission to his apostles to "go ye into all the world, and preach the gospel to the whole creation." (Mark 16: 15.) Luke had said "that repentance and remission of sins should be preached in his name unto all the nations, beginning from Jerusalem." (Luke 24: 47.) The historical record of the redemption of man would be incomplete without the history of the apostles laboring under this commission. This book gives a record of some of the apostles in their obedience to the commission. It is in this book that we have the all-important question, *"What must I do to be saved?"* and the answer given by inspired men. It is in this book that we learn the terms of salvation; this makes it an important book. There is no other book in the New Testament where this question, *"What must I do to be saved?"* is asked and answered.

The Acts gives a history of the first thirty years of the church; this was the story of the first generation of Christians. It begins with Pentecost in A.D. 33, and ends with the close of Paul's imprisonment in Rome in A.D. 63 or 64. During this period Rome was ruled by the successors of Octavius; the rule of Octavius had scarcely ended before the imperial throne began to be the prize of the most successful soldier. Palestine was subjected to many changes. Herod Agrippa I was slowly gaining the rule over all Palestine; the first twelve chapters of the Acts narrate the first twelve years of the history of the church. Tiberius, Caligula, and Claudius were emperors in Rome. It is necessary to keep these events in mind in reading the first part of the Acts.

All believers in the Bible regard the Acts as a genuinely historical work and accurate in its details; it is a trustworthy history, and judged from almost every possible standpoint of historical criticism it is a solid, respectable, and in many respects an extraordinary work. It fills a unique place in the scheme of redemption; the Holy Spirit gave this book to us; hence, we need to give it a place in our thoughts.

V. CHRONOLOGY

There is always an element of uncertainty in chronological events of the Bible. This is especially true when the Bible does not give the dates of the events. No one should be dogmatic in fixing the time or chronology of events in the Bible. The dates of certain events recorded in the Acts are fixed by contemporary historians. For example, the death of Agrippa II at Caesarea, as mentioned in Acts 12: 23, occurred, according to Josephus, in A.D. 44. Another instance is the recall of Felix, the Roman governor, which occurred, according to Josephus, in A.D. 60 or 61. From these two dates as starting points, the chronology of Acts can be approximately constructed, but there is no certainty about

the dates of many of the events narrated by Luke. The following
table will be helpful to the student of the Acts:

CHRONOLOGY OF EVENTS

A.D.	Events	Roman Emperors
33	The Day of Pentecost (Acts 2)	Tiberius, A.D. 14-37
36	Martyrdom of Stephen (Acts 7)	
37	Conversion of Paul (Acts 9)	
	Conversion of Cornelius (Acts 10, 11)	Caligula, A.D. 37-41
44	Martyrdom of James (Acts 12: 2)	
44-49	Paul's first missionary journey as far as Lystra and Derbe, returning to Antioch (Acts 13, 14)	Claudius, A.D. 41-54
50 or 51	Apostolic council in Jerusalem (Acts 15)	
51-53	Paul's second missionary journey through Asia Minor and Greece (Acts 15: 40 to 18: 22)	
54-57	Paul's third missionary journey, including three years at Ephesus (Acts 18: 23 to 21: 17)	Nero, A.D. 54-68
57	Paul's last visit to Jerusalem	
53-60	Paul's captivity in Caesarea	
61	Paul's voyage to Rome	
61-63	Paul's captivity in Rome	

COMMENTARY ON THE ACTS

PART ONE

HISTORY OF THE CHURCH: PETER AS THE CHIEF ACTOR

SECTION ONE
INSTRUCTION TO THE APOSTLES; ASCENSION OF CHRIST; DESCENT OF THE HOLY SPIRIT
1:1 to 2:13

1. THE FORTY DAYS
1:1-5

1 The [1]former treatise I made, O Theophilus, concerning all that Jesus began both to do and to teach, 2 until the day in which he was received up,

[1]Gr. *first*

---

1 **The former treatise I made, O Theophilus,**—The "former treatise" is the first treatise that Luke wrote; this was the Gospel according to Luke. Here is a continuation of the subject matter with which Luke closed his first volume. This is volume two of his writings. "Theophilus" is addressed in the Gospel according to Luke as "most excellent Theophilus." It is not known who he was; some think that he was a man of honorable estate, and that Luke addressed both of his books to him; others think that as "Theophilus" means "friend of God," or "lover of God," Luke is writing to all who love God; that he adopted this name to indicate any believer in Christ. However, this is improbable. "Theophilus" is a Greek name probably applied to some Roman citizen.

concerning all that Jesus began both to do and to teach,—This gives the scope of Luke's first or "former treatise." He had "traced the course of all things accurately from the first" (Luke 1: 3), and wrote in detail about all that Jesus "began both to do and to teach." God and Christ begin, but there is no ending in their working; Jesus began working and teaching in the Gospel according to Luke, and he is still working through the Holy Spirit in his church. The works of Jesus and the teachings of him go together;

after that he had given commandment through the Holy Spirit unto the
apostles whom he had chosen: 3 to whom he also ²showed himself alive after

²Gr. *presented*

---

he lived his life and preached his doctrine; the entire earthly ministry is summed up by Luke in all "that Jesus began both to do
and to teach." It is significant that Luke here puts what Jesus did
before that which he taught; Jesus preached his own life. It was
lived before his disciples and then taught to them. This is the way
that Jesus placed it. "Whosoever therefore shall break one of
these least commandments, and shall teach men so, shall be called
least in the kingdom of heaven: but whosoever shall do and teach
them, he shall be called great in the kingdom of heaven." (Matt.
5: 19.)

2 **until the day in which he was received up,**—The ascension
of Jesus was the end of his earthly ministry; soon his heavenly
ministry would begin; hence, this finds a place both in the gospel
and in the Acts. The first two chapters of Luke record a brief account of the birth and childhood of Jesus, and then from the third
chapter to the end of his record Luke gives what Jesus did and
taught from his entrance on his public work to his ascension. The
ascension of Christ took place "after that he had given commandment through the Holy Spirit unto the apostles whom he had chosen." Jesus is represented in the Bible as acting by the special aid
of the Holy Spirit; hence, he is said (Acts 10: 38) to have been
anointed with the Holy Spirit, and (Luke 4: 1) to have been full
of the Holy Spirit. God gave the Spirit to Jesus not "by measure." (John 3: 34.) An account of his choosing the twelve
apostles is found in Matt. 10: 2-4; Mark 3: 13-19; Luke 6: 13-16.

3 **to whom he also showed himself alive**—After his resurrection Jesus remained on earth "by the space of forty days" before
he ascended. He made many appearances to his apostles during
this time; we have a record of some of these appearances in Matthew, Mark, Luke, and John. Jesus presented himself to them
under different circumstances in such a way that they could not
doubt that he had been raised from the dead. "By many proofs,"
he established the fact of his resurrection. The resurrection was
the evidence that Jesus' death was not mere martyrdom, but **trium-**

his passion by many proofs, appearing unto them by the space of forty days, and speaking the things concerning the kingdom of God: 4 and, ³being assembled together with them, he charged them not to depart from Jerusalem, but to wait for the promise of the Father, which, *said he,* he heard from me:

³Or, *eating with them*

---

phant atonement. The resurrection was to be the subject of the preaching of the apostles; hence, they were left without a doubt as to his resurrection. The King James Version uses the word "infallible," but the Revised Version omits it with the assumption that a proof implies certainty. "After his passion" means after his suffering and death. "Passion" is from the Greek "pathein," and is used absolutely of Christ's suffering. (Acts 17: 3; 26: 23.) During the forty days there are more than ten definite appearances mentioned; Jesus was not with them continually as he was before his death.

The ascension was ten days before Pentecost when the Holy Spirit came; Moses was in the mount at the giving of the law forty days (Ex. 24: 18), and Jesus fasted forty days (Matt. 4: 2) just after his baptism. We are given the subject that Jesus discussed while with his apostles; he spoke to them "the things concerning the kingdom of God." "The kingdom of God" appears thirty-three times in the Gospel according to Luke; fifteen times in Mark; four times in Matthew, who elsewhere has "the kingdom of heaven"; one time in John; and six times in the Acts. No distinction is to be made between "the kingdom of God" and "the kingdom of heaven."

4 **and, being assembled together with them, he charged them**—Among those things that Jesus taught his disciples during this period of forty days was "repentance and remission of sins should be preached in his name unto all the nations, beginning from Jerusalem: . . . but tarry ye in the city, until ye be clothed with power from on high." (Luke 24: 47-49.) The law was to go forth from Zion, and the word of God from Jerusalem. (Isa. 2: 3.) The apostles were all Galileans far from home and in danger (John 20: 19), but as Jesus had been denied the home comforts of Nazareth (Luke 4: 16), so his disciples were all to remain in Jerusalem until the Holy Spirit came. It is called "the promise of my Father." (Luke 24: 49; John 16: 16-27; 15: 26.) Jesus

5 for John indeed baptized with water; but ye shall be baptized ⁴in the Holy
Spirit not many days hence.

⁴Or, *with*

had also emphasized this promise. (Luke 12: 11, 12; John 14 to
16.)

5 **for John indeed baptized with water;**—John baptized "with
water," but Jesus promised that his apostles should "be baptized in
the Holy Spirit not many days hence." This baptism in the Holy
Spirit is *the* promise of the Father. It was a promise made in the
Old Testament which Peter quoted at Pentecost. Some of the
apostles, if not all, had been disciples of John, and had heard John
make the promise. (Matt. 3: 11; Mark 1: 8; Luke 3: 16; John
1: 26.) Some had heard of the new birth. (John 3: 3-5.) Now
they were to know what it really meant, as they already knew in
part. (John 20: 22.) It is called a "baptism" to indicate the
abundant and overwhelming outpouring of the Spirit which over-
whelmed the spirit of the apostles in the Holy Spirit. "Water"
was the element in which John baptized, and "the Holy Spirit"
was the element in which the apostles were to be baptized.

2. COMMISSION TO THE APOSTLES
1: 6-8

6 They therefore, when they were come together, asked him, saying,

6 **They therefore, when they were come together,**—At one
of the appearances of Jesus, during these forty days, probably his
last appearance before his ascension, while they were all together,
his apostles asked him: "Lord, dost thou at this time restore the
kingdom to Israel?" This shows that even after the resurrection
of Jesus his apostles did not understand the nature of his kingdom.
It was clear in their minds that he came to establish a kingdom, but
they were still laboring under the misconception that his kingdom
would be an earthly one. The word "restore" as used here is from
the Greek, "apokathistaneis," and as a double compound, it means
"to restore to its former state." The apostles asked him if he
would restore the political kingdom to the Jews as it was in the
days of David and other kings. Here is proof that the apostles

Lord, dost thou at this time restore the kingdom to Israel? 7 And he said unto them, It is not for you to know times or seasons, which the Father hath [5]set within his own authority. 8 But ye shall receive power, when the Holy

[5]Or, *appointed by*

needed "the promise of my Father" before they began to spread the message of the risen Christ; they could not preach the gospel of the kingdom until they understood the nature of the kingdom. The apostles still looked for a political kingdom, and needed the enlightenment of the Holy Spirit and the power of the Holy Spirit to proclaim the gospel.

7 **And he said unto them, It is not for you to know**—Jesus passed over for the moment the nature of the kingdom and spoke more definitely as to the point which they made emphatic "at this time." They had asked Jesus whether he would "at this time" restore the kingdom to Israel; so Jesus tells them that it was not for them now "to know times or seasons." He had repeatedly taught them the nature of his kingdom before he was crucified, but they had failed to comprehend his meaning; now during the forty days that he remained here after his resurrection and before his ascension, they asked him about the time of restoring the kingdom. "Times and seasons" was not for them to know now; they must wait until the Holy Spirit comes to guide them into a fuller knowledge of the truth and the nature of his kingdom. "The Father hath set within his own authority" the time when the kingdom would be established. Christ named neither the day nor the hour: he wanted his apostles to watch and pray, and wait: they were to wait in the school of the pious, but not many days. God had at his own disposal the time for the kingdom to begin its work. Jesus does not teach them at this time the time or the character of the great future events which the Father has reserved under his own control. This is true of the second coming of Christ (Mark 13: 32), where Jesus recognizes the Father's reservation of the question of time to himself exclusively.

8 **But ye shall receive power, when the Holy Spirit is come upon you:**—They should receive power, or strength; the power was from on high (Luke 24: 49), or it was the promise of the Father, which was the baptism of the Holy Spirit; they needed

Spirit is come upon you: and ye shall be my witnesses both in Jerusalem, and in all Judaea and Samaria, and unto the uttermost part of the earth. 9

this in order to do their work. They were not to have a profitless knowledge as they had asked for, but they were to have the power to bear witness for Jesus and convince people of the truth of his kingdom; they needed strength which was to come from a great promise. They needed the power and wisdom which their adversaries could neither gainsay nor resist; in this way they would be enabled to become Christ's witnesses. Their question was ample proof of their need of this new "power." "Power," as used here, comes from the Greek "dunamin," and is used frequently with reference to the Holy Spirit. All needed power to equip them for the work that they were to do would be furnished by the Holy Spirit; hence, it was by the Holy Spirit's agency that the apostles were to preach the gospel to the entire world.

and ye shall be my witnesses—Here Jesus gives a program of their missionary work. They are to begin in Jerusalem, and then advance to Judea, or the region round about Jerusalem; then they are to advance into Samaria, or the country beyond Judea, and continue in an ever-widening circle until they have reached "the uttermost part of the earth." The commission as here given to bear witness for Christ was to go beyond the limits of Palestine; even to the ends of the earth, they were to spread the gospel. The apostles were to go throughout the known world; wherever they could find, or make, an opportunity, they were to bear their testimony respecting Jesus. The providence of God would be with them, and the Holy Spirit would direct them, so that they could thus make the gospel known throughout the world. "Ye shall be my witnesses" throughout the world; the peculiar mission of the church is to preserve to the world the living memory of a risen Christ. Further sections of the book of Acts record how this was done.

3. ASCENSION OF JESUS
1: 9-11

And when he had said these things, as they were looking, he was taken up;

9 **And when he had said these things,**—While his words were yet in their ears (Luke 24: 51), and while their eyes were still

and a cloud received him out of their sight. 10 And while they were looking stedfastly into heaven as he went, behold, two men stood by them in white apparel; 11 who also said, Ye men of Galilee, why stand ye looking into

gazing on him, the ascension took place. They were to be witnesses of it, and they saw it plainly and could describe it vividly and accurately. Jesus was first raised from the earth in visible manner, and as he continued to rise higher and higher, their eyes followed him ascending; a cloud received him and surrounded and enclosed him and removed him out of their sight. Jesus had instructed them as their Prophet and Teacher; he had laid his command on them as their King; and now as their great High Priest he is to bless them as they bear witness for him throughout the world. Matthew and John (except indirectly in John 6: 62) do not mention the ascension. Mark and Luke very briefly record the fact. There is no display, no expletives or exclamations, in narrating this wonderful event; the fact is stated in a simple, direct, natural way that emphasizes its truthfulness. Jesus went up to Mount Olivet just before the ascension, though he could have ascended just as well from a plain or in a valley.

10 **And while they were looking stedfastly into heaven**—The astonished disciples continued looking up where Jesus had disappeared, as if hoping to see him again. Suddenly "two men stood by them in white apparel." The past perfect active indicative of "paristemi," an intransitive form, is used here, and means literally, "had taken a stand by them." The apostles did not see these two angels until they were standing beside them; they had human forms and white clothing. The angels at the tomb are described in a similar way. (Mark 16: 5; Luke 24: 4; John 20: 12.)

11 **who also said, Ye men of Galilee,**—The angels addressed the apostles as "men of Galilee"; they were all Galileans now; all the apostles except Judas Iscariot were Galileans, and five of them came from the village of Bethsaida. The angels asked: "Why stand ye looking into heaven?" There was work to be done for Jesus; they are to return to the city of Jerusalem and wait for the descent of the Holy Spirit. The angels further instruct them that "this Jesus, who was received up from you into heaven, shall so come in like manner as ye beheld him going into heaven." The angels connect the ascension with the second advent; the ascension of

heaven? this Jesus, who was received up from you into heaven, shall so come in like manner as ye beheld him going into heaven.

Jesus is thus made a promise of his second coming. No representative of Jesus will come the second time, for "this Jesus" that they saw disappear shall reappear. He is to come "in like manner" as he ascended. Jesus himself foretold (Matt. 26: 64) that he should hereafter come "on the clouds of heaven."

4. WAITING FOR THE PROMISE
1: 12-14

12 Then returned they unto Jerusalem from the mount called Olivet, which is nigh unto Jerusalem, a sabbath day's journey day off. 13 And when they were come in, they went up into the upper chamber, where they were abid-

---

12 **Then returned they unto Jerusalem**—The usual name in the Bible for this mountain is "mount of Olives," and is used eleven times in the New Testament. (Matt. 21: 1; Mark 13: 3; Luke 22: 39; John 8: 1.) "Olivet" is the Greek word here meaning "olive orchard" or "olive yard." This mountain was "nigh unto Jerusalem." The Mount of Olives is on the east of Jerusalem, and must be passed by those who go from Jerusalem to Bethany; hence, Luke's expression, "He led them out until they were over against Bethany." (Luke 24: 50.) No one knows the exact spot on the Mount of Olives from which Jesus ascended; it was "a sabbath day's journey off." Different parts of the Mount of Olives were, of course, more or less distant from Jerusalem. "A sabbath day's journey" was about two thousand yards, or about three-quarters of a mile from the city wall. Luke says here that the Mount of Olives was a Sabbath day's journey from Jerusalem, not that Jesus was precisely that distance when he ascended. Bethany was on one side of the Mount of Olives, at the foot of the mountain, on the east side, "about fifteen furlongs off" (John 11: 18), or nearly two miles from Jerusalem, and the ascension was "over against Bethany." (Luke 24: 50.)

13 **And when they were come in,**—When the apostles came into the city of Jerusalem from the ascension, "they went up into the upper chamber." Some claim that this "upper chamber" was the same room that was occupied by Jesus when he ate the pass-

ing; both Peter and John and ¹James and Andrew, Philip and Thomas, Bartholomew and Matthew, ¹James *the son* of Alphaeus, and Simon the Zealot, and Judas *the ²son* of ¹James. 14 These all with one accord continued steadfastly

¹Or, *Jacob*
²Or, brother.   See Jude 1

over, which is described both by Mark and Luke as a "large upper room." (Mark 14: 15; Luke 22: 12.) This was in a private house, as is indicated in Luke 22: 11; and not in the temple, as is indicated in Luke 24: 53. "The upper chamber" is a phrase which suggests a well-known place, and this is as definite as we can make it. In this room the eleven were abiding, not in the sense of dwelling, but of sojourning; they were waiting for the promise of the Father. Here we have a list of the apostles; this is the fourth record or list of these names found in the New Testament.

The four lists of the apostles in the New Testament are as follows:

	Matt. 10: 2-4	Mark 3: 16-19	Luke 6: 14-16	Acts 1: 13
1.	Peter	Peter	Peter	Peter
2.	Andrew	James	Andrew	John
3.	James	John	James	James
4.	John	Andrew	John	Andrew
5.	Philip	Philip	Philip	Philip
6.	Bartholomew	Bartholomew	Bartholomew	Thomas
7.	Thomas	Matthew	Matthew	Bartholomew
8.	Matthew	Thomas	Thomas	Matthew
9.	James of Alphaeus	James of Alphaeus	James of Alphaeus	James of Alphaeus
10.	Thaddaeus	Thaddaeus	Simon the Zealot	Simon the Zealot
11.	Simon the Zealot	Simon the Zealot	Judas of James	Judas of James
12.	Judas Iscariot	Judas Iscariot	Judas Iscariot	(Matthias)

The list of apostles is grouped by fours into three groups; Peter heads all the lists as leader; Philip heads the list of the second group in all four of the lists; and James of Alphaeus heads the list of the last group in all four of the lists. Luke varies his roll in his gospel and Acts; Andrew follows Peter in the gospel, and in Acts he is the fourth; while John is the fourth in the gospel and second in Acts. Luke changes the order in the second group, but the arrangement is the same in the third group. Peter, James, and John are the only apostles whose names are mentioned again in the Acts; they are mentioned here at the beginning of the history of the church. When the roll is called by Luke in Acts the name of Judas Iscariot is omitted.

in prayer, [3]with the women, and Mary the mother of Jesus, and with his brethren.

[3]Or, *with* certain *women*

14 **These all with one accord continued stedfastly in prayer,** —The disciple company consists of four separately mentioned classes of persons: (1) the eleven apostles; (2) certain devout women, including Mary the mother of Jesus; (3) the brethren of Jesus, James, Joses (Joseph), Simon, and Judas (Matt. 13: 55; Mark 6: 3); (4) the other disciples of Jesus. The Greek word for "one accord," "homothumadon," means more than being together in one outward society; it means concord or oneness of mind and of spirit. They were together "in one place" because they had one purpose, and were of oneness of soul. They "continued stedfastly in prayer"; that is, they let nothing interfere with their prayers. They had been told to wait for the fulfillment of the promise, and that it would not be many days, so they spent their time in prayer. This was the best preparation that they could make for the great event of the descent of the Holy Spirit. This is the last mention that we have of Mary the mother of Jesus; the New Testament leaves her on her knees in prayer waiting, with the others, for the descent of the Holy Spirit.

5. SELECTION OF MATTHIAS
1: 5-26

15 And in these days Peter stood up in the midst of the brethren, and said (and there was a multitude of [4]persons *gathered* together, about a

[4]Gr. *names.* See Rev. 3. 4

15 **And in these days Peter stood up**—Peter had denied his Lord after the keys of the kingdom of heaven were committed unto him, but we now find him in his old place impetuously speaking for the apostles. He had been forgiven, and had received a special message sent to him by the risen Saviour (Mark 16: 7), and a special charge given him (John 21: 15-18). He is here strengthening his brethren; he does not apologize for the sin of Judas, but rather reminds them that "he was numbered among us, and received his portion in this ministry." Some think that Peter was the oldest of the apostles; hence, he took the lead. There "was a multitude of

hundred and twenty), 16 Brethren, it was needful that the scripture should
be fulfilled, which the Holy Spirit spake before by the mouth of David concerning Judas, who was guide to them that took Jesus. 17 For he was numbered among us, and received his [5]portion in this ministry. 18 (Now this
man obtained a field with the reward of his iniquity; and falling headlong, he

[5]Or, *lot*

persons gathered together, about a hundred and twenty." The
word for "gathered" is not in the Greek here, but it does occur in
Matt. 22: 34, and it seems to be the same idea in Luke 17: 35.
The entire number of disciples is not mentioned as being one
hundred and twenty, but that number was gathered together in Jerusalem; evidently there were others scattered through the country. (1 Cor. 15: 6.) There is no significance in the number "one
hundred and twenty."

16 **Brethren, it was needful that the scripture should be fulfilled,**—"Brethren" literally means "men, brethren, or brother
men." Women are included in this address, though "andres" refers only to men. Peter reminds them that the prophecy given by
David through the Holy Spirit concerning Judas must be fulfilled.
He evidently refers to Psalm 41: 9, which referred first to Ahitho-
phel, and in John 13: 18 to Judas; hence, Peter here indirectly
states that David wrote Psalm 41. Judas led the company of Jews
and Romans to the Garden of Gethsemane to betray Jesus. Peter
here found three things foretold, which had to be fulfilled: (1) that
the traitor was to be one of themselves; (2) what his fate would
be; (3) that his office from which he had been ejected was to be
filled by another.

17 **For he was numbered among us,**—Peter is not ashamed to
state that one of the twelve betrayed the Master; inspiration has
been true to the fact and recorded this betrayal. One might think
that it would be injurious to the cause of Christ to record the fact
that one of his disciples betrayed him; however, Judas fulfilled the
conditions of the prophecy. (Psalms 41: 9; 109: 2-5.) Judas
had a mouth of deceitfulness, the lying tongue, the groundless
enmity, the requital of evil for good; yet he was numbered among
the twelve apostles.

18 **(Now this man obtained a field with the reward**—Judas
"obtained" this field, or acquired it indirectly with the money
which he received for the betrayal of Jesus. (Matt. 26: 14-26;

burst asunder in the midst, and all his bowels gushed out.   19 And it became
known to all the dwellers at Jerusalem; insomuch that in their language that
field was called Akeldama, that is, The field of blood.)   20 For it is written
in the book of Psalms,

> [6]Let his habitation be made desolate,
> And let no man dwell therein: and,
> [7]His [8]office let another take.

[6]Ps. 69. 25
[7]Ps. 109. 8
[8]Gr. *overseership*

27: 3-8.)   Verses 18 and 19 are not a part of Peter's speech, but
seem to have been parenthetically included in Luke's account.
The field was bought with the money that Judas received for be-
traying the Savior; he brought it back and threw it at the feet of
the chief priest, and they took the money and purchased this property; they would not put the money in the treasury. (Matt. 27:
5-8.)   This field was bought by the chief priest in order to bury
strangers in it.   Matthew further says: "That field was called, The
field of blood."   (Matt. 27: 3-8.)   Luke here states that Judas fell
"headlong" and "burst asunder in the midst, and all his bowels
gushed out."   Matthew states that Judas "went away and hanged
himself."   (Matt. 27: 5.)   There is no contradiction here, as he
could have hanged himself and then fallen and "burst asunder."
Evidently in his attempt to hang himself the traitor's body fell and
was mangled as described here by Luke.

19 **And it became known to all the dwellers at Jerusalem;**
—The fate of Judas and the way in which the purchase money was
obtained caused the name to be changed from "the potter's field"
to "The field of blood," and all people recognized the appropriate-
ness of this name.   "Akeldama" is the Aramaic word which Peter
explained to mean "The field of blood."   "Aramaic" was the cor-
rupt Hebrew which was spoken in Palestine at that time.

20 **For it is written in the book of Psalms,**—Peter here
quotes from Psalm 69: 25 and Psalm 109: 8.   He changes the
plural of the first quotation into the singular as David was speaking of many enemies of his own, and Judas was the instrument
through which the many enemies of Jesus work out their will;
hence, the punishment which came upon Judas as the chief of-
fender.   Peter illustrates and points to its fulfillment in prophecy.
The disciples would be disturbed at the treachery of Judas, but
Peter answers by pointing to predictions in the Psalms which

21 Of the men therefore that have companied with us all the time that the Lord Jesus went in and went out *among us, 22 beginning from the baptism of John, unto the day that he was received up from us, of these must one become a witness with us of his resurrection. 23 And they put forward two,

*Or, *over*

---

proved that none of these things were accidental; they were known long before by Jehovah. "His office let another take" means that another must be selected to fill the place that Judas was selected to fill.

21, 22 **Of the men therefore that have companied**—The apostles were to be witnesses of Jesus; Peter here states the conditions required in the one who is to be appointed to take the place of Judas. He mentions two things; namely, that they should have been a disciple of Jesus "from the baptism of John," and that they should have accompanied him after his resurrection. This is another way of saying that one should have known and followed Jesus from the first of his personal ministry to his trials, death, burial, resurrection, and ascension. These apostles were careful in selecting the successor to Judas' place; the one selected must be a competent witness; no one can be selected who is not an eyewitness of the things to which he must testify, so that his knowledge may be firsthand and his evidence trustworthy. Peter had quoted from the Psalms that the place was vacant and that another should fill it; hence, he proceeded at once under the guidance of God to complete this task.

23 **And they put forward two, Joseph called Barsabbas,—** With the qualifications before them, "they" began their search for one who met all qualifications. They found two who met these qualifications. It is supposed that these two were selected from the company that was assembled. It is not clear as to who is included in "they"; some think that the entire assembly selected or found the two who were qualified; others think that only the apostles were included in the "they." Those who take the view that the assembly selected the two who had the qualifications draw the conclusion that the church may select its officers today. They should remember that the church had not been established at this time, and that this is no precedent for selecting officers in the

Joseph called Barsabbas, who was surnamed Justus, and Matthias. 24 And
they prayed, and said, Thou, Lord, who knowest the hearts of all men, show
of these two the one whom thou hast chosen, 25 to take the place in this
ministry and apostleship from which Judas fell away, that he might go to his

church. "Joseph called Barsabbas" also bore the name "Justus";
he was a well-known disciple at that time, and had been a companion of Jesus for three or more years, but we know nothing further
about him. There have been different interpretations as to the
meaning of his name; we cannot make him the same as "Barnabas" mentioned in Acts 4: 36. "Matthias" is the contracted form
of "Mattathias," and is the equivalent of the Greek, "Theodore,"
which means "gift of God."

24 **And they prayed, and said, Thou, Lord,**—Luke here
gives only the substance of the prayer that was prayed; it is very
probable that Peter led in this prayer, and that they all prayed with
him. Some claim that this prayer was addressed to Jesus, and
others that it was addressed to God. "Lord" may refer to God
and Christ. It is the same Greek word that Peter used four times in
answering Jesus (John 21: 15-17, 21), and that the eleven used
after the resurrection in speaking to Jesus (Acts 1: 6). Jesus had
not at this time become the Mediator and High Priest, as his
church had not been established. "Who knowest the hearts of all
men" literally means who "heart knowing all men." There is a
similar expression applied to God: "Jehovah searcheth all hearts"
(1 Chron. 28: 9) and "I, Jehovah, search the mind, I try the
heart" (Jer. 17: 10). Since God knows the hearts of all men, he
is asked to "show of these two the one whom thou hast chosen."
It is clear that the Lord had chosen; that he was to make known
which one should take the place of Judas. The Lord knew the
heart; they knew only the men with their qualifications; hence,
they asked the Lord to "show" or "point out" by some visible or
other means which one of the two he had chosen. They wanted
only the one that the Lord had chosen.

25 **to take the place in this ministry**—It is clear that they desire one to take Judas' place and to become an apostle with them;
they want him to participate in the office of the apostleship "from
which Judas fell away" that he might go to his own place. Judas
had been chosen to the place by Jesus, but he was disqualified by

on place. 26 And they gave lots ¹⁰for them; and the lot fell upon Matthias; and he was numbered with the eleven apostles.

¹⁰Or, *unto*

---

his wickedness and went to his own place, and now another must
be chosen by the authority of God to take his place.

26 **And they gave lots for them**—The Jews were familiar with
the process of casting lots; this method of decision by lot was an
Old Testament custom.   The land of Canaan was divided and assigned to the different tribes by lot. (Num. 26: 55.)   The guilt of
Achan seems to have been determined by lot (Josh. 7: 14); the
king of Israel, Saul, was selected by lot (1 Sam. 10: 20, 21); the
same method was used in determining the "scapegoat" (Lev. 16:
8).   Prov. 16: 33 indicates how the lot was cast.   There are different ways by which the lot was cast, but we need not discuss
these. The only thing practical here is that the apostles placed the
responsibility of the selection on the Lord, and he made the choice;
so Matthias was chosen by the Lord, "and he was numbered with
the eleven apostles."   The Greek word for "numbered" is not the
same as in verse 17, but is a word used in one form to signify the
person who was selected.   Some have doubted as to whether the
apostles were guided by the Holy Spirit in selecting Matthias;
they claim that Matthias was never an apostle.

6. DESCENT OF THE HOLY SPIRIT
2: 1-13

1 And when the day of Pentecost ¹¹was now come, they were all together

¹¹Gr. *was being fulfilled*

---

1 **And when the day of Pentecost was now come,**—The apostles had now been waiting about a week "for the promise of the
Father."   There were three annual feasts of the Jews—the Passover, Pentecost, and the Feast of Tabernacles.   The Passover
commemorated the salvation of the first born in Egypt; the Pentecost celebrated the beginning of their harvest; and the Feast of
Tabernacles commemorated their sojourn in the wilderness.
There were four names given to this feast: (1) "Feast of Harvest"
(Ex. 23: 16); (2) "Feast of the First-Fruits" (Lev. 23: 17;

in one place. 2 And suddenly there came from heaven a sound as of the
rushing of a mighty wind, and it filled all the house where they were sitting.

Num. 28: 26); (3) "Feast of Weeks" (Ex. 34: 22; Deut. 16:
10); (4) "Pentecost." The last name is found only in the New
Testament; it came fifty days after the Passover, and came on the
first day of the week. In many respects it was considered the
greatest feast of the year, and brought more people into Jerusalem
than any of the other feasts. Some have contended that it commemorated the giving of the law upon Mount Sinai as it was, as
they claimed, fifty days from the time they left Egypt to the giving
of the law. There is no reference in the scriptures to this event in
connection with this feast. At this time the Jews were scattered
among all the civilized nations of the earth; many had come to the
Passover, and had remained over to keep the Feast of Pentecost;
also many came to this feast that had not attended the Feast of the
Passover. On this day probably more Jews were in Jerusalem
than at any other day in the year. This was a memorable day with
the Jews, and became the birthday of the church. It was an opportune time for the Holy Spirit to come as a fulfillment of the
promise made by Jesus. All things are now ready; Jesus had ascended to the Father about a week before this, after telling the
apostles to wait in Jerusalem for the Holy Spirit; they had spent
much of the time in prayer, and were now ready for the advent of
the Holy Spirit. "They were all together in one place." We do
not know what place this was; probably it was the same room
where they had spent the week.

2 **And suddenly there came from heaven**—While the group
was waiting for the promise of the Holy Spirit, suddenly a sound
came "as the rushing of a mighty wind." There is no evidence
that there was "a mighty wind," but the sudden sound was like
that of a storm or hurricane. The sound "filled all the house
where they were sitting." This describes the posture that they occupied at the moment that this sound came. This sound "came
from heaven" as of a violent wind rushing along; this was the first
miracle or manifestation of the great event.

3 And there appeared unto them tongues [12]parting asunder, like as of fire; and it sat upon each one of them. 4 And they were all filled with the Holy Spirit, and began to speak with other tongues, as the Spirit gave them utterance.

[12]Or, *parting among them.*   Or, *distributing themselves*

3 **And there appeared unto them tongues**—This was the second miracle of the visible manifestation of the descent of the Holy Spirit. There appeared "tongues parting asunder," or tongues parting among them; it seems that there was one great sheet of light, and that this broke up into different parts called "tongues," and rested on each one of them. This was not "fire"; it was "like as of fire"; it is not said that there was either fire or wind; there was a noise and there were tongues; but there was felt neither blast nor burning. The noise was like a gust of wind borne violently along, and bringing with it tongues of flame which, distributing themselves among the disciples, settled for a moment on the head of each. There were not "cloven tongues," but there was one tongue that rested upon each person. Some have contended that the tongue on each person was parted or forked, but this is not the meaning of the Greek word.

4 **And they were all filled with the Holy Spirit,**—Here we have the third event—they were "filled with the Holy Spirit." The first was the sound which affected the ear, the second was the tongues which affected the eye, and now the Holy Spirit came upon them. These three events, the sound "from heaven," the appearance unto them "tongues parting asunder," and "all filled with the Holy Spirit," came close together, but whether in quick succession or all together at the same moment cannot be determined with certainty. As a result of the Holy Spirit's coming upon them they "began to speak with other tongues, as the Spirit gave them utterance." It seems clear that the Holy Spirit here came only upon the apostles; they were Galileans, and verse 7 says that those who were speaking were Galileans. It is not to be understood that the company of one hundred and twenty mentioned in chapter 1 were all filled with the Holy Spirit, because not all of these were Galileans. They were speaking as "the Spirit gave them utterance." They were not uttering unintelligible sounds nor using mere jargon of syllables with no meaning; their sentences were clear and

5 Now there were dwelling at Jerusalem Jews, devout men, from every nation under heaven. 6 And when this sound was heard, the multitude came together, and were confounded, because that every man heard them speaking in his own language. 7 And they were all amazed and marvelled, saying,

---

their words distinct, so that "every man heard them speaking in his own language." Hence, they used such language and such words as could be understood. There were probably twelve to fifteen different languages or dialects spoken by the multitude on this day; there were fifteen countries and provinces named, but we do not know whether there was a different dialect for each country.

5 **Now there were dwelling at Jerusalem Jews,**—Only a small portion of the Jews lived in Jerusalem or Palestine at this time; the greater number were natives of other lands dwelling in large colonies or in small communities. "Dwelling at Jerusalem" literally means "there were being housed in Jerusalem," either temporarily or permanently in the city, Jews who were devout, religious men; they had a sacred regard for the law of Moses and the worship according to that law. "Devout men" literally means "taking hold well"; that is, "cautious," "fearing." The Jews were widely scattered over the Roman Empire at this time, and only the "devout" ones would make the long journey to Jerusalem to keep this feast.

6 **And when this sound was heard,**—There has been much discussion as to the meaning here; some think that the "sound as of the rushing of a mighty wind" was heard and brought the multitude together; others think that their speaking "with other tongues" was noised abroad and thus brought the multitude together. It could have been both; the miraculous manifestation, both of the physical appearance of the sound like that of a violent tempest and that of the speaking of tongues, when noised abroad, brought the curiosity-seeking multitude together. It is clear that the multitude did not come together until after the Holy Spirit had come upon the apostles. As the multitude assembled they were amazed, or caused to stand out by themselves, with wide open astonishment. The wonder grew and grew and spread and spread until the whole city had been brought together. This furnished the occasion for the proclamation of the gospel.

Behold, are not all these that speak Galilaeans? 8 And how hear we, every man in our own language wherein we were born? 9 Parthians and Medes and Elamites, and the dwellers in Mesopotamia, in Judaea and Cappadocia, in Pontus and Asia, 10 in Phrygia and Pamphylia, in Egypt and the parts of Libya about Cyrene, and sojourners from Rome, both Jews and proselytes,

7, 8 And they were all amazed and marvelled,—"Amazed" and "marvelled" are from different Greek words, and describe the state of confusion and astonishment that prevailed over the multitude. In their bewildered and astonished condition they were unable to account for such conditions, and asked: "Are not all these that speak Galilaeans?" This was one of the main forms of their exclamations; these men who were speaking were from only one province, and yet they were speaking the different dialects of all the people represented. Some think that the entire company of a hundred and twenty were speaking, but this is not sustained by the evidence, as all of those speaking were recognized to be Galileans. Greek was almost universally spoken over the whole of the eastern part of the Roman Empire, but most districts had their own dialect; Aramaic was spoken in Palestine, and the people of Lycaonia had a language of their own; hence, Luke meant to say that the utterances of the disciples, inspired by the Holy Spirit, were made in a variety of dialects or languages.

9-11 Parthians and Medes and Elamites, and the dwellers— The countries mentioned here are in geographical order; the Parthians and Medes and Elamites lived far eastward beyond the Tigris River and the Caspian Sea; the Jews had been scattered there for several hundred years. "The dwellers in Mesopotamia" are mentioned next, and they lived between the Tigris and Euphrates Rivers; "Mesopotamia" means "between the rivers." The Jews had been taken as captives there; the Babylonian captivity was "between the rivers," and some of the Jews never returned from that captivity. Next the Judeans are mentioned, because they designated a dialect of southern Palestine as distinguished from that of Galilee. Next in order are mentioned five provinces in Asia Minor; they are Cappadocia, Pontus, Asia, Phrygia, and Pamphylia; Cappadocia is in the southeastern portion of Asia Minor; Pontus is in the northeastern part bordering the Black Sea; Asia, meaning not the continent nor Asia Minor, but a smaller territory, the Roman province of that name which included

11 Cretans and Arabians, we hear them speaking in our tongues the mighty works of God. 12 And they were all amazed, and were perplexed, saying one to another, What meaneth this? 13 But others mocking said, They are filled with new wine.

---

the little countries of Mysia, Lydia, and Caria, bordering on the Aegean Sea and opposite to Greece. Phrygia and Pamphylia were located a little south of the central part of Asia Minor. Egypt is next mentioned, which was in Africa, south of the Mediterranean Sea, and Libya was west of Egypt, bordering the Mediterranean Sea. Many Jews dwelt in all these countries in Egypt as well as in Asia Minor; large colonies of Jews dwelt in Egypt, so that a Greek version of the Old Testament, called the Septuagint, had been made at Alexandria in the third century before the Christian Era. "Sojourners from Rome" were thought to be Romans who were proselytes or dwelling in Jerusalem for trade. "Jews" means those born of Jewish parents; "proselytes" means those who were born of Gentile parents, or were of mixed parentage, partly Jewish and partly Gentile, but had become converts to the Jewish religion. It cannot be determined whether both classes came from all the countries or from Rome only. It is sure that sojourners at Rome are included. Cretans were from the island of Crete in the Mediterranean Sea; the Arabians were the Jews who had settled in Arabia; a large number of Jews had settled in Arabia.

12, 13 **And they were all amazed, and were perplexed,**—The effect that these wonderful things had on the multitude is here briefly described by the words "amazed, and were perplexed." They were confounded, "perplexed," and "amazed" at what they saw and heard. They turned in their amazement to each other and asked: "What meaneth this?" Literally their question meant: "What will this be," or "become." They believed that it was a sign or omen that signified something remarkable, but they did not know what to think of it. This question also describes a further state of their feeling—they were, in addition to being confounded, perplexed, and amazed, awe-struck. Some attempted to dismiss the matter with the suggestion that "they are filled with new wine." "New wine" is from the Greek "gleukous," which means "sweet wine," but was considered highly intoxicating; "sweet wine" kept a year was very intoxicating. There is some discussion as to who the "others" were; some had asked, "What meaneth this?" but "others" mocked and accused them of being "filled with new wine." Some think that those who made this accusation were other than those who had been mentioned. However, it seems that in the confusion and amazement some asked the question and others made the accusation; they were not agreed as to the cause of the manifestations which they saw and heard.

SECTION TWO

THE CHURCH AT JERUSALEM
2 : 14 to 6 : 7

1. PETER'S ADDRESS
2 : 14-36

14 But Peter, standing up with the eleven, lifted up his voice, and spake forth unto them, *saying,* Ye men of Judaea, and all ye that dwell at Jerusalem, be this known unto you, and give ear unto my words. 15 For these are not drunken, as ye suppose; seeing it is *but* the third hour of the day; 16 but this is that which hath been spoken through the prophet Joel:

---

14 **But Peter, standing up with the eleven,**—Each step in the progress of the history is important; Peter had been selected to be the spokesman, for to him had been committed the "keys of the kingdom of heaven" (Matt. 16: 19); he had waited in Jerusalem until the Holy Spirit had come; he, with the others, was now ready to testify for Jesus. Through the miraculous manifestations the multitude had assembled and were anxious to know the cause of these momentous manifestations. They have given Peter an opportunity, or an invitation to speak, and he stood "up with the eleven" and made his address. Peter and the eleven make the twelve apostles now. Peter becomes the spokesman for the twelve. The large crowd and the confusion of tongues demanded loud speaking; hence, he "lifted up his voice." By this means he demanded the attention in order that he might say to them what the Holy Spirit prompted him to speak. He first addressed the "men of Judaea," or literally, men, Judeans, and dwellers at Jerusalem; he addressed them in a respectful way and received a respectful hearing.

15, 16 **For these are not drunken, as ye suppose;**—Peter first clears the situation; he removes the accusation that some had brought against them; this must be done before he can proceed with the more important things which the Spirit was to speak through him. The apostles had spent the time of vigilant waiting in prayer, as all devout Jews were accustomed to doing before the worship at Pentecost; hence, the charge that they were drunken was a serious one at this time, more serious than at other seasons; for, in the eyes of the Jews, it was a greater sin to be drunken at

17   ¹And it shall be in the last days, saith God,
      I will pour forth of my Spirit upon all flesh:
      And your sons and your daughters shall prophesy,
      And your young men shall see visions,
      And your old men shall dream dreams:
18   Yea and on my ²servants and on my ³handmaidens in those days
      Will I pour forth of my Spirit; and they shall prophesy.
19   And I will show wonders in the heaven above,
      And signs on the earth beneath;
      Blood, and fire, and vapor of smoke:
20   The sun shall be turned into darkness,
      And the moon into blood, ·
      Before the day of the Lord come,
      That great and notable *day*:
21   And it shall be, that whosoever shall call on the name of the Lord
         shall be saved.

¹Joel, 2. 28 ff.
²Gr. *bondmen*
³Gr. *bondmaidens*

this time than at others. The impetuous Peter is now calm and courageous; he flatly denies the charge that he and his comrades are drunken. The charge had been made without proof; hence, circumstances were strongly against the assumption of his accusers. It was in the morning hour of prayer, only the third hour of the day; no Jew, certainly no devout Jew, would eat or drink before this hour was past. Men that got drunk did so at night, and this was only nine o'clock in the morning. The accusation was so absurd that Peter passes it by with the emphatic denial and the observation that all could make. He now points them to the real cause of all that they had heard and seen. He directed the attention of these pious Jews to one of their own prophets, Joel.

17-21 **And it shall be in the last days, saith God,**—This quotation from Joel is one of the scriptures that the Jews relied upon to prove the coming of the Messiah; they were correct in their understanding that it referred to the Messiah's kingdom, but they were in error with respect to Jesus as being that Messiah. He claimed to be, but they rejected his claim; he proved that he was the Messiah, but they refused to accept the proof; they did not believe the evidence. "The last days" had come, and God had poured "forth of my Spirit," and a literal fulfillment was at that time taking place in their very midst. The "wonders in the heaven above, and signs on the earth beneath," were taking place at that time. "The sun shall be turned into darkness"; this had been done

22 Ye men of Israel, hear these words: Jesus of Nazareth, a man approved of God unto you by ⁴ mighty works and wonders and signs which God did by him in the midst of you, even as ye yourselves know; 23 him, being deliv-

⁴Gr. *powers*

at the crucifixion of Jesus. (Luke 23: 45.) "Before the day of the Lord come, that great and notable day," has received various interpretations. The darkening of the sun with all the physical phenomena that go with it may have a primary fulfillment in the destruction of Jerusalem; this expression usually designates some time of fearful judgments. Whatever the prophecy of Joel may mean, Peter said that what was occurring at that time were the things which Joel said would come to pass in "the last days," and hence "the last days" were now upon them. At this time "whosoever shall call on the name of the Lord shall be saved." In the midst of these alarming events and wonders and terrible phenomena that foretold awful judgments, opportunity would be given to all who would "call on the name of the Lord" to be saved. That time was now, and they should begin calling upon the name of the Lord. The promise of deliverance, the "door of hope," had now come to them, and the blessings were conditioned on their calling on the name of the Lord.

22 Ye men of Israel, hear these words:—Peter's sermon may be divided into three divisions: (1) an explanation of the outpouring of the Holy Spirit with the fulfillment of the promise as made by Joel; (2) a description of the Lord upon whom they should call; and (3) a pointed appeal to acknowledge the Messiahship of Jesus who had been crucified, buried, raised from the dead, and ascended back to the Father. The first part of Peter's address begins with verse 14 and closes with verse 21; the second part begins with verse 22 and closes with verse 28; the third part begins with verse 29 and closes with verse 36.

Jesus of Nazareth, a man approved of God—In the audience there are those who knew Jesus as "the Nazarene," so he uses the title so that they could not misunderstand him. When Jesus asked the Jews and Romans in the Garden of Gethsemane whom they sought, they answered: "Jesus of Nazareth." (John 18: 5, 7.) Jesus was not only "a man approved of God," but he was proved

ered up by the determinate counsel and foreknowledge of God, ye by the
hand of ⁵lawless men did crucify and slay: 24 whom God raised up, having
loosed the pangs of death: because it was not possible that he should be hold-

⁵Or, *men without the law.* See Rom. 2. 12

---

to be from God. "Approved," as used here, means to "show to be
true," or "to prove" to be true. All the miracles of Jesus are here
included in "mighty works and wonders and signs"; three words
to cover all that God did through Jesus. They could not deny the
miracles wrought by Jesus.

23 **him, being delivered up by the determinate counsel**—
This shows that Jesus was delivered by the Jews to the Roman authorities according to a definite plan that had been outlined by the
prophets. Jesus willingly, when his hour came, gave himself into
the hands of his enemy, and let them do what they would with him.
God had willed the death of Jesus (John 3: 16) and the death of
Judas (Acts 1: 16), but that fact did not clear Judas of the responsibility and guilt (Luke 22: 22). Judas acted as a free moral
agent; hence, Peter could say that "ye by the hand of lawless men
did crucify and slay." This places guilt upon those who took part
in the crucifixion of Jesus. The Jews cried, "Crucify, crucify him"
(Luke 23: 21), and Pilate attempted to constrain them, but finally
gave sentence against Jesus. Peter here made a bold charge
against his hearers. They charged Peter and the other apostles
with being drunk, but he charged them with the crucifixion of their
Messiah.

24 **whom God raised up, having loosed the pangs of death:**—
They had, with the hands of lawless men, crucified the Son of
God, but God had raised him from the dead; what they did to
Jesus is put in contrast with what God did for him. The works of
man are frequently put in contrast with the works of God. This
strong antithesis is emphasized frequently in the preaching of the
apostles. When the time came, or when his hour arrived, God delivered Jesus into the hands of the wicked Jews; when they crucified him, God raised him from the dead, because it was not possible
for the powers of death to keep him in the grave. It was as much
the "determinate counsel and foreknowledge of God" to raise Jesus
from the dead as it was to deliver him into the hands of lawless

en of it. 25 For David saith concerning him.
    [6]I beheld the Lord always before my face;
    For he is on my right hand, that I should not be moved:
26   Therefore my heart was glad, and my tongue rejoiced;
    Moreover my flesh also shall [7]dwell in hope:
27   Because thou wilt not leave my soul unto Hades,
    Neither wilt thou give thy Holy One to see corruption.
28   Thou madest known unto me the ways of life;
    Thou shalt make me full of gladness [8]with thy countenance.
29 Brethren, I may say unto you freely of the patriarch David, that he both

[6]Ps. 16. 8 ff.
[7]Or, *tabernacle*
[8]Or, *in thy presence*

men to be crucified. There had been rumors of the resurrection in Jerusalem of Jesus, but Peter now stands without equivocation and declares the fact of his resurrection.

25-28 For David saith concerning him,—Peter here quotes Psalm 16: 8-11; he attributes his prophecy to David. It is noticed that quotations in the New Testament from the Old Testament are not "word for word" and punctuation exact; often the Holy Spirit gives the meaning and not the exact words. David often spoke concerning himself, but the Holy Spirit who spoke through David also spoke of Christ; hence, a prophecy would have a primary fulfillment and an ultimate fulfillment. The sepulcher of David was in the city of Jerusalem. (1 Kings 2: 10; Neh. 3: 16.) The site of David's tomb was then known to every Jew. David as a prophet took upon himself the task to speak of the Messiah as he was guided by the Holy Spirit; hence, he was not speaking altogether of himself when he referred to his flesh seeing corruption. "Hades" means the "unseen world." David died and was buried and his tomb was in their midst; his body had decayed; hence, David could not have spoken of himself, but of the Messiah. Peter now argued that this prophecy of David that his body should not see corruption could not have referred to David himself, but to the Messiah.

29-31 Brethren, I may say unto you freely—Here begins the third part of Peter's address. He shows them that David died and was buried within the city of Jerusalem, and that his tomb was with them and that his body had decayed; hence, David as a prophet did not apply the language to himself, but being a prophet he

died and was buried, and his tomb is with us unto this day. 30 Being therefore a prophet, and knowing that God had sworn with an oath to him, that of the fruit of his loins [9]he would set *one* upon his throne; 31 he foreseeing *this* spake of the resurrection of the Christ, that neither was he left unto Hades, nor did his flesh see corruption. 32 This Jesus did God raise up, [10]whereof we all are witnesses. 33 Being therefore [11]by the right hand of God exalted, and having received of the Father the promise of the Holy Spirit, he hath

---

[9]Or, one *should sit*
[10]Or, *of whom*
[11]Or, *at*

---

knew that God had sworn with an oath to him, that of the fruit of his loins he would set one upon his throne. Peter here refers to Psalm 132: 11. Furthermore, Peter argues that God has fulfilled that oath and promise to David and that Christ was raised from the dead to sit on David's throne. Peter here declares that David knew that in Psalm 16: 10 he was describing the resurrection of the Messiah. David as king occupied the throne of the nation of Israel, the national people of God. The Messiah, who was to descend from him, was in like manner to be King of God's people, his spiritual people; hence, the Messiah was to sit on David's throne ruling the people of God. The royal government among the Lord's national people was, properly speaking, a theocracy; that is, a government of which God was considered the Supreme Ruler, while the earthly king was God's agent. Christ or the Messiah was to sit on David's throne, or to be his successor, by becoming the King of God's spiritual people.

32 **This Jesus did God raise up,**—Again, the Jews crucified Jesus, but God raised him up and has made the apostles witnesses of that resurrection. Peter now had proved that the prophecy was not fulfilled in David, and could not refer to him, or to an earthly king or person long after him; but it did refer to the Messiah. Then he affirmed that God did raise up Jesus from the dead, and proceeded to prove that this Jesus is the Christ. The "we" who "are witnesses" of the resurrection includes the twelve apostles, and may include other disciples who had seen Jesus after his resurrection. (1 Cor. 15: 6.)

33 **Being therefore by the right hand of God exalted,**—God had raised Jesus from the dead that he might sit on David's throne, which is here called "the right hand of God exalted." Jesus was not only raised from the dead, like Lazarus or the

poured forth this, which ye see and hear. 34 For David ascended not into the heavens: but he saith himself,
   [1]The Lord said unto my Lord, Sit thou on my right hand,
35   Till I make thine enemies the footstool of thy feet.
36 Let [2]all the house of Israel therefore know assuredly, that God hath made him both Lord and Christ, this Jesus whom ye crucified.

[1]Ps. 110. 1
[2]Or, every house

---

daughter of Jairus to die again, but he was raised from the dead to be exalted to the right hand of God. Again we see the contrast between what the Jews had done for Christ and what God had done. There is a similar phrase in Psalm 98: 1: "His right hand, and his holy arm, hath wrought salvation for him." He had promised that if he returned to the Father he would send the Holy Spirit; since he had returned to the Father he has now sent the Holy Spirit. The physical manifestations which so confused and astonished the multitude were evidences that the Holy Spirit had come and they saw and heard these things.

34, 35 **For David ascended not into the heavens:**—Peter further argues and proves that the prophecy here did not apply to David. He quotes Psalm 110: 1. David had not ascended into the heavens, but Jesus had. It is clear that David understood this to refer to some other than himself; David with the Holy Spirit saw the Messiah come to the earth, suffer and die, be buried, raised from the dead, and ascend back to the Father, and seated at his right hand. This prophecy of David as to the Lord had been fulfilled. Some in that audience could recall that a few weeks before this time the Pharisees had been confused by a question about the meaning of this same passage, and they could not answer Jesus; if they had answered him truly they would have conceded his claim. (Matt. 22: 42-45.)

36 **Let all the house of Israel therefore know**—"Let all the house of Israel" is equivalent to saying "let every house of Israel"; this appeal could be made only to Israel, for they only had known the prophecies, and they only had received the promises. "Know assuredly" is equivalent to believing the evidence that Peter had given to establish the fact that Jesus of Nazareth was the Messiah and therefore the Son of God. This was another way of telling them to believe on the Lord Jesus Christ. The fact that they were

to believe was that God had "made him both Lord and Christ, this Jesus whom ye crucified." Jesus who had been crucified, God had raised from the dead, exalted him to heaven, and set him on his own right hand; in this way God had shown that Jesus was the Messiah. He has been made "Lord" or ruler; he has all authority in heaven and on earth; he also had been made "Christ," which means the Anointed One. This concluded Peter's address; it closed with an appeal to believe the evidence that had been presented.

2. THE FIRST CONVERTS
2: 37-41

37 Now when they heard *this,* they were pricked in their heart, and said unto Peter and the rest of the apostles, Brethren, what shall we do? 38 And

---

37 **Now when they heard this,**—The effect of Peter's address is now briefly narrated; it was a wonderful address and there were wonderful results. The simple declaration of facts, together with prophecies which supported the claim of Jesus as the Savior of the world, had such an effect on the hearts of the people that many were moved. "They were pricked in their heart," which means that they were stung with remorse at the exceeding wickedness of their crime in the crucifixion; they must have been amazed at the stupid blindness with which they had acted. The leaders and the people had closed their eyes to the teaching of the prophecies which had spoken of their Messiah. "Pricked" is from the verb "katanusso," which means "to pierce, to sting sharply, to stun, to smite." Peter's sermon carried conviction, and they felt keenly the sting of their conviction; hence, they asked Peter "and the rest of the apostles," "What shall we do?" This shows that they regarded the other apostles with Peter as witnesses for Christ. Since he had brought conviction to them, surely Peter and the rest of the apostles would know what to do. They had been with Jesus; they had seen him and talked with him since his resurrection; they had seen him as he ascended; surely the Messiah would leave some word with them as to what they should do in order to receive remission of their sins. They recognize that there is something that they must do.

Peter *said* unto them, Repent ye, and be baptized every one of you in the name
of Jesus Christ unto the remission of your sins; and ye shall receive the gift

---

38 And Peter said unto them, Repent ye, and be baptized—
This is possibly one of the most mooted scriptures in the New Testament; many theological controversies have been based on this verse. It should be remembered that after being convinced that Jesus was the Messiah and knowing that they had crucified him, they asked what they must do. This verse gives the answer to that question. While much controversy has been had about the meaning of the answer, it is plain and simple enough. These believers are told to "repent ye." John had taught repentance and Jesus had taught repentance. He had included repentance in the commission. (Luke 24: 47.) "Repent" had been the clarion cry of John in the wilderness (Matt. 3: 2); it was the gospel call of Jesus (Mark 1: 15); it was the demand of the apostles as they went out on their limited commission (Mark 6: 12). They were not only to repent, but they were to "be baptized." In giving the commission, Jesus said: "He that believeth and is baptized shall be saved." John and Jesus had both preached baptism; Jesus had placed baptism in the commission; hence, the apostle Peter, guided by the Holy Spirit, gave the answer and told them what they should do. "Repent ye" is singular, while "be baptized every one of you" is in the plural. There is here also a change from the second to the third person; this change shows a break in the thought; the first thing to do is make a radical and complete change; this is done in repentance; then let each one be baptized "in the name of Jesus Christ." This is the same as the command in Matt. 28: 19. There is no distinction between "eis to onoma" and "en toi onomati" with "baptizo," since "eis" and "en" are really the same word in origin. In Acts 10: 48 "en toi onomati Iesou Christou" occurs, but "eis to onoma" is found in Acts 8: 16; 19: 5. The use of "onoma" means in the name or with the authority of one, as "eis onoma prophetou" (Matt. 10: 41) as a prophet, in the name of a prophet.

unto the remission of your sins;—The Greek is "eis aphesin ton hamartion humon"; this is the phrase over which there has been so much controversy. It seems to be clear. After Peter convinced the multitude that they had crucified the Messiah and that

of the Holy Spirit. 39 For to you is the promise, and to your children, and

---

God had exalted him and that he was now at the right hand of God, in this state they asked: "What shall we do?" Evidently they were asking what to do to obtain remission of sins. Peter answers them and tells them to do two things—repent and be baptized. This is to be done by every one of them "in the name of Jesus Christ," "eis aphesin ton hamartion humon" "unto the remission of your sins." Much depends on the meaning of "eis"; some have claimed that it means "because of"; hence, they claim that baptism is "because of the remission of sins"; or one receives remission of sins before baptism. Others claim that "eis" means "for," "in order to," "unto" the remission of sins. Repentance and baptism are both "eis aphesin ton hamartion humon." Herewith is submitted the best scholarship on the translation of "eis" and its accompanying phrase.

MEANING OF "EIS" IN ACTS 2 : 38

Translation	Name	Denomination	Work
"for the putting away"	Abbot	Church of England	"Commentary on Acts"
"for, to or toward"	Alexander	Presbyterian	"Commentary on Acts"
"unto, for, in order to"	Axtell	Baptist	"Shepherd's Handbook"
"for, unto"	Benson	Methodist	"Commentary on Bible"
"for, unto"	Bickersteth	Church of England	"Commentary on Acts"
"end toward which"	Butcher	Presbyterian	"Shepherd's Handbook"
"in reference to"	Adam Clarke	Methodist	"Commentary on Bible"
"unto, to"	Dill	Baptist	"Shepherd's Handbook"
"is always prospective"	Ditzler	Methodist	"Wilkes-Ditzler Debate"
"aim, purpose"	Godet	Presbyterian	"Shepherd's Handbook"
"purpose"	Goodwin	Congregationalist	"Shepherd's Handbook"
"in order to"	Harkness	Baptist	"Shepherd's Handbook"
"the object to be obtained"	Harmon	Methodist	"Shepherd's Handbook"
"unto, in order to receive"	Harper	Baptist	"Shepherd's Handbook"
"unto"	Hovey	Baptist	"Commentary on John"
"unto, to this end"	Jacobus	Presbyterian	"Commentary on Acts"
"denotes object"	Meyer	Lutheran	"Commentary on Acts"
"with a view to"	McLintock	Methodist	McLintock & Strong Encyclopedia
"unto"	Rice		"Commentary on Acts"
"might receive"	Schaff	Presbyterian	"Shepherd's Handbook"
"in order to"	Strong	Methodist	"Shepherd's Handbook"
"unto, to the end"	Summers	Methodist	"Commentary on Acts"
"into, to, toward"	Thayer	Congregationalist	Greek-English Lexicon
"in order to"	Willmarth	Baptist	Baptist Quarterly, 1878

ye shall receive the gift of the Holy Spirit.—Peter, by the Holy Spirit, promised two things on the condition that they repented and were baptized in the name of Jesus Christ—"the remission of your sins" and "the gift of the Holy Spirit." Much controversy exists as to whether this meant the Holy Spirit as a gift in

to all that are afar off, *even* as many as the Lord our God shall call unto him. 40 And with many other words he testified, and exhorted them, saying,

---

that measure that the apostles now enjoyed, or whether "the gift of the Holy Spirit" was the ordinary measure that belonged to all Christians. It seems that some of the early Christians received miraculous measure of the Holy Spirit, and that this is what Peter meant. Joel had been quoted by Peter as being fulfilled at this time; hence, the Spirit dispensation was now beginning and those who obeyed the gospel would receive all the blessings promised by this dispensation.

39 **For to you is the promise, and to your children,**—"The promise" is the promise mentioned above; it was what Christ had termed "the promise of the Father" (Acts 1 : 4), and described as the baptism "in the Holy Spirit not many days hence." This promise carried with it the blessings of salvation in Christ and all that accompanied a faithful life in his service. "To your children" includes the Jews, and "all that are afar off" includes the Gentiles; hence, all flesh would receive the blessings of the Holy Spirit. The limitations were set by the qualifying clause, "even as many as the Lord our God shall call unto him." The Lord calls people by his gospel: "Whereunto he called you through our gospel, to the obtaining of the glory of our Lord Jesus Christ." (2 Thess. 2: 14.) "Whosoever shall call upon the name of the Lord shall be saved. How then shall they call on him in whom they have not believed? and how shall they believe in him whom they have not heard? and how shall they hear without a preacher?" (Rom. 10: 13, 14.) "And they shall all be taught of God. Every one that hath heard from the Father, and hath learned, cometh unto me." (John 6: 45.) This shows how they are to learn of Jesus and how they are to call upon him. The gospel is to be preached which makes known Christ to the world; people hear it and believe it; they obey its commands and receive its blessings; in this way they come to God through Christ.

40 **And with many other words he testified,**—Luke did not record all that Peter said on this occasion; he gave a brief outline of the address that Peter made. The address may be formally arranged as follows:

Save yourselves from this crooked generation. 41 They then *that received his word were baptized: and there were added *unto them* in that day about three thousand souls. 42 And they continued stedfastly in the apostles'

*Or, *having received*

PETER'S ADDRESS

Introduction:
1. Defense of the Apostles
2. Explanation of the Events
I. The Theme—Jesus Is the Christ
II. The Proof
1. The Works of Jesus
2. His Resurrection
a. Quotation from David
b. Exposition of Quotation
c. The Witness of the Disciples
3. The Gift of the Holy Spirit Promised

Peter exhorted the people to "save" themselves from "this crooked generation." Peter's "many other words" exhorted the people to accept Jesus as the Messiah. "Crooked" is from the Greek "skolias," which is a word opposite of "orthos," which means "straight"; they were "crooked" mentally, morally, and spiritually, since they were unbelieving Jews who had crucified their Messiah.

41 **They then that received his word were baptized:**—Some ancient manuscripts omit the word "gladly," and the Standard Version follows the oldest manuscripts. They received the word by believing and obeying the gospel. People receive Christ today by receiving his teachings. Jesus said: "He that receiveth whomsoever I send receiveth me; and he that receiveth me receiveth him that sent me." (John 13: 20.) "He that heareth you heareth me; and he that rejecteth you rejecteth me; and he that rejecteth me rejecteth him that sent me." (Luke 10: 16.) To hear the apostles was to hear Christ, and to hear Christ was to hear God who sent him; hence, when they received the words of the apostles spoken by the Holy Spirit they were hearing the words of Christ, and therefore the word of God. They were baptized; all who received the word were baptized; the Holy Spirit through Peter had com-

manded them to be baptized. Those who were baptized were
"added unto them"; that is, those who were baptized were added
together, added to the church; there were "about three thousand
souls." Some think that these three thousand were added to the
hundred and twenty, but since the phrase "unto them" is in italics,
or supplied, they were simply added together.

3. THE UNITY OF THE CHURCH
2 : 42-47

teaching and ⁴fellowship, in the breaking of bread and the prayers.
43 And fear came upon every soul: and many wonders and signs were
⁴Or, *in fellowship*

---

42 **And they continued stedfastly in the apostles' teaching**
—These new disciples were not fickle; they "continued" in those
things which they were taught. Here are mentioned four things in
which they continued: (1) "apostles' teaching," (2) "fellowship,"
(3) "in the breaking of bread," and (4) "the prayers." The
teaching here mentioned is that which Jesus commissioned when
he told his apostles to teach all the baptized ones everything that
he had commanded. (Matt. 28: 20.) "Fellowship" here means
that common interest and mutual participation in those things
which concern the welfare of each other. "Breaking of bread"
comes from "klasei," which is used only by Luke, and only in the
phrase "breaking of bread"; the kindred verb for "break" occurs
often, but, like the noun, only of breaking bread; hence, it is used
to designate the celebration of the Lord's Supper. "The prayers"
means that all the services were accompanied with prayer; only
stated times were given to prayer under the law, but now the
prayers are offered continually, at any time and all time. (See
Luke 5: 33.)

43 **And fear came upon every soul:**—Wonder and amazement
pervaded the entire group; the attention of the public was attracted
to the disciples. "Fear" is used here in the sense of deep reverence and awe. "Many wonders and signs were done through the
apostles." The mockers were put to silence and awe came over
them, and they were deterred from further opposition, even though
they did not repent. The apostles were able to work many miracles,

done through the apostles.[5] 44 And all that believed were together, and had all things common; 45 and they sold their possessions and goods, and parted them to all, according as any man had need. 46 And day by day, continuing stedfastly with one accord in the temple, and breaking bread at home, they

[5]Many ancient authorities add *in Jerusalem; and great fear was upon all*

---

though no particular one is described at this point except the one in the next chapter, and that one is noticed only because it is connected with the arrest of the apostles.

44, 45 **And all that believed were together,**—Some have thought that this means that they lived together in one house, but this is impossible since three thousand were converted on this day. It simply means that they "were together" in mind, in purpose, in faith, and in heart. It refers to the unity of spirit and mind and not so much to unity of organization. They "had all things common." This clause seems to convey the idea of community of goods, lands, and possessions. It does not mean that everyone sold everything that was possessed, but that all held their possessions as a trust for the good of all. Christianity teaches that we are responsible for the welfare of each other and that we should render service, money, and everything for the welfare of others. "But whoso hath the world's goods, and beholdeth his brother in need, and shutteth up his compassion from him, how doth the love of God abide in him?" (1 John 3: 17.) Many of these Jews had come from a distance and had brought but little with them; their sojourn was longer than they expected; hence, they did not have sufficient supplies. In this condition those who did have gladly shared with those who had not.

46, 47 **And day by day, continuing stedfastly with one accord**—This was not "communism," but the disciples had their property at the disposal of the common good as it was needed. The disciples were still worshipping in the temple, as no wide separation had as yet come between the Christians and Jews. They broke their bread at home, and rejoiced in all of the temporal blessings that God had given to them. Those who contributed of their means to those who had not rejoiced in the opportunity to help others; while those who received help rejoiced that there were those who loved them and were able to help them. It was an occasion of all rejoicing together. The description of these early disciples closes

took their food with gladness and singleness of heart, 47 praising God, and having favor with all the people. And the Lord added ⁶to them day by day those that ⁷were saved.

⁶Gr. *together*
⁷Or, *were being saved*

---

with their praising God and finding "favor with all the people." "And the Lord added to them day by day those that were saved." The word "church" is left out of the Standard Version and "to them" is expressed; hence, the meaning is that those who heard the word, believed it, repented of their sins, and were baptized, were by this process added together, and thus formed the church. Every step was taken by divine guidance, and all rejoiced in the unity of the faith and in the love and fellowship of each other. As we leave this instructive chapter we are impressed with the power of the gospel as preached by Peter. We also are impressed with the simple procedure of the apostles in thus forming the church. The church is now functioning under the direction of the apostles, guided by the Holy Spirit. We see how people become Christians and we see them living the Christian life. Luke, the historian, is ready now to proceed further with the expansion of the church.

4. THE LAME MAN HEALED
3: 1-10

1 Now Peter and John were going up into the temple at the hour of

---

1 Now Peter and John were going up into the temple—This miracle is selected from among the many miracles that the apostles wrought because it brought the apostles into conflict with the authorities; opposition and persecution started at this time; this miracle led to the arrest of the apostles, which was the beginning of a religious persecution as relentless, bloody, and violent as any that is known in the history of the church. "Peter and John" are now associated, and went up "into the temple at the hour of prayer." Peter and John were sent together to prepare the Passover meal (Luke 22: 8); they were together at the sepulcher (John 20: 3); they were together fishing after the crucifixion (John 21: 7); and John helped Peter to get into the palace of the high priest (John 18: 16). Again they were together now going into the temple at

prayer, *being* the ninth *hour.* 2 And a certain man that was lame from his mother's womb was carried, whom they laid daily at the door of the temple which is called Beautiful, to ask alms of them that entered into the temple; 3 who seeing Peter and John about to go into the temple, asked to receive an alms. 4 And Peter, fastening his eyes upon him, with John, said, Look on

---

the ninth hour, "the hour of prayer." "The ninth hour" was about three o'clock, according to our count, in the afternoon. These apostles continued to observe the hour of prayer according to the law of Jewish worship; it also furnished them the occasion to preach to the people who came to worship at that hour.

2, 3 **And a certain man that was lame**—It was customary for the afflicted and maimed to be placed near the place of worship; this was especially true when they depended upon public charity for their living. People were more liberal when going to worship or at worship, and these unfortunates, with their friends, took advantage of the situation. This lame man was born with some malformation of his ankles or feet; he was unable to walk and his friends carried him and placed him "daily at the door of the temple"; hence, he was a well-known and familiar character. He was placed at the "gate" or "door" that "is called Beautiful." There were nine gates used as entrance into the court, four, respectively, on the north and the south, and one on the east side; the west side had no gate. A part of the court was called the "court of women" to distinguish it from "the court of men." It is thought that this gate "called Beautiful" was an entrance which led from the "court of the Gentiles" to the "court of the women." This is the only mention in the Bible of the door which is "called Beautiful." When the lame man saw "Peter and John" as they were about to enter the temple, he "asked to receive an alms." "Alms" is singular number, and was in early times spelled "almesse"; the beggar simply asked for "a gift" or "gifts." At this time he knew nothing of Peter and John except that they were Jews and had come to the temple to worship.

4, 5, **And Peter, fastening his eyes upon him,**—Peter and John looked at the lame beggar; they looked with such a gaze that it would attract attention; then Peter said to him: "Look on us." This emphasized his attention on the apostles. He

us. 5 And he gave heed unto them, expecting to receive something from them. 6 But Peter said, Silver and gold have I none; but what I have, that give I thee. In the name of Jesus Christ of Nazareth, walk. 7 And he took him by the right hand, and raised him up: and immediately his feet and his ankle-bones received strength. 8 And leaping up. he stood, and began to walk;

expected "to receive something from them." The expectation had been aroused by their gazing upon him and the command for him to look upon them; he naturally expected to receive some gift. He desired to receive something and this desire helped to heighten his expectation. The serious and earnest manner of the apostles confirmed his expectation.

6 **But Peter said, Silver and gold have I none;**—The apostles had no worldly wealth; they were endued with power to perform miraculous cures. They could use this power "in the name of Jesus Christ"; hence, they commanded him to "walk." Peter and John had no money; the possessions which had been sold did not belong to the apostles; such things were used for the common welfare and not for the personal use of the apostles. "Walk" is from the original "peripapei," and has the idea of to begin to walk and then go on walking; the beggar is thus commanded to do that which he had never done in his life. Peter was willing and anxious to give him what he could. We do not know how much time had passed since the day of Pentecost, and it is probable that this was not the first miracle that Peter had wrought. (Acts 2: 43.) Peter speaks as one who has had experience; his language is firm and carries assurance. "In the name of Jesus Christ of Nazareth" is a common phrase and connects the Christ with the Jesus of Nazareth. According to John's account, the name "Nazareth" was included in the title of the superscription on the cross (John 19: 19); we know that the place was of no repute in the eyes of the Jews (John 1: 46). The obscure origin as well as the shameful death of Jesus was a stumbling block to the Jew. There were other people named "Jesus"; there was but one "Jesus of Nazareth."

7 **And he took him by the right hand,**—He was encouraged by the extension of Peter's hand, and as it was grasped by the right hand of the lame man, Peter raised him to his feet. It seems that Peter had to pull him up on his feet before he would attempt to walk. Luke was a physician; and he uses words that a physician

and he entered with them into the temple, walking, and leaping, and praising God. 9 And all the people saw him walking and praising God: 10 and they took knowledge of him, that it was he that sat for alms at the Beautiful Gate of the temple; and they were filled with wonder and amazement at that which had happened to him.

---

would use; he knows how a physician would deal with his patient and he gives one of those minute coincidences which go to prove that Luke the physician was the author of the Acts. The lame man "immediately" began to walk as "his feet and his ankle-bones received strength." Here again we see the physician's description of the incident. Some think that it should be "the soles of his feet" received strength.

8 **And leaping up, he stood, and began to walk;**—Again Luke gives a detailed description of the exercises that he took; he leaped up; then he stood for a moment and gained his equilibrium, then he began to walk. The progressive steps show the progress that he made. As he was assured that he could walk he went into the temple. The man had been lame from birth and did not know how to walk; it seems that he began by a jump, then a walk and went into the temple repeating the new exercises, and praised God. He was so joyful over the fact that he could walk that he "walking, and leaping," went to the place to praise God. He did not go into the holy place of the temple, as only priests had access to it. He was thankful for the blessing and was now ready to worship God.

9, 10 **And all the people saw him walking**—This was the hour of prayer in the afternoon; many people had assembled or were coming to the temple for worship; they observed the man and knew that it was the one that they had seen begging at the gate. This miracle showed that the apostles had the power to heal; the man who had been healed did not praise the apostles, but God; he gave God the praise for his being able to walk. There was abundance of witnesses to testify that he had been healed; they saw and could not deny that which they saw had been done. This would beget respect and confidence in the apostles as the witnesses for Christ. Everyone believed that this man who was now walking and leaping about the temple courts was the same person as the cripple; there was no charge of pretense or deception about the healing; there were too many witnesses, too many knew the facts

about the deformed man for anyone to question the fact of the
wonderful cure. This filled the people with wonder and amazement.
It was a sign from heaven as the Jewish rulers on a former occasion had demanded of Jesus. (John 6: 30.) The conduct of the
man clearly showed that he was now perfectly healed.

5. PETER'S ADDRESS TO THE MULTITUDE
3: 11-26

11 And as he held Peter and John, all the people ran together unto them
in the [8]porch that is called Solomon's, greatly wondering. 12 And when
Peter saw it, he answered unto the people, Ye men of Israel, why marvel ye
at this [9]man? or why fasten ye your eyes on us, as though by our own

[8]Or, *portico*
[9]Or, *thing*

---

11 **And as he held Peter and John, all the people ran**—In his
gratitude he held to Peter and John; he would not let them go.
These apostles had been the agents through whom he had received
the blessing; he wished all to know to whom he was indebted for
his great blessing. While he kept near Peter and John, and as the
people looked upon the man that had been healed, they must also
behold Peter and John. This would draw attention to Peter and
John. In the amazement of the occasion the people gathered or
literally "ran together," and assembled "in the porch that is called
Solomon's." Solomon's porch was on the east side of the temple;
it was a covered colonnade and was named for Solomon; it overlooked the Kedron valley. Some think that it was built by Solomon, hence its name. The people assembled here to see what
would further occur, and see the men who had wrought such a
miracle.

12 **And when Peter saw it, he answered unto the people,—**
When the people assembled, this gave Peter an audience, and he
began at once to preach to them. He had the attention of the people, because the man who had been held was before them. He
made three chief points: (1) the miracle was the work of God to
glorify Jesus; (2) the Jews denied Jesus from ignorance, but he
fulfilled the prophecy; (3) therefore they should repent and be
saved by the gospel. He addressed them as "men of Israel"; this

power or godliness we had made him to walk? 13 The God of Abraham, and of Isaac, and of Jacob, the God of our fathers, hath glorified his [10]Servant Jesus; whom ye delivered up, and denied before the face of Pilate, when he had determined to release him. 14 But ye denied the Holy and Righteous One, and asked for a murderer to be granted unto you, 15 and killed the [1]Prince of life; whom God raised from the dead; [2]whereof we are

[10]Or, *Child.* See Mt. 12. 18; Is. 42. 1; 52. 13; 53. 11
[1]Or, *Author*
[2]Or, *of whom*

---

was a respectful address. He then interrogated them as to the cause of their astonishment. He claimed no credit for what had been done, and did not want them to think that they had healed the man by their own power and godliness. It is noticed that Peter includes John in his speech. This denial that Peter makes clears the way to ascribe unto God all honor and glory.

13 **The God of Abraham, and of Isaac, and of Jacob,**—God had revealed himself to Moses as "the God of Abraham, and of Isaac, and of Jacob." (Ex. 3: 6.) Peter by mentioning these patriarchs stirred reverence in their hearts; this was a good way to begin his sermon. It was the very God of the patriarchs who had sent Jesus of Nazareth, and the same God who had glorified him. Jesus is mentioned here as "his Servant Jesus." This phrase occurs in Isa. 42: 1; 52: 13 about the Messiah except the name "Jesus," which Peter adds; many think that this should be translated "child." Perhaps there were some in the audience who had cried out against Jesus: "Crucify, crucify him." Hence, the charge that they had "delivered up, and denied before the face of Pilate." We learn here that Pilate "had determined to release him." It is clear from Luke 23: 16-20 that Pilate had determined to release Jesus, but the multitude was persuaded by the rulers to ask Pilate to release Barabbas and crucify Jesus. (Matt. 27: 20; Mark 15: 11-14.) Hence, the charge that Peter brought against them.

14, 15 **But ye denied the Holy and Righteous One,**—These Jews understood that this had reference to the Messiah. (Psalm 16: 10.) The demoniacs called him by this title. (Mark 1: 24.) In prophecy he is also called "the Just," or "Righteous One." (Isa. 45: 21; Zech. 9: 9.) A sharp contrast is here drawn between what the Jews did to Jesus and what God did to him; they "killed the Prince of life," but "God raised" him from the dead.

witnesses. 16 And ³by faith in his name hath his name made this man
strong, whom ye behold and know: yea, the faith which is through him hath
given him this perfect soundness in the presence of you all. 17 And now,
brethren, I know that in ignorance ye did it, as did also your rulers. 18 But

³Or, *on the ground of*

Frequently we have this contrast brought out by the apostles; they
denied Jesus, but God owned him; they crucified him, but God
raised him from the dead. If the resurrection could have been denied, they would have done so. They could not deny the crucifixion of Jesus, neither could they deny the resurrection. The apostles were witnesses to this fact.

16 **And by faith in his name**—By faith in the name of "the
Prince of life" "hath his name made this man strong." The man
was not healed by the faith of the apostles, but by the faith of the
apostles and the faith of the man. The apostles had faith in Jesus;
they had faith in his power, and that he would give them power to
heal the man. The man had faith in the apostles and in Jesus, for
he praised God for his blessing. "Name" is equivalent to
"power"; hence, "in the name of Jesus" is equivalent to "by his
power." This crippled man was above forty years old (Acts 4:
22), and he must have heard of the miracles that Jesus did and
those the apostles were then doing. (Acts 2: 43.) Peter here insisted upon three things that proved a divine agency in the miracle: (1) their knowledge of the man's previous condition; (2) the
completeness of the cure; (3) the public, open manner of the healing; it was done "in the presence of you all."

17 **And now, brethren, I know that in ignorance**—Their ignorance is admitted; but their ignorance does not clear them of
guilt. The Jews could have known that Jesus was the Messiah;
they should have known that he was; but the fact still remains that
they were ignorant of his divinity. Jesus while on the cross
prayed: "Father, forgive them; for they know not what they do."
(Luke 23: 34.) Paul persecuted the church in ignorance, and he
said: "I obtained mercy, because I did it ignorantly in unbelief."
(1 Tim. 1: 13.) Their ignorance did not justify their crime, nor
excuse them; but it was ground for calling on them to repent.

the things which God foreshowed by the mouth of all the prophets, that his Christ should suffer, he thus fulfilled. 19 Repent ye therefore, and turn again, that your sins may be blotted out, that so there may come seasons of refreshing from the presence of the Lord; 20 and that he may send the

18 **But the things which God foreshowed**—All the prophets had foretold the coming of Christ; as the types under the law foreshowed the Christ, so the prophets pointed the people to the Messiah. Even the crucifixion was foretold; Christ frequently told his apostles that he would die for the sins of the world. Their crime, though real, was carrying out God's purpose. (John 3: 16; Acts 2: 23; 17: 3; 26: 23.) Their crime in crucifying Jesus did not prevent the fulfillment of what God foreknew and foretold; in fact, their crime was foretold. Even in their ignorance and wickedness the Jews were contributing toward the fulfillment of the prophecy. Peter emphasized the fulfillment of the prophecies before this Jewish audience.

19 **Repent ye therefore, and turn again,**—Peter repeats in substance in this address what he had said in Acts 2: 38. Verse 38 of chapter 2 is a parallel of this verse. There he had given evidence that Christ was the Son of God; they were convinced or believed his evidence; they asked what to do; Peter told them to repent and be baptized, in the name of or by the authority of Christ, unto the remission of their sins, and then they should receive the gift of the Holy Spirit. Here he tells them to "repent" and "turn again" "that your sins may be blotted out," "so there may come seasons of refreshing from the presence of the Lord." In both statements, after they believed, they were commanded to "repent"; in the first they were told to "be baptized," but in the second they are told to "turn again"; in the first they are told that their repentance and baptism were "unto the remission of your sins," but here after repentance and turning again they are promised "that your sins may be blotted out." Evidently the blotting out of sins is equivalent to the remission of sins, and being baptized is tantamount to turning again. "Blotted out" literally means "to wipe out, rub off, erase, smear out." "Seasons of refreshing," literally from the Greek, "anapsuxis," "to cool again or refresh," or "cooling, reviving with fresh air." The "seasons of refreshing" depend on their repentance and turning again and having their sins erased or forgiven.

Christ who hath been appointed for you, *even* Jesus: 21 whom the heaven
must receive until the times of restoration of all things, whereof God spake
by the mouth of his holy prophets that have been from of old. 22 Moses
indeed said, ⁴A prophet shall the Lord God raise up unto you from among

⁴Dt. 18. 15

---

20 and that he may send the Christ—This verse has called
forth much controversy. The coming of Christ the second time
seems to be the meaning here. What would their repentance and
turning again have to do with the coming of Christ? Evidently the
coming again of Christ, like the coming of the times of refreshing,
depends upon their repentance and turning again; as people were
converted, conditions would be more favorable for the coming
again of Christ. Christ came the first time to redeem the world;
his second coming will complete that redemption.

21 whom the heaven must receive until the times—This
Jesus who is here promised to return must remain in heaven until
the "times of restoration of all things." Peter has told them that
this Jesus whom they had crucified had ascended back to heaven,
and that now the heaven must receive and retain until the time for
his return; the Messiah is to reign over God's people until he returns. "Times of restoration" comes from the Greek, "apokatasta-
seos," and is a double compound word composed of "apo," "kata,"
and "histemi," and is only used here in the New Testament; it
seems to be a technical medical term, and means complete restoration to health. The first coming of Christ marked the beginning of
the period of restoration, and the second coming marks the end of
that period; all who are converted and live the Christian life repro-
duce the Christ life in his church until all things are ready for the
final restoration. The scope or the prophecies included both the
first and the second coming of Christ, and therefore included the
period known as the "restoration" of all things. The prophecies
were those mentioned by Zacharias in Luke 1: 70; the writer there
referred to such Messianic predictions as Psalm 111: 9; Jer. 25: 5,
6; 30: 10; Dan. 9: 24-26.

22 Moses indeed said, A prophet shall the Lord God—This
prophecy may be found in Deut. 18: 15-19, and Peter quotes it
without many variations from the Septuagint, Greek version of the
Old Testament; Moses was a lawgiver, leader, ruler, and deliverer,

your brethren ⁵like unto me; to him shall ye hearken in all things whatsoever he shall speak unto you. 23 ⁶And it shall be, that every soul that
shall not hearken to that prophet, shall be utterly destroyed from among the
people. 24 Yea and all the prophets from Samuel and them that followed

⁵Or, *as* he raised up *me*
⁶Dt. 18. 19

as well as a prophet; his prophecy had not been fulfilled. The
Jews acknowledged that this had reference to the Messiah; they
asked John the Baptist: "Art thou the prophet?" John answered
that he was not; and they asked him then: "Why then baptizest
thou, if thou art not the Christ, neither Elijah, neither the prophet?" (John 1: 21-25.) Here Peter identifies "the prophet" with
the Christ; this is exactly what the Jews had done. The Messiah
was to be one from among the Jews; he was to bring blessings to
every nation on the earth. They should obey this prophet "in all
things whatsoever" he should command them. Just as the children
of Israel were to obey Moses, their deliverer, lawgiver, ruler, their
leader, so the people now are to obey Christ as he is their Deliverer from sin, their Lawgiver, their Leader, their King, and Prophet.

23 **And it shall be, that every soul that shall not hearken—**
Jesus said that Moses wrote of him. "For if ye believed Moses, ye
would believe me; for he wrote of me." (John 5: 46.) The Jews
could not obey Moses without obeying Christ, since Moses commanded them to obey the prophet that God would raise up from
among them like unto him. The one who refused to obey this
prophet, the Christ, should "be utterly destroyed from among the
people." This declares that God himself would visit punishment
upon those who refused to accept Christ. It was plainly expressed
in the law that an apostate Israelite should be cut off from the people. (Ex. 12: 15, 19; 22: 20; Num. 19: 13.) The New Testament
language is that "shall be cast forth into the outer darkness"
(Matt. 8: 12); "shall suffer punishment, even eternal destruction
from the face of the Lord and from the glory of his might" (2
Thess. 1: 9). This expresses the fearful consequences of rejecting
Christ.

24 **Yea and all the prophets from Samuel—**Samuel was not
the first prophet in Israel; Enoch was the first prophet that we

after, as many as have spoken, they also told of these days. 25 Ye are the sons of the prophets, and of the covenant which God [7]made with your fathers, saying unto Abraham, [8]And in thy seed shall all the families of the earth be blessed. 26 Unto you first God, having raised up his [9]Servant, sent him to bless you, in turning away every one of you from your iniquities.

[7]Gr. *covenanted*
[8]Gen. 12. 3; 22. 18; 26. 4; 28. 14
[9]Or, *Child.* See Mt. 12. 18; Is. 42. 1; 52. 13; 53. 11

---

read about in the Bible (Jude 14, 15); Samuel was the founder of the school of the prophets; hence, Peter says that "all the prophets from Samuel" and those who came after him "told of these days." Samuel and every school of the prophets taught of the Messiah, and hence the days of which Peter now spoke. These prophets predicted the blessings or judgments that were to come, and especially the glories of the Messianic reign, the outpouring of the Holy Spirit, and "these days." They could not reject Peter's address without rejecting the Christ, and in rejecting the Christ they would be rejecting all of their prophets.

25 Ye are the sons of the prophets, and of the covenant— The Jews were "the sons of the prophets," and were members "of the covenant," not in the sense of being lineal descendants of the prophets, but in the sense of being heirs to all promises, predictions, and blessings of the covenant. The promise here referred to was first made to Abraham (Gen. 12: 3; 18: 18; 22: 18); and later to Isaac and Jacob (Gen. 26: 4; 28: 14). The prophet had arisen, of whom Moses had spoken, and all the promises made in the Abrahamic covenant belonged to these hearers whom Peter addressed; they were the heirs of the temporal blessings of this covenant and had access to the spiritual blessings through faith in Christ. The Abrahamic promise included "all the families of the earth"; this would include the Gentiles as well as the Jews, but as Peter's hearers were Jews, special application is here made to them.

26 Unto you first God, having raised up his Servant,—Some translations have "his Son" instead of "his Servant." The Greek is "tou paida autou," as in verse 13, as the Messiah was God's servant. This is in harmony with Isa. 42: 1; Matt. 12: 18. The conclusion of the whole matter is that salvation will come to them through their faith in Jesus and their turning from sin. In this address Peter gave the evidence that the lame man had been healed by the power of Jesus whom they had crucified and whom God had raised from the dead; he has ascended back to the Father and there will remain until the restoration of all things. Peter bore a threefold testimony concerning Christ: (1) he is the power by which all miracles are worked (verses 12-17); (2) the redeemer of all souls (verses 18-21); (3) the fulfillment of all the prophecies (verses 22-26).

6. FIRST PERSECUTION—PETER AND JOHN IMPRISONED
4: 1-22

1 And as they spake unto the people, [10]the priests and the captain of the temple and the Sadducess came upon them, 2 being sore troubled because they taught the people, and proclaimed in Jesus the resurrection from the

[10]Some ancient authorities read *the chief priests*

1, 2 **And as they spake unto the people,**—Peter and John had gone up to the temple at the ninth hour, which was the hour of prayer, and had healed the lame man; this excited and brought a multitude of people together in Solomon's porch of the temple, and Peter explained to the multitude the healing of the lame man and proceeded to preach Jesus as the Christ to them. The Jewish authorities felt the charge of crucifying the Messiah; they must either confess their guilt or suppress the testimony against them. Some of them chose to stop Peter and John from bearing testimony that Jesus of Nazareth was the Christ, the Messiah promised. The "Sadducees" joined the rulers in suppressing the testimony. The Sadducees did not believe in the resurrection of the dead; hence, when the resurrection of Jesus was preached, it antagonized them and they were ready to help suppress the doctrine of the resurrection. As the kingdom of God advances under the ministry of the apostles, the kingdom of darkness is also aroused, and sets itself in active opposition. The priests were divided into twenty-four courses, each of which served a week in the temple; the priests mentioned here are probably those on duty for that week. "The captain of the temple" was the ruler of the house of God (1 Chron. 9: 11; 2 Chron. 31: 13; Neh. 11: 11); he was a priest whose duty was to command the guard of Levites stationed in the temple; he posted the sentinels at night and preserved peace during the day; his presence implied that the authorities were afraid of a disturb-

dead. 3 And they laid hands on them, and put them in ward unto the morrow: for it was now eventide. 4 But many of them that heard the word
believed; and the number of the men came to be about five thousand.

---

ance from the crowd surrounding the apostles. The distinction
between Pharisees and Sadducees had grown out of national differences dating from the time of the captivity; they were a small
but powerful party of the priestly nobles who were supported by
the temple dues, and had come to regard religion as a matter of
profitable living rather than a service to God. They disliked any
popular movement which might disturb the steady accumulation of
temple revenues; they saw in the preaching of Jesus that their
source of revenue would be diminished.

3 **And they laid hands on them,**—To lay "hands on them"
was to arrest them; so they were arrested and put in "ward" or in
prison; probably the prison was one of the chambers of the temple;
Peter and John had gone up to the temple at the hour of prayer,
and now they find themselves at "eventide" in prison. They were
put in prison until the next morning, as no trial could take place
before the next day. They often quoted Jer. 21: 12, but violated
this with respect to the trial of Jesus; the day closed with the
twelfth hour or sunset.

4 **But many of them that heard the word**—In contrast with
the opposition "many of them that heard the word believed."
"The number of the men came to be about five thousand"; it is
noticed here that "the number of the men" became about five thousand; this says nothing about the number of women. Two questions have been raised here: (1) Did five thousand believe for the
first time that day? (2) Did the whole number of Christians now
become five thousand? Were five thousand converted here? or
were there only two thousand converted here? and the two thousand added to the three thousand on Pentecost made the number
five thousand? The best scholarship is in favor of two thousand
converted on this occasion, and so the number "came to be about
five thousand." It is very likely that others were converted besides those mentioned on Pentecost and those at this time, as some
time had elapsed between Pentecost and this day. The church increased rapidly.

5 And it came to pass on the morrow, that their rulers and elders and scribes were gathered together in Jerusalem; 6 and Annas the high priest *was there*, and Caiaphas, and John, and Alexander, and as many as were of the kindred of the high priest. 7 And when they had set them in the midst,

5, 6 **And it came to pass on the morrow,**—The apostles are now put on trial before the Sanhedrin; this was the highest court of the Jewish nation; "the morrow," or the day, had dawned and they could proceed legally with their trial. We have here mentioned the different classes who composed the Sanhedrin. The Sanhedrin was supposed to be composed of twenty-four chief priests, or rulers of the twenty-four courses into which the priests had been divided, and twenty-four elders and twenty-four scribes; this would make the number of the Sanhedrin to be seventy-two; the high priest was ex officio a member of the Sanhedrin. It seldom had its full quota. "Annas" is mentioned in Luke 3: 2 with Caiaphas as being both of them high priests; Annas was father-in-law of Caiaphas (John 18: 13), and had some rank above Caiaphas. This is accounted for from the fact that while by the Jewish law the office of high priest was held for life, it was shifted at pleasure by the Roman authorities; hence, while but one would be the high priest according to Jewish law, the office might have passed to several others by the authority of the Romans, who deposed and appointed whom they pleased. Here Annas is designated as the high priest (in the eye of the Jewish law the only one), while Caiaphas is named also as holding the title under the Romans. John and Alexander were relatives of Annas and Caiaphas, and must have been well known. There were also present "many as were of the kindred of the high priest." Some think that these were the members of the family of the high priest whose ancestors had lately enjoyed the high priesthood. Some authorities claim that Annas lived to see five sons and a son-in-law high priests, and for nearly fifty years enjoyed the real power of the high priesthood. Caiaphas was a Sadducee, and since he had been made high priest by the Roman authorities, he was willing to do anyting that the Roman authorities demanded.

7 **And when they had set them in the midst,**—When the Sanhedrin assembled that morning, and all of the kindred of the

they inquired, By what power, or in what name, have ye done this? 8 Then Peter, filled with the Holy Spirit, said unto them, Ye rulers of the people, and elders, 9 if we this day are examined concerning a good deed done to an impotent man, [11]by what means this man is made whole; 10 be it known unto

[11]Or, *in whom*

high priest were present, they "set them in the midst." The Sanhedrin usually sat in a semicircle in the room, and the accused and witnesses occupied a place in the center. When Peter and John were thus placed, they were asked: "By what power, or in what name, have ye done this?" "By what power" means the same as "in what name"; some think that they meant to ask: "What sort of power, or in what kind of name," have ye done this? It was impossible to deny the cure; the lame man now healed was in their midst; so the Sadducees asked for the authority or source of power for doing what they had done. This was the very question that the apostles wanted, for it would give them the best opportunity to preach Christ unto them.

8, 9 **Then Peter, filled with the Holy Spirit,**—It seems that they were filled with the Holy Spirit for the present occasion; they had been promised such aid when they should be brought before rulers for the sake of Christ. (Mark 13: 11; Luke 12: 12; 21: 14, 15.) "Ye rulers of the people, and elders," is a very respectful way of addressing the Sanhedrin. Christianity demands that we be respectful even to our enemies; the apostles set the example of being respectful to rulers. The high court or Sanhedrin consisted of seventy-two persons of rank; hence, the apostles recognize and honor the rank of the members of the Sanhedrin. Peter now puts the case on its merits and forces the Sanhedrin to pass judgment on their doing a good deed to an unfortunate man. Surely these honorable men will not object to the apostles doing "a good deed" to "an impotent man." They cannot object to the good deed without putting themselves against doing that which is good. Next they will want to know by what authority this good deed was done. They have a right to inquire into this matter, and the apostles are anxious to tell them that it is by the authority of Jesus of Nazareth who was crucified, but who has been raised from the dead.

you all, and to all the people of Israel, that in the name of Jesus Christ of
Nazareth, whom ye crucified, whom God raised from the dead, *even* in [12]him
doth this man stand here before you whole. 11 He is [13]the stone which was
set at nought of you the builders, which was made the head of the corner.
12 And in none other is there salvation: for neither is there any other name

[12]Or, *this* name
[13]Ps. 118. 22

---

10 **be it known unto you all,**—Peter is not ashamed or afraid
to give the greatest publicity to what he had done and taught; he is
anxious for the entire membership of the Sanhedrin and all who
were present to know. He at once tells them that the man was
made whole "in the name of Jesus Christ of Nazareth"; he also is
bold enough to accuse them of crucifying this Jesus, and that God
had raised him from the dead. They had asked, "By what power,
or in what name," and Peter now tells them that it was "in the
name of Jesus Christ of Nazareth." "Jesus" means Savior;
"Christ" means the anointed, the Messiah who was predicted in
the Old Testament; "of Nazareth" designates which Jesus, as the
one that they had crucified and the one that God had raised from
the dead. Peter thus charges the Sanhedrin of the high crime of
crucifying the Messiah. Instead of the Sanhedrin placing Peter
and John on trial, these apostles now put the Sanhedrin on trial;
they are forced to defend the crime which they had committed or
acknowledge their guilt.

11 **He is the stone which was set at nought**—Reference is
here made to Psalm 118: 22; Jesus is the stone which was set at
nought. Jesus had already made application of this Psalm to himself. (Matt. 21: 42.) Both Paul and Peter later referred to this
prophecy and applied it to Christ. (Eph. 2: 20; 1 Pet. 2: 4-6.)
The Sanhedrin as the rulers of the people had rejected Christ and
refused to build upon him, but he has now become the "chief corner stone." Their rejection of Christ went to prove him to be the
true stone of whom the prophets spoke.

12 **And in none other is there salvation:**—We must admire
the boldness of Peter and John as they stood in the midst of the
Sanhedrin and declared that even the members of the Sanhedrin
could be saved only by accepting this Jesus of Nazareth whom they
had condemned and crucified. This Jesus is the author of all salvation; the miraculous cure of this lame man and all others is only

under heaven, that is given among men, wherein we must be saved.
13 Now when they beheld the boldness of Peter and John, and had perceived that they were unlearned and ignorant men, they marvelled; and they

the lower department of his salvation; he is to save not only the
body, but the soul. Although the Sanhedrin had rejected Christ
once, Peter tells them that there is given them an opportunity to
repent; he also informs them that there is no "other name under
heaven, that is given among men," wherein people must be saved.
There is no second Savior; Jesus the Christ is the only Savior.
The Jews hoped to be saved because they were of Abraham's seed
(John 8: 33-39), or because they claimed to trust in Moses (John
5: 45, 46). But Abraham and Moses pointed to the Christ whom
they had rejected. It is important that the gospel be preached since
there was none other in whom there is salvation "wherein we must
be saved." In the Greek the "we" is the last word in the Greek
sentence; it means "we"—priests, elders, scribes, fishermen—all of
us here must be saved by faith and obedience in the Christ.

13 **Now when they beheld the boldness of Peter and John,**
—It was an inspiring scene to see the Sanhedrin assembled in a
semicircle, sitting in their dignity and clothed with the highest authority granted unto the Jewish race, and observe two prisoners,
Peter and John, standing accused by the Sanhedrin, to turn and
bring such grave charges against the Sanhedrin! It took courage
to do this; the members of the Sanhedrin observed their boldness
and observed that they were "unlearned and ignorant men."
"Unlearned," as used here, means unlettered men without technical training in the professional rabbinical schools of Hillel or
Shammai; Jesus himself was regarded as not having learned letters. (John 7: 15.) "Ignorant," as used here, is "one in a private station, as opposed to one in office or in public affairs; therefore, one without professional knowlege, a layman; hence, generally ignorant, ill-informed." These apostles were not cultured and
trained in the schools of that day, but they had a knowledge far superior to all of the culture and education and training of the members of the Sanhedrin. They were caused to wonder or marvel at
such boldness.. "They took knowledge of them, that they had been

took knowledge of them, that they had been with Jesus. 14 And seeing the man that was healed standing with them, they could say nothing against it. 15 But when they had commanded them to go aside out of the council, they conferred among themselves, 16 saying, What shall we do to these men? for that indeed a notable ¹miracle hath been wrought through them, is manifest to all that dwell in Jerusalem; and we cannot deny it. 17 But that it spread no further among the people, let us threaten them, that they speak henceforth

¹Gr. *sign*

with Jesus." They began to recognize them as men that had seen and had been associated with Jesus.

14 **And seeing the man that was healed standing**—The lame man was standing there before their eyes in proof of what Peter had said. They did not pretend to deny the miracle, neither were they prepared to acknowledge the real source of his cure. They had nothing to say; their mouths were closed; no argument could be made and no accusation could they charge against the apostles. What would they do under such circumstances?

15, 16 **But when they had commanded them to go aside**—In their confused state they asked the apostles to retire so that they could confer among themselves as to what was the best thing to do. They acknowledged that a notable deed had been done and that they could not deny it, and they knew that such publicity had been given to it that "all that dwell in Jerusalem" knew of it. Instead of asking what they should do to be saved, they asked how they should stop the apostles from preaching in the name of Jesus. They acknowledged that they could not deny what had been done, which implies that they would have denied if they could have done so successfully.

17 **But that it spread no further among the people,**—These admissions were made to each other in the absence of the apostles, and an agreement was reached that they "threaten them" that they speak no more "in this name." This was done that "it spread no further among the people." "Spread," as used here, means "be distributed." It is the same idea as expressed in 2 Tim. 2: 17: "Their word will eat as doth a gangrene," or literally, "will have distribution or spreading" as a gangrene. There was no inquiry as to the truth of their salvation, but an anxious inquiry as to how they could put a check on these apostles. They assumed that the teaching of the apostles was pernicious and that it must be sup-

to no man in this name. 18 And they called them, and charged them not to speak at all nor teach in the name of Jesus. 19 But Peter and John answered and said unto them, Whether it is right in the sight of God to hearken unto you rather than unto God, judge ye: 20 for we cannot but speak the things which we saw and heard. 21 And they, when they had further

pressed; their only concern was as to the best way to suppress it; hence, they proposed to threaten the apostles and not let them teach any more.

18 **And they called them, and charged them**—After reaching a decision in the absence of the apostles, they summoned the apostles again into their presence and made known to them the decision that they were "not to speak at all nor teach in the name of Jesus." The two words, "speak" and "teach," are used to make the command more rigid; the original conveys the idea that they were not to let the name of Jesus pass their lips again. They severely threatened them and charged them that they were not to use "the name of Jesus" at all.

19, 20 **But Peter and John answered and said unto them,**— This reply of the apostles shows the strong ground which they took; God spoke by the miracle which they had done, and the Sanhedrin, however authorized, had no right to contradict God. It was the business of the Sanhedrin to inquire whether Peter and John were speaking by the authority of God, but their right extended no further; they had no right to suppress anything that God authorized to be taught. Peter and John again put a matter to the Sanhedrin that it could not answer. They asked "whether it is right in the sight of God to hearken unto you rather than unto God." The Sanhedrin was in a dilemma. If the Sanhedrin said it is right to hearken unto God when God authorizes the thing to be done, then the apostles would continue to speak in the name of Jesus; but if the Sanhedrin should say that it was right to hearken unto its decision, then it would be teaching to go contrary to the authority of God. Peter gave them to understand that they would continue to obey the authority of God regardless of the decision and threats of the Sanhedrin. This was an open defiance of the authority of the Sanhedrin, when it conflicted with the authority of God. This was also an implication that the authority of the Sanhedrin was in defiance of the authority of God. The Sanhedrin threatened them, let them go, finding nothing how they might punish them, because of the people; for all men glorified God for that which was done. 22 For the man was more than forty years old, on whom this ¹miracle of healing was wrought.

was to learn that there were some things that it could not do; it could not put to silence the apostles.

21 **And they, when they had further threatened them,**—The Sanhedrin was put to silence; they had no further arguments to offer, charges to make, or warnings to give; they repeated with emphasis the threatenings that had been made. They "further threatened them"; that is, they added further threatenings to those that had been first announced. They let them go free, not because they were reconciled to them, or that they acknowledged that the apostles were right, but because they were unable to find in a legal way how "they might punish them." The Sanhedrin did not inflict punishment because "of the people." They were afraid of the people; they did not want the people to rise up against the rulers; the miracle was so manifest and so well known that "all men glorified God for that which was done." Hence, the people would be ready to take the part of the apostles against their persecutors. The enemies of Jesus also feared the people. (Mark 12: 12.) It would be dangerous for the rulers to deal severely with the apostles in the face of such public enthusiasm.

22 **For the man was more than forty years old,**—There was a reason for the age of the man being given. He had been lame all his life; he was not a child, but a man fully matured, and had been in this condition so long his acquaintance was extensive. This made the case a notable one in favor of the apostles and the cause of Christianity. The rulers were helpless except to threaten; the truth and the apostles had triumphed this time. All human cures had been exhausted and failed; the apostles with the power of Jesus had triumphed in the case.

7. PETER AND JOHN SET FREE; REPORT TO THE DISCIPLES; THEIR PRAYER
4: 23-31

23 And being let go, they came to their own company, and reported all that the chief priests and the elders had said unto them. 24 And they, when they heard it, lifted up their voice to God with one accord, and said, O ²Lord, ³thou that didst make the heaven and the earth and the sea, and all that in them is: 25 ⁴who by the Holy Spirit, *by* the mouth of our father David thy servant, didst say,

²Gr. *Master*
³Or, *thou art he that did make*
⁴The Greek text in this clause is somewhat uncertain

23 **And being let go, they came to their own company,**—
Here we have a turn in the history. The apostles so soon as they were released "came to their own company." They came to the Christians and reported "all that the chief priests and the elders had said unto them." They reported what the chief priests and elders had said in threatening them; and it is also possible that they reported just what they had said to the Sanhedrin. Peter and John had been tried before the Jewish court and they had been triumphant in their defense; they now reported all to the other Christians. The entire company of Christians now numbered several thousand. It is noted that the Sanhedrin is here called "the chief priests and the elders."

24 **And they, when they heard it,**—When the disciples heard the report of Peter and John, they "lifted up their voice to God with one accord." They all prayed to God; they were united in their prayer. Did one lead and the others repeat aloud the petition after him? Was there a general form of prayer already known to all? Or did one lead and the others join mentally or by responses with "Amen"? We do not know just how they proceeded; we only know that "with one accord" they addressed God as the one who had made "the heaven and the earth and the sea." This prayer addressed Jehovah as the Creator and Governor of the universe. The same God who made the world has prophesied of Christ and provided against all his enemies.

25, 26 **who by the Holy Spirit,**—Again we have reference made to Psalm 2: 1, 2, and it is ascribed to David. Reference here made to this Psalm shows that it was prophetic, and had reference to Christ in whom it is so remarkably fulfilled. "Why did the

[5]Why did the [6]Gentiles rage,
And the peoples [7]imagine vain things?
26   The kings of the earth set themselves in array,
And the rulers were gathered together,
Against the Lord, and against his [8]Anointed:
27 for of a truth in this city against thy holy [9]Servant Jesus, whom thou
didst anoint, both Herod and Pontius Pilate, with the [6]Gentiles and the peoples of Israel, were gathered together, 28 to do whatsoever thy hand and thy

[5]Ps. 2. 1, 2
[6]Gr. nations
[7]Or, meditate
[8]Gr. Christ
[9]Or, Child. See marginal note on ch. 3. 13

Gentiles rage" had reference to the nations who were not of Israel,
and "the peoples" generally are included by the Jews; hence, both
Jew and Gentile "raged" against Christ. The Greek for "rage" is
"ephruaxan," and literally means "to neigh like a horse, to prance
or stamp the ground, to put on lofty airs." This is the only time
the word is used in the New Testament. "Imagine" is from the
Greek "emeletesan," and means "to practice, to caution, as orators
and rhetoricians." "The kings of the earth" mean the rulers and
governors, and include the Jewish "Sanhedrin" with all its mighty
power. All of the forces were "gathered together" against "the
Lord, and against his Anointed." The Psalm is quoted and applied to Jesus as the Christ, and the heathen or Roman soldiers,
the people of the Jews, kings of the earth such as Herod and Pontius Pilate, and the rulers, or Sanhedrin, were all opposed to
Christ.

27, 28 **for of a truth in this city**—The apostles continued their
prayer with the assembly of disciples and made mention of the opposition "against thy holy Servant Jesus"; some translate "holy
Child Jesus." God had anointed him with the Holy Spirit at his
baptism; hence, he was the "Christ," as "Christ" means
"anointed." (Isa. 42: 1; 52: 13; Zech. 3: 8.) "Herod and Pontius Pilate, with the Gentiles and the peoples of Israel," were gathered together and put Jesus to death. He was brought before
Herod and Pilate in his mock trials; he was subjected to trial before the Sanhedrin; the Jews and Roman soldiers conspired together to put Jesus to death. The actors in this dreadful tragedy
had no design to fulfill prophecy; they only acted of their own free
will, and were guilty of the greatest crime known to man, yet they
were doing that which fulfilled the predictions concerning them.

counsel foreordained to come to pass. 29 And now, Lord, look upon their threatenings: and grant unto thy [10]servants to speak thy word with all boldness, 30 while thou stretchest forth thy hand to heal; and that signs and wonders may be done through the name of thy holy [9]Servant Jesus. 31 And when they had prayed, the place was shaken wherein they were gathered together; and they were all filled with the Holy Spirit, and they spake the word of God with boldness.

[10]Gr. *bondservants*

The death of Jesus was a fulfillment of prophecy and was necessary to his resurrection.

29, 30 And now, Lord, look upon their threatenings:—The apostles prayed for courage to go on and preach the gospel, for God to continue his power with them in working miracles and confirming his word, and for God to be with them as they continued to speak boldly in the name of Jesus. They were under the heavy threatenings of the Sanhedrin; they wanted to be protected from the threatenings of the opposition so they could continue freely to testify for Christ. This was to be done by God's stretching "forth thy hand to heal." By exerting his miraculous power in healing the sick and the lame, God would be confirming what the apostles preached; this was all to be done "through the name of thy holy Servant Jesus." The apostles did not pray for safety or deliverance from the threats, or that their persecutors be crushed; they asked as "bondservants" for boldness to speak the word and continue the work which they had begun. They prayed that the "signs and wonders" should prove to the people the power of Jesus.

31 And when they had prayed,—God answered their prayers by this physical manifestation; the "place was shaken" where they had assembled with the other disciples. Also "they were all filled with the Holy Spirit," which was a renewal of the Holy Spirit received on Pentecost. The apostles were strengthened anew by the Spirit's influence; they rose above the fear of the rulers' threats, and continued with boldness to bear testimony in the name of Jesus. It should be observed that these pious men went to the Lord in prayer under these trying circumstances. It is encouraging to Christians to have the fellowship and companionship of others in the work of the Lord; the apostles went to this company of disciples. It may be observed also that the enemies of God cannot thwart the purposes of God. They continued to speak "the word of God with boldness" wherever occasion presented itself.

8. UNITY OF THE CHURCH; POSSESSIONS FOR COMMON GOOD
4 : 32-37

32 And the multitude of them that believed were of one heart and soul: and not one *of them* said that aught of the things which he possessed was his own; but they had all things common. 33 And with great power gave the apostles their witness of the resurrection of the Lord Jesus[11]: and great

[11]Some ancient authorities add *Christ*

32 **And the multitude of them that believed**—The disciples of Christ now numbered several thousand; they were all in and around Jerusalem; they had not been scattered at this time. The entire company were united; they "were of one heart and soul." They were many in number, but one in spirit. One of the most striking things that may be said about the early church was its perfect oneness of heart and soul. It is not possible to make a clear distinction between "heart" and "soul." "Kardia," as used here, means not only the seat of the affections, but the center of the entire complex being, physical, moral, and intellectual. "Psuche" is frequently used in the New Testament to mean "life." (Matt. 2: 20; 20: 28; Acts 20: 10; Rom. 11: 3.) Those who owned property regarded it not as their own, but freely used it for the common weal of others; they "had all things common." The property was held for the common use, but the rights of property were not abolished, nor the individual holding of property declared to be wrong. This was an emergency, and all were willing and anxious to use whatever they possessed for the common good.

33 **And with great power gave the apostles their witness**— The apostles bore witness to the resurrection with great power; the resurrection was the offensive doctrine to the Sadducees; it was the very heart of the gospel; hence, the apostles bore witness to what they had seen and heard. They kept on giving their witness with power after the answer to their prayer. "Great power" means the force of argument accompanied with spiritual power. "Great grace was upon them all." The entire membership of the church found favor with each other and with others. The lives

grace was upon them all. 34 For neither was there among them any that
lacked: for as many as were possessors of lands or houses sold them, and
brought the prices of the things that were sold, 35 and laid them at the apostles' feet: and distribution was made unto each, according as any one had
need.
36 And Joseph, who by the apostles was surnamed Barnabas (which is,

---

that they were now living commended them to others. The original word for "grace" is the same as the word for "favor" in Acts
2: 47. Hence, the same idea is expressed; therefore, great favor
was felt toward the Christians on the part of the people generally.

34, 35 **For neither was there among them**—No one among
them was allowed by his brethren to be in want, for no one among
them was in want. Those who owned the property sold it and used
the money to relieve those who were in destitute circumstances. It
should be remembered that a great company of Jews had assembled in Jerusalem for the Passover, and then remained over for the
Pentecost feast. They brought possessions enough to last them
until this feast had passed. But many of them had been converted
and continued their sojourn in Jerusalem until their supply had
been exhausted. They were now new creatures in Christ; they
had begun a new life; they had new hopes and new purposes; they
had not learned the full meaning of Christianity. Some of them
were in need, not because they had been idle, neither because they
had squandered their possessions, nor yet because they were shift-
less; but their means had been exhausted and they now were in
need. In this emergency those who had possessions were ready
to distribute as each had need. There is no "communism" practiced
here; there was no denial of property rights, nor an encouragement to idleness; but an emergency had arisen and they had
enough of the spirit of Christ to supply the needs of those who
were in distress.

36, 37 **And Joseph, who by the apostles was surnamed Barnabas**—"Barnabas" is derived from two Hebrew words which
mean "son of teaching" or "preaching"; the two Greek words,
here translated "son of consolation," may also mean "son of
preaching or exhortation." His name was "Joseph"; he is here
mentioned as one illustration of those who are mentioned in verse
34, who sold his possessions and brought the money to the apostles
for them to distribute it as there was need. The apostles named

being interpreted, Son of [12]exhortation), a Levite, a man of Cyprus by race,
37 having a field, sold it, and brought the money and laid it at the apostles'
feet.

[12]Or, *consolation*. See Lk. 2. 25; ch. 9. 31; 15. 31; 2 Cor. 1. 3-7, in the Gr.

---

this Joseph "Barnabas," and he is known better by this name than
any other. It seems clear from this fact that all did not actually
sell their property, but were ready to do so as the need arose; but
Barnabas actually sold his field and gave to the apostles the price.
It is very likely that as a preacher his gift was in persuasion and
exhortation. In Acts 11: 23 the very word "parekalei," which
means "exhorted," is used of Barnabas. Paul describes such a
preacher in 1 Cor. 14: 3. He is in a broad sense of the word
called an apostle. (Acts 14: 14.) He was of the tribe of Levi
and a native of Cyprus, which was an important island in the Mediterranean Sea. He was a Levite and "a man of Cyprus by race,"
which means that he was a Jew and was born in Cyprus of Jewish
parents; the Greek literally means "a Levite, a Cyprian by birth";
he was both a Jew and a Cyprian.

9. ANANIAS AND SAPPHIRA
5: 1-11

1 But a certain man named Ananias, with Sapphira his wife, sold a posses-

---

1 **But a certain man named Ananias, with Sapphira his
wife,**—Luke now turns to the dark side of the picture in the history of the early church; he selected two illustrations of those who
sold lands and possessions; he has just described what Barnabas
did, and now turns to another case which is put in contrast. "A
certain man named Ananias" and his wife Sapphira sold a piece of
land. "Ananias" was a name very familiar among the Jews; it
means "the grace of the Lord." "Sapphira" means "beautiful";
her name is mentioned twice in connection with the sin. "With
Sapphira his wife" is the way Luke presents her. The two illustrations here were intended to be brought in contrast, as the conjunction "but" introduces this sentence; these illustrations lose
some of their force by the division into chapters; this division was
not made by Luke.

sion, 2 and kept back *part* of the price, his wife also being privy to it, and brought a certain part, and laid it at the apostles' feet. 3 But Peter said, Ananias, why hath Satan filled thy heart to [13]lie to the Holy Spirit, and to keep back *part* of the price of the land? 4 While it remained, did it not remain thine own? and after it was sold, was it not in thy power? How is it

[13]Or, *deceive*

---

2 **and kept back part of the price,**—Ananias took the lead in this sin, but his wife knew of it and entered into the sin with him; they pretended to deliver up the entire amount which they had received for the land. His wife was fully acquainted with his purpose and agreed to join him in practicing the deception. The praise that Barnabas received for what he had done was too much for Ananias; he wanted to obtain the same praise, but he was not willing to make the sacrifice that Barnabas made; he wanted praise for giving all while he had given only a part. He started "the Ananias Club" which has given a different meaning to his name—"Jehovah hath been gracious."

3 **But Peter said, Ananias, why hath Satan filled thy heart**— This is the first sin recorded against any member of the church; it may not be the first sin that any of them committed, but it is the first one of which we have a record. We do not know how old the church was at this time, since we do not know how long it had been since Pentecost. We are not told how Satan filled the heart of Ananias to "lie to the Holy Spirit." We do know that Ananias permitted Satan to fill his heart; Ananias was held responsible for what he did, and therefore, he permitted Satan to prompt him to do the evil. There seems to be an inspiration of the devil as well as an inspiration of the Holy Spirit. We may infer here that Satan is a real being acting upon and influencing men to do evil; that Ananias had the power to resist Satan's influence, or he should not have been punished. Peter accused him of lying by keeping back a part of the price, and attempting to deceive; he thus attempts to deceive the Holy Spirit, since the apostles were filled with the Holy Spirit.

4 **While it remained, did it not remain thine own?**—It was the property of Ananias and his wife; they volunteered to sell it; the price was in their hands, and they could do with it what they pleased. This shows that the disciples who owned property were

that thou hast conceived this thing in thy heart? thou hast not lied unto
men, but unto God. 5 And Ananias hearing these words fell down and gave
up the ghost: and great fear came upon all that heard it. 6 And the ¹young
men arose and wrapped him round, and they carried him out and buried him.
7 And it was about the space of three hours after, when his wife, not

¹Gr. *younger*

---

not forced or commanded to dispose of that property; those who
did so showed liberality and charity. Peter impresses upon him
that he had not "lied unto men, but unto God." The community
of goods was not compulsory; it was permitted and encouraged because of the emergency of the case; Peter does not say that Ananias had not lied unto men at all, but that the gravity of his offense
was that he thought to deceive God.

5, 6 **And Ananias hearing these words**—Ananias died by the
special visitation of God as a punishment for his hypocrisy and his
attempt to deceive men in whom the Holy Spirit eminently dwelt,
and thus attempting to deceive the Holy Spirit and God. "Great
fear came upon all that heard it." This statement of Luke does not
have reference merely to the time between the death of Ananias
and Sapphira, but was made by the historian to show the effect that
the death of Ananias had on all of the disciples. Some of the
"young men arose" and carried the body of Ananias out and buried
it. The circumstances required a speedy burial; neither the place
nor the circumstance would admit of much formal preparation for
a funeral. It was customary among the Jews to bury on the same
day that death occurred; coffins or caskets were not in use at that
time, and they simply "wrapped him round" with possibly his
mantle that he had worn. This was done without delay and without sending his wife word. It is very likely that all was done
under the direction of the apostle Peter. The age and ability of
the younger men made them suitable persons to bury the body.
Some think that Luke described the wrapping with bandages as a
physician would bandage a broken limb; however, others think
that the young men used their own mantles in preparing the body
for this speedy burial.

7 **And it was about the space of three hours**—It would seem
strange that the death of the husband and the burial of his body
should take place and his wife, Sapphira, not know anything about

knowing what was done, came in. 8 And Peter answered unto her, Tell me whether ye sold the land for so much. And she said, Yea, for so much. 9 But Peter *said* unto her, How is it that ye have agreed together to try the Spirit of the Lord? behold, the feet of them that have buried thy husband are at the door, and they shall carry thee out. 10 And she fell down imme-

---

it. The custom, hot climate, and the strong sense of defilement from contact with a dead body would all tend to hasten burial, besides the sense of awe caused by the manner of his death. The three hours would give time for the burial and for the young men to return from the burial. His wife came in about this time. We do not know where they were at this time, but probably in some well-known meeting place in Jerusalem.

8 **And Peter answered unto her,**—It seems that before she had learned of the death of her husband Peter asked her if the land had been sold for a certain price; he very likely specified the price that Ananias had mentioned. Sapphira answered the question and designated that price. "Yea, for so much." Peter may have pointed to the pile of money that Ananias brought in when he asked her the question. Peter's question would awaken her conscience and prompt her to tell the truth; but instead of confessing her sin she confirmed the lie told by Ananias.

9 **But Peter said unto her, How is it that ye have agreed together**—Sapphira was given the opportunity to confess her wrong and correct it, but she persisted in the sin. Peter then asked why she had agreed with Ananias "to try the Spirit of the Lord." Here Peter refers to "the Holy Spirit" as "the Spirit of the Lord," because the Lord had sent the Holy Spirit. He then called her attention to the fact that the young men who had buried her husband had just returned, and that "they shall carry thee out." It seems that this case, whether intentional or not, was to "try the Spirit of the Lord," or put the Holy Spirit to the test to see whether the apostles or Holy Spirit could detect any hypocrisy or deception. Such was the nature of their conduct that it involved a doubt whether their sin would ever be known, or a disbelief as to the knowledge and holiness of God. So deep was their sin, so utterly regardless were they of the presence of God, that they committed this crime against the Holy Spirit. Peter an-

diately at his feet, and gave up the ghost: and the young men came in and found her dead, and they carried her out and buried her by her husband. 11 And great fear came upon the whole church, and upon all that heard these things.

nounced to her that her death would immediately take place.

10 **And she fell down immediately at his feet,**—Very close to the place where her husband had died and close to the place where the money was piled, Sapphira died. Her death, like that of Ananias, was regarded as supernatural. The young men who had buried her husband came in and "found her dead," and carried her out and "buried her by her husband." Literally, they buried her "face to face to her husband." The swift judgment of God was visited upon her, thus impressing upon all in the church the fearfulness of sin.

11 **And great fear came upon the whole church,**—The church was purified of this awful sin. "If any man destroyeth the temple of God, him shall God destroy; for the temple of God is holy, and such are ye." (1 Cor. 3: 17.) Fear came upon "the whole church." Here for the first time in Acts we find "ekklesia," from which we get the word church. The word is used twice in Matthew (16: 18) where it is used to designate all believers in Christ and (18: 17) where it is used to designate the local body. In Acts 7: 38 it is used to designate the whole congregation of Israel, while in Acts 19: 32 it is used to designate a public assembly in Ephesus; but in Acts 8: 3 it is applied to the church which Saul was persecuting in their homes when not assembled.

10. SIGNS AND WONDERS
5: 12-16

12 And by the hands of the apostles were many signs and wonders wrought among the people; and they were all with one accord in Solomon's

12 **And by the hands of the apostles**—Frequently we have the signs and wonders attributed to "the hands of the apostles." The awful judgment upon Ananias and Sapphira was followed by "many signs and wonders" which were "wrought among the people." Just as the exclusion of Achan was followed by victories of Israel at Ai (Josh. 7 and 8), so these signs and wonders followed

²porch. 13 But of the rest durst no man join himself to them: howbeit the
people magnified them; 14 ³and believers were the more added to the Lord,

²Or, *portico*
³Or, *and there were the more added* to them, *believing on the Lord*

---

the cleansing of the church by the death of Ananias and Sapphira.
"Signs and wonders"—in Acts 2: 43 it is put "wonders and signs."
Miracles in the New Testament are described by four names—
"signs," "works," "wonders," and "powers." They are "signs" of
the presence and power of God, of the truth of divine revelation;
"works" include all the doings of God which are supernatural;
"wonders" give the astonishing manifestations of God, attracting
men's attention to him; "powers" because they reveal the almighty
power of God to help and save. Again we find the disciples "all
with one accord in Solomon's porch." They assembled here when
attracted by the healing of the lame man a few days before this.
(Acts 3: 11.)

13 **But of the rest durst no man join himself**—The miracles
of the apostles had such an effect on the multitude that "no man"
attempted to "join himself to them." Who are meant by "the
rest"? It seems to stand in contrast with "all" in verse 12. If it
does, then "the rest" might refer to Pharisees, rulers, and the
crowd generally; but others think that it has reference to the apostles, and that the other disciples stood in awe of them and did not
come near them. Christians and others were smitten with terror at
the death of Ananias and Sapphira; and awed by the power of the
apostles to know the secret thoughts of persons as shown by Peter
discerning their falsehood, and seeing they were putting the Holy
Spirit to the test in planning to deceive him, felt afraid to come
near the apostles, and kept at a distance from them. While the
people feared to join themselves to their company, yet they magnified them for the superhuman knowledge and power they showed.

14 **and believers were the more added to the Lord,**—"Prose-
tithento" is the Greek from which we get "added"; "mallon" is the
Greek for "more." It means literally that believers "kept being
added." "Both of men and women" describes the "believers";
only believers were added to the Lord; no infants or irresponsible
persons were added to the Lord. The distinction between "andres"

multitudes both of men and women; 15 insomuch that they even carried out the sick into the streets, and laid them on beds and ⁴couches, that, as Peter came by, at the least his shadow might overshadow some one of them. 16 And there also came together the multitude from the cities round about Je-

⁴Or, *pallets*

---

and "gunaikes," or "men and women," may be considered in connection with "andres" in Acts 4: 4. To be added "to the Lord" is to be "added to the church"; and "to be added to the church" is to be "converted"; hence, only converted ones were added to the church.

15 **insomuch that they even carried out the sick**—This verse seems to look back to verses 12 and 13, which show that the membership increased, together with the influence of the church, as the "many signs and wonders" were wrought. Miracles were wrought, the disciples met together as a distinct body in Solomon's porch, the membership was much increased, so that they brought forth the sick for miraculous healing by the apostles. The places of public resort were not sufficient to accommodate the great number that came for healing. They carried their sick "into the streets, and laid them on beds and couches," so that as Peter passed by, "at the least his shadow might overshadow some one of them," and they be healed. In his daily passing to and fro they hoped to be healed even by his shadow; that is, the power of the Holy Spirit would heal them through even Peter's shadow. This shows the great fear and reverence that the people had for the apostles who could work such miracles; it also shows the faith that they had in God through the preaching of Peter and John.

16 **And there also came together the multitude**—Not only were the sick brought to the apostles from Jerusalem, but the "multitude from the cities round about Jerusalem" brought their sick and those who were vexed with "unclean spirits," and "they were healed every one." This states more clearly and fully the details of what had been stated in verse 12. It was a manifestation "of signs and wonders" greater than any before mentioned in the history of the church thus far. Jesus had said: "He that believeth on me, the works that I do shall he do also; and greater works than these shall he do; because I go unto the Father." (John 14: 12.) Here was a fulfillment of this promise by Jesus. "Unclean

rusalem, bringing sick folk, and them that were vexed with unclean spirits:
and they were healed every one.

---

spirits" mean those who are possessed with demons. Some think
that they were fallen angels who, being depraved themselves, seek
to make others depraved. (Zech. 13: 2; Luke 4: 33.) The sick
and the demoniacs are here as in Luke 6: 18 distinguished. The
demoniacs may be associated with the sick as they usually are, for
one possessed of a demon suffered bodily from the possession, and
was relieved when the demon was cast out. It is noted that there
were no favors, but all were cured.

11. PETER AND JOHN IMPRISONED AGAIN
5: 17-25

17 But the high priest rose up, and all they that were with him (which is
the sect of the Sadducees), and they were filled with jealousy, 18 and laid

---

17 **But the high priest rose up,**—Here we see another step
taken by the enemies of the early church. Peter and John had
been thrust into prison overnight to await their trial in the morning. (Acts 4: 3.) The "high priest" was probably Annas, who is
named as high priest (Acts 4: 6), or it may have been Caiaphas,
who was acting high priest at the time by Roman authority.
According to the law, Annas was high priest until his death.
(Num. 35: 25, 28, 32.) "Rose up" has been variously interpreted; some think that it simply means to rise from one's seat or
bed (Matt. 9: 9; Mark 1: 35; Luke 4: 29); others give it a figura-
tive meaning as to be raised from the dead (Matt. 17: 9; Mark 6:
14; Luke 9: 8); still others give it the meaning to follow a course
without giving some reason for doing so. It seems here that this is
the meaning; Annas with the Sadducees, who were opposed to the
resurrection from the dead, began anew the persecution of the
apostles. "Sect of the Sadducees" means those who taught against
the resurrection and held to other tenets of faith. "Sect" comes
from "hairesis," which means "to choose an opinion, parties, factions." (1 Cor. 11: 19; Gal. 5: 20.) It is also applied to the
Pharisees (Acts 15: 5; 26: 5) and to Christians (Acts 24: 5-14;
28: 22).

hands on the apostles, and put them in public ward. 19 But an angel of
the Lord by night opened the prison doors, and brought them out, and said,
20 Go ye, and stand and speak in the temple to the people all the words of

---

18 and laid hands on the apostles,—Peter and John were arrested and this time they were put "in public ward"; that is, in the
public prison. They were not put in prison for punishment, but
for detention until they could be examined; however, they were
made to associate with all sorts of criminals in this prison. The
arrest is described in the same words as before—"laid hands" on
them. (Acts 4: 3.)

19 **But an angel of the Lord by night**—This is put in contrast with what the high priest and Sadducees did for them; they
put them in prison, but "an angel of the Lord" visited, comforted,
and delivered them. There are at least six distinct acts ascribed to
angels by Luke in the Acts. (5: 19; 8: 26; 10: 3; 12: 7, 23; 27:
23.) "Angel" is found twenty times in Acts. The angel here
opened the prison doors and released the apostles. This act on the
part of the angel gave courage and confidence to the apostles; it
astonished, perplexed, and awed the Sadducees and prepared the
way for the release of the apostles; it confirmed the faith of the
disciples and held the favor of the people. The "angel" did more
than merely open the prison door; he "brought them out" and
gave them a command.

20 **Go ye, and stand and speak in the temple**—The angel
commanded them, after releasing them from prison, to go and
"stand and speak in the temple." That is, they were to take their
places as usual, and with courage stand and teach. They were not
to linger, but go at once; they were to go to the temple and speak
"to the people all the words of this Life." They were to speak the
words of eternal life which Christ revealed; speak the words of the
resurrection life, which the Sadducees denied. Peter once had said
of Jesus: "Thou hast the words of eternal life." (John 6: 68.)
These words were committed to the apostles, and the angel now
bids them speak these words to all the people. Jesus not only had
the words of eternal life, but he gives life to those who obey him.
(2 Tim. 1: 10; 1 John 5: 11.) "I am the way, and the truth,

this Life. 21 And when they heard *this*, they entered into the temple about daybreak, and taught. But the high priest came, and they that were with him, and called the council together, and all the senate of the children of Israel, and sent to the prison-house to have them brought. 22 But the officers that came found them not in the prison; and they returned, and told, 23 saying, The prison-house we found shut in all safety, and the keepers standing at the doors: but when we had opened, we found no man within.

---

and the life," said Jesus. (John 14: 6.) "In him was life; and the life was the light of men." (John 1: 4.)

21 **And when they heard this, they entered into the temple**— The apostles did not delay; they went early, "about daybreak," and began teaching those who came to the temple at that early hour. They had been forbidden by the Sanhedrin to speak any more in the name of Christ, but seemingly in defiance to all authority of men they continue to preach the resurrection. The high priest assembled the Sanhedrin and "called the council together, and all the senate of the children of Israel," and made ready to try the apostles. The high priest came, and "they that were with him," meaning the Sadducees; men of influence were also invited to be present; it seems that they wanted to have a strong and influential meeting. "The senate" is from the Greek "ten gerousian," and means the old men. After the council with its prominent men had assembled they "sent to the prison-house" to have the apostles brought to them. All things were ready for the trial, but the presence of the prisoners; hence, they sent for them.

22, 23 **But the officers that came found them not**—The officers must have been greatly surprised when they came to the prison and found the prison doors closed and fastened as the guard had left them, but no prisoners within. It must have been a foolish feeling for them to be guarding an empty prison, or to go for prisoners who were already free and publicly preaching in the temple. These "officers" were not Roman soldiers, but Jewish civil officers or servants of the Sanhedrin. There were no marks of prison doors being broken nor the walls battered; everything was in good order, but the prisoners were absent. It seems that the angel had miraculously opened the prison doors and brought the prisoners out without the guards or keepers knowing anything about it.

24 Now when the captain of the temple and the chief priests heard these words, they were much perplexed concerning them whereunto this would grow. 25 And there came one and told them, Behold, the men whom ye put in the prison are in the temple standing and teaching the people. 26 Then

24 **Now when the captain of the temple**—The Standard Version omits "high priest," and mentions only the "captain of the temple and the chief priests"; the "captain" was the ruler of the house of God; he was not a military officer, but had charge of the guard of priests and Levites who watched the temple at night. "The chief priests" were the heads of the classes or courses of the priests. There were twenty-four divisions of priests and each division had its "chief." The Sanhedrin was composed of chief priests, elders, and scribes. All were confused as well as perplexed about the affair; they did not know how the prisoners had escaped, but that which concerned them most was what would be the final outcome of preaching the name of Jesus.

25 **And there came one and told them,**—As the Sanhedrin was thrown into a state of confusion and astonishment when the report that the prisoners were gone reached it, there came another report which added to the state of perplexity; this report was that the apostles were "in the temple standing and teaching the people." They had been put in prison for preaching Christ; an angel had released them without the authorities knowing it; and now to their great surprise the apostles were in the temple doing that which they had been forbidden to do and in seeming defiance of the authority of the Sanhedrin. The apostles were at their old work, fearlessly teaching the people in the temple. The fearless apostles were too powerful to be roughly treated and the Sanhedrin did not know what to do.

12. PETER'S ADDRESS TO THE SANHEDRIN
5: 26-32

went the captain with the officers, and brought them, *but* without violence;

26 **Then went the captain with the officers,**—The apostles were rearrested by the captain and officers, and "without violence" brought before the Sanhedrin. They did not bind the apostles, but

for they feared the people, lest they should be stoned. 27 And when they
had brought them, they set them before the council. And the high priest
asked them, 28 saying, We strictly charged you not to teach in this name:
and behold, ye have filled Jerusalem with your teaching, and intend to bring

---

with all consideration for them they brought them before the council. There were at this time several thousand Christians; nearly
all of these were still in Jerusalem, and the Sanhedrin was in the
minority, and "feared the people"; they were afraid that the people
would stone them. This shows the great influence that the number
of disciples had over the Jewish authorities. Peter and John not
only stood very high in the estimation of the people, but they were
quite popular at this time. The officers and Sanhedrin were not
concerned about what was right, but rather what was expedient.

27, 28 **And when they had brought them,**—Peter and John
were not afraid to be brought before the Sanhedrin; they knew
that they had followed a course that seemed to defy the authority
of the council, but they knew that they were in the right; this
made them bold to continue their course. When they were
brought before the Sanhedrin, they were "set" in the place of the
accused in the presence of the Sanhedrin. The accused usually
stood in the semicircle and made their defense. The spokesman
for the Sanhedrin, probably the high priest, said: "We strictly
charged you not to teach in this name." The apostles knew the
charge, but knew that God was with them in what they were
doing. Instead of obeying the charge of the council, they were
now charged with having "filled Jerusalem" with their teaching.
So many had heard and obeyed the gospel that they could truly say
that Jerusalem had been filled with the teachings of Jesus. They
further explained to the apostles or charged them that they intended "to bring this man's blood upon us." The blood of Jesus
was already upon them; the Sanhedrin had condemned him to
death and had asked Pilate to confirm its decision; it now feels the
guilt, but is not ready to repent. The simple and obvious answer
is that the teachings of the apostles, in view of the Sanhedrin,
tended to arouse the people, so that they would avenge the death of
Jesus upon their rulers. They were ready enough to accept that
responsibility before Pilate (Matt. 27: 25), but now they are not

this man's blood upon us. 29 But Peter and the apostles answered and said,
We must obey God rather than men. 30 The God of our fathers raised up
Jesus, whom ye slew, hanging him on a tree. 31 Him did God exalt [5]with
his right hand *to be* a Prince and a Saviour, to give repentance to Israel,

---

[5]Or. *at*

---

willing to accept the responsibility. Caiaphas, or the high priest,
did not mention the name of Jesus, but spoke of him as "this man."

29 **But Peter and the apostles answered**—It seems from this
that there were other apostles than Peter and John, but no others
have been mentioned. Peter, speaking for the apostles and for all
disciples, said: "We must obey God rather than men." Here
Peter, as in Acts 4: 19, states the principle that should govern all
Christians. When there is a conflict between the authority of God
and men, we must obey God; God comes first; obedience to his
authority takes precedence over all other authorities. Here the
conflict is between obedience to the Sanhedrin or obedience to
God. Peter, without any evading or equivocation, states posi-
tively, clearly, and emphatically that he and the other apostles are
going to obey God.

30 **The God of our fathers raised up Jesus,**—Again there is
brought in sharp contrast what the rulers had done to Jesus and
what God had done; they had falsely charged him, mockingly condemned him, and shamefully crucified him, but God had raised him
from the dead. "Epi xulou" is the Greek for "tree"; it originally
meant "wood, timber." (Luke 23: 31; Acts 5: 30; 10: 39; 1 Pet.
2: 24.) The term "slew," in the original, means "to take in hand,
manage, to lay hands on, manhandle, kill." He was put to death
by crucifixion on the cross. This describes what man had done to
him.

31 **Him did God exalt with his right hand**—To continue the
description as to what God had done for him, he has been exalted
and is now at the right hand of God as "a Prince and a Saviour."
"A Prince," as having authority and so must be obeyed; he has all
authority in heaven and on earth; as "a Saviour," he uses his authority to give salvation unto all who obey him. Jesus is now
Prophet, Priest, and King; he is a Savior to those only who accept
him as their Lord. He gives "repentance to Israel, and remission
of sins." Repentance is given by teaching them to turn from their

and remission of sins. 32 And we are witnesses ¹of these ²things; ³and *so is* the Holy Spirit, whom God hath given to them that obey him.

sins and by granting the opportunity unto them; remission of sins is granted to those who obey his will. Jesus has been raised from the dead and exalted to the right hand of God that he might be the King and Savior of those who put their trust in him.

32 **And we are witnesses of these things;**—The apostles were witnesses of the crucifixion, the resurrection, and the ascension; these three main topics were emphasized in the preaching of the apostles. Peter also states that the Holy Spirit is also witness of the things which they preached, "whom God hath given to them that obey him." The Holy Spirit is given to those only who obey him. This is the conclusion of Peter's second address to the council. So we have the Holy Spirit and the apostles as witnesses for Christ and against the Sanhedrin. The three lines of his defense were as follows: (1) We must obey God; (2) the facts in the life of Jesus show that we have not obeyed God; (3) the Holy Spirit is witness with us of all these things. Hence, if the apostles were wrong, the Holy Spirit was wrong.

13. SPEECH OF GAMALIEL
5: 33-42

33 But they, when they heard this, were cut to the heart, and were

33 **But they, when they heard this, were cut to the heart,**— This expresses the effect that Peter's address had on the council; instead of being convinced and turning from their evil course, they were "cut to the heart," but not of the conviction of their sins. Instead of blessing the apostles for speaking to them the word of life, or preaching to them the gospel, they were "minded to slay them." The original, "dieprionto," means "to saw into, to cut into, to saw asunder"; here it is rage that cuts into their hearts, not conviction of their sins as in Acts 2: 37. There is one other use of this term, in the speech of Stephen (Acts 7: 54) we have the same expression.

minded to slay them. 34 But there stood up one in the council, a Pharisee named Gamaliel, a doctor of the law, had in honor of all the people, and commanded to put the men forth a little while. 35 And he said unto them, Ye men of Israel, take heed to yourselves as touching these men, what ye are about to do. 36 For before these days rose up Theudas, giving himself out to be somebody; to whom a number of men, about four hundred, joined themselves: who was slain; and all, as many as obeyed him, were dispersed, and came to nought. 37 After this man rose up Judas of Galilee in the days

---

34 **But there stood up one in the council,**—There are four things said about Gamaliel here: (1) He was one of the council, a member of the Sanhedrin; (2) he was a Pharisee; if not the most influential, he was a leader among the Pharisees, while many of the other members were Sadducees; (3) he was a doctor of the law, or a teacher of the law; (4) he was respected and honored by all the people. The council feared the people, and as Gamaliel had such influence with the people it was prudent for them to hear him; hence, he asked that the apostles be put out so that he could address the council himself in the absence of the apostles.

35 **And he said unto them, Ye men of Israel,**—Gamaliel addressed them as "men of Israel"; these were common words of address to the council. Gamaliel proceeded then to give a timely warning as to what should be done with the apostles. He calls upon them to take heed to themselves as to what they were about to do. This does not mean that some danger is about to befall them, but that they should be careful or cautious about reaching a decision.

36 **For before these days rose up Theudas,**—Gamaliel now shows his wisdom by reminding them of some illustrations that mere pretenders will come to nought. Much discussion has been raised as to who Theudas was and what he did. It does not matter who he was; they were familiar with him and knew just what he had done. Josephus mentions a Theudas, who was a leader in an insurrection, but he could not have been this Theudas, for his rebellion was fifteen years later than this time. The times were full of revolts and rebellions, and as not less than three insurrectionary leaders were called Judas, and four Simon, there may have been two of the name of Theudas. This Theudas led about four hundred off, and was finally slain with his company.

37 **After this man rose up Judas of Galilee**—This Judas was

of the enrolment, and drew away *some of the* people after him: he also perished; and all, as many as obeyed him, were scattered abroad. 38 And now
I say unto you, Refrain from these men, and let them alone: for if this
counsel or this work be of men, it will be overthrown: 39 but if it is of God,
ye will not be able to overthrow them; lest haply ye be found even to be
fighting against God. 40 And to him they agreed: and when they had called
the apostles unto them, they beat them and charged them not to speak in the

---

one of those who led an insurrection about the time of the "taxing"
or "enrolment." Josephus mentions a Judas of Galilee who made
a revolt against the Roman enrollment which was ordered while
Cyrenius or Quirinus was governor; he also mentions that his sons
were executed, but does not tell what became of Judas; however,
Gamaliel says here that "he also perished," and all that were with
him were either killed or scattered abroad.

38, 39 **And now I say unto you,**—Gamaliel, after reciting
these illustrations of those who had failed in their efforts to reform
or rebel, gives his advice. He now says, "Let them alone"; that is,
literally, "stand off" or "aloof and suffer them" to go on. He gives
his reasons or argument for his advice. He advises that their work
can be left to the dealing of God, which, in case of Theudas and
Judas, as cited, had brought the wicked counsels to nought.
Furthermore, if these men were doing the work of God, they
would be fighting against God to oppose them. This was a shrewd
argument for Gamaliel, and was suited to the critical case of the
apostles; Gamaliel does not imply that he was a secret disciple of
Jesus or that he leaned toward the apostles. Gamaliel's reasoning
seems to be clear; from the cases mentioned he inferred that if these
apostles had no other basis but such as those that Theudas and
Judas had, they would come to nought and the Sanhedrin would
have no use to oppose them; but on the other hand, if the work
that the apostles were doing was of God, it would be vain for the
council to oppose it—nay, worse, for it would be in vain, and even
worse than that, they would be found fighting against God.

40 **And to him they agreed:**—The argument of Gamaliel had
influence on the Sanhedrin; the council yielded; the apostles were
recalled; to give vent to their malice, and perhaps in their thought,
to atone somewhat for this concession to moderate measures, they
beat the apostles, and then repeated their futile injunction to speak
no more in the name of Jesus; then they let them go. This Gama-

name of Jesus, and let them go. 41 They therefore departed from the presence of the council, rejoicing that they were counted worthy to suffer dishonor for the Name. 42 And every day, in the temple and at home, they ceased not to teach and to ⁴preach Jesus *as* the Christ.

---

⁴Gr. *bring good tidings of.* See ch. 13. 32; 14. 15

---

liel was the same one who had taught Saul of Tarsus. Some think that Saul was present; if so, what did he think of the counsel of his old professor? The members of the Sanhedrin may have felt that their honor was at stake, and that, if the apostles departed untouched, they themselves would be regarded as having proceeded against innocent men; hence, to save their honor and the honor of the court, and to make the impression that the apostles were guilty of some offense, they were scourged. This was a frequent, though a very disgraceful, punishment among the Jews. Jesus had warned his apostles of such treatment. (Matt. 10: 17.)

41 **They therefore departed from the presence of the council,**—The apostles considered it an honor to be followers of Jesus "by evil report and good report." (2 Cor. 6: 8.) Jesus had prepared them to meet ill treatment. (John 15: 20.) The apostles departed from the Sanhedrin "rejoicing that they were counted worthy to suffer dishonor for the Name." No greater indignity could be put upon them than to be subjected to judicial scourging; such treatment would fill many with indignation, anger, or grief over the terrible injustice they suffered; but the apostles counted themselves fortunate, and they considered it an honor to suffer for Christ.

42 **And every day, in the temple and at home,**—The apostles continued to disregard the authority of the Sanhedrin and to obey God; they continued to teach in the temple and in every house. The two fields of apostolic work here mentioned are the public teaching at the temple, and the private teaching at home. Where crowds gathered and the disciples met, they continued to teach. The mission of the church is to carry the gospel to those who do not have it, and to edify itself in the things of God. This may be done by teaching "from house to house" (Acts 20: 20) and publicly in the temple. "Teach" and "preach" are used here to describe the nature of the work of the apostles; "didaskontes" is the

original for "teaching," and "euaggelizomenoi" is the original for "preaching" or "evangelizing." This is the first use of the specific word for "preach" in the Acts; it is the same word from which the English term "evangelize" comes, and means to proclaim good news. It is used frequently by Luke and Paul. (See Luke 2: 10; 9: 6; 1 Thess. 3: 6; Rom. 1: 15; 1 Cor. 15: 1; Gal. 1: 23; Eph. 2: 17.) From the scourging the apostles went to preach Christ as the Savior of the world.

14. THE SEVEN CHOSEN
6: 1-7

1 Now in these days, when the number of the disciples was multiplying, there arose a murmuring of the ⁵Grecian Jews against the Hebrews, because

---

⁵Gr. *Hellenists*

---

1 **Now in these days, when the number of the disciples—** Luke, as a faithful historian, now narrates further development of the church; a gradual unfolding of gospel principles is made in the preaching of the gospel, and a gradual development in the organization of the church. The church was established on Pentecost; the historian now reaches a point where the church is four or five years old. The increase in the number of disciples brought about a complication of affairs, and gave an opportunity for the apostles to arrange in a more systematic order for the work and discipline of the large and growing number of disciples. "Now in these days" is a phrase of indefinite time; it is generally understood that the ascension took place about A.D. 30; some think that it was in A.D. 29 and others in A.D. 33; the date is immaterial. The first six chapters of Acts are generally supposed to cover a history of four or five years; hence, at this time the church would be that old. This was a period of great prosperity, as the number of disciples increased daily. "A murmuring" or "muttering" or complaining arose among "the Grecian Jews against the Hebrews." "Grecian Jews" were "Hellenists," or Jews who were born and reared in another country than Palestine; "Hebrews" were the Jews who were of pure Jewish blood and spoke the Hebrew language. Paul said that he was "a Hebrew of Hebrews" (Phil. 3: 5), which meant that he was of pure Hebrew blood and that he spoke the Hebrew language. The cause of this complaint was because the widows among

their widows were neglected in the daily ministration. 2 And the twelve called the multitude of the disciples unto them, and said, It is not [6]fit that we should forsake the word of God, and [7]serve tables. 3 [8]Look ye out therefore,

---

[6]Gr. *pleasing*
[7]Or, *minister to tables*
[8]Some ancient authorities read *But, brethren, look ye out from among you*

"the Grecian Jews" were "neglected," or "overlooked," in "the daily ministration." This "murmuring" or whispering of discontent is a sin frequently condemned in the New Testament. (Phil. 2: 14; 1 Pet. 4: 9.) This complaint seems to have been against the apostles, as they had charge of the funds that had been contributed. (Acts 4: 35, 37; 5: 2.) "Daily ministration" shows that there was a daily distribution of things which were needed. This sin of neglect is the second sin that is recorded against any member of the church.

2 **And the twelve called the multitude**—Here we have "the twelve" apostles mentioned, showing that for these few years of the church all twelve of the apostles were still at Jerusalem. This shows that Matthias was regarded as one of the apostles, for it would take him to complete the list of "the twelve." (Acts 1: 26.) The number of disciples here is spoken of as "the multitude of the disciples." The apostles stated that it was not best, or satisfactory, for them to give their time to ministering to tables, "serve tables." They had a higher and more important work to do—preaching the word. In order for them to "serve tables" they would necessarily have to "forsake the word of God" in part at least. "Tables," as used here, does not mean money tables as in John 2: 15, but rather the tables used in the common daily distribution of the food. "Ministration" is from the Greek "diakonia," and means the same as "to serve." The Greek word "diakonia," or "diakonos," as used here, has the same meaning as used in Phil. 1: 1 and 1 Tim. 3: 8-13; it is usually translated "deacon." There are three English words in our version by which "diakonos" is translated; they are "minister," "servant," and "deacon." Sometimes it is translated "bond servant" or "bondman"; it is frequently used to designate a "minister of the gospel." (1 Cor. 3: 5; 2 Cor. 3: 6; Eph. 3: 7.) The word "deacon" is almost a transcription of "diakonos." (Phil. 1: 1; 1 Tim. 3: 8-12.) It is also applied to Phoebe. (Rom. 16: 1.)

brethren, from among you seven men of good report, full of the Spirit and of wisdom, whom we may appoint over this business. 4 But we will continue stedfastly in prayer, and in the ministry of the word. 5 And the saying

3 **Look ye out therefore, brethren,**—The term "look ye out" means to "look at" in order to select, to "seek out" as persons for office. The entire multitude of disciples was instructed to do this. They were to select "from among" themselves "seven men." There is no significance in the number "seven" except that it is a sacred number and usually implies completeness. This number was considered sufficient for the work that they were to do. The qualifications are specified; they were to be "men of good report," "full of the Spirit," and men "of wisdom"; these "we" may appoint over this business. The first qualification "of good report" is important; it is mentioned in Acts 10: 22; 16: 2; 1 Tim. 5: 10. The second qualification was that they were to be "full of the Spirit"; this phrase is frequently used in regard to spiritual gifts and miraculous powers. (Acts 2: 4; 4: 8.) Furthermore, they were to be men "of wisdom," which means that they were to have practical sagacity, good sense, and sound judgment. "Whom we may appoint" has received much discussion. Some think that the "we" has reference only to the apostles; others think that it includes the entire church and apostles; since the apostles are directing in this, it seems clear that it includes only the apostles.

4 **But we will continue stedfastly in prayer,**—"We" here designates the same "we" in the preceding verse; it is clear that it includes the apostles. The apostles would "continue stedfastly"; that is, would adhere to that which they had been doing. (Rom. 12: 12; Col. 4: 2.) The apostles had been spending much time in prayer; they determined to continue "in prayer"; this does not merely mean private prayer, but here in the sense of public worship. (Acts 16: 13.) If the apostles, filled with the Holy Spirit, needed to continue "stedfastly in prayer," how much more do we need to pray! "The ministry of the word," in which they were to steadfastly continue, means serving as preaching and teaching the word. Here, again, we have the word "diakonia," as used in verse 1, but here it has reference to preaching as the special ministry with which the apostles were concerned.

pleased the whole multitude: and they chose Stephen, a man full of faith and
of the Holy Spirit, and Philip, and Prochorus, and Nicanor, and Timon, and
Parmenas, and Nicolaus a proselyte of Antioch; 6 whom they set before the
apostles: and when they had prayed, they laid their hands upon them.

---

5 **And the saying pleased the whole multitude:**—The suggestion made by the apostles met with the hearty approval of "the
whole multitude." There was no dissent in the meeting; they
unanimously concurred in the direction given by the apostles, and
proceeded according to their direction. They chose Stephen, Philip, Prochorus, Nicanor, Timon, Parmenas, and Nicolaus. All
these names are from the Greek language, and indicate the gener-
osity of the Hebrew portion of the multitude in putting this matter
in the hands of "the Grecian Jews" from whom the complaint had
come. "Stephen" is mentioned first as he was the most conspicuous of the group; "Philip" is the next one mentioned. We have a
record of Stephen and also of Philip in the later history of the
church; but we do not have any mention of the others after their
appointment. Philip is to be distinguished from Philip the apostle.
This Philip is "Philip the evangelist." (Acts 21: 8.) Some of
Philip's labors in Samaria and elsewhere are mentioned in the
Acts; Stephen was the first martyr; and some think that Nicolaus
is mentioned in Rev. 2: 6-15. The other four names are not referred to elsewhere in the New Testament. Some have contended
that the Greek names do not prove that these were all from the
"Grecian Jews"; they think that three of the seven were Hebrews,
three Grecians, and one a proselyte.

6 **whom they set before the apostles:**—After the selection of
these seven men who were qualified as mentioned in verse 3, they
were placed before the apostles who prayed and "laid their hands
upon them." Much discussion has been had as to the form of "or-
daining" these men. The imposition of hands was a practice of
long standing among the Jews. Jacob laid hands on the sons of
Joseph (Gen. 48: 13, 14); it is recorded also that Moses laid
hands on Joshua (Deut. 34: 9); the Levites were set apart to the
service of the tabernacle by the imposition of hands (Num. 8:
10); hands were laid on the scapegoat to impart to it the sins to
be carried away (Lev. 16: 21). The laying on of hands was a symbol of the impartation of the gifts and graces which were needed to

7 And the word of God increased; and the number of the disciples multiplied in Jerusalem exceedingly; and a great company of the priests were obedient to the faith.

---

qualify them for their new duties; this was accompanied with prayer that God would bestow the necessary gifts upon them. Some have thought that this is the beginning of the officers in the church known as "deacons"; it may be, but these men are not called deacons. We do not know whether they were appointed in this case of emergency, and ceased when the supplies were exhausted, or when the church was scattered abroad. (Acts 8: 1.) It is claimed that they did the work of "deacons," and that their work is described by the same Greek word that is used for "deacons"; this may be true, but the fact remains that they are nowhere in the New Testament called "deacons."

7 And the word of God increased;—"Increased," as used here, is from "euxanen," which means "kept on growing all the more" because the apostles were now relieved from the daily ministration of the food. The number of disciples "multiplied" as the result of the increased activities of the apostles in preaching the word. "Multiplied" is from the original "eplethuneto," which means that the preaching of the apostles and the multiplication of the number of disciples kept pace with each other. "A great company of the priests were obedient to the faith." The priests were usually Sadducees; it was a sad day for Annas and Caiaphas and all the sect of the Sadducees (Acts 5: 17) when such a large number of priests became obedient to the faith. Three things are mentioned here to show the progress of the church: "the word of God increased," "the number of the disciples multiplied," and "a great company of the priests were obedient to the faith." "Obedient to the faith" is equivalent to obeying the gospel; "faith" here means "faith in Jesus Christ as the Son of God, the gospel."

SECTION THREE

GOSPEL PREACHED IN JUDEA AND SAMARIA
6: 8 to 8: 25

1. STEPHEN ARRESTED AND TRIED
6: 8-15

8 And Stephen, full of grace and power, wrought great wonders and signs among the people. 9 But there arose certain of them that were of the synagogue called *the synagogue* of the ⁹Libertines, and of the Cyrenians, and of the Alexandrians, and of them of Cilicia and Asia, disputing with Stephen.

---

⁹Or, *Freedmen*

---

8 **And Stephen, full of grace and power,**—Stephen was described as "a man full of faith and of the Holy Spirit" when he was selected; here he is described as being "full of grace and power." "Grace" is used here in the sense of favor with God; "power" does not merely mean strength and fortitude, but some unusual power, enabling him to be the instrument of doing great wonders or miracles among the people. It is thought that Stephen was a "Grecian Jew," who had accepted Christ; he worked "great wonders and signs among the people."

9 **But there arose certain of them**—This verse has confused many commentators, and given them no little trouble. "The synagogue of the Libertines" were the Jews who were one time slaves, but had been given their liberty. Some think that they were merely Jews of Rome, who had been taken there as captives by Pompey. "Libertines" comes from the Latin which means "freedman," or "the son of a freedman." It is said that there were two hundred eighty synagogues in Jerusalem; these places of worship and study were in all the cities of later times where there were Jews enough to maintain one. Luke here speaks of five such synagogues in Jerusalem—"Libertines," "Cyrenians," "Alexandrians," "Cilicia," and "Asia." There were probably enough "Hellenists" in Jerusalem to have five such synagogues. Cyrene was in Africa, about halfway between Carthage and Alexandria; it contained a large number of Jews, who constituted one-fourth of its entire population. (Mark 15: 21; Acts 13: 1.) Alexandria was the capital of Egypt, and was founded by Alexander the Great. In no city

10 And they were not able to withstand the wisdom and the Spirit by which he spake. 11 Then they suborned men, who said, We have heard him speak blasphemous words against Moses, and *against* God. 12 And they stirred up the people, and the elders, and the scribes, and came upon him, and seized him, and brought him into the council, 13 and set up false witnesses, who

save Jerusalem were there so many Jews, nor had they so much power anywhere out of Palestine; the Septuagint translation of the Old Testament had been made at Alexandria for Jews there. Cilicia was at the southeast corner of what is now called Asia Minor; it contained a large number of Jews; Asia in the New Testament always means the northwest corner of Asia Minor, which had Ephesus for its capital. Stephen engaged all of these synagogues in controversy about Christ.

10 **And they were not able to withstand the wisdom**—Stephen was "full of grace and power," and representatives of these synagogues were unable to meet his arguments. He spoke with such fearlessness, clearness of argument, understanding of the prophecy, and power of the Spirit that his speech was irresistible.

11 **Then they suborned men, who said,**—"Suborned" is from "hupoballo," which originally meant "to put under like a carpet, to bring men under one's control by suggestion or money." Here it means that they put these men forward in an underhand way for fraud. These men for money or for some wicked motive bore witness that they had heard Stephen "speak blasphemous words against Moses, and against God." They brought the same accusation against Christ. (Matt. 26: 65; Mark 2: 7.) Punishment for blasphemy against God was death by stoning. (Lev. 24: 16; Deut. 13: 6-10.) They charged Stephen with blaspheming Moses, and concluded their charge that he had blasphemed God.

12, 13 **And they stirred up the people,**—The original, "sunekinesan," means they shook the people together like an earthquake. The wrangling Libertines and the others of verse 9 were the leaders of this mob against Stephen; with the testimony of these false witnesses they "stirred up" the people; the elders and the scribes rushed upon Stephen and brought him into the council. After Stephen was brought into the presence of the council, again they "set up false witnesses" who testified that "this man ceaseth not to speak words against this holy place, and the law." They

said, This man ceaseth not to speak words against this holy place, and the law: 14 for we have heard him say, that this Jesus of Nazareth shall destroy this place, and shall change the customs which Moses delivered unto us. 15 And all that sat in the council, fastening their eyes on him, saw his face as it had been the face of an angel.

---

enlarged upon the testimony that was first borne; this time they add that Stephen not only blasphemed Moses and God, but that he spoke "words against this holy place," meaning Jerusalem, or the temple. They made wild charges against Stephen that he had spoken against the law and the temple; it is supposed that they had reference to what Stephen had spoken in their synagogues.

14 **for we have heard him say,**—Probably Stephen had warned the people that if they persisted in their opposition to Jesus their city and temple would be destroyed. Jesus himself had made declarations of the same import. (Matt. 26: 61; Luke 19: 41-44.) They perverted what Jesus had said, and now they put a wrong construction on what Stephen says. Jesus had predicted the destruction of the temple, but it was to be done by the Gentiles. The enemies of Stephen were unable to meet his arguments, and they resorted to violent means; this was a confession that they could not withstand his arguments. Their charges were false, and they proceeded upon false accusations.

15 **And all that sat in the council,**—Probably Saul of Tarsus sat in this council with others and saw the face of Stephen shine as though "it had been the face of an angel." His face was lighted up with divine radiance. The members of the council literally gazed upon him as if they had seen "the face of an angel." Even his enemies saw his face as if it were the face of an angel, but they were too wicked to turn from their evil course. The face of Moses shone in a similar way when he came down from the mountain. (Ex. 34: 30; 2 Cor. 3: 7.) We do not know where Peter and John were at this time; it seems that Stephen stood alone before the Sanhedrin as did Jesus; however, he was not alone, for he saw Jesus standing at the right hand of God. (Acts 7: 56.) There was little that Peter and John could do at this time; Gamaliel did not interpose this time, for the Pharisees were behind the charges against Stephen.

2. STEPHEN'S DEFENSE
7: 1-53

1 And the high priest said, Are these things so? 2 And he said, Brethren and fathers, hearken: The God of glory appeared unto our father Abraham, when he was in Mesopotamia, before he dwelt in Haran, 3 and said unto

1 **And the high priest said,**—Stephen's defense, at first view, is a condensed outline of Jewish history from the call of Abraham to the temple. It will be observed that in all the prominent periods of their history God did not confine himself to the Holy Land, nor to the temple; he appeared to Abraham in Mesopotamia, to Joseph and Israel in Egypt, to Moses in the wilderness of Sinai; hence, God's glorious appearings to their fathers were outside of the land of Canaan, and before the temple had an existence. "The high priest" presided over the Sanhedrin; the council had felt uneasy for some time, as the history of the church reveals; its members had felt for a while quite satisfied on the death of Jesus, but when his resurrection was preached and proved so conclusively by the testimony of the apostles, and when the church had multiplied in such great numbers, the Sanhedrin now was most uncomfortable. The high priest asked Stephen with regard to the charges that the council made against him: "Are these things so?" This is mild language, more so than that addressed to Christ. (Matt. 26: 62.) His question to Stephen was equivalent to the question: "Guilty or not guilty?" This gave Stephen the opportunity to make his defense.

2 **Brethren and fathers, hearken:**—Stephen addressed the council in a very respectful way; he included the bystanders as "brethren," and the council as "fathers." Paul made a similar address. (Acts 22: 1.) "The God of glory appeared unto our father Abraham" before he dwelt in Haran. Stephen begins by calling Abraham "our Father," and the narrative proceeds to set forth the successive steps of God's dealing toward them under the Abrahamic covenant. No vision is recorded in the Old Testament of God's appearance to Abraham in Mesopotamia, but it is implied, as it is said that God brought him out of Ur of the Chaldees. (Gen. 11: 31; 15: 7; Neh. 9: 7.) In Gen. 12: 1, Abram is said to have been called after he dwelt in Haran. "Mesopotamia" is the region between the rivers Tigris and Euphrates.

him, Get thee out of thy land, and from thy kindred, and come into the land
which I shall show thee. 4 Then came he out of the land of the Chaldaeans,
and dwelt in Haran: and from thence, when his father was dead, *God* removed him into this land, wherein ye now dwell: 5 and he gave him none
inheritance in it, no, not so much as to set his foot on: and he promised that
he would give it to him in possession, and to his seed after him, when *as yet*
he had no child. 6 And God spake on this wise, that his seed should sojourn

---

3 **and said unto him, Get thee out of thy land,**—Stephen here
gives the divine instruction which is given in Gen. 12: 1.
Abraham was called out of Ur with the special object of removing
him away from the influence of his idolatrous surroundings. His
people served other gods there. (Josh. 24: 2.) He was to leave
his native land and his kinspeople and go into a land which Jehovah would show him. He was not told where he should go; and
"by faith Abraham . . . went out, not knowing whither he went."
(Heb. 11: 8.)

4 **Then came he out of the land**—Abraham left Mesopotamia
and took with him his father Terah and Lot; they dwelt in Haran
about five years. Terah was seventy years old when Abram was
born (Gen. 11: 26); and Abraham was seventy-five when he left
Haran (Gen. 12: 4). Then Terah would have been one hundred
forty-five years old at that time; but Terah lived to be two
hundred five. (Gen. 11: 32.) Thus it is supposed that Terah
must have lived about sixty years after Abraham started for Canaan. There are several explanations offered, as Stephen refers
to Terah's spiritual death by relaxing into idolatry. However,
the most satisfactory explanation is that critics wrongly assume
Abram to be the eldest son of Terah, whereas he may have been
the youngest, and Haran, who died in Ur, may have been the eldest,
or even Nahor.

5 **and he gave him none inheritance in it,**—Abraham did not
get the land for a living possession; it was promised to him for his
heirs; he bought a burial place for his wife Sarah. (Gen. 23: 20;
50: 13.) This gave him no right of possession to live there. He
buried his wife in the cave of Machpelah; this was his only possession. This promise was made to Abraham that his seed should in-
herit the land even before Abraham had an heir. (Gen. 12: 7; 13:
15, 16.)

6 **And God spake on this wise,**—These promises were made to

in a strange land, and that they should bring them into bondage, and treat them ill, four hundred years. 7 And the nation to which they shall be in bondage will I judge, said God: and after that shall they come forth, and serve me in this place. 8 And he gave him the covenant of circumcision: and so *Abraham* begat Isaac, and circumcised him the eighth day; and Isaac *begat* Jacob, and Jacob the twelve patriarchs. 9 And the patriarchs, moved with jealousy against Joseph, sold him into Egypt: and God was with him,

Abraham while he had no child, that "his seed should sojourn in a strange land." This sojourn should result in their bondage and evil treatment for "four hundred years." It was God's plan to delay the fulfillment of the promise. The four hundred years may be stated in round numbers as in Ex. 12: 40, 41. Paul says that the law came four hundred thirty years after the promise (Gal. 3: 17); so that the four hundred thirty years of Ex. 12: 40 probably included the patriarchs' residence in Canaan (Gen. 15: 13, 14; Ex. 3: 12).

7 **And the nation to which they shall be in bondage**—This nation was Egypt. God said that he would judge this nation, and this was done when he told Moses from the burning bush that Israel should come out of Egypt and serve him "in this place," meaning Mount Horeb. Thus the council was reminded that Israel was to worship Jehovah in Sinai, and not alone in the temple, nor alone in Canaan.

8 **And he gave him the covenant of circumcision:**—"The covenant of circumcision" was the covenant that God made with Abraham to give his posterity this land. The seal or sign of this covenant was circumcision; it was the covenant marked by circumcision. (Gen. 17: 9-14; Rom. 4: 11.) The covenant of circumcision was given the year before Isaac was born. (Gen. 17: 21.) "The eighth day"—each male child should be circumcised on the eighth day. Isaac, Jacob, and the twelve patriarchs, or sons of Jacob, were circumcised.

9 **And the patriarchs, moved with jealousy against Joseph,** —"Jealousy" here comes from the original "zelosantes," which means "to burn or boil with zeal, and then with envy." (Acts 5: 17.) The brothers of Joseph were excited to envy against him because of Jacob's partiality toward him. (Gen. 37: 3, 4.) They sold him into Egypt. (Gen. 37: 25-28.) However, God was with

10 and delivered him out of all his afflictions, and gave him favor and wisdom before Pharaoh king of Egypt; and he made him governor over Egypt and all his house. 11 Now there came a famine over all Egypt and Canaan, and great affliction: and our fathers found no sustenance. 12 But when Jacob heard that there was grain in Egypt, he sent forth our fathers the first time. 13 And at the second time Joseph was made known to his brethren; and Joseph's race became manifest unto Pharaoh. 14 And Joseph sent, and

him. (Gen. 39: 2, 21.) Stephen is merely giving an outline of the story which occupies much space in Genesis.

10 and delivered him out of all his afflictions,—For a record of this, see Gen. 41: 38-45, 54. God was with him in all of his afflictions in Egypt, and finally elevated him "before Pharaoh king of Egypt." He was finally made governor over Egypt and all of Pharaoh's house. "Pharaoh" is not a name of a king, but a title, the Egyptian title meaning "a great house."

11 Now there came a famine over all Egypt—Here another stage in the history is noted as part of the same plan of providential development in the case of the covenant people. The famine is recorded in Gen. 41: 54; it was very severe. Stephen reaches the climax by saying, "Our fathers found no sustenance." Notice that Stephen continues to speak of "our fathers," which identifies him with the council and all who were present. "Sustenance" is from the original "chortasmata," and means "to feed with grass or herbs." In the New Testament it includes food for men and animals, but in Gen. 24: 25, 32 it is fodder for the cattle, a first necessity for owners of herds of cattle.

12 But when Jacob heard that there was grain in Egypt,— Jacob heard that there was "grain" in Egypt. The Greek for corn or grain is "sitia," and means grain, such as wheat and barley, but not our maize or Indian corn; it is an old word for provisions, victuals. Jacob remained in Canaan while ten of his sons went into Egypt the first time.

13 And at the second time Joseph was made known—While Joseph was ruler over Egypt the famine occurred; he controlled the distribution of the grain; he had been in Egypt many years and his brothers did not recognize him and he did not make himself known unto them the first time. The second time Joseph was made known to his brethren, and Pharaoh assisted Joseph in making arrangements to bring his father into Egypt.

called to him Jacob his father, and all his kindred, threescore and fifteen souls. 15 And Jacob went down into Egypt; and he died, himself and our fathers; 16 and they were carried over unto Shechem, and laid in the tomb that Abraham bought for a price in silver of the sons of [1]Hamor in Shechem. 17 But as the time of the promise drew nigh which God vouchsafed unto Abraham, the people grew and multiplied in Egypt, 18 till there arose another king over Egypt, who knew not Joseph. 19 The same dealt craftily with our race, and ill-treated our fathers, that [2]they should cast out

[1]Gr. *Emmor*
[2]Or, *he*

14 **And Joseph sent, and called to him Jacob**—Gen. 45: 17-21 gives an account of Joseph's sending for his father; Jacob, with all of his kindred, "threescore and fifteen souls," went down into Egypt. Stephen counts some grandchildren of Joseph and so makes it seventy-five, whereas Gen. 46: 26 has sixty-six, and then the next verse makes it seventy, including Jacob and Joseph with his two sons.

15, 16 **And Jacob went down into Egypt;**—Jacob went into Egypt and lived there seventeen years and died; his body was brought out of Egypt and buried in the cave of Machpelah, where Abraham and Sarah, Isaac and Rebekah were buried, and where he had buried Leah. Abraham had bought the cave of Machpelah as a burying place from Ephron the Hittite at Hebron (Gen. 23: 16); while Jacob bought a field from the sons of Hamor at Shechem (Gen. 33: 19; Josh. 24: 32). Abraham had built an altar at Shechem when he entered Canaan. (Gen. 12: 6, 7.)

17, 18 **But as the time of the promise drew nigh**—The promise here referred to may be that made to Abraham in Gen. 12: 7, "Unto thy seed will I give this land"; or it may refer to the one recorded in Gen. 15: 16, "And in the fourth generation they shall come hither again." "The people grew and multiplied in Egypt," and prospered until "there arose another king over Egypt, who knew not Joseph." This "Pharaoh" did not remember with gratitude nor acknowledge Egypt's obligation to Joseph. Stephen may have quoted from Ex. 1: 8 at this point.

19 **The same dealt craftily with our race,**—"Dealt craftily" is from the Greek "katasophizomai," which means "to make wise, to become wise, then to play the sophist"; however, in the New Testament it is used to mean "to use fraud, craft, deceit." Pharaoh required the children of Israel to "cast out their babes to the end

their babes to the end they might not ³live. 20 At which season Moses was born, and was ⁴exceeding fair; and he was nourished three months in his father's house: 21 and when he was cast out, Pharaoh's daughter took him up, and nourished him for her own son. 22 And Moses was instructed in all the wisdom of the Egyptians; and he was mighty in his words and works.

³Gr. *be preserved alive*
⁴Or, *fair unto God.* Comp. 2 Cor. 10. 4

they might not live." It seems that Pharaoh, besides the command to cast every infant son into the river Nile, treated the Hebrews with such rigor that, through dread of training up any children to endure their own hard lot, they in some instances abandoned their daughters also to death. The purpose and plan of this king was to keep the nation of Israel from multiplying and growing stronger; hence, he required the parents to abandon their children and let them die. (Ex. 2: 2, 3.) Pharaoh was afraid that the Israelites would multiply so fast and become so strong that they would rebel against the Egyptian king.

20 **At which season Moses was born,**—Amram of the tribe of Levi and the family of Kohath married Jochebed and had at least two children before Moses was born, Miriam and Aaron. It is not known whether these children were born before the king's decree was issued; but it is known that Moses was born while this decree was in force and his mother, Jochebed, refused to obey the king's orders and preserved Moses because he "was exceeding fair." He was nourished at home for three months in defiance of the new Pharaoh's orders.

21 **and when he was cast out,**—Jochebed, after nourishing him for three months in her own house, made preparations for him to be found by Pharaoh's daughter with the hope that she would spare the child. Pharaoh's daughter came down and found the child and "nourished him for her own son." Stephen had been accused of blaspheming Moses; he refutes the charge by reverently rehearsing the history of Moses, and also shows how God guarded all these changes; this emphasized the proof that his providential care would now, as in the past, overrule all the changes to advance his kingdom.

22 **And Moses was instructed in all the wisdom**—Moses was "mighty in his words and works," which refers to his later life; he said of himself: "Oh, Lord, I am not eloquent, . . . I am slow of

23 But when he was well-nigh forty years old, it came into his heart to visit his brethren the children of Israel. 24 And seeing one *of them* suffer wrong, he defended him, and avenged him that was oppressed, smiting the Egyptian: 25 and he supposed that his brethren understood that God by his hand was giving them [5]deliverance; but they understood not. 26 And the day following he appeared unto them as they strove, and would have set them at one

[5]Or, *salvation*

speech, and of a slow tongue." (Ex. 4: 10.) The priestly caste in Egypt was noted for its knowledge of science, astronomy, medicine, and mathematics; this reputation was proverbial. (1 Kings 4: 30.) It was said of Jesus that he "was a prophet mighty in deed and word before God and all the people." (Luke 24: 19.) Jesus was a prophet like unto Moses. (Acts 3: 22.)

23 **But when he was well-nigh forty years old,**—Moses was forty years old at this time; Ex. 2: 11 says that "when Moses was grown up," and Heb. 11: 24 says "when he was grown up." The Jews understood this to mean forty years which he had spent as the son of Pharaoh's daughter; then he was in Midian forty years; then forty years in the wilderness, making his age one hundred twenty years. "It came into his heart" to visit his brethren at this time when he was forty years of age; we are not told how he was impressed with the thought of delivering his brethren from Egyptian bondage at this time.

24, 25 **And seeing one of them suffer wrong,**—While down in the land of Goshen visiting his brethren he saw an Egyptian, presumably a taskmaster, smiting one of his brethren, and Moses slew the Egyptian and hid his body in the sand. (Ex. 2: 12.) He may not have intended to kill the Egyptian, but having done so, he concealed his body in the sand. He "went out the second day" and "two men of the Hebrews . . . striving together" (Ex. 2: 13), and rebuked the one that was in the wrong. He thought that his brethren "understood that God by his hand was giving . . . deliverance" to the children of Israel. They did not understand; neither is there anything said in Exodus about his intentions at this time. God intended to deliver them by the hand of Moses, but Moses was not prepared at this time to become their deliverer; neither was this the way that God would deliver them.

26 **And the day following he appeared unto them as they strove,**—Here Moses attempted to establish peace between two of

again, saying, Sirs, ye are brethren; why do ye wrong one to another? 27 But he that did his neighbor wrong thrust him away, saying, Who made thee a ruler and a judge over us? 28 Wouldest thou kill me, as thou killedst the Egyptian yesterday? 29 And Moses fled at this saying, and became a sojourner in the land of Midian, where he begat two sons. 30 And when forty years were fulfilled, an angel appeared to him in the wilderness of mount Sinai, in a flame of fire in a bush. 31 And when Moses saw it, he wondered

his brethren, but they did not understand his intentions. Stephen knew that they were familiar with the history. As they were of the same race, and both under oppression, it was not in harmony with the relationship for them to be fighting among themselves; some think that there is implied here the fact that they should reserve their strength to contend together against the common enemy.

27, 28 **But he that did his neighbor wrong**—The one that was in the wrong resented the correction and reminded him what he had done to the Egyptian. A record of this is found in Ex. 2: 14. It does not appear that Moses assumed any authority over them; it seems that they should have understood what Moses was doing and should have been in sympathy with him. However, Moses saw that what he had done to the Egyptian was known, and that his brethren would not accept him as their deliverer.

29 **And Moses fled at this saying,**—When Pharaoh heard what Moses had done, "he sought to slay Moses." (Ex. 2: 15.) Moses became a sojourner in the land of Midian. "Midian" was a son of Abraham by Keturah. (Gen. 25: 2.) His descendants occupied the region extending from the eastern shore of the Gulf of Akabah to the borders of Moab on the one side, and to the vicinity of Sinai on the other. Here he married Zipporah, daughter of Jethro, the priest of Midian. (Ex. 2: 16 22.) He had two sons by Zipporah, born while he was in Midian.

30 **And when forty years were fulfilled,**—Moses sojourned in Midian in the region about Mount Sinai forty years. While there, an angel appeared to him and summoned him by the signal of "a flame of fire in a bush." This corresponds with the statement in Ex. 7: 7 that Moses was eighty years old when he appeared before Pharaoh, and one hundred twenty years old when he died. (Deut. 29: 5; 31: 2; 34: 7.) The angel appeared to Moses at the end of the forty years' sojourn in the land of Midian.

at the sight: and as he drew near to behold, there came a voice of the Lord, 32 I am the God of thy fathers, the God of Abraham, and of Isaac, and of Jacob. And Moses trembled, and durst not behold. 33 And the Lord said unto him, Loose the shoes from thy feet: for the place whereon thou standest is holy ground. 34 I have surely seen the affliction of my people that is in Egypt, and have heard their groaning, and I am come down to deliver them: and now come, I will send thee into Egypt. 35 This Moses whom they refused, saying, Who made thee a ruler and a judge? him hath God sent *to be*

31, 32 **And when Moses saw it,**—A flame of fire in a bush would not excite wonder; but if the flame kept on burning and the bush was not consumed, it would excite attention. (Ex. 3: 2.) Moses approached the bush to discover the cause of this wonder. When he did so, a voice was heard, saying, "I am the God of thy fathers, the God of Abraham, and of Isaac, and of Jacob." This is the way that God called him; Moses thus further becomes acquainted with God. When Moses heard the voice, he "trembled, and durst not behold." It was a fearful thing to stand in the presence of God. The angel here is termed Jehovah himself; the angel was a messenger of Jehovah.

33 **And the Lord said unto him,**—Jehovah told Moses to take off his shoes as he was standing on holy ground; Jehovah was represented there by the angel and the bush that was aflame. Moses was in the presence of God; hence, he should remove his sandals. It was considered an act of reverence to remove the shoes; this is still considered an act of reverence in the eastern country. We remove the hat as an act of respect and reverence. They removed their sandals.

34 **I have surely seen the affliction of my people**—This is what Jehovah said to Moses as Moses stood there in reverence for the presence of Jehovah. (Ex. 3: 7.) God had seen the affliction of his people; he saw how they were treated by the Egyptians. He had foretold this suffering. (Gen. 17; Neh. 9: 9; Psalm 106: 44, 45; Isa. 63: 7-14.) Here Moses is directed as a leader to deliver Israel from Egyptian bondage. Stephen is honoring Moses in all of the history that he recites.

35 **This Moses whom they refused, saying,**—Here Stephen emphasizes that this Moses who was rejected forty years previous to this time now has the command to go back to Egypt and deliver

both a ruler and a ¹deliverer with the hand of the angel that appeared to him in the bush. 36 This man led them forth, having wrought wonders and signs in Egypt, and in the Red sea, and in the wilderness forty years. 37 This is that Moses, who said unto the children of Israel, ²A prophet shall God raise up unto you from among your brethren, ³like unto me. 38 This is he that

¹Gr. *redeemer*
²Deut. 18. 15
³Or, *as* he raised up *me*

Israel from bondage. Many think that he was not commissioned the first time to deliver Israel. The council must have seen the parallel suggested in Stephen's words; their fathers had rejected Moses, yet God sent him; so they rejected Jesus, but God sent him to deliver them. Moses is called here a "deliverer"; he is also called a "ruler." There is a deadly parallel between Moses and Christ that the Sanhedrin must see; they must also see that they are doing to Christ and his disciples just what was done to Moses. Moses was ruler, lawgiver, deliverer, and prophet; Christ was all this to the people, but they rejected him. Moses was encouraged and supported by the angel which represented the presence of God.

36 **This man led them forth, having wrought wonders—** Moses and Aaron went before Pharaoh and wrought miracles; the ten plagues brought on Egypt were among the "wonders and signs" which Moses wrought in Egypt; but not all of these "wonders and signs" were done in Egypt. Some of them were "in the Red sea," and for forty years in the wilderness. Though rejected, Moses delivered the afflicted Israelites; so Christ wrought many "wonders and signs" among the people, yet he was rejected and crucified. Again, they must see the point in Stephen's recital of this history.

37 **This is that Moses, who said—**After reciting the history of Moses up to this point, Stephen now tells the council that Moses said: "A prophet shall God raise up unto you from among your brethren, like unto me." Peter had quoted this same prophecy (Acts 3: 22, 23) when speaking in the temple, and applied it to Christ. The Sanhedrin must have been familiar with the application of this prophecy to Christ. Stephen now reminds the council that Moses himself declared that at some future time God would raise up a great prophet like unto Moses. "This" Moses is used five times here in Stephen's speech. (Verses 35, 36, 37, 38, 40.)

was in the ⁴church in the wilderness with the angel that spake to him in the mount Sinai, and with our fathers: who received living oracles to give unto us: 39 to whom our fathers would not be obedient, but thrust him from them, and turned back in their hearts unto Egypt, 40 saying unto Aaron, Make us gods that shall go before us: for as for this Moses, who led us forth out of the land of Egypt, we know not what is become of him. 41 And

---

⁴Or, *congregation*

Stephen's purpose is to show that "this Moses" whom he honored had predicted the Messiah as a prophet like himself, and that this fulfillment was to be found in Jesus of Nazareth. Hence, they are opposing Moses, and he is loyal to Moses; but they, in rebellion to Moses, were falsely accusing Stephen.

38 **This is he that was in the church in the wilderness**—This prophecy is found in Psalm 22: 22; there it is "assembly"; it is also quoted in Heb. 2: 12, and is there translated "congregation"; here in Stephen's speech it is translated "church." It is the same Greek word, "ekklesiai," and is better translated "congregation." Moses is here represented as receiving the law from an angel, as in Heb. 2: 2; Gal. 3: 19, and so was a mediator between the angel and the people; but Jesus is the mediator of a better covenant. (Heb. 8: 6.) Exodus does not speak of an angel; there Moses received the law from Jehovah. "Living oracles" means life-giving oracles, divine utterances. (Rom. 3: 2; Heb. 5: 12; 1 Pet. 4: 11.) Moses was with the congregation and with the angel on Mount Sinai, where the law, called "lively" or "living oracles," literally "living words," was given.

39, 40 **to whom our fathers would not be obedient,**—At Mount Sinai, while Moses was up in the mountain for forty days, the people asked Aaron to make a calf of gold for them to worship; they did not know what had become of Moses. They acknowledged that he had brought them out of Egypt. Here again is a contrast between the way Israel treated Moses and the honor God placed upon him; Israel refused Moses as a deliverer, and wanted to go back to the bondage of Egypt. They "turned back in their hearts unto Egypt," but did not really go back into Egypt. They did go back to the idolatry of Egypt in calling for Aaron to make them "gods." (Ex. 16: 3; 17: 3; Num. 14: 4; Ezek. 20: 8.)

they made a calf in those days, and brought a sacrifice unto the idol, and rejoiced in the works of their hands. 42 But God turned, and gave them up to serve the host of heaven; as it is written in the book of the prophets,
> ⁵Did ye offer unto me slain beasts and sacrifices
> Forty years in the wilderness, O house of Israel?
> 43 And ye took up the tabernacle of Moloch,
> And the star of the god Rephan,
> The figures which ye made to worship them:
> And I will carry you away beyond Babylon.

⁵Amos 5. 25 ff.

The pillar of cloud and of fire went before the Israelites as a symbol of God's presence (Ex. 13: 21, 22; Num. 10: 34, 36; Neh. 9: 12), but they wished a symbolic representation of Jehovah more striking to their sensual hearts, so long accustomed as they had been to the image worship of the Egyptians. They spoke language of contempt about Moses. They did not know what had become of him, and perhaps did not care.

41 **And they made a calf in those days,**—This verse describes their idolatrous worship. Aaron made the calf and also the people made it. (Ex. 32: 3, 35.) Stephen calls it "the idol." The people said it was their way of worshiping Jehovah. It is thought that they made "a calf" of gold because they were accustomed to seeing the Egyptians worship the bull Apis at Memphis as the symbol of Osiris, the sun. The Egyptians had another sacred bull, Mnevis, at Heliopolis. The Israelites "rejoiced in the works of their hands." They rejoiced in the calf they had made, as if it were Jehovah whom they professed to worship. Idolatry is so foolish! (Isa. 44: 9-20.)

42, 43 **But God turned, and gave them up**—The Israelites forsook God, and he gave them up to their idolatrous ways after pleading with them and warning them for many long years. "Gave them up" is from the original "paredoken"; this same form occurs three times like clods on a coffin in a grave in Rom. 1: 24, 26, 28, where Paul speaks of God giving the heathen up to their lusts. They worshiped the host of heaven (Deut. 17: 3; 2 Kings 17: 16; 21: 3; 2 Chron. 33: 3, 5; Jer. 8: 2; 19: 13); which means the sun, moon, and stars. This quotation is from Amos 5: 25-27. Stephen makes application here in such a way as to impress upon

44 Our fathers had the tabernacle of the testimony in the wilderness, even as he appointed who spake unto Moses, that he should make it according to the figure that he had seen. 45 Which also our fathers, in their turn, brought in with [6]Joshua when they entered on the possession of the [7]nations, that God thrust out before the face of our fathers, unto the days of David; 46 who found favor in the sight of God, and asked to find a habitation for the God of

[6]Gr. *Jesus.* Comp. Heb. 4. 8
[7]Or, *Gentiles.* Comp. ch. 4. 25

the Sanhedrin the wickedness of the people and God's giving them up to follow their own idolatrous hearts. "Tabernacle of Moloch" is the place of worshiping Moloch; Moloch was the god of the Amorites, to whom children were offered as live sacrifices; it was an image with a head of an ox with arms outstretched in which children were placed, and underneath fire was placed so as to consume the offering. "The star of the god Rephan" is supposed to be the star Saturn to which the Egyptians and others gave worship. Israel turned away from Jehovah and turned to these idols. For these sins the Israelites were to be carried beyond Babylon, or as some versions read, "beyond Damascus"; however, "beyond Damascus" to the Jewish mind meant Babylon.

44 **Our fathers had the tabernacle of the testimony**—"The tabernacle of the testimony" has reference to the tabernacle in the wilderness. (Ex. 25: 22; 38: 21.) The Ten Commandments were placed in the ark of the covenant, and the ark was kept in the most holy place. Stephen seems to pass on from the conduct of Israel to his other argument that God is not necessarily worshiped in a particular spot. Moses had been called up in the mountain and had been given a pattern of the tabernacle, and even warned: "See, saith he, that thou make all things according to the pattern that was showed thee in the mount." (Heb. 8: 5.) So the place of worship was at the tabernacle, but as the tabernacle was moved around, the place of worship changed. Stephen is preparing to show that they have changed from the religious customs of Moses themselves.

45, 46 **Which also our fathers, in their turn,**—The tabernacle with all of its equipment was built in the wilderness, and at the death of Moses, after their sojourn of forty years in the wilderness, Joshua became the leader and led the Israelites across the river

Jacob. 47 But Solomon built him a house.   48 Howbeit the Most High
dwelleth not in *houses* made with hands; as saith the prophet,
49   ⁸The heaven is my throne,
        And the earth the footstool of my feet:
        What manner of house will ye build me? saith the Lord:
        Or what is the place of my rest?
50   Did not my hand make all these things?

⁸Is. 66. 1 f.

Jordan into the promised land. The tabernacle was brought across
the river Jordan and used in the land of Canaan for a long period.
They continued to use the tabernacle until the days of David;
King David made preparation to build a permanent house for Jehovah. He was not permitted to build this house.

47 **But Solomon built him a house.**—David had found favor
with Jehovah; he was raised to sit on the throne and made king
over Israel; God established David's kingdom (1 Sam. 13: 14;
Psalm 89: 20-37); but he would not permit David to build the
temple (2 Sam. 7: 2ff). David's son Solomon was permitted to
build the temple; David gave to Solomon material that he had collected for the temple, and also the pattern. Solomon then built the
temple (2 Sam. 7: 2ff.). David's son Solomon was permitted to
built and ready for use.

48-50 **Howbeit the Most High dwelleth not in houses**—
Though Solomon built a magnificent house, yet he did not suppose
that Jehovah could be circumscribed within the walls of the temple.
Jehovah God "dwelleth not in houses made with hands." These
were the words of Solomon when the temple was dedicated. (1
Kings 8: 26, 27, 43; 2 Chron. 6: 18, 39.) Stephen here quoted
from Isa. 66: 1, 2, which emphasizes that Jehovah cannot be confined to a material building, but his throne is in heaven and the
earth is his footstool; hence, no house could contain him. No
house could be large enough and magnificent enough to contain
him who made the universe. The argument seems to be that if the
universe which God made could not contain him, how much less
this temple which had been made by the hands of man. This is
what Solomon said in his prayer at the dedication of the temple.
(2 Chron. 6: 18.)

51 Ye stiffnecked and uncircumcised in heart and ears, ye do always resist the Holy Spirit: as your fathers did, so do ye. 52 Which of the prophets
did not your fathers persecute? and they killed them that showed before of
the coming of the Righteous One; of whom ye have now become betrayers

---

51 Ye stiffnecked and uncircumcised in heart—It is thought
that Stephen was interrupted at this point; hence, the turn that his
address takes. "Stiffnecked" is from "sklerotracheloi," which is a
compound word and means that they were hard in neck; that they
would not bow the neck to Jehovah; they were stubborn.
"Uncircumcised in heart and ears" means that they were not willing to believe or obey in their hearts; neither were they willing to
hear with their ears. Circumcision was a sign that they submitted
to God; hence, uncircumcised in heart would mean that in heart
they would not submit to God, and therefore were not God's people. "Ye do always resist the Holy Spirit"; they resisted the Holy
Spirit by rejecting the words that the Holy Spirit spoke through
Stephen to them. "Resist" is from the Greek "antipiptete," which
means "to fall against, to rush against." This is the only place
that it is used in the New Testament, but it is used in the Old Testament which is here quoted. (Num. 27: 14.) Hence, the meaning is that they had fallen against the Holy Spirit as one would
against an enemy. Stephen had completed his historical argument
and he now makes an application of it.

**52, 53 Which of the prophets did not your fathers perse-
cute?**—There is an implied charge here that they had persecuted
all of the prophets, and that they were still persecuting the disciples of Jesus. This was the same spirit that their fathers had in
persecuting the prophets. He simply charges them as possessing
the same evil spirit that the fathers had when they persecuted the
prophets and "killed them that showed before of the coming of the
Righteous One." The prophets that foretold of Christ were persecuted and killed; hence, when the "Righteous One" came as a fulfillment of those prophecies, they continued to exercise the spirit of
persecution and destroyed him. Stephen becomes more pointed in
his application and says: "Of whom ye have now become betrayers
and murderers." This was a fearful indictment against the council
and all who sympathized with the council. Stephen's accusation

and murderers; 53 ye who received the law [9]as it was ordained by angels, and kept it not.

------

[9]Or, *as the ordinance of angels*. Gr. *unto ordinances of angels*

------

here is so fearful that the Sanhedrin will not let it pass. He further states that they had "received the law as it was ordained by angels, and kept it not." This has reference to the law of Moses; the one whom they had charged Stephen with blaspheming. Yet they were blaspheming Moses and the law by persecuting the disciples of Christ. Instead of trying Stephen, Stephen put the Sanhedrin on trial. Four thoughts stand out in this address of Stephen; it is well to note the lines of argument that he has presented before leaving his address. The first thought is that God's dealings with his people showed continual progress; the end was not reached by a single leap, but by development. As proof of this he recited the story of Abraham, to whom the land was promised; he did not reach the promised land until some years after he was called, and he did not get the covenant of circumcision till later. The second thought is that the temple is not exclusively holy; he makes this stand out so clearly that his hearers could not fail to get it. God had appeared to Abraham in a heathen land, in Mesopotamia; Joseph had his entire glorious career in Egypt; Jacob, because of the famine, had gone down into Egypt. In another heathen land Moses found God. The signs and wonders were done in Egypt, in the Red Sea, and in the wilderness. The law was given from Mount Sinai, another foreign country. The third thought showed the long-suffering of God and his many mercies, though the people had gone into idolatry. Joseph was ill-treated by his brethren; their rejection of Joseph was a parallel to the rejection of Christ by the Jews. They rebelled against Moses, and in the same way they had rebelled against Christ who was the Messiah and the one who fulfilled the prophecies. The fourth point was that he showed the falsity of the charge that they had made against him by quoting so frequently from Moses and the prophets. In a burst of impassioned words he charges the council and the race of Jews with its long-continued crime, its murder of the "Righteous One," and its outrage of the law given by angels.

3. STEPHEN'S DEATH
7 : 54 to 8 : 2

54 Now when they heard these things, they were cut to the heart, and they gnashed on him with their teeth. 55 But he, being full of the Holy Spirit, looked up stedfastly into heaven, and saw the glory of God, and Jesus

---

54 Now when they heard these things,—"These things" refer to what Stephen had said in his defense, and especially to the things that he had said in verses 51-53. "They were cut to the heart," which literally means "sawn through," as in Acts 5: 33. They were not convicted of their sin; they hardened their heart and turned from the truth. This was the effect that Stephen's speech had on them; he became the occasion for their hardening their hearts. "They gnashed on him with their teeth." This was an expression of the frenzy of rage, only restrained by a brute-like grinding of the teeth. Stephen's address had the same effect on his auditors that Peter's address had on the Sadducees. Stephen had sent a saw through the hearts of the Pharisees, and they with a loud noise, and a grinding and gnashing of their teeth, like a pack of hungry, snarling wolves, rushed upon Stephen. No uglier sight could be pictured than we have here of these frenzied, religious people.

55 But he, being full of the Holy Spirit,—There is a wide contrast in the spirit manifested by Stephen and that of the members of the Sanhedrin. Again it is stated that Stephen was "full of the Holy Spirit," and what he said and did was guided by the Holy Spirit. Stephen "looked up stedfastly into heaven." He turned his face heavenward and away from such ugly expressions as could be seen on the faces of these frenzied people. As he looked into heaven he "saw the glory of God," which was a vision of God and his glory. Stephen also saw "Jesus standing on the right hand of God." At this time Jesus was "standing" as if he had arisen to encourage Stephen in his contention for Christ. This is the only reference to the attitude of Jesus as "standing" after he ascended to heaven. Jesus is usually represented as "sitting" in the majesty and sovereignty of his glory. No one else saw the vision but Stephen, and there is no use to speculate as to the reality of it.

standing on the right hand of God, 56 and said, Behold, I see the heavens opened, and the Son of man standing on the right hand of God. 57 But they cried out with a loud voice, and stopped their ears, and rushed upon him with one accord; 58 and they cast him out of the city, and stoned him: and the witnesses laid down their garments at the feet of a young man named Saul. 59 And they stoned Stephen, calling upon *the Lord,* and saying, Lord

---

56 **Behold, I see the heavens opened,**—Stephen described his vision there to this frenzied people. Some think that Stephen here referred to the words of Jesus as recorded in Matt. 26: 64. Stephen here refers to Christ as "the Son of man"; this was a name frequently used by Christ when speaking of himself, but never by any other speaker or writer, save Stephen. Such a vision must have comforted Stephen and enabled him to receive with meekness the affliction of stoning.

57, 58 **But they cried out with a loud voice,**—The charge that Stephen had made against them, that they had killed Jesus, was made very irritating now by the declaration that Stephen saw Jesus so exalted. It was an offensive proclamation of the doctrine of the resurrection, which the Sadducees denied; it was also reasserting that the crucified Jesus was coequal with God. They must have regarded this statement of Stephen as one of the strongest examples of blasphemy, spoken here in the presence of the Sanhedrin; hence, they "stopped their ears, and rushed upon him with one accord." The word for "stopped" literally means to hold their ears together with their hands, as if to say that they would not listen to such blasphemous words. No trial was had; no vote was taken; no question was raised about what was the right thing to do; they rushed upon him as the hogs did down the cliff when the demons entered them. (Luke 8: 33.) They rushed him out of the city with their wild violence "and stoned him." They were scrupulous to observe the letter of the law with murder in their hearts. (Lev. 24: 10-16; Num. 15: 35, 36; 1 Kings 21: 13; Heb. 13: 12.) "Witnesses" laid down their garments at the feet of a young man named Saul. This is the first mention that we have of Saul. The witnesses had to cast the first stone. (Deut. 17: 7; John 8: 7.) They laid aside the outer garments to have free access with their arms.

59 **And they stoned Stephen,**—As Stephen prayed, he was stoned; the witnesses against him had taken off their outer gar-

Jesus, receive my spirit.   60 And he kneeled down, and cried with a loud
voice, Lord, lay not this sin to their charge.   And when he had said this, he
fell asleep.

---

ments and Saul had kept the clothes of those who did the prelimi-
nary stoning. (Deut. 17: 7.) It has been discussed frequently as
to whether the Sanhedrin passed sentence on Stephen; some think
that there was no decision or judgment rendered, and that the
Sanhedrin with others became infuriated at Stephen's speech and
rushed upon him, took him out of the city, and stoned him without
any formal trial or decision. Others think that a decision was rendered hastily and the execution as hastily carried out. Another
difficulty has been discussed, and that is that the Jews could not put
to death anyone they tried; the Sanhedrin could pass the judicial
sentence of death, but could not carry it out. (John 18: 31.)
They could pass the sentence of death (Matt. 26: 66; Mark 14:
64), and were as guilty as if they had executed their sentence.
Stephen's prayer was made to Jesus to receive his spirit. The
prayer to Jesus was equivalent to calling on the Lord. (Acts 9:
21; 22: 16; 1 Cor. 1: 2.) Jesus had encouraged his disciples to
expect mansions of rest. (John 14: 2.) He had also spoken of
everlasting habitations (Luke 16: 9), or "eternal tabernacles."
This is similar to Jesus, as he expired on the cross. "Father, into
thy hands I commend my spirit: and having said this, he gave up
the ghost." (Luke 23: 46.)

60 **And he kneeled down, and cried with a loud voice,—**
Again Stephen's prayer is similar to that of his Lord's (Luke 23:
34), "Father, forgive them; for they know not what they do."
The spirit of Christ is a spirit of forgiveness; it leads us to love
our enemies and to bless them that curse us, and to pray for them
who despitefully use us. (Matt. 5: 44.) As they pelted his body
with stones, Stephen took the posture of kneeling in prayer. His
last moments were spent in prayer; "and when he had said this, he
fell asleep." "Fell asleep" is from the Greek "ekoimethe," which
is used to denote "to put to sleep"; our English word "cemetery"
comes from this Greek word, and means "the sleeping place of the
dead." This is an appropriate figure for the death of the saints.
Jesus used the term "sleep" for "death." (Matt. 9: 24; Mark 5:

1 And Saul was consenting unto his death.
And there arose on that day a great persecution against the church which
was in Jerusalem; and they were all scattered abroad throughout the regions

---

39; John 11: 11, 12.) Paul also used the term "sleep" for death.
(1 Cor. 15: 18, 51; 1 Thess. 4: 13, 14.)

1 **And Saul was consenting unto his death.**—"Saul" is later
the apostle Paul; he was present when Stephen was stoned and held
the clothes of those who stoned Stephen. He was not only "consenting unto his death," but the Greek shows that he approved of it
and that he took pleasure in the death of Stephen. Later he so
confessed (Acts 22: 20), and encouraged the killing of the first
Christian martyr (Rom. 1: 32). Saul was willing to be known
as really participating in the transaction. The first picture that we
have of Saul is that he is engaging in the murder of the first Christian martyr. At that time he is described as "a young man" (Acts
7: 58), which may be interpreted as thirty or forty years old; this
term and kindred ones were used with greater latitude than we
now use them. In Paul's letter to Philemon (verse 9) he calls
himself "the aged"; this letter was written probably in A.D. 62 to
64. The martyrdom of Stephen is generally placed in A.D. 34 or
35. If Paul was between sixty and seventy years of age when he
wrote to Philemon, he was between thirty and forty at the death of
Stephen.

And there arose on that day a great persecution—This was
the first of a number of waves of persecution that swept over the
early church. This persecution of Stephen was the first of such
violent opposition to the church; the martyrdom of Stephen acted
like the first taste of blood to a wild beast. "They were all scattered abroad"; the word "all" is used in a general sense, meaning,
in popular language, "very many." They were scattered
"throughout the regions of Judaea and Samaria." Samaria was
the middle division of Palestine at that time, and was just north of
Judea; it lay between Judea on the south and Galilee on the north.
"Except the apostles"; that is, all were scattered except the apostles who remained with the small remnant of the church in Jerusalem. We are not told why the apostles remained in Jerusalem at

of Judaea and Samaria, except the apostles. 2 And devout men buried Stephen, and made great lamentation over him. 3 But Saul laid waste the

---

this time; they were guided by the Holy Spirit, and God had some
purpose in their remaining at Jerusalem.

2 **And devout men buried Stephen,**—"Devout" comes from
the Greek "eulabeis," and is used only four times in the New Testament. (Luke 2: 25; Acts 2: 5; 8: 2; 22: 12.) "Devout," as
used in Acts 10: 2, comes from the Greek "eusebes." It is not
known whether these "devout men" who buried Stephen were
Christians; some think that they were Jews who were kindly disposed toward Christianity. However, others think that they were
Christians because they "made great lamentation over him."
"Lamentation" here comes from "kopeton," and means "to beat
the breast." This is the only place it is used in the New Testament. This was a distinguished honor paid to Stephen; there
were those who deeply lamented his death and willingly bore testimony to his worth.

4. DISCIPLES SCATTERED
8: 3, 4

church, entering into every house, and dragging men and women committed
them to prison.

---

3 **But Saul laid waste the church,**—The first seven chapters
of Acts give a history of the origin or beginning of the church and
its development in Jerusalem; so far all of the events narrated
about the church occurred in the city of Jerusalem. It seems that
for the first three to five years the church was confined to Jerusalem, but after the martyrdom of Stephen, the persecuting spirit,
which had already so often attempted to silence the apostles, became more decided and even unrelenting. It prevailed to such an
extent that the Christians were induced in large numbers to leave
the city, and go abroad even beyond their own country. (Acts 11:
19.) The persecution which was designed to crush the rising
cause of the gospel was overruled by God into an occasion of its
rapid advancement. The followers of Christ, wherever they went,
made known the gospel, and multitudes were converted to Christ.
The history from now on takes us to regions beyond Jerusalem.

4 They therefore that were scattered abroad went about ¹preaching the

¹Comp. marg. note on ch. 5. 42

Saul was a leader in the persecution. He not only persecuted Christians publicly, but visited homes, and "dragging men and women" out of their homes, "committed them to prison." He was empowered, as he himself said (Acts 26: 10), by the chief priests to persecute Christians.

4 **They therefore that were scattered abroad**—It is probable that the events took place in A.D. 37; this was the year in which Tiberius died and Caligula succeeded him. There was a time when there was no Roman governor in Judea, and the Jewish factions reigned supreme. Hence, the opponents of Christianity visited Christian homes and thrust Christian men and women into vile prisons, and then brought them before the elders in the synagogue, who tried to force them to deny Jesus; on their refusal some of them were put to death (Acts 22: 4; 26: 10), others were beaten (Acts 26: 11), and all suffered many outrages (1 Tim. 1: 13). They that "were scattered abroad went about preaching the word." They traveled far and wide through various regions; they did not confine themselves to the Jewish territory, but some of them went as far as Phoenicia, the island of Cyprus, and Antioch in Syria. (Acts 11: 19.) By going beyond the Jewish territory they would be in less danger of being pursued by the hostility of the chief priests, and might hope to enjoy comparative security. It is probable that some went as far as Rome, for Andronicus and Junias were disciples before Paul's conversion. (Rom. 16: 7.) "Preaching the word" is from the Greek "euaggelizomenoi ton logon," and means "evangelizing" or "gospelizing" the word. All of those scattered were emergency preachers; they were men stirred to activity by zeal for the Lord. They visited the country, towns, and villages, and even went into the homes of those who would permit them, and told them about Jesus, the Savior of the world. We see here another illustration of the providential law, which appears to be an irretrievable calamity and it is not only overruled, but designed from the beginning to promote the very cause which it seems to threaten with disaster and defeat.

5. PHILIP IN SAMARIA
8: 5-8

word. 5 And Philip went down to the city of Samaria, and proclaimed unto them the Christ. 6 And the multitudes gave heed with one accord unto the things that were spoken by Philip, when they heard, and saw the signs which

5 **And Philip went down to the city of Samaria,**—This Philip was one of the seven selected at Jerusalem to help look after the Grecian widows in the daily ministration. (Acts 6: 5.) He was also called later "Philip the evangelist." (Acts 21: 8.) So this was not Philip the apostle, for the twelve apostles remained at Jerusalem. The apostles are mentioned in Acts 8: 14 in distinction from Philip. We do not have Philip the apostle mentioned any more in Acts. "The city of Samaria" is located in the country of Samaria; so there was a city and a country by the same name. The city of Samaria was built by Omri, king of Israel. (1 Kings 16: 24.) It became the capital of the kingdom of the ten tribes, or northern kingdom. It was destroyed several times and rebuilt. Philip "went down" to this city; Jerusalem was situated on a higher elevation than Samaria. He "proclaimed unto them the Christ." He preached that Jesus was the Messiah, the Son of God, and the Savior of the world. The Samaritans of half-heathen descent accepted and professed a corrupted Judaism; they looked for the Messiah, who was to rebuild the temple on Mount Gerizim, and restore everywhere the law of Moses. (John 4: 25.) This is the first instance cited of the expansion noted in verse 4; proclaim is here translated from "ekerussen," which means "to preach and keep on at it." It is different from "euaggelizomenoi" in verse 4, where the good news is spread. To proclaim Christ is to preach the gospel. Samaria had been expressly named by Christ as a region in which his disciples were to bear witness of him. (Acts 1: 8.)

6 **And the multitudes gave heed with one accord**—"Gave heed" is from "proseichon," which means that they kept holding the mind on the things which were spoken by Philip; it carried the meaning of "spellbound." The entire multitude "with one accord" listened attentively to what Philip preached and were astonished at the signs which he did. Great throngs of people crowded around Philip and listened with eager attention; the Holy Spirit aided the

he did. 7 ²For *from* many of those that had unclean spirits, they came out, crying with a loud voice: and many that were palsied, and that were lame, were healed. 8 And there was much joy in that city.

preaching of the word with "signs" or miracles. These miracles were to be the "signs" that the message which Philip preached was from God; they were such as could leave no doubt in the minds of those who witnessed them.

7, 8 **For from many of those that had unclean spirits,**—The kind of miracles mentioned were such that there could be no doubt that God had wrought them. "Unclean spirits" were cast out and came out "with a loud voice"; this would attract the attention of the multitude to the one who was afflicted. The cry may have been a testimony to the Messiahship of Christ. (Mark 3: 11; Luke 4: 41.) Then again it may have been just an inarticulate shout of rage; it is to be noticed that demoniac possession is clearly distinguished in this passage from ordinary disease, for "many that were palsied, and that were lame, were healed." Under the general name "palsied," several infirmities may be included; sometimes it meant apoplexy, which affected the whole body, and sometimes a paralysis of a part of the body. The preaching, and the curing of the disease, caused much joy in that city.

6. SIMON THE SORCERER
8: 9-13

9 But there was a certain man, Simon by name, who beforetime in the city used sorcery, and amazed the ³people of Samaria, giving out that him-

³Gr. *nation*

9 **But there was a certain man, Simon**—"Simon" was a common name among the Jews; it is a contraction from "Simeon." There are ten men mentioned in the New Testament by this name. This Simon is known as "Simon Magus," or "Simon the sorcerer." There were many sorcerers, or those who deceived the people by certain tricks and deceptions. Nothing further is known of this Simon except what is mentioned here. He had used sor-

self was some great one: 10 to whom they all gave heed, from the least to
the greatest, saying, This man is that power of God which is called Great.
11 And they gave heed to him, because that of long time he had amazed

cery for some time and had "amazed the people of Samaria," and
had pretended himself to be "some great one." Simon was an impostor, and it is amazing how gullible people are in the presence of
such deceivers. He practiced his magic arts and pretended that he
could do wonderful things. Simon has become a famous character
in the early history of the church in Samaria. His pretended miracles were not discovered by the people; they thought that he was
what he claimed to be, "some great one."

10 **to whom they all gave heed,**—It seems that he had been
successful in practicing his magic art until he had deceived all the
people in that country. They listened to him from the "least to the
greatest," and all praised him, thinking that the "power of God
which is called Great" was exercised through him. They were led
to regard him as having a most intimate connection with the Deity,
and as having power to affect seriously the destiny of men.

11 **And they gave heed to him,**—Tradition has it that Simon
went about accompanied by a woman named Helena who was also
a "power of God." He taught a great first principle, hidden but
omnipresent; this principle manifested itself in *two different ways*
—as an active and spiritual principle and as a passive and receptive principle. The first is the good, the latter the evil; the first is
the great "power of God" manifesting itself from the recovery of
the other or passive receptive principle. Simon himself was the incarnation of the active principle, which made for salvation; Helena
was the incarnation of the passive reception principle. Her life of
degradation was a type of the deterioration of the visible universe,
and her recovery by Simon was the process of salvation by the
great power of God made visible. This dualism, with its simple,
almost childish, symbolism, its male and female principles, its opposition of good and evil, was the source out of which Simon constructed his system. Simon had so amazed the people by his pretended supernatural powers that they gave heed to him in whatsoever he did or claimed.

them with his sorceries. 12 But when they believed Philip ¹preaching good tidings concerning the kingdom of God and the name of Jesus Christ, they were baptized, both men and women. 13 And Simon also himself believed: and being baptized, he continued with Philip; and beholding signs and great ⁴miracles wrought, he was amazed.

⁴Gr. *powers*

---

12 **But when they believed Philip preaching**—When Philip went among these deluded people and preached Jesus as the Messiah and the Savior of the world, and accompanied his preaching with the real "signs" or miracles, they believed him. Philip's miracles were put in direct contrast with the pretended works of Simon; Philip cast out demons, cured the palsied, and healed the crippled so that the people could see what he had done. Many of them were thus healed and knew that there was no deception practiced by Philip. It is noted that when they believed, "they were baptized, both men and women." On Pentecost after they believed Peter's preaching, they asked what to do, and they were told that they should repent and be baptized "unto the remission of your sins." (Acts 2: 38.) Hence, in every instance where people turned to the Lord, or believed the gospel, they were baptized.

13 **And Simon also himself believed:**—Simon heard Philip and saw what Philip did; he "believed: and being baptized," he continued for some time with Philip. There was no difference between the faith of Simon and that of the other people in Samaria. "Simon also himself believed": he believed the same thing that the others believed, and he was baptized as were the others. Jesus had said: "He that believeth and is baptized shall be saved." (Mark 16: 16.) Simon "believed" and was "baptized"; hence, he had the remission of his sins, for Jesus had said that the one who believed and was baptized should be saved. "He continued with Philip," and saw the "signs and great miracles wrought" by Philip. "Continued" is from the Greek "proskartereo," and is used in Acts 1: 14; 2: 42, 46, and means originally "to persist obstinately in." For some time at least he continued with Philip, hearing his preaching and seeing the miracles that he wrought. He saw the wide contrast in what Philip was doing and what he had pretended

to do. He was "amazed" or astonished at what Philip was able to do ; he saw the reality of working miracles by the hand of Philip.

7. PETER AND JOHN IN SAMARIA
8 : 14-25

14 Now when the apostles that were at Jerusalem heard that Samaria had received the word of God, they sent unto them Peter and John: 15 who, when they were come down, prayed for them, that they might receive the Holy Spirit: 16 for as yet it was fallen upon none of them: only they had

14 **Now when the apostles that were at Jerusalem**—The apostles were still at Jerusalem, though the church had been scattered. The apostles heard the good news of the success that Philip had in Samaria, and it was thought best to send someone there with apostolic authority to encourage and confer on the believers some extraordinary gifts of the Holy Spirit; so Peter and John were sent. It must have been an occasion of rejoicing on the part of the apostles when they heard that the Samaritans had received the gospel of Christ. (Matt. 10: 5; Acts 1: 8.) It should be noticed that the apostles "sent" Peter and John as their messengers; it will be recalled also that John had at one time sought to call down fire on a Samaritan village. (Luke 9: 54.)

15 **who, when they were come down,**—Peter and John went down to Samaria and prayed for the disciples there; they prayed "that they might receive the Holy Spirit." There were special gifts of the Holy Spirit which could be given by the apostles; these gifts would confirm the disciples in the faith. Sometimes they were imparted by the laying on of hands. These gifts are to be distinguished from the baptism of the Holy Spirit.

16 **for as yet it was fallen upon none of them:**—"It was fallen upon" none of them; "pneuma" is the word for "spirit" here, and the translation should be "he," rather than "it"; it is not a correct form to use "it" for the Holy Spirit. The Holy Spirit is a member of the Godhead and is a personality, or spiritual being; Jesus frequently referred to him with the personal pronoun and the masculine gender. (John 14: 16, 17; 15: 26; 16: 13, 14.) These Samaritans had only been "baptized into the name of the Lord Jesus"; hence, they had received remission of sins, but had not received a miraculous measure of the Holy Spirit.

been baptized into the name of the Lord Jesus. 17 Then laid they their hands on them, and they received the Holy Spirit. 18 Now when Simon saw that through the laying on of the apostles' hands the Holy Spirit was given, he offered them money, 19 saying, Give me also this power, that on whomsoever I lay my hands, he may receive the Holy Spirit. 20 But Peter said

[5]Some ancient authorities omit *Holy*

17 **Then laid they their hands on them,**—The laying on of hands did not occur at Pentecost (Acts 2: 4, 33) nor in Acts 10: 44; these were baptisms of the Holy Spirit, and were administered by the Lord; the Holy Spirit given by the laying on of hands was a measure of the Holy Spirit not so full as 'the baptism. Some have concluded that the Holy Spirit in its miraculous form could be given only by the apostles; hence, Peter and John had to go to Samaria. We do not know that all who believed in Samaria received this miraculous endowment of the Holy Spirit; neither do we know whether Simon received this measure. Some have concluded that Simon and all the believers in Samaria had hands laid on them and a miraculous measure of the Holy Spirit bestowed upon them, but the evidence is not clear and does not warrant such a conclusion.

18, 19 **Now when Simon saw that through the laying on**— There was something that Simon could see in the bestowal of the gift of the Holy Spirit; he observed a transference of power from the apostles to the believers. Simon wanted the power to bestow gifts upon others; he "offered them money" for the power to bestow miraculous gifts upon others. Simon had been for some time practicing magic arts and deceiving the people; but now he thought that he could obtain with money the power not only to work miracles himself, but to give others the power to work miracles. Simon had not as yet risen above the mercenary spirit. Simon's whole attitude is that of a professional trickster or deceiver; he fancied that he could by money be instructed how to acquire, use, and impart, all in the way of trade, these powers. From this act of Simon's comes our word "simony," the crime of buying, selling, or bargaining for spiritual functions.

20 **But Peter said unto him,**—Peter was filled with holy and righteous indignation at Simon's proposition; he used language as

unto him, Thy silver perish with thee, because thou hast thought to obtain the gift of God with money. 21 Thou hast neither part nor lot in this ⁶matter: for thy heart is not right before God. 22 Repent therefore of this thy wickedness, and pray the Lord, if perhaps the thought of thy heart shall

---

⁶Gr. *word*

strong as we find anywhere in Peter's teaching or writings; "thy silver perish with thee" was the condemnation; this expresses his abhorrence of the proposal and shows Simon the imminent danger to which he was exposed with such a condition of heart. Peter also sounded a solemn warning to him of the end that would befall him if he followed such a course. Simon thought that the gift of God could be purchased with money; he is to learn that the blessings of God, and especially the power to bestow miraculous gifts on others, cannot be had with money.

21 **Thou hast neither part nor lot in this matter:**—"Lot" comes from the Greek "kleros," and means "part"; it means that Simon should have no "part" in the matter of bestowing the Holy Spirit on others. "Part nor lot," the first denoting any share or portion, and the second one determined or assigned. "In this matter" literally means in this word (Luke 1: 4; Acts 15: 6), and has direct reference to the power of communicating the Holy Spirit. However, some think that it has reference to the preaching of the gospel; hence, they would say that Simon had no part in preaching the gospel; the context seems not to bear out this thought. "For thy heart is not right before God," or "straight"; Simon's heart was not "right," or "straight," or "straightforward," as it ought to be, but was seeking crooked, perverse, and secret ways. (Matt. 3: 3; Mark 1: 3; 2 Pet. 2: 15.)

22 **Repent therefore of this thy wickedness,**—Peter here gives the second law of pardon—the law of forgiveness to the erring Christian. He is commanded to "repent," and "pray" for forgiveness. Simon as a Christian had made the mistake of thinking that he could purchase the communication of the Holy Spirit to others with his money; hence, Peter tells him to repent "of this thy wickedness"; this shows what wickedness he was to repent of; his former sins had been forgiven, and now he is guilty of another sin, and it is this one that he is instructed to repent of and "pray the Lord" that "the thought of thy heart shall be forgiven thee."

be forgiven thee. 23 For I see that thou ⁷art in the gall of bitterness and in
the bond of iniquity. 24 And Simon answered and said, Pray ye for me to
the Lord, that none of the things which ye have spoken come upon me.

⁷Or, *wilt become gall* (or, *a gall root*) *of bitterness and a bond of iniquity.* Comp.
Deut. 29. 18; Heb. 12. 15

Again we see that the sin of which he was to repent was "the
thought of thy heart" of thinking that he could purchase that
power with his money. "If perhaps" means that there is some
chance of his forgiveness; though his sin was great, yet if he would
repent and pray God there is a hope of his being cleansed of it.
Some think that Peter had in mind the sin mentioned by Jesus in
Matt. 12: 31, but Peter does not close the door of hope here. "If
perhaps" means "if it be possible," or since it is possible.

23 **For I see that thou art in the gall of bitterness**—"Gall,"
as used here, is an emblem of exceeding great wickedness; "gall"
is from the Greek "cholas," and means to pour out a yellowish
green bile or gall; it is used only twice in the New Testament—
here and in Matt. 27: 34. "Gall and wormwood" (Deut. 29: 18) ;
in Heb. 12: 15 we have a "root of bitterness," or a bitter root;
"bond of iniquity" means that he would be in the bondage of sin
and under the curse of the sin. The ancients considered that the
gall of noxious reptiles was the source of their venom, and Peter
warns Simon that unless repentance comes he will become worse
and worse until he becomes all venom; Simon is warned that unless he repents a chain or band of iniquity will enslave him. This
was a dangerous condition for him to be in.

24 **And Simon answered and said,**—Simon saw the danger
that he was in; evidently he repented and prayed God, and even
asked Peter to pray for him, as though his own prayer was not
sufficient to obtain forgiveness. Simon is anxious to escape the
penalty for his sin, and hopes that Peter can avert it; Peter had by
the Holy Spirit diagnosed his case correctly. Simon was a converted man, but was in sin at this point. We are led to believe
that Simon surely repented and corrected his life. The inspired
record drops the matter here and draws the curtain, so that we see
Simon no more. Some claim that Simon was never penitent, and
therefore never forgiven; they say that there is no evidence that
Simon ever prayed for himself. However, the fact that he asked

25 They therefore, when they had testified and spoken the word of the Lord, returned to Jerusalem, and ¹preached the gospel to many villages of the Samaritans.

---

¹Gr. *brought good tidings*. Comp. ch. 5. 42

Peter to pray for him seems to imply that he was praying for himself. Surely he would not ask Peter to do for him what Peter had commanded him to do for himself.

25 They therefore, when they had testified—Peter and John had been sent down to Samaria to encourage those who had believed and to bestow such miraculous gifts upon the believers as the Holy Spirit deemed wise to confirm the word of the Samaritans. Luke the historian has lingered on the case of Simon, and now, having disposed of that notable case, states that Peter and John preached the word of the Lord to them while there and then returned to Jerusalem. However, they "preached the gospel to many villages of the Samaritans." The preaching of the gospel among the Samaritans was not confined to the city where it had begun, but extended to many of the smaller towns through which Peter and John passed on their return to Jerusalem. Peter and John furthered the work of Philip among the Samaritans; Luke closes the record of Philip's work in Samaria, and he is next directed to go to the Ethiopian eunuch.

SECTION FOUR

CONVERSION OF THE EUNUCH, SAUL, AND
CORNELIUS
8 : 26 to 12 : 25

1. CONVERSION OF THE EUNUCH
8 : 26-40

26 But an angel of the Lord spake unto Philip, saying, Arise, and go
²toward the south unto the way that goeth down from Jerusalem unto Gaza:

²Or, *at noon.* Comp. ch. 22. 6

---

26 **But an angel of the Lord spake unto Philip,**—The historian now turns from the brief record of the work of Peter and
John in Samaria to the further work that the Holy Spirit had for
Philip. It is not stated how the angel of the Lord spoke unto Philip, and there is no use in our guessing at it. It is enough to know
that the message was conveyed to Philip in language that Philip
understood and obeyed. The command was given to Philip in Samaria. He was commanded to "arise, and go toward the south
unto the way that goeth down from Jerusalem unto Gaza." He is
not required to go to Jerusalem, but to get upon the road leading
from Jerusalem to Gaza. Gaza is one of the oldest places mentioned in the Bible; it first occurs in Gen. 10: 19, as a frontier
town of the Canaanites, and later as the southernmost of the five
cities of the Philistines, to whom it really belonged, even after it
was formally assigned to Judah. (Josh. 15: 47; Judges 1: 18.)
Palestine was divided into three divisions at this time—Galilee was
the extreme northern division, Samaria was the middle division,
and Judea the southern division. Gaza was in Judea. Gaza was
about sixty miles southwest from Jerusalem, and had been destroyed in 96 B.C., but was rebuilt, and was a city of importance at
this time. Philip would pass west of Jerusalem on his way from
Samaria and would intercept the road between Jerusalem and
Gaza; this was a journey of from sixty to seventy miles. "The
same is desert." It has been a matter of much dispute as to
whether this means the way was desert or whether the city was
deserted; some have contended that the city was deserted at this
time; however, others think that Gaza was not deserted until later.

the same is desert. 27 And he arose and went: and behold, a man of Ethiopia, a eunuch of great authority under Candace, queen of the Ethiopians, who
was over all her treasure, who had come to Jerusalem to worship; 28 and he
was returning and sitting in his chariot, and was reading the prophet Isaiah.

This phrase is considered as not being the language of the angel,
but is the language of Luke the historian. There were two roads,
some think three, from Jerusalem to Gaza; Philip was told to take
the "desert" road, probably the one by Hebron which went
through the desert hills of southern Judea. Any place which was
thinly peopled and unfit for cultivation was called "desert"; hence,
the angel sent Philip to a desert road, in which he was not likely to
encounter travelers much less to meet with such an adventure as
did there befall him. It is "desert" in the sense of being uninhab-
ited, and not in the sense of there being no water.

27 **And he arose and went:**—Philip obeyed promptly the instruction received from the angel. Attention is now directed to "a
man of Ethiopia, a eunuch of great authority under Candace,
queen of the Ethiopians." It is not known whether the eunuch was
a Jew or a proselyte of the Jewish religion. He was certainly zealous in going the long distance to Jerusalem to worship. He is introduced to us as "a man of Ethiopia." "Ethiopia" is the general
term for that part of Africa now known as Nubia and Abyssinia;
this portion of Africa was ruled for a long time by queens.
"Candace" was the general title of their queens, as rulers of Egypt
were called "Pharaoh," and those of Rome were called "Caesar."
This eunuch had "great authority," as he was "over all her treasure." Hence, he was the treasurer of this country, and had been
honored with great authority. Eunuchs were often employed by
oriental rulers in high stations; they were not allowed to be Jews
in the full sense, but only proselytes of the gate. (Deut. 23: 1.)
This eunuch seems to have held the same office under Candace that
Blastus held in the court or family of Herod Agrippa. (Acts 12:
20.) The word "treasure," as used here, means royal treasure.
The purpose of his visit to Jerusalem is clearly stated; he went
there "to worship"; this meant that he went to worship according
to the law of Moses.

28 **and he was returning and sitting in his chariot,**—"Returning" seems to be a favorite Greek verb with Luke. (Acts 1:

29 And the Spirit said unto Philip, Go near, and join thyself to this chariot.
30 And Philip ran to him, and heard him reading Isaiah the prophet, and
said, Understandest thou what thou readest? 31 And he said, How can I,

12; 8: 25.) It seemed that he was returning by way of Egypt to
his own country; his first stage or journey was from Jerusalem to
Gaza. He was riding in his chariot. He was "sitting in his chariot" and "was reading the prophet Isaiah." "Was reading" is
from the original "aneginosken," which means that he was reading
aloud as Philip "heard him" reading. This was common among
the orientals; some think that he had purchased this roll of Isaiah
in Jerusalem and was reading from the Septuagint Version. The
Jews when on a journey were accustomed to employ their time in
reading their scriptures. One of the commands enjoined by the
rabbis upon the Jews was that a Jew, when on a journey without a
companion, should study the law. He was reading "the prophet
Isaiah."

29 **And the Spirit said unto Philip,**—It should be noted that
the Holy Spirit spoke to the preacher, not to the one to be converted; Philip is directed to "go near, and join" himself to the
chariot. If the eunuch had been from some eastern country he
might have been riding a camel; but chariots were common in
Egypt. Here we get the first intimation of Philip's journey to this
section of the country; he is to interview the man who is riding in
this chariot. Philip may have been standing there waiting for further direction when the eunuch came along.

30 **And Philip ran to him, and heard him reading**—Philip
obeyed promptly the command given by the Holy Spirit. It
should be noted here that there have been cooperating three agencies to bring to the eunuch a knowledge of the gospel—namely, an
angel, the Holy Spirit, and Philip the preacher. The angel and the
Holy Spirit have not spoken to the man to be converted; they have
cooperated in bringing Philip to the eunuch. Philip heard the
eunuch reading; hence, the eunuch was reading aloud. Philip may
have recognized the scripture that was being read. He asked:
"Understandest thou what thou readest?" It will be noticed furthermore that "Philip ran" to the eunuch; that is, he hastened to
do what the Holy Spirit commanded. Here was a soul uncon-

except some one shall guide me? And he besought Philip to come up and sit with him. 32 Now the passage of the scripture which he was reading was this,

> [3]He was led as a sheep to the slaughter;
> And as a lamb before his shearer is dumb,
> So he openeth not his mouth:
> 33   In his humiliation his judgment was taken away:
> His generation who shall declare?
> For his life is taken from the earth.

---

[3]Is. 53. 7 f.

---

verted, and an opportunity is given to convert him. Philip's question refers to the meaning and application of the words that the eunuch was reading. The eunuch did not know that the very words that he was reading were a prophecy concerning Jesus. It is very likely that he had heard something of Jesus while he was in Jerusalem; surely he would have heard something about Christianity while there. It is always a profitable question to ask when one is reading: "Understandest thou what thou readest?" Reading is of very little profit if one does not understand what is read.

31 **And he said, How can I,**—The eunuch felt the need of someone to guide him in understanding what he was reading; his question here seems to imply, "How can you expect a stranger without aid to understand what puzzles your most learned doctors?" "Guide me" is the expression which is employed for the guidance given by a teacher to a pupil. Jesus used this expression frequently in reproaching the blind guidance which the scribes and Pharisees were giving to the people who came to them for instruction. (Matt. 15: 14; Luke 6: 39.) He uses also the same word for the guidance of the Holy Spirit. (John 16: 13.) He then asked Philip to join him and instruct him. He seems to have recognized in Philip one who could guide him; he desired to learn and graciously invited Philip "to come up and sit with him" in the chariot. This shows that the eunuch was an anxious inquirer of the truth, but bewildered and ready to be taught.

32, 33 **Now the passage of the scripture**—"The passage" is from the Greek "perioche," and means either of the section or the contents of the scripture; the eunuch was reading one particular passage, which we know as Isa. 53: 7, 8. This quotation is taken from the Septuagint Version, which varies some from the Hebrew

34 And the eunuch answered Philip, and said, I pray thee, of whom speaketh the prophet this? of himself, or of some other? 35 And Philip opened his mouth, and beginning from this scripture, *preached unto him Jesus. 36 And

*See marg. note on ch. 5. 42

text. This scripture describes the sufferings of an innocent and unresisting person; what perplexed the eunuch was to whom this referred. The declaration means that in his humiliation his right to justice was taken away; and who will be heirs or followers of him since his life was violently taken away? The Messiah patiently submitted, without murmuring to the ignominy and death; he made no complaint, though treated violently and unjustly; he was submissive, like the innocent lamb. Jesus was taken away from prison and from judgment; he was taken away to death by a violent judicial procedure. Pilate had declared that he found no fault in him. (Luke 23: 4; John 18: 38; 19: 6.) Jesus could have claimed a verdict of "not guilty"; but he let this sentence or judgment pass without claiming protection under it. The question is asked: "His generation who shall declare? for his life is taken from the earth." The idea of extinction is conveyed here, but his apostles and disciples were to declare his generation; the apostles were to bear witness of him, and the Holy Spirit was sent to bear witness of him, and he was now ready to do so through Philip to the eunuch.

34 **And the eunuch answered Philip,**—The point of difficulty in the mind of the eunuch was to whom did this scripture in Isaiah refer. Of whom is the prophet speaking? This question was very interesting, and perhaps more so, because of what the eunuch had heard in Jerusalem. We do not know whether he began obscurely to connect this passage with what he may have heard concerning Jesus; hence, he at once frankly asked Philip the question. He was encouraged to do so by the interest that Philip manifested in him, and by Philip's accepting the invitation to ride with him.

35 **And Philip opened his mouth,**—This question gave Philip the opportunity to instruct the eunuch; he had a good text, and an anxious learner. Philip knew, and he was as anxious to teach the eunuch as the eunuch was to learn. He began with this scripture

as they went on the way, they came unto a certain water; and the eunuch saith, Behold, *here is* water; what doth hinder me to be baptized?⁵ 38 And

⁵Some ancient authorities insert, wholly or in part, ver. 37 *And Philip said, If thou believest with all thy heart thou mayest. And he answered and said, I believe that Jesus Christ is the Son of God*

and "preached unto him Jesus." "Preached unto him Jesus" comes from the Greek "eueggalisato autoi ton Iesoun," which is the Greek for "evangelize." Philip had no doubt about the Messianic meaning of this passage, and he knew that Jesus was the Messiah. Philip "evangelized unto him Jesus"; he taught him about Jesus. Philip showed that the language of Isaiah had been fulfilled in Jesus of Nazareth, and particularly the manner of his death, and then his resurrection and the ascension. To "preach" Jesus is to preach his commands. Philip in preaching Jesus not only preached his death, burial, resurrection, but the commission that he gave to his apostles just before his ascension. Philip preached the terms of remission of sins.

36 **And as they went on the way,**—They continued to ride along the way, Philip preaching Jesus and the eunuch listening intensively. This was a most serious and important occasion; the eunuch hears Philip preach the commands of the gospel; and as they went along, "they came unto a certain water." It is to be noted that they "came" to this water. We must suppose that Philip traveled for some time with the eunuch, for it would take some time to teach the eunuch all that he needed to know about Jesus. Much discussion has been had as to where the eunuch was baptized. Luke does not tell us, hence we do not know. We do know that they "came unto a certain water," and that there was enough water for Philip and the eunuch to go "down into the water." Philip had preached Jesus in such a way that the eunuch learned that he should be baptized. No inspired preacher of the gospel then preached Jesus without preaching the baptism that Jesus commanded; no gospel preacher today can preach Jesus without preaching the command to be baptized.

(37 **And Philip said, If thou believest with all thy heart,**)— Verse 37 is left out of the Standard Version, but a footnote is inserted, saying that "some ancient authorities insert, wholly or in part, verse 37." It was found in one manuscript in the latter half of the second century, as it was quoted by "Irenaeus," who was

he commanded the chariot to stand still: and they both went down into the
water, both Philip and the eunuch; and he baptized him. 39 And when they
came up out of the water, the Spirit of the Lord caught away Philip; and
the eunuch saw him no more, for he went on his way rejoicing. 40 But Phil-

---

active from the year A.D. 170 to A.D. 210. It is supposed that this
verse was written in the margin and later was transcribed as a part
of the original text. Even if the verse be an interpolation, and
should be left out, it does not change in any way the thought;
nothing is added by retaining the verse so far as doctrine is concerned, and nothing certainly is lost by omitting the verse.
However, the early records that contain it show that very early in
the history of the church such a question was asked and such answer was given.

38 **And he commanded the chariot to stand still:**—Evidently
the eunuch had a chariot driver, since he "commanded the chariot"
to stop. When the chariot stopped, "they both went down into the
water"; it was necessary that they go down into the water in order
to do what was commanded to be done. The purpose of their
going down into the water was to baptize the eunuch. Philip had
preached Jesus to the eunuch and he had learned from such
preaching that he was to be baptized; he also had learned or knew
that it was necessary to go down into the water to be baptized. Both
the baptizer and the one to be baptized went into the water, and
Philip baptized the eunuch after they went down into the water.
The eunuch must have laid aside his garments and descended into
the water and was buried in baptism "in the name of our Lord
Jesus"; this was the authority for Philip's baptizing the eunuch.

39 **And when they came up out of the water,**—They did not
come up from the "edge of the water," but up "out of the water."
(Mark 1: 10.) Philip had done what he was directed to do; he
had been led to the eunuch who was an unconverted man, and was
ready to receive the truth. Philip had preached to him the truth of
the gospel; he had heard it, believed it, and had been baptized;
now he had the promise of Jesus that "he that believeth and is baptized shall be saved." (Mark 16: 16.) Philip was now "caught
away" by "the Spirit of the Lord." Some look at this as a miracle; however, Philip was "caught away" from the eunuch by the
Holy Spirit in the way that he was led to the eunuch. The Greek

ip was found at Azotus: and passing through he ⁴preached the gospel to all
the cities, till he came to Caesarea.

---

for "caught away" is "herpasen," which sometimes means suddenly and miraculously carried away. Hence, according to the
view of some, he was literally snatched away from the presence of
the eunuch as was Elijah. (1 Kings 18: 12; 2 Kings 2: 11; Ezek.
3: 12, 14; 2 Cor. 12: 2, 4.) The eunuch saw Philip no more, but
went on his way rejoicing in the salvation that he had found in
Christ. The next and only other account that we have of the eunuch is not in the Bible but in tradition; Luke draws the curtain
here and we see the eunuch no more.

40 **But Philip was found at Azotus:**—"Azotus" is the name
for the ancient city of the Philistines, "Ashdod." It was about
thirty miles from Gaza, on the way to Joppa. Philip "preached
the gospel to all the cities, till he came to Caesarea." Philip did
evangelistic service through the country there "till he came to Caesarea," where he made his home and headquarters (Acts 21: 8)
and was known as the "evangelist." It will be noted that Philip
preached the gospel "to all the cities" in that section of the country. The route which Philip would naturally take on this journey
led through Lydda and Joppa and we may trace the effects of his
preaching in the appearance in Acts 9: 32, 36.

2. CONVERSION OF SAUL
9: 1-19

1 But Saul, yet breathing threatening and slaughter against the disciples of

---

1 **But Saul, yet breathing threatening and slaughter**—Saul
was first mentioned in Acts 7: 58, and again in Acts 8: 1-3; now
we come to his conversion. There we find him as a persistent persecutor of the church; here we find him "yet breathing threatening
and slaughter against the disciples of the Lord." His attitude and
conduct is put in contrast to that of Philip by the conjunction
"but." Some translations have "and," but others seem to translate
"eti" as "yet," as if some time had elapsed between the death of
Stephen and the events that we are now to consider. "Breathing

the Lord, went unto the high priest, 2 and asked of him letters to Damascus unto the synagogues, that if he found any that were of the Way, whether men or women, he might bring them bound to Jerusalem. 3 And as he journeyed,

---

threatening and slaughter" does not mean "breathing out," but "breathing in" or "breathing on." It means that the very breath that Saul breathed encouraged him on to persecute the disciples of Christ. The figure is like a war horse who sniffs the smell of battle; he becomes anxious to persecute Christians. We are not told of any other death than that of Stephen, but we are led to believe that many others were put to death. Surely Saul's anger was greatly excited by the success of the early church, and with great zeal he put forth every effort possible to stop the progress of the church. He was orderly about what he was doing, as he had the authority of the "high priest."

2 and asked of him letters to Damascus—It is probable that the high priest here mentioned was Caiaphas, who was a chief of the Jews and exercised authority in such matters. "Letters to Damascus" means that Saul was granted authority to persecute Christians along the way and in the city of Damascus. Saul, a Pharisee, makes request of a Sadducee (the high priest) to persecute the disciples of Christ. Julius Caesar and Augustus had granted the high priest and Sanhedrin jurisdiction over Jews in foreign cities; so later Paul said that he received his authority to go to Damascus from the priests (Acts 26: 10) and "the estate of the elders" (Acts 22: 5); that is, the Sanhedrin. It seems that Paul had finished his persecution in Jerusalem and now wishes to extend it beyond to Damascus. "Damascus" is said to be the oldest city in the world; it was about a hundred and fifty miles northeast from Jerusalem and watered by the river Abana. A great number of Jews dwelt in this city; it seems that Christians had found refuge from Saul's persecution in Judea and had gone to Damascus. Paul's language in Acts 26: 11 seems to imply that Damascus is merely one of the other "foreign cities" to which he carried the persecution. "The Way" is frequently used by Luke to describe Christianity as "the Way" of life. (Acts 19: 9, 23; 22: 4; 24: 14, 22.) Luke also speaks of the way of salvation (Acts 16: 17) and "the way of the Lord" (Acts 18: 25). Jesus called

it came to pass that he drew nigh unto Damascus: and suddenly there shone round about him a light out of heaven: 4 and he fell upon the earth, and heard a voice saying unto him, Saul, Saul, why persecutest thou me? 5 And

---

himself "the way" (John 14: 6), the only way to the Father. Paul had authority to arrest both men and women and bring them to Jerusalem to be tried before the Sanhedrin.

3, 4 **And as he journeyed, it came to pass**—We are not told what mode of travel Paul used in making this journey to Damascus. He probably used the best mode that could be had at hand, which was horseback, or on a camel or ass or mule, or in a chariot; he would make the journey by land. There were two roads by which Saul could make his journey—one the caravan road which led from Egypt to Damascus, and kept near the coast line of Palestine till it struck eastward to cross the Jordan at the north point of the Sea of Galilee; to connect with this road Saul would have had first to go westward from Jerusalem to the sea. The other road led through Neapolis and crossed the Jordan south of the Sea of Galilee, and passed through Gadara and on northeastward to Damascus. We do not know which road Saul traveled. As he "drew nigh unto Damascus" there suddenly "shone round about him a light out of heaven." In Acts 22: 6 we are told that the time of day was "about noon" when the vision was seen, and in Acts 26: 13 Paul says that "at midday" the light was "above the brightness of the sun." The midday glare of the sun in that country was exceedingly bright, yet the glory of Christ as seen by Paul far surpassed the glory of the sun. Paul, smitten with blindness, "fell upon the earth," and "heard a voice saying," "Saul, Saul, why persecutest thou me?" This voice was clear and distinct to him, but seems to have been a mysterious sound to others; the voice spoke in the Hebrew tongue. (Acts 26: 14.) In all three of the accounts given by Luke he uses the transliteration of the Hebrew way of spelling Saul, "Saoul," while in every other case the Greek form "Saulos" is used. The disciples of Christ are one with him. (Matt. 10: 40; 25: 40, 45; Luke 10: 16; John 15: 1-5.) Hence, to persecute Christians was to persecute Christ; Saul thought that he was persecuting the disciples of an impostor who had been cru-

he said, Who art thou, Lord? And he *said,* I am Jesus whom thou persecutest: 6 but rise, and enter into the city, and it shall be told thee what thou must do. 7 And the men that journeyed with him stood speechless, hearing

---

cified as a malefactor. He now is to see that he was persecuting the Messiah by persecuting his disciples.

5, 6 **And he said, Who art thou, Lord?**—"Lord" is here used in reverence and in response to the question; this title could not have been used at this moment in all the fullness of its meaning. It seems to mean: "Whose voice do I hear?" The response came at once: "I am Jesus whom thou persecutest." In Acts 22: 8 Paul gives the fuller form of the sentence: "I am Jesus of Nazareth, whom thou persecutest." By using this name Saul could gain a direct knowledge of the voice that was speaking to him, and know that he was persecuting Christ in persecuting his disciples. The voice is very specific, denoting definitely and accurately just what Saul was doing in persecuting Christians; it carried a conviction as well as preferring a charge. This voice told him that he should go into the city and there he would be instructed as to "what thou must do." In Acts 26: 16-18 we have what Ananias told Saul. The Authorized Version adds "it is hard for thee to kick against the pricks"; that is, it is hard to kick against the "pricks" or goads used to spur an ox.

7 **And the men that journeyed with him**—We are not told how large a company Saul had with him; hence, there is no use to guess at the number. "Stood speechless" simply means that they came to a stop; in Acts 26: 14 they are described as "all fallen to the earth," but there is no contradiction here. "Speechless" means they were mute. Those that were with Paul heard "the voice, but beholding no man," but in Acts 22: 9 we have the statement "but they heard not the voice of him that spake to me." There is no contradiction here. They heard the voice, but did not understand what it said; hence, in that sense they did not "hear" the voice. Those with Paul heard the sound, but did not understand the words; they saw the light, but did not see the form of the Christ; they had fallen to the ground and remained motionless.

the °voice, but beholding no man. 8 And Saul arose from the earth; and when his eyes were opened, he saw nothing; and they led him by the hand, and brought him into Damascus. 9 And he was three days without sight, and did neither eat nor drink.

10 Now there was a certain disciple at Damascus, named Ananias; and the Lord said unto him in a vision, Ananias. And he said, Behold, I *am here,* Lord. 11 And the Lord *said* unto him, Arise, and go to the street

---

°Or, *sound*

---

8 **And Saul arose from the earth;**—When Saul, who had fallen to the earth with the others, arose "his eyes were opened," but "he saw nothing." Some translations say he "saw no man." His eyes were open, but he did not have the power to discern or see clearly objects that were before him. He was led "by the hand, and brought" into Damascus. Saul at this time presents a sad and pathetic picture; Saul, the persecutor, clothed with authority from the Sanhedrin, now becomes the convicted, blind, and helpless one, and has to be led with the authority with which he was clothed, in this helpless condition, into the city of Damascus to wait for further instruction.

9 **And he was three days without sight,**— In his helpless condition Saul the persecutor is led into Damascus. He has now reached his destination; he had left Jerusalem to go to Damascus. Little did he think that he would enter Damascus in such a helpless and humbled condition. He began praying, and for "three days" he was "without sight," and did "neither eat nor drink." Verse 11 tells us that he was praying. The mental anguish for a time overpowered the natural craving for food.

10 **Now there was a certain disciple at Damascus,**—This disciple was named "Ananias"; it was a common name among the Jews, and is to be thought of as meaning "Jehovah is gracious." This Ananias had the respect of both Jews and Christians in Damascus (Acts 22: 12); he was "a devout man according to the law," and "well reported of by all the Jews that dwelt there." Here he is described as "a certain disciple"; the disciple that baptized Saul was no high dignitary in the church; he was just "a certain disciple."

11 **And the Lord said unto him,**—We do not know when or how Ananias became a disciple; he may have been one of those converted on Pentecost; the Lord spoke to him in a vision; he was

which is called Straight, and inquire in the house of Judas for one named Saul, a man of Tarsus: for behold, he prayeth; 12 and he hath seen a man named Ananias coming in, and laying his hands on him, that he might receive his sight. 13 But Ananias answered, Lord, I have heard from many of this man, how much evil he did to thy saints at Jerusalem: 14 and here he

told to go to the street "which is called Straight" and inquire at the house of Judas for Saul; he was further instructed that Saul was praying. This street was called "Straight," and is said to extend in a direct line from east to west, and was a mile long. Ananias received from the Lord in the vision direct and accurate information so that he could locate Saul without delay. Ananias was ready to render service in the name of the Lord; we do not have him mentioned anywhere else except in Acts 22: 12, which is in connection with the conversion of Saul. Nothing is further known about Judas where Saul was sojourning; he may have been one of the Christians, or he may have been one to whom Paul had letters. We are not told for what he was praying; probably he was praying for his sight and for more light in a spiritual way.

12 and he hath seen a man named Ananias—The Lord in this vision told Ananias where to find Saul, and also told him that Saul had seen "a man named Ananias coming in," and that he would lay his hands on him that he might receive his sight. It seems that there had been two simultaneous visions—Saul had received one and Ananias the other. Ananias was now told just what he should say and do to Saul. In Acts 22: 13-16 Saul is told what he should do; he received his sight at that time, and was informed that he should become a witness for Christ and should suffer many things for him. He was told to arise and be baptized, "and wash away thy sins."

13, 14 But Ananias answered, Lord,—Ananias hesitated because he had heard "from many of this man"; he had heard of the bitter persecution that Saul had waged against "thy saints at Jerusalem"; he had also heard of Saul's "authority from the chief priests" to persecute Christians in Damascus. Here we learn that the disciples were called "saints"; that is, "sanctified ones," early in the history of the church. Paul frequently uses this word and applies it to Christians. This is the first time that the word is used and applied to Christians; Saul was deeply impressed with this

hath authority from the chief priests to bind all that call upon thy name. 15
But the Lord said unto him, Go thy way: for he is a ¹chosen vessel unto me,
to bear my name before the Gentiles and kings, and the children of Israel:
16 for I will show him how many things he must suffer for my name's sake.
17 And Ananias departed, and entered into the house; and laying his hands

¹Gr. *vessel of election*

word and addressed at least six of his epistles to those who were
"called saints." "Saints" mean the same as those who "call upon
thy name."

15 **But the Lord said unto him, Go thy way:**—Ananias is assured of the vision and its meaning, and is commanded to obey it.
The instruction is that Saul was to be "a chosen vessel" unto the
Lord, and that he was to bear his name "before the Gentiles and
kings, and the children of Israel." Here Saul is said to perform the
task of being a witness for Christ to three classes—namely, "Gentiles," "kings," and "the children of Israel." "Chosen vessel" simply means "a vessel of choice or selection"; Jesus chose Saul before Saul had chosen Jesus as his Lord. He makes Saul an
earthen vessel (2 Cor. 4: 7), an unworthy vessel for so great a
treasure. His chief work was to be among the Gentiles. (Gal. 2:
7, 8; Eph. 3: 6-12.) Saul fulfilled this commission in going before
kings when he appeared before Agrippa at Caesarea (Acts 26: 1-
32); perhaps he went before Emperor Nero at Rome, and pleaded
his cause before the tribunals of the Roman governors, Sergius
Paulus, Gallio, Felix, and Festus (2 Tim. 4: 16, 17).

16 **for I will show him how many things he must suffer**—
Saul had made others suffer for Christ; he had persecuted them
even unto death; now he is to suffer more than he has caused others to suffer. He said in his address to the elders of the church at
Ephesus that "the Holy Spirit testifieth unto me in every city, saying that bonds and afflictions abide me." (Acts 20: 23.) In writing to the church at Corinth later Paul gave a long list of persecutions and sufferings which he had endured for Christ. (2 Cor. 6:
4-10; 11: 23-28.)

17 **And Ananias departed, and entered**—Ananias now was
convinced that he would obey the vision, and he at once departed
to find the man who needed his services. He entered into the house
and placed his hands on Saul and said: "Brother Saul," the Lord

on him said, Brother Saul, the Lord, *even* Jesus, who appeared unto thee in the way which thou camest, hath sent me, that thou mayest receive thy sight, and be filled with the Holy Spirit. 18 And straightway there fell from his eyes as it were scales, and he received his sight; and he arose and was baptized; 19 and he took food and was strengthened.

And he was certain days with the disciples that were at Damascus. 20

---

who appeared to you on the way has sent me to you that "thou mayest receive thy sight, and be filled with the Holy Spirit." Ananias addressed him as "brother"; whether this was because of the Jewish relation, or because of their relation in Christ is not made clear; it has been the occasion of much discussion. This comes about by not knowing at what point Saul was converted. Saul was not converted until he was baptized into Christ; forgiveness of sins, with Saul, took place after his obedience to the gospel, just as it did with all others. Paul says that he and others were baptized into Christ. (Rom. 6: 3, 4.) Hence, as Paul had not been baptized into Christ when Ananias first addressed him, he must have addressed him as a fellow member of the Jewish family.

18, 19 **And straightway there fell from his eyes**—Immediately when Ananias came to Saul and placed his hands upon him, Saul received his sight. His vision came to him suddenly as if "scales" had fallen from "his eyes." The original for "scales" is "lepides," and comes from the verb "lepo," which means "to peel." Luke does not say that actual "scales" fell from the eyes of Saul, but that it felt that way to him as his sight was restored to him. Saul "arose and was baptized"; it seems that he was baptized by Ananias (Acts 22: 16), and his sins were forgiven, and he could claim promises of salvation through faith in Christ. Some think that this left a permanent defect in Paul's eyes; however, there is no direct evidence of it. Saul at once "took food and was strengthened." He had been fasting for three days, and now since he has been refreshed in soul, he is also refreshed in body. He remained with the disciples in Damascus for "certain days"; we do not know how long he remained there; it is probable that he spent these days in private devotion and in private intercourse with the disciples. "Certain days" is a phrase used by Luke to mean a short space of time. (Acts 10: 48; 15: 36; 16: 12; 24: 24; 25: 13.)

3. PAUL'S PREACHING AT DAMASCUS
9: 20-22

And straightway in the synagogues he proclaimed Jesus, that he is the Son of God. 21 And all that heard him were amazed, and said, Is not this he that in Jerusalem made havoc of them that called on this name? and he had come hither for this intent, that he might bring them bound before the chief

20 **And straightway in the synagogues**—The "certain days" were very profitable days to Saul who is now converted; he visited without delay the synagogues and "proclaimed Jesus, that he is the Son of God." The preaching of Jesus to the Jews was a stumbling block; nevertheless, Saul now boldly went into the synagogues and where he could have opportunity told the people that Jesus of Nazareth who had been crucified, buried, and raised from the dead was the Messiah of the Old Testament scriptures. Strange indeed that he who had gone to Damascus to punish those who believed in Christ is now proclaiming him from the synagogues. Henceforth, Saul is ready to stand on this platform: "Jesus is the Christ, the Son of God."

21 **And all that heard him were amazed,**—Those who heard Saul were "amazed"; that is, they continued to sense in themselves astonishment at this violent reversal in Saul the persecutor; they were not so much astonished at what he preached as they were at the sudden turn that had taken place in the preacher. They began to inquire: "Is not this he that in Jerusalem made havoc of them that called on this name?" Saul's fame as a leader in persecution had even reached Damascus. He "made havoc of them" who believed on Jesus. "Made havoc" is from the Greek "northesas," which means "to lay waste"; hence Saul laid waste the church in Jerusalem by his persecution. He had even gone to Damascus with "this intent," that if he found disciples of Christ he would bind them and bring them before the chief priests. All knew why Saul had come to Damascus, and all now knew that he preached Jesus as the Son of God. Some think that Saul, when he left Jerusalem to go to Damascus, had instructed the rulers of the synagogue or the Sanhedrin had instructed the synagogue to receive Saul as the agent of persecution; but now they are greatly astonished that instead of waging his persecution he proclaims the divinity and Messiahship of Jesus.

priests. 22 But Saul increased the more in strength, and confounded the
Jews that dwelt at Damascus, proving that this is the Christ.

---

22 But Saul increased the more in strength,—Saul's conversion would necessarily excite opposition to those who had not accepted Christ; Saul necessarily had to give his reasons for the
change, and his reasons for believing that Jesus was the Christ, the
Son of God. Opposition would increase against him, and Saul
would necessarily have to increase "the more in strength" until he
was able to demonstrate without any doubt that Jesus was the
Christ. He was strengthened for this great task. (Rom. 4: 22;
Phil. 4: 13; 1 Tim. 1: 12; 2 Tim. 2: 1; 4: 17.) "Proving" is
from the Greek "sunbibazon," and means that Saul put things side
by side, and so making a comparison and forming a conclusion that
Jesus was the Christ. Saul not only grew in Christian life, but he
also grew as a preacher of the gospel. He not only proved that
Jesus is the Christ, but he "confounded the Jews," which means
that they were "poured together, commingled."

4. PAUL PERSECUTED; ESCAPED IN A BASKET
9: 23-25

23 And when many days were fulfilled, the Jews took counsel together to

---

23 And when many days were fulfilled,—"Many days" here
denote an indefinite period of time; some think that it includes at
least three years; they draw this conclusion from Gal. 1: 17, 18,
where Paul says, that he "went away into Arabia; and again I returned unto Damascus. Then after three years I went up to Jerusalem." The order of events seemed to have been as follows: (1)
Saul struck down on the road to Damascus near the city (Acts 9:
3-8); (2) three days of blindness and prayer to God in the house
of Judas on the street called Straight (verse 9); (3) sight restored, baptized, and received some measure of the Holy Spirit
(verses 10-19); (4) preached that Jesus is the Christ in the synagogues with such power and spiritual force that the Jews were
confounded (verses 19-22); (5) sudden departure to Arabia for
solitary communion with God (Gal. 1: 17, 18); (6) back to Damascus; (7) conspiracy to slay him (verse 23); (8) escape to Je-

kill him: 24 but their plot became known to Saul. And they watched the gates also day and night that they might kill him: 25 but his disciples took him by night, and let him down through the wall, lowering him in a basket.

---

rusalem (verse 25); (9) disciples afraid of him (verse 26); (10) Barnabas vouches for his conversion (verse 27); (11) takes the place of Stephen and preaches to the Hellenists (verse 29); (12) conspiracy to slay him (verse 29); (13) sent to Caesarea, and thence to Tarsus (verse 30).

24 **but their plot became known to Saul.**—The Jews were not able to withstand Saul's arguments, and hence resorted to persecution. They plotted to kill Saul; they "watched the gates also day and night," thinking that he might attempt to escape, and they would fall on him and kill him. It seems that the governor of the city used the garrison of soldiers to watch the gates so that Saul would not escape. "In Damascus the governor under Aretas the king guarded the city of the Damascenes in order to take me: and through a window was I let down in a basket by the wall, and escaped his hands." (2 Cor. 11: 32, 33.) It may be that the Jews prevailed upon Aretas to furnish the guard to keep Saul from escaping. The Jews were powerful in Damascus, and hence would have a great influence on Aretas.

25 **but his disciples took him by night,**—Saul was successful in convincing some that Jesus was the Son of God; here "his disciples," that is, the disciples that Saul had made by preaching the gospel, were also disciples of Christ. One night they let Saul down "through the wall, lowering him in a basket." Some think that he was let "through a window." The Greek is "dia tou teichous," and is explained by Saul in 2 Cor. 11: 33 as being "through a window"; or "dia thuridos," which means a window that opened into the house on the inside of the wall. Rahab let the spies escape "by a cord through the window." (Josh. 2: 15.) "In a basket" is from "en sphuridi," and is the word used when the four thousand were fed. (Matt. 15: 37; Mark 8: 8.) Large baskets were made of reeds, and are distinguished from the smaller kind. This escape by night by the help of the men whom he had come to destroy was an occasion that Saul never forgot.

5. PAUL AT JERUSALEM
9 : 26-29

26 And when he was come to Jerusalem, he assayed to join himself to the disciples: and they were all afraid of him, not believing that he was a disciple. 27 But Barnabas took him, and brought him to the apostles, and declared unto them how he had seen the Lord in the way, and that he had

26 **And when he was come to Jerusalem,**—We do not know just how long it has been since Saul left Jerusalem; it seems that the Jewish authorities there had lost sight of him; evidently they had not known of his long disappearance into Arabia and his second period of preaching in Damascus. Saul attempted to "join himself to the disciples," but they were not willing to receive him. There had been political changes in Judea since the persecution began three years before; a change of emperors and of policy had taken place, so that Jews were themselves being persecuted, and had little time to persecute the Christians. Communication with Damascus was slow and difficult; this was especially true on account of the hostility which had arisen between Aretas the ruler of Damascus and Herod the ruler of Judea. Saul's escape had been too hurried for him to obtain letters of commendation; he was in Damascus but a short time after his conversion, and the disciples in Jerusalem had not heard from him for more than two years, and could not be sure that he had continued in the faith. Some think that the meaning here is that they doubted Saul's sincerity; this was his first visit to Jerusalem since he left as a persecutor.

27 **But Barnabas took him,**—Barnabas, who introduced Saul to the apostles, has already been mentioned as a Levite of Cyprus (Acts 4: 36) and, from the nearness of Cyprus to Cilicia and the distinction of the schools of Tarsus, some have thought that Barnabas may have been known to Saul before they came to Jerusalem. Barnabas declared to the apostles that Saul had seen the Lord; it was necessary for Saul, like the other apostles, to have seen the Lord in order to be a witness of the resurrection; hence, his sight of the risen Christ is always brought forward. Barnabas also declared to the apostles that Saul had preached boldly "in the name of Jesus" in Damascus. It seems that at this time Barnabas presented Saul only to Peter and James (Gal. 1: 18, 19), the repre-

spoken to him, and how at Damascus he had preached boldly in the name of Jesus. 28 And he was with them going in and going out at Jerusalem, 29 preaching boldly in the name of the Lord: and he spake and disputed against the ²Grecian Jews; but they were seeking to kill him. 30 And when the

²Gr. *Hellenists*

sentative leaders; the other apostles may have been away on preaching tours as we know Peter and John had been. It seems that Saul conversed with Peter and James. This James is called "the Lord's brother," and may be said to have been the half brother of Jesus. Peter was convinced that Saul had been converted and kept him as a guest for "fifteen days." Saul had gone to Jerusalem to see Peter, but not to receive a commission from him. He received his commission to preach from the Lord. (Gal. 1: 1-5, 11-17.)

28, 29 **And he was with them going in and going out**—Saul remained quietly at the home of Peter for fifteen days (Gal. 1: 18, 19), and visited others at that time. It seems that Barnabas and Peter and James opened all the doors for Saul and the fear of the disciples ceased; they received him as a brother in the Lord. Saul, now in the city of Jerusalem, preached boldly "in the name of the Lord." He came in contact especially with "the Grecian Jews," or Hellenists. It should be remembered that it was as the leader of the Hellenistic Jews of the synagogue (Acts 6: 9) that Saul had first appeared in the history of the disciples of Christ. Saul is seeking to undo the evil that he had then done by preaching to them the faith which he had then opposed, and presenting the very arguments and truths that had been most prominent in Stephen's address. Saul could not preach Christ to these Jews without antagonizing them. He did not shrink, but spoke boldly to them as did Stephen; they resisted his teaching and sought to kill him as they had done Stephen. Saul was no coward; he did not merely run from the enemy, but escaped that he might continue preaching the gospel as God's power to save.

6. PAUL IN TARSUS; CHURCH EDIFIED
9: 30, 31

brethren knew it, they brought him down to Caesarea, and sent him forth to
Tarsus.
31 So the church throughout all Judaea and Galilee and Samaria had

---

30 **And when the brethren knew it,**—The fact that the disciples in Jerusalem helped Saul to escape shows that they had received him into their fellowship and were willing to help him in every way possible, consistent with the teachings of Christ. The brethren assisted him in leaving Jerusalem, and "they brought him down to Caesarea." Caesarea was the seaport on the Mediterranean coast, and was on the great road from Tyre to Egypt, and about halfway betweeen Joppa and Dora; it was about seventy miles from Jerusalem. It was the seaport from which Saul could set sail for Tarsus. It seems that the brethren accompanied Saul down to Caesarea. Saul gives a different reason in Acts 22: 17 for leaving Jerusalem; God revealed to him in a vision that another sphere of work awaited him. In Gal. 1: 21 Saul tells us that he went from Jerusalem to Syria and Cilicia; hence, some have inferred that the "Caesarea" mentioned here is "Caesarea Philippi," which was situated at the foot of Mount Hermon, on the direct road to lower Syria. Tarsus was Saul's birthplace; he tells us that he was "a Jew, of Tarsus in Cilicia, a citizen of no mean city." (Acts 21: 39.) Saul tells us that he was engaged in preaching the gospel in that region (Gal. 1: 21-23), and we are led to believe that he was eminently successful (Acts 15: 23, 41). Some think that during this period Saul converted to Christ some of his own relatives (Rom. 16: 7, 11, 21), and possibly his sister and her son (Acts 23: 16). Although Saul was denied the privilege of preaching Christ in Jerusalem, yet an open door was before him in other regions.

31 **So the church throughout all Judaea**—Some versions read "churches," but the Greek is "ekklesia," and is in the singular; at this time there were churches scattered over Judea, Galilee, and Samaria (Gal. 1: 22), but Luke either regards the disciples in Palestine as still members of the one great church in Jerusalem or he employs the term "ekklesia" in a geographical or collective sense covering all of Palestine. "Church" is used in the strictly local

peace, being [3]edified; and, walking [4]in the fear of the Lord and [4]in the comfort of the Holy Spirit, was multiplied.

[3]Gr. *builded up*
[4]Or, *by*

sense in Acts 8: 1, 3 and in Matt. 18: 17, and in the general spiritual sense in Matt. 16: 18. Here "the church throughout all Judaea and Galilee and Samaria had peace"; this seems to be used in the general sense. The church was edified: such preachers of the gospel and teachers would edify the church: not a line of the New Testament had been written at this time and all of the teaching was oral, yet the church was greatly "edified." The term "edified" comes from the Greek "oikodomoumene," and means "to build up a house"; this term or figure is used frequently by Paul; Peter speaks of "a spiritual house." (1 Pet. 2: 5.) Great political changes had taken place at this time which worked advantageously to the peace of the church. Petronius was appointed governor of Syria in A.D. 40, and a firm government was restored; in the same year Emperor Caligula ordered his statue to be set up in the temple at Jerusalem, and the Jews had to use all their energy to prevent this form of idolatry. In A.D. 41, Herod Agrippa I was made ruler in Judea and Samaria; all these events would prevent the persecution which had taken place with impunity during the three or four preceding years of anarchy; this would give opportunity for the disciples of Christ to have peace and to continue to edify the church and enjoy "the comfort of the Holy Spirit." The "peace" here means a freedom from war and persecution, whether from Jews or Romans; "being edified" refers to a growth in the knowledge of Christ and a gain in spiritual power; "was multiplied" refers to increase in number of places to which the gospel was successfully carried, and to the gain in the number of disciples also where the gospel had been proclaimed.

7. PETER CURES AENEAS
9: 32-35

32 And it came to pass, as Peter went throughout all parts, he came

32 And it came to pass, as Peter went throughout all parts,
—Luke in arranging his materials gave an account of Peter and

down also to the saints that dwelt at Lydda. 33 And there he found a certain man named Aeneas, who had kept his bed eight years; for he was palsied. 34 And Peter said unto him, Aeneas, Jesus Christ healeth thee: arise,

---

John going trom Jerusalem down to Samaria, and there bestowing
spiritual gifts upon the Samaritans and then mentioning the incidents connected with Simon the sorcerer; here we left Peter in
Samaria. Next Luke gave an account of Philip and the eunuch,
and then an account of the conversion of Saul and the incidents
that followed. He now returns to Peter. So far this section of the
book of Acts may be described as the acts of Peter; however, it is
evident that only a part of the general outline of work that Peter
did is given. Luke does not follow Peter's course, as in a biogra-
phy, but confines himself to tracing the steps by which he had been
led to the part he played in the great work of the conversion of the
Gentiles. In leaving Samaria Peter "went throughout all parts,"
and finally "came down also to the saints that dwelt at Lydda."
Here again we have "the saints" mentioned. "Lydda" is the same
as "Lod" in the Old Testament. (1 Chron. 8: 12; Ezra 2: 33;
Neh. 7: 37; 11: 35.) Lydda was about ten miles from Joppa, and
was on the highway between Jerusalem and Joppa; it was a day's
journey from Jerusalem.

33 **And there he found a certain man named Aeneas,**—This
name implies that he belonged to the Hellenistic section of disciples. As Peter went about doing good he was led to this man.
He had been sick for eight years; he "had kept his bed eight
years"; Luke being a physician tells us the specific disease with
which he was afflicted; he was "palsied"; "palsy" is a contraction
of the word "paralysis." The term is used by the ancient physicians in a much wider sense than by our modern men of science; it
included not only what we call paralysis, but also catalepsy and tet-
anus; that is, cramps and lockjaw. Since he was bedfast for eight
years, the miracle of his cure would be more famous.

34 **And Peter said unto him, Aeneas,**—As in the cure of the
cripple at the temple (Acts 3: 6), Peter makes known that he is
but the messenger of Christ, and that the power to heal comes
through Christ. We do not know whether Aeneas was a disciple,

and make thy bed. And straightway he arose. 35 And all that dwelt at
Lydda and in Sharon saw him, and they turned to the Lord.

but it seems reasonable to infer that he was among "the saints,"
and that Peter was brought to him. He is commanded to "arise,
and make thy bed." Literally, he was commanded to spread his
bed for himself; he was commanded to do that which others for
years had done for him. This was proof that he could take care of
himself, and immediately he obeyed Peter. This shows that the
cure was miraculous. No doubt Peter remembered the time when
four men brought a man with the same disease to Christ at Capernaum and that Jesus had commanded the man to "arise, take up
thy bed, and go unto thy house." (Mark 2: 1-11.)

35 **And all that dwelt at Lydda**—This miracle had a wonderful effect on the people in Lydda; "Sharon" was not a city or
town, but was a section of country about thirty miles long from
Joppa to Caesarea. Those who saw Aeneas healed were now
ready to accept the preaching of Peter; they "turned to the Lord,"
which means that they heard the gospel, repented of their sins,
were baptized into Christ, and were thus numbered among "the
saints," or added to the church.

8. PETER RAISES DORCAS
9: 36-43

36 Now there was at Joppa a certain disciple named Tabitha, which by
interpretation is called [5]Dorcas: this woman was full of good works and

_____

[5]That is, *Gazelle*

_____

36 **Now there was at Joppa a certain disciple named Tabitha,**—Joppa was on the Mediterranean coast and about ten miles
from Lydda; there was "a certain disciple" there who bore the
name of "Tabitha," which is also interpreted to mean "Dorcas."
Dorcas is called a disciple that it may be seen that under the gospel
there is no distinction between male and female. (Gal. 3: 28.)
"Tabitha" is the Aramaic form of a Hebrew proper name which
means "a gazelle" (Sol. 4: 5), as does the Greek word "Dorcas."
Dorcas is described as being a woman "full of good works and
almsdeeds." There is nothing said about a husband, and so it is
inferred that she was unmarried. Dorcas is the second woman

almsdeeds which she did. 37 And it came to pass in those days, that she fell sick, and died: and when they had washed her, they laid her in an upper chamber. 38 And as Lydda was nigh unto Joppa, the disciples, hearing that Peter was there, sent two men unto him, entreating him, Delay not to come on unto us. 39 And Peter arose and went with them. And when he was come, they brought him into the upper chamber: and all the widows stood by

---

mentioned by name after Pentecost; the first one mentioned is Sapphira. (Acts 5 : 1.) We are not told what "the good works" were that Dorcas had done; however, they showed Peter "the coats and garments which Dorcas made," and probably these were made for the poor and widows who in that country were a most unfortunate class. Dorcas continued to do such good work while she lived.

37 **And it came to pass in those days,**—Luke does not tell the disease with which Dorcas suffered and died; some have thought that it was due to her overexertion in helping others; this is merely a conjecture. The body was placed in an upper room, according to Jewish custom, and was prepared for burial. She was not buried with that rapidity with which Ananias and Sapphira were buried. Perhaps an evidence of faith is seen in the delayed burial as the sequence shows.

38 **And as Lydda was nigh unto Joppa,**—Peter was at Lydda and Dorcas lived at Joppa. The friends of Dorcas had heard that Peter was at Lydda, and "sent two men unto him," entreating him to come to Joppa without delay. Lydda was nine or ten miles from Joppa; it was too late to send for a physician, but not too late to send for Peter. We are not told why they sent for Peter; some have thought that they anticipated what Peter would do. They knew that Peter had wrought some great miracles in the name of Jesus, though we have no record thus far of his raising anyone from the dead. They were very urgent in their request for Peter to come without delay; they wanted him to hasten, as every hour of delay tended toward the decay of the body.

39 **And Peter arose and went with them.**—Peter responded at once to the urgent request and returned with the two men who had come for him. When he arrived without delay they took him "into the upper chamber" where the body of Dorcas was. "All the widows stood by him weeping," and displayed to him some of the

him weeping, and showing the coats and garments which Dorcas made, while she was with them. 40 But Peter put them all forth, and kneeled down, and prayed; and turning to the body, he said, Tabitha, arise. And she opened her eyes; and when she saw Peter, she sat up. 41 And he gave her his hand, and raised her up; and calling the saints and widows, he presented her

"coats and garments which Dorcas made" while she was alive. "The widows" were either the poor widows whom Dorcas had helped, or those who had been associated with her in the good work with which her life was filled. "Coats" is from the Greek "chitonas," and means "the shirt-like undergarment or tunic"; "garments" is from the Greek "himatia," which means the outer garment, the mantle. Dorcas had made these and the widows were displaying them as an appeal to Peter to help them in some way. This presented a very vivid and pathetic picture; to see the prostrate body of Dorcas lying cold and stiff in death, and to see the work of her hands which had blessed and helped so many, and to hear the grief-stricken widows sobbing in sorrow for the loss of their friend and sister; it must have made a very strong appeal to Peter.

40 **But Peter put them all forth, and kneeled down,**—Surely Peter remembered what his Lord had done at the house of Jairus. (Mark 5: 40; Luke 8: 54.) After putting all out of the room, Peter kneeled down and prayed. Peter's praying alone in the presence of the corpse reminds one of the prayer of Elijah (1 Kings 17: 20); and that of Elisha (2 Kings 4: 33). After praying Peter turned "to the body" and said: "Tabitha, arise." Here Peter displayed sublime faith in the name of the Christ, for he commanded the dead to come to life. He is following closely the example of Jesus which he had observed at the house of Jairus. Peter had been present three times when Jesus had raised the dead: (1) the raising of Jairus' daughter (Mark 5: 40, 41); (2) the raising of the son of the widow at Nain (Luke 7: 11-15); (3) the raising of Lazarus (John 11: 36-44). The dead obeyed the voice of Peter, and Tabitha opened her eyes, and "when she saw Peter, she sat up." She arose as one awaking from sleep. "She sat up" is from "anakathizo," and is used only here and in Luke 7: 15; it is a medical term often used.

41 **And he gave her his hand,**—Peter extended his hand to her and assisted her by raising her up. She was now alive and Peter

alive. 42 And it became known throughout all Joppa: and many believed on the Lord. 43 And it came to pass, that he abode many days in Joppa with one Simon a tanner.

rendered her what assistance she needed, Jesus took Jairus' daughter's hand before she was restored to life. After she had been restored to life and was now in normal condition, he called "the saints and widows," and presented Dorcas to them. "Saints and widows" are mentioned here, not that the "widows" were not "saints," but the widows are mentioned to distinguish them from the main body of disciples, who are here called "saints," because the widows were the more grieved at the death of Dorcas.

42 **And it became known throughout all Joppa:**—The result of this miracle was to confirm the preaching of the gospel. This was a notable incident and it became known to all those who dwelt in Joppa, and as a result of this, "many believed on the Lord." The faith of the disciples was strengthened and others believed on the Lord. The effect of this miracle was similar to that of the raising of Lazarus from the dead. (John 11: 45.) It does not say "all," as in the case of Lydda and Sharon (verse 35), as Joppa was a large place, and all the inhabitants did not come to witness the miracle.

43 **And it came to pass, that he abode many days in Joppa** —Again we have "many days," which means a considerable time. (Acts 8: 11; 9: 23.) Peter abode in the house of a man by the name of Simon; his occupation was that of a tanner. Since we do not know the length of time expressed by "many days," and as it may mean ten days, ten months, or ten years, we cannot calculate, with any accuracy, the chronology of the events. The trade of "a tanner" was held abominable to the Jews, as he would have to handle unclean animals. It seems that Peter was gradually getting away from his Jewish prejudices; this will help to prepare him for the vision that is recorded in the next chapter.

9. PETER'S VISION
10: 1-16

1 Now *there was* a certain man in Caesarea, Cornelius by name, a centu-

1, 2 **Now there was a certain man in Caesarea,**—Caesarea at this time was the most prominent city in Palestine, and was virtu-

rion of the ¹band called the Italian *band*, 2 a devout man, and one that feared God with all his house, who gave much alms to the people, and prayed to God always. 3 He saw in a vision openly, as it were about the ninth hour of the day, an angel of God coming in unto him, and saying to him, Cornelius.

¹Or, *cohort*

ally the capital; it was built by Herod the Great as a seaport, which he had founded on the ruins of Samaria; it was named "Caesarea" after Caesar Augustus. "Cornelius" is a Roman name, and this "certain man" may have been a descendant of the great Cornelian family of Rome; however, there were many Romans bearing this name. He was "a centurion," which means that he was a leader of a hundred soldiers; "centurion" comes from the Latin "centurio," and means one hundred. "Of the band called the Italian band," means that the soldiers that made or composed this "band" or "cohort" were from Italy; the Italian cohorts were sent to any part of the empire where they were needed. It is possible that the soldiers of this cohort could have been Roman citizens who lived in Caesarea. Cornelius is described as being "devout," "one that feared God with all his house," one "who gave much alms to the people," and one who "prayed to God always." It seems that he worshiped God with all earnestness and devotion, and taught his house to do the same; he was liberal in that the Jewish people among whom he was stationed needed help and he gave of his means to help them; he continued praying to God and seemed to be anxious for greater knowledge of God's way. However, this good man, Cornelius, was an unsaved man; he was unconverted.

3 **He saw in a vision openly,**—Cornelius was not in a trance, but was engaged in prayer when an angel appeared to him. He was not in a dream, but "saw in a vision" the angel. The Greek "oramati" means "something seen"; it is not the same word as used for Peter's "trance" in verse 10. The Jews had three regular hours of prayer; the hour when the evening sacrifice was offered in the temple was the hour also of prayer, and this was the time when Cornelius was praying. It was supposed to be about three o'clock in the afternoon. Cornelius did not call the messenger "an angel," but the men sent to Peter spoke of an angel.

4 And he, fastening his eyes upon him, and being affrighted, said, What is it, Lord? And he said unto him, Thy prayers and thine alms are gone up for a memorial before God. 5 And now send men to Joppa, and fetch one Simon, who is surnamed Peter : 6 he lodgeth with one Simon a tanner, whose house

4 And he, fastening his eyes upon him,—Cornelius looked steadfastly at the angel, and became frightened and exclaimed: "What is it, Lord?" It seems that Cornelius recognized the angel of God as a messenger from God; hence, he addressed the angel as "Lord." Such a messenger coming so unexpectedly frightened Cornelius. The angel responded and told Cornelius that his "prayers" and his "alms" had "gone up for a memorial before God." "Memorial" means a remembrance; it comes from the Greek "mnemosuon," and is used only one other time in the New Testament by Jesus concerning the act of Mary of Bethany. (Matt. 26: 13; Mark 14: 9.) The prayers of Cornelius had ascended like incense and were remembered by God; he had faith to pray to God that God would in some way answer his prayer.

5, 6 And now send men to Joppa,—The angel gives Cornelius definite instruction as to what he should do; Peter was at Joppa, and the angel instructs Cornelius to send men to Joppa and "fetch one Simon, who is surnamed Peter." The information that Cornelius is to receive must come through human agency. Note the several particulars mentioned by the angel; men are to go to Joppa; they are to bring a man by the name of Simon; this Simon was called Peter; he lodged with another Simon who was a tanner; Simon the tanner lived "by the sea side." The Jewish name, "Simon," is mentioned, and then the name "Peter," which describes minutely the preacher for whom he should send. Next the city where he was sojourning, and the name and occupation of the man with whom Peter was dwelling; then the exact location of the house is given. With these minute and accurate directions the messengers of Cornelius could find Peter without any delay. Philip the evangelist was probably in Caesarea. (Acts 8: 40.) Why was not Philip called? We are not told; however, Peter had "the keys of the kingdom of heaven" (Matt. 16: 19), and he is to give by the Holy Spirit the conditions of salvation to the Gentiles; Peter is to open the door to the Gentiles.

is by the sea side. 7 And when the angel that spake unto him was departed,
he called two of his household-servants, and a devout soldier of them that
waited on him continually; 8 and having rehearsed all things unto them, he
sent them to Joppa.

9 Now on the morrow, as they were on their journey, and drew nigh
unto the city, Peter went up upon the housetop to pray, about the sixth

---

7, 8 And when the angel that spake unto him—So soon as
the angel had finished his message to Cornelius, preparation began
to be made to carry out in detail all that had been commanded.
Cornelius selected "two of his household-servants, and a devout
soldier" and dispatched them immediately. The angel "departed,"
apparently as a man would walk away; it is not said that he "van-
ished" as Jesus did after his resurrection. (Luke 24: 31.)
Cornelius promptly selected men whom he could trust—two of his
household servants and a devout soldier. Probably the two servants were to bear the message to Peter and the soldier was to
act as guard for them. It seems that they started that evening, and
would be able to arrive at Joppa, thirty miles away, the next day
soon after midday. Cornelius "rehearsed all things" to these men
before he dispatched them to Joppa. It seems that Cornelius put
great faith in the message of the angels, and also equal faith in
these three men whom he sent for Peter; he recited to them his
vision and conversation with the angel; they reverently listened to
him and hastened to obey his orders.

9 Now on the morrow, as they were on their journey,—The
roofs of the houses in that country were built flat, and there was a
stairway on the outside that led to the roof. The roof of the house
was the place where worship and conversation were usually had.
Samuel chose this place for his conference with Saul before he
anointed him king. (1 Sam. 9: 25, 26.) The housetop was used
for religious purposes also. (Jer. 19: 13; Zeph. 1: 5.) We see
from verses 23 and 24 that the journey from Joppa to Caesarea
occupied more than one day, so that the vision of Cornelius took
place on the day before the trance of Peter, and the messengers
had time almost to accomplish their journey before Peter was prepared to receive them; the distance between Caesarea and Joppa
was thirty Roman miles. Peter had gone upon the housetop to
pray; it was about the sixth hour, or about noon. The Jews had

hour: 10 and he became hungry, and desired to eat: but while they made ready, he fell into a trance; 11 and he beholdeth the heaven opened, and a certain vessel descending, as it were a great sheet, let down by four corners upon the earth: 12 wherein were all manner of fourfooted beasts and creeping things of the earth and birds of the heaven. 13 And there came a voice

three periods in the day for prayer—third hour or nine o'clock, sixth hour or noon, and the ninth hour or three o'clock in the afternoon.

10 and he became hungry,—"Hungry" comes from the Greek "prospeinos," and means "very hungry"; that is, exceedingly hungry. His appetite for food was very strong; he "desired to eat." His hunger and longing for food was so strong that it was beyond his control; it was about noon and they were making ready the noon meal in Simon the tanner's house. While in this extremely hungry condition, "he fell into a trance." "Trance" here comes from the Greek "ekstasis," which means that "an ectasy came upon him," in which trance he passed out of himself and from which one came to himself. (Acts 11: 5; 12: 11; 22: 17.) A trance is different from a vision. In a "trance" the bodily senses are dormant or inactive, while in a "vision" the bodily senses are active and awake. Peter had a mental vision, but not a dream, for the trance differs from the dream.

11, 12 and he beholdeth the heaven opened,—In this trance Peter saw as it were "a certain vessel descending" like a great sheet, which was let down through the opened heaven by four corners to the earth. What Peter saw was an extended sheet, the four corners of which were held up, as it were, by cords let down from the four extremities of the opened sky. Enclosed as it were in this great sheet were "all manner of fourfooted beasts and creeping things of the earth and birds of the heaven." The classification here included sheep, oxen, swine, and all other "fourfooted beasts" and creeping things of all kinds and all kinds of birds; there was a mixture of both clean and unclean animals. The vision represented the whole animal creation, yet fish are not mentioned; perhaps fish are not mentioned because the sheet had no water, though they were clean and unclean. (Lev. 11: 9; Deut. 14: 9.) It will be noted that there are three groups named: fourfooted beasts, creeping things, and birds; these three great groups were in the

to him, Rise, Peter: kill and eat. 14 But Peter said, Not so, Lord; for I
have never eaten anything that is common and unclean. 15 And a voice
came unto him again the second time, What God hath cleansed, make not
thou common. 16 And this was done thrice: and straightway the vessel was
received up into heaven.

---

sheet, and "all kinds" of each group. "Wild beasts" is omitted in
the best texts.

13 **And there came a voice to him,**—As Peter was hungry before he fell into the trance, here is presented the means of satisfying his hunger, and by the command in which he is directed to kill
without distinction among all that he sees, this would indicate that
the law of Moses concerning the choice among living creatures, or
the distinction between clean and unclean animals, had been abro-
gated. Peter was told to "rise"; that is, from his knees in prayer,
or his reclining posture. The animals were clean and unclean, but
the clean animals had become unclean by contact with the unclean,
and Peter is told by a voice from heaven to break the Mosaic law,
and in his eating do away with the distinction between Jew and
Gentile.

14 **But Peter said, Not so, Lord;**—Peter refused to ease his
hunger by violating the law by which he had been governed as a
Jew; he had never "eaten anything that is common and unclean."
This was one of the distinctions which separated the Jews from the
Gentiles; but Peter is to learn that there is a better, truer distinction between God's people than that of choosing diferent kinds of
animals for food. Peter showed his usual abrupt determination by
the answer that he gave; he is polite but firm in his refusal; he
gives his reason for his firm decision. He had never violated this
law and he firmly declares that he will not do so now.

15, 16 **And a voice came unto him again the second time,**—
After Peter's clear and emphatic refusal, the voice stated, "What
God hath cleansed, make not thou common." The lesson for Peter
was clear; he should not make "common" that which God had
"cleansed." "And this was done thrice." Does this mean that the
whole vision was repeated three times, or that the voice gave the
command three times? Some claim that the whole scene was repeated three times; but many others understand that the voice
came three times to emphasize the one lesson: Peter was not to

call the Gentiles "common" or "unclean" when God had arranged to give to them the blessings of salvation through Christ. It seems that the vessel was let down from heaven only once, and then taken back "up into heaven." Peter was to learn that all nations might be admitted to the kingdom of God upon the same terms of the gospel.

10. CORNELIUS CONVERTED
10 : 17-48

17 Now while Peter was much perplexed in himself what the vision which he had seen might mean, behold, the men that were sent by Cornelius, having made inquiry for Simon's house, stood before the gate, 18 and called and asked whether Simon, who was surnamed Peter, were lodging there. 19 And while Peter thought on the vision, the Spirit said unto him, Behold, three men seek thee. 20 But arise, and get thee down, and go with them,

17, 18 **Now while Peter was much perplexed**—It seems that Peter came out of "the trance" and was disturbed or confused as to what was meant by the vision. He seems to have understood the vision, but did not know the application or spiritual significance of it. While he was in this "perplexed" state, the three men who had come from Caesarea were at the gate of Simon the tanner's house, and making inquiry as to whether "Simon, who was surnamed Peter," was stopping there. The messengers from Cornelius, by inquiry, had found the lodging place of Peter and were making inquiry for him. Luke, the writer, takes pains to make clear the close connection of providential guidance in the successive steps that have brought the messengers of Cornelius from Caesarea to Peter in Joppa. Peter saw a little later very clearly that these were all providential and designed coincidences controlled by the hand of God.

19 **And while Peter thought on the vision,**—As Peter was trying to solve the mystery, the Holy Spirit said to him: "Behold, three men seek thee." Peter was turning over the vision in his mind and seeking for its significance, and the Holy Spirit now intercedes and directs him. The "voice" no longer seemed to come from heaven to the outward ear, but was heard as not less divine in the secret recesses of his soul, and he is further directed as to what he should do.

20 **But arise, and get thee down,**—Peter is told that he should not hesitate or doubt as to the meaning of the strange vi-

nothing doubting: for I have sent them. 21 and Peter went down to the
men, and said, Behold, I am he whom ye seek: what is the cause wherefore
ye are come? 22 And they said, Cornelius a centurion, a righteous man and
one that feareth God, and well reported of by all the nation of the Jews, was
warned *of God* by a holy angel to send for thee into his house, and to hear
words from thee. 23 So he called them in and lodged them.

---

sion; he is to understand that it came from God and that he
should follow it. He was to walk, as it were, blindfold, but he
should trust in the assurance of faith in the hand that was guiding
him. As once before (John 13: 7) Peter knew not yet what his
Lord was doing, but was to know hereafter; Peter and the messengers from Cornelius were alike acting under the guidance of God.
We see here the divine hand in bringing the preacher of the gospel
into the presence of the unsaved. The two visions of Cornelius in
Caesarea and of Peter in Joppa occurred in teaching the same
truth: God calls Jews and Gentiles to salvation through the same
gospel.

21 **And Peter went down to the men,**—Peter at once went
down from the housetop and said to the messengers from Cornelius, "I am he whom ye seek: what is the cause wherefore ye are
come?" Peter was as yet ignorant of the reason of their coming.
He had learned three things: (1) that God was about to teach him
some new truth, but the precise character of it was dimly seen;
(2) that the Holy Spirit had sent these three messengers to him;
(3) that he was to go with them. The reason for their coming
Peter could learn from the men; the light they would throw upon
the vision was gradually to appear clearer and clearer to him.

22 **And they said, Cornelius a centurion,**—The messengers
from Cornelius began at once and very briefly and pointedly told
Peter the full message that they had brought from Cornelius. They
described Cornelius as a "centurion, a righteous man and one that
feareth God, and well reported of by all the nation of the Jews."
After describing Cornelius they then told Peter that God had
warned him "by a holy angel to send" for Peter that he might
"hear words" from him. Very likely this reminded Peter of another centurion whose name is not recorded, who was stationed at
Capernaum, and had built a synagogue for the Jews. (Luke 7: 5.)
There was a message from God that Peter had that Cornelius

And on the morrow he arose and went forth with them, and certain of
the brethren from Joppa accompanied him.   24 And on the morrow ²they
entered into Caesarea.   And Cornelius was waiting for them, having called

---

²Some ancient authorities read *he*

---

needed to hear; Peter had the gospel as God's power to save, and
Cornelius was an unsaved man; hence, he needed to hear the
words that Peter had for him.

23 **So he called them in and lodged them.**—Here, according
to the translators of the Standard Version, should close the twen-
ty-second verse. The New Testament was divided into verses by
Robert Stephen in A.D. 1551, and his division into verses has been
observed since that time; but it would have been better to have included the words here in verse 22, and that division would have
corresponded to the paragraph division.

And on the morrow he arose—Peter had lodged the three men
overnight and was ready the next morning to start on the journey
from Joppa to Caesarea.   He selected six Jewish brethren to go
with him. (Acts 11: 12.)   These six brethren are called "they of
the circumcision that believed."   Peter took them for his companions that he might, if need be, afterwards appeal to them for testimony of what was done, and to explain why he had acted as he
did.   Probably he informed them of the message which the servants of Cornelius had brought, and of the vision that he had seen
in the trance, as well as what the Holy Spirit had said to him.

24 **And on the morrow they entered into Caesarea.**—After
keeping the three men overnight Peter arranged with six Jewish
brethren to go with him to Caesarea; they arrived in Caesarea the
second day about three o'clock after they left Joppa.   It seems that
it took Peter and his company longer to make the journey from
Joppa to Caesarea than it had taken the three men from Caesarea
to arrive in Joppa.   Cornelius was waiting for them to arrive; he
did not know just what time Peter and his company would arrive,
but he had "called together his kinsmen and his near friends" to
hear what Peter had to say. They returned to Caesarea the fourth
day after Cornelius sent the messengers. (Verse 30.)   It is very
probable that Peter and his company did not leave Joppa so early
and promptly as we might expect, since they did not arrive in Cae-

together his kinsmen and his near friends. 25 And when it came to pass that Peter entered, Cornelius met him, and fell down at his feet, and [1]worshipped him. 26 But Peter raised him up, saying, Stand up; I myself also am a man. 27 And as he talked with him, he went in, and findeth many come together: 28 and he said unto them, Ye yourselves know [2]how it is an unlawful thing for a man that is a Jew to join himself or come unto one of another na-

---

[1]The Greek word denotes an act of reverence, whether paid to a creature or to the Creator
[2]Or, how unlawful it is for a man &c.

---

sarea until about three o'clock the following day. It will be noted that only the kinsmen of Cornelius "and his near friends" were present when Peter arrived.

25 And when it came to pass that Peter entered,—When Peter entered the house of Cornelius, Cornelius graciously met him, "and fell down at his feet, and worshipped him." Cornelius regarded Peter as a messenger from God and sought to do honor to him; "worshipped" is from the Greek "prosekunesen," and means a high degree of reverence and not actual worship, for Cornelius was not an idolator, and would not have worshipped Peter as a god. However, it seems that Peter understood Cornelius to be worshiping him.

26 But Peter raised him up,—It seems clear that Peter understood that Cornelius was not merely doing him homage, but that his acts were intended as worship; hence, he corrected Cornelius and told him to "stand up," and then added, "I myself also am a man." Peter did not want to receive the homage that Cornelius was offering, for such belonged not to man, but to God alone.

27 And as he talked with him,—The introduction and conversation began without, for they talked together and then Peter went in. When he came in he found "many come together"; the conversation without had taken some time as the term "talked with him" implies a long conversation; the "many" who were in the house shows the influence and prominence of Cornelius.

28 and he said unto them, Ye yourselves know—Peter now gives an explanation for his entering the house of Cornelius, a Gentile; he appeals to the knowledge of Cornelius and his friends, and they thus knew the strict regulations that the Jews observed in their association with the Gentiles. Peter says that "it is an unlawful thing" for a Jew "to join himself or come unto one of another tion; and *yet* unto me hath God showed that I should not call any man common or unclean: 29 wherefore also I came without gainsaying, when I was sent for. I ask therefore with what intent ye sent for me. 30 And Cornelius said, Four days ago, until this hour, I was keeping the ninth hour of prayer in my house; and behold, a man stood before me in bright apparel, 31 and saith, Cornelius, thy prayer is heard, and thine alms are had in re-

---

nation." "Unlawful" comes from "athemitos," which means contrary to law or custom; it is used in this form only twice in the New Testament; Peter uses the term both times, here and in 1 Pet. 4: 3; it means a violation of established order. The position in which Peter found himself was strangely unfamiliar, so much so that he can scarcely help apologizing, even to Romans, for his conduct. The separative ceremonial law, partly Mosaic, and partly traditional with the Jews, had built up a barrier which was difficult to overcome. However, God had showed Peter by the vision on the housetop that he should call no "man common or unclean." Perhaps Peter saw this clearer now than he had done before.

29 **wherefore also I came without gainsaying,**—Peter had been deeply impressed with the lesson that had been taught him, and so soon as he learned what God wanted him to do without "gainsaying," or "without answering back," or doubting he obeyed and came at once. "I ask therefore with what intent ye sent for me." No time is wasted, no delay is had; Peter at once inquires why Cornelius, a Gentile, had sent for him. Perhaps Peter had not been instructed by the Holy Spirit; it was left for Cornelius to reveal his vision to Peter. In this way Peter could take his own vision and that of Cornelius and put them together and learn what God wanted him to do.

30, 31 **And Cornelius said, Four days ago,**—This statement, "four days ago," has been interpreted several ways, partly due to different readings of the Greek text; some read, "From the fourth day until this very hour, the ninth, I was praying in my house; and behold a man stood in my presence in bright garments." The Greek text appears to mean that four days before Cornelius was praying until the ninth hour, the very hour of the day which it was when he was talking to Peter. This makes the time of Peter's arrival to be after the ninth hour of the day. Cornelius relates his experience to Peter, the six Jewish brethren, and the kinsmen and

membrance in the sight of God. 32 Send therefore to Joppa, and call unto
thee Simon, who is surnamed Peter; he lodgeth in the house of Simon a
tanner, by the sea side. 33 Forthwith therefore I sent to thee; and thou hast
well done that thou art come. Now therefore we are all here present in the
sight of God, to hear all things that have been commanded thee of the Lord.
34 And Peter opened his mouth, and said,
    Of a truth I perceive that God is no respecter of persons: 35 but in every

---

near friends who had assembled. These verses can best be understood and studied in connection with the other accounts given together in verse 3. There is no new point emphasized in the rehearsal given here by Cornelius.

32 **Send therefore to Joppa,**—Here also Cornelius repeats
what is stated in verses 5 and 6 with no additional thought. The
Authorized Version adds: "Who, when he cometh, shall speak
unto thee." However, this phrase does not appear in the best
Greek texts.

33 **Forthwith therefore I sent to thee;**—Cornelius had been
instructed to send for Peter and he did not delay, but sent the
three men the same afternoon that he had received the instruction.
He commends Peter for coming so promptly by saying: "Thou
hast well done that thou art come." He thus commends Peter and
encourages him in the task that is now before Peter by saying:
"We are all here present in the sight of God, to hear all things that
have been commanded thee of the Lord." Cornelius not only commends Peter for his courage in breaking away from Jewish customs, but he takes no offense at the implied superiority of the Jews
over the Gentiles; he tells Peter that his circle of close friends are
present to hear the message from God that Peter has. This audience was fertile soil for the preaching of the gospel to the Gentiles.
They were not only "present in the sight of God," but they were
there "to hear all things" that God commanded to be done.
Cornelius recognizes Peter as being a messenger of God, and hence
he has a message from God.

34, 35 **And Peter opened his mouth, and said,**—"Opened his
mouth" is a solemn form of beginning an address, and is used frequently in the New Testament. (Matt. 5: 2; 13: 35; Acts 8: 35;
18: 14.) "Of a truth I perceive that God is no respecter of persons." Peter now is fully convinced that God had sent an angel to
Cornelius and had given him the vision on the housetop that he

nation he that feareth him, and worketh righteousness, is acceptable to him.
36 ³The word which he sent unto the children of Israel, preaching ⁴good
tidings of peace by Jesus Christ (he is Lord of all)—37 that saying ye yourselves know, which was published throughout all Judaea, beginning from

³Many ancient authorities read *He sent the word unto*
⁴Or, *the gospel*

might know that God was no respecter of persons; that the barrier
between Jew and Gentile had been removed in Christ. God is no
"respecter of persons," but he is a respecter of character. A "respecter of persons" is one who receives or treats others, not according to what they are, but according to their outward circumstances,
such as wealth or social position, nationality, or color. All men
alike need salvation; God loves all men and Christ died for all;
there is one and the same plan of salvation for all; hence, those
who faithfully comply with the terms of salvation receive it. Peter
now understands that the Gentiles are to enjoy salvation in Christ
as are the Jews. God had sent him among the Gentiles and had
prepared him by a vision for the venture, and he had learned that
he, a Jew, had not defiled himself in God's sight by association
with the Gentiles. Peter had also learned that the Gentile was the
same in the sight of God as the Jew, and that God would treat him
in the same way.

36 **The word which he sent unto the children of Israel,**—Peter further learns that the gospel which came to the Jews was also
intended to go to the Gentiles, for "he is Lord of all." "The
word" which was preached concerning Christ by John the Baptist,
and then by Christ and his apostles, and now by the disciples of
Christ, was the gospel or "good tidings of peace" which should be
enjoyed in Christ. Since the gospel is a gospel of peace, obedience
to it reconciles both Jew and Gentile in Christ. Christ is the Savior, not only of the Jews, but of Gentiles, of the entire world.

37 **that saying ye yourselves know,**—Peter affirms that Cornelius and his company knew something about Jesus of Nazareth;
Caesarea was in Palestine and all Palestine had learned of Jesus.
Cornelius may have been in Jerusalem during the personal ministry of Christ; at any rate, Peter affirms that Cornelius knew of
him since it had been "published throughout all Judaea, beginning
from Galilee." During the personal ministry of Christ he had

Galilee, after the baptism which John preached; 38 *even* Jesus of Nazareth, how God anointed him with the Holy Spirit and with power: who went about doing good, and healing all that were oppressed of the devil; for God was with him. 39 And we are witnesses of all things which he did both in the country of the Jews, and in Jerusalem; whom also they slew, hanging

---

evangelized Judea and Galilee; since the death of Christ the apostles had preached in Jerusalem, Judea, and Samaria, and those who were scattered from Jerusalem had gone everywhere preaching the word. (Acts 8: 1, 4.) Peter limits the publication of this gospel to the time of John's baptism. The oral gospel of the apostles began with the baptism of John and ended with the death of Christ, so far as the limited commission was concerned. The works of Christ were so public and so widespread that some knowledge of them had come to Cornelius; hence, Peter has a foundation upon which to instruct Cornelius.

38 **even Jesus of Nazareth, how God anointed him**—To distinguish which Jesus, Peter designates that it is "Jesus of Nazareth." God had anointed him with the Holy Spirit and had given him power to work miracles. He was anointed with the Holy Spirit when he was baptized. (Luke 3: 22.) After his baptism he "went about doing good," and exercising the power that God had given him in "healing all that were oppressed of the devil." Those who had evil spirits and demons were oppressed by the devil. Peter here recognized the reality of the devil. The reason assigned for his being able to do this was that "God was with him." Nicodemus had confessed that "no one can do these signs that thou doest, except God be with him." (John 3: 2.)

39 **And we are witnesses of all things which he did**—Jesus had made his apostles his witnesses. (Acts 1: 8.) The apostles had followed him from his early ministry to his crucifixion; they had seen him after his resurrection and saw him ascend to the Father; hence, they could be his witnesses "both in the country of the Jews, and in Jerusalem." They had borne witness of him in Jerusalem and in Judea. Peter could say to Cornelius that he had heard of these things, but his apostles had *seen* them; Peter knew them at firsthand, so he was a competent witness. He could say that he knew when, where, to whom, and under what circumstances all these things which Cornelius had heard about were

him on a tree. 40 Him God raised up the third day, and gave him to be
made manifest, 41 not to all the people, but unto witnesses that were chosen
before of God, *even* to us, who ate and drank with him after he rose from
the dead. 42 And he charged us to preach unto the people, and to testify
that this is he who is ordained of God *to be* the Judge of the living and the

done. The Jews, in whose country and chief city these good
things were done, slew this Jesus of Nazareth, "hanging him on a
tree." Peter had used this expression once before. (Acts 5: 30.)
Peter represented in Acts 2: 23 the crucifixion as an act of the rulers and people of Jerusalem, and not of the Roman governor.

40, 41 **Him God raised up the third day,**—Again Peter brings
in contrast what the people did for Jesus of Nazareth and what
God did for him—the people crucified him, but God raised him
from the dead; the people were working contrary to God. Not
only were the apostles witnesses, but God himself bore witness of
Jesus by raising him from the dead. The Jews thought that they
had destroyed Jesus by crucifying him, but this only gave God the
occasion to prove more conclusively that Jesus was the Messiah,
his Son. Peter makes it clear that Jesus appeared to the apostles,
and not to "all the people," but just to chosen witnesses; these witnesses were not deceived, for they "ate and drank with him after
he rose from the dead." It is difficult for us to understand how
Jesus could eat and drink after the resurrection as is stated here by
Peter and also in Luke 24: 41-43; yet Peter makes it clear that
there was no possible way by which these witnesses could be deceived.

42 **And he charged us to preach unto the people,**—Not only
were Peter and others to be witnesses for Christ, but they were to
preach him to others; in fact, they were to preach the gospel to the
whole creation. (Mark 16: 15.) Here Peter shows Cornelius his
commission from Christ to preach what he had seen and heard and
experienced. Among the things that he should preach was that
Christ died for the sins of the world, that he was buried and raised
from the dead and made his ascension back to the Father, and that
he was "ordained of God to be the Judge of the living and the
dead." Christ is now the Judge; his life and character are the
standard by which every man is to judge himself; he shows the

dead. 43 To him bear all the prophets witness, that through his name every
one that believeth on him shall receive remission of sins.
　　44 While Peter yet spake these words, the Holy Spirit fell on all them
that heard the word. 45 And they of the circumcision that believed were

---

ideal way to live; he is also to be the Judge at the last day.
"Judge of the living and the dead" covers all past, present, and future.

　　43 **To him bear all the prophets witness,**—All the prophets
pointed to Jesus. Peter had declared "all the prophets from Samuel and them that followed after, as many as have spoken, they also
told of these days." (Acts 3: 24.) The important thing that the
prophets bore witness to, and that the apostles were witnesses of, is
"that through his name every one that believeth on him shall receive
remission of sins." Peter has made the claim that the entire Old
Testament prophecy bore witness to the universality of the gospel,
and that the condition of salvation was through obedience to
Christ. The remission of sins is through the name of Jesus and
belongs to those who believe on him; Peter had preached before
that there is no "other name under heaven, that is given among
men, wherein we must be saved." (Acts 4: 12.) On the day of
Pentecost Peter had told believers, when they asked what to do,
that they should "repent ye, and be baptized . . . in the name of
Jesus Christ unto the remission of your sins." (Acts 2: 38.)

　　44 **While Peter yet spake these words,**—We may know that
Cornelius and his company were listening with deep interest to
Peter, with emotions as intense as those which possessed anyone,
and suddenly "the Holy Spirit fell on all them that heard the
word." He did not come by the laying on of hands, but came on
these Gentiles as he did on the day of Pentecost on the Jews.
(Acts 11: 15.) Peter had not formally finished his address when
the interruption of the Holy Spirit came. Joel had prophesied that
God would "pour forth of my Spirit upon all flesh" (Acts 2: 17),
and the Jews had received the Holy Spirit on Pentecost, and now
he comes upon the Gentiles; hence, "all flesh" had now received
the Holy Spirit, for the race of man was divided at that time into
Jew and Gentile.

amazed, as many as came with Peter, because that on the Gentiles also was poured out the gift of the Holy Spirit. 46 For they heard them speak with tongues, and magnify God. Then answered Peter, 47 Can any man forbid the water, that these should not be baptized, who have received the Holy Spirit as well as we? 48 And he commanded them to be baptized in the name of Jesus Christ. Then prayed they him to tarry certain days.

45 **And they of the circumcision that believed**—Peter had taken six Jewish brethren with him; they are spoken of here as "they of the circumcision." From this point on Luke refers to the two classes of disciples, Jewish and Gentile. The Jewish disciples who had accompanied Peter from Joppa were amazed because the Gentiles had received the gift of the Holy Spirit. The miracle proved what Peter had said with a fullness of proof for which Peter himself perhaps was not prepared; these Gentiles had faith and the miraculous manifestation of the Holy Spirit may be called a baptism of the Holy Spirit.

46, 47 **For they heard them speak with tongues,**—"With tongues" means that they spoke with new and strange tongues as they did on the day of Pentecost. (Acts 2: 4, 11.) They were praising God with these new tongues. There was the same kind of need of the outward manifestation of the Holy Spirit at this time that there was on Pentecost. The speaking of tongues always accompanied the baptism of the Holy Spirit. This convinced Peter, and he asked who could forbid "the water, that these should not be baptized." He gave as his reason that they had received the Holy Spirit as the Jews had; hence, they were entitled to all the privileges of the gospel. They had believed Peter's testimony; hence, had believed on Jesus; it is evident that they were penitent of all their sins because they could not be saved with their sins; now they are to be baptized. Baptism was one of the prerequisites to remission of sins.

48 **And he commanded them to be baptized**—Peter was speaking by the authority of God; he was speaking by the Holy Spirit; hence, God through Peter commanded them to be baptized "in the name of Jesus Christ." Peter and the six Jewish brethren who were present could baptize this company in a short time, but Peter commanded others to do the baptizing. Paul refrained from baptizing some, as may be inferred from his letters to the Corinthians. (1 Cor. 1: 14-17.) Peter may have acted from a similar

motive. After they were baptized they earnestly requested that Peter and the Jewish brethren "tarry certain days" with them. The implication is that Peter remained with Cornelius some time.

11. PETER JUSTIFIES HIS PREACHING TO GENTILES
11: 1-18

1 Now the apostles and the brethren that were in Judaea heard that the Gentiles also had received the word of God. 2 And when Peter was come up to Jerusalem, they that were of the circumcision contended with him, 3 saying, Thou wentest in to men uncircumcised, and didst eat with them. 4 But

1 **Now the apostles and the brethren**—The distance from Caesarea, the home of Cornelius, to Jerusalem was about seventy miles. We do not know how long after the conversion of Cornelius and his household until the news reached Jerusalem; Cornelius had invited Peter and the other brethren to "tarry certain days" with him, and the implication is that they did so. The news of the conversion of Cornelius, and especially the news of Peter's going into the house of a Gentile, was startling to Jewish Christians; they had, as yet, not learned that the gospel was for the Gentiles as well as the Jews; neither had they heard of the vision that Peter had and the command to go to the Gentiles. It seems that the news came to Jerusalem and the other Judean churches before Peter had left Caesarea.

2, 3 **And when Peter was come up to Jerusalem,**—Peter was accompanied by the six Jewish brethren who had gone with him from Joppa to Caesarea, and now came with him to Jerusalem. We may now see the purpose Peter had in taking these six Jewish brethren with him to Caesarea; they were to be witnesses with him, and it seems that Peter had gone to Jerusalem to defend himself and to impart to the church there the news of the reception of the Gentiles. "They that were of the circumcision," or the Jewish Christians, "contended" with Peter, and brought the accusation against him that he went "in to men uncircumcised, and didst eat with them." "Contended" is from the Greek "diekrinonto," and here means "to separate oneself apart, to take sides against, to make a cleavage." So Peter is at once put on the defense; it is clear here that Peter was not regarded as any kind of "pope" or overlord. The Jewish Christians must have contended that the distinction between Jew and Gentile should be maintained in the

Peter began, and expounded *the matter* unto them in order, saying, 5 I was in the city of Joppa praying: and in a trance I saw a vision, a certain vessel descending, as it were a great sheet let down from heaven by four corners; and it came even unto me: 6 upon which when I had fastened mine eyes, I considered, and saw the fourfooted beasts of the earth and wild beasts and creeping things and birds of the heaven. 7 And I heard also a voice saying unto me, Rise, Peter; kill and eat. 8 But I said, Not so, Lord: for nothing common or unclean hath ever entered into my mouth. 9 But a voice answered

church; hence, they should not mix socially with Gentiles, the uncircumcised, nor eat with them. "Uncircumcised" means men having not been circumcised; it is used here as a contemptuous expression; they did not object to Peter's preaching to the Gentiles, but they did object to his going into the house and eating with them.

4-6 **But Peter began, and expounded the matter**—When Peter came before the other "apostles" and "brethren," he explained in a very deliberate and detailed way that he had been convinced that God wanted the gospel preached to the Gentiles. He gave the facts that convinced him, thinking that the arguments that convinced him would convince others that the Gentiles should have the blessings of the gospel. A great work had been done in the name of Christ and Peter is called on to defend himself for his part in it. Peter's mildness and patience in explaining the entire matter to them was put in contrast with the heat and excitement that his accusers manifested. Peter's rehearsal was so simple and truthful that it carried conviction. He told exactly where he was, what he was doing, and all things connected with his trance.

7-10 **And I heard also a voice saying unto me,**—There was a clear issue between Peter with respect to his conduct and the other apostles and brethren; the charge was: "Thou wentest in to men uncircumcised, and didst eat with them." (Verse 3.) This issue involved the one of bringing Gentiles into the church without their becoming Jews. Luke, the writer, through the Holy Spirit, deemed it wise to give the two records of this set of events—the one in chapter 10 and the other here. This shows that great importance and significance was attached to the event. God himself, the God of the Jews, had directed Peter to do what he had done. (Verses 5-10.) God had convinced Peter with a vivid illustration while Peter was in a trance. (Verse 6.) God had directed Cor-

the second time out of heaven, What God hath cleansed, make not thou common.   10 And this was done thrice: and all were drawn up again into heaven.   11 And behold, forthwith three men stood before the house in which we were, having been sent from Caesarea unto me.   12 And the Spirit bade me go with them, making no distinction.   And these six brethren also accompanied me; and we entered into the man's house: 13 and he told us how he had seen the angel standing in his house, and saying, Send to Joppa, and fetch Simon, whose surname is Peter; 14 who shall speak unto thee words, whereby thou shalt be saved, thou and all thy house.   15 And as I began to speak, the Holy Spirit fell on them, even as on us at the beginning.   16 And

nelius to send for Peter; to confirm the fact, an angel was sent to Cornelius bidding him send for Peter.   These Gentiles had become Christians without becoming Jews; the Holy Spirit had come upon them as he had upon the Jews on Pentecost.   While Jesus was on earth teaching the Jews had asked him for "a sign from heaven," and now Peter gives these disciples a sign from heaven. (Matt. 16: 1; Luke 11: 16.)

11-14 **And behold, forthwith three men stood**—Peter rehearsed the matter in the detailed order that the events occurred, so that his report of them might impress the minds of his hearers, as the events themselves did to his own mind.   Peter's vision had scarcely ended when these three men from Caesarea called for him. "Forthwith three men stood before the house in which we were." Further evidence was that the Holy Spirit commanded Peter to go with them, "making no distinction."   That is, Peter should go to the Gentiles with the gospel as freely as he would to the Jews; "these six brethren" accompanied Peter and were now present to bear witness that the Gentiles had received the Holy Spirit and to testify just what Peter had done.   So Peter confessed to the charge that was brought against him, and the other six were guilty of the same charge. Peter has made it clear that he did not go to the Gentiles and eat with them of his own initiative; he went under the direct orders of God and the Holy Spirit; these six Jewish brethren could bear witness to this fact.

15 **And as I began to speak,**—Cornelius had been told by the angel that Peter, when brought from Joppa, would "speak unto thee words, whereby thou shalt be saved, thou and all thy house." (Verse 14.)   Now Peter began to speak these words unto this good, yet unsaved, man; he had not been speaking very long (Acts 10: 34-44) when the Holy Spirit came upon the company assem-

I remembered the word of the Lord, how he said, John indeed baptized with water; but ye shall be baptized ¹in the Holy Spirit. 17 If then God gave unto them the like gift as *he did* also unto us, when we believed on the Lord

¹Or, *with*

bled at Cornelius' house as he had "on us at the beginning." The "beginning" mentioned here was Pentecost. Peter recalls very vividly the events at Pentecost; this was the beginning of the church; it was the beginning of the preaching of the gospel in its fullness; it was the beginning of the work of the apostles under the Great Commission; it was the beginning of the Christian dispensation. The Holy Spirit came upon these Gentiles as it did upon the Jews "at the beginning." According to the best chronologists, Pentecost occurred A.D. 30 to 33, and the conversion of Cornelius took place about A.D. 40; hence, it has been eight or ten years since Pentecost; the church was eight or ten years old at the conversion of Cornelius. The coming of the Holy Spirit upon the household of Cornelius was a baptism of the Holy Spirit. There had been nothing like this since Pentecost; hence, Peter says that the Holy Spirit came on the house of Cornelius as it did on the Jews "at the beginning." Therefore, there had been no baptism of the Holy Spirit since Pentecost; if there had been Peter could have referred to the numerous other incidents and not have had to go back to Pentecost. This also shows that the baptism of the Holy Spirit was not to convert people, for Peter would only have had to refer to any case of conversion to prove his point.

16 **And I remembered the word of the Lord,**—When the Holy Spirit came on the Gentiles, Peter remembered how Jesus had said: "John indeed baptized with water; but ye shall be baptized in the Holy Spirit." (Acts 1: 5.) The baptism of the Holy Spirit was a mark of the divine acceptance of Gentiles as disciples. If God had conferred on the Gentiles the baptism of the Holy Spirit, how can man refuse to them all the blessings of the gospel? How can Christian Jews call men common and unclean upon whom God has bestowed the baptism of the Holy Spirit?

17 **If then God gave unto them the like gift**—Here Peter reached the climax of his argument; he and other Jewish Chris-

Jesus Christ, who was I, that I could withstand God? 18 And when they heard these things, they held their peace, and glorified God, saying, Then to the Gentiles also hath God granted repentance unto life.

tians could not refuse those whom God had accepted; he could not withstand God. The argument is clear and forceful. To reject the Gentiles and refuse to let them enjoy all the blessings of the gospel would be to "withstand God." If God gave to them the same gift which he gave to the Jews on believing on the Lord Jesus Christ, Peter could not reject the Gentiles. The argument forces the other apostles and brethren to withdraw their charge against Peter, or commend him for what he had done, and rejoice with him in the conversion of the Gentiles.

18 **And when they heard these things,**—The accusation against Peter was withdrawn; the wrangling ceased; the critics even "glorified God." They rejoiced that God had "granted repentance unto life" to the Gentiles as well as to the Jews. Peter now sees in this incident the same principle for which Paul contended at a later date. (Acts 15: 8.) The Jews were now satisfied that God had called Gentiles as well as Jews; it is clear here that the Jews could not live as Jews and be Christians, and that the Gentiles could not live as Gentiles and be Christians; that "there can be neither Jew nor Greek, there can be neither bond nor free, there can be no male and female; for ye all are one man in Christ Jesus." (Gal. 3: 28.)

12. CHURCH IN ANTIOCH FOUNDED
11: 19-21

19 They therefore that were scattered abroad upon the tribulation that arose about Stephen travelled as far as Phoenicia, and Cyprus, and Antioch,

19 **They therefore that were scattered abroad**—Luke, the historian, here picks up the thread of events where he left it in Acts 8: 1. All the thousands of disciples that had been converted at Jerusalem were scattered abroad except the apostles; the persecution of the church began with the martyrdom of Stephen, and some of those who were scattered abroad went "as far as Phoenicia, and Cyprus, and Antioch." These, however, preached the gospel "to none save only to Jews." The persecution which fol-

speaking the word to none save only to Jews. 20 But there were some of them, men of Cyprus and Cyrene, who, when they were come to Antioch, spake unto the ²Greeks also, ³preaching the Lord Jesus. 21 And the hand of

---

²Many ancient authorities read *Grecian Jews.* See ch. 6. 1
³See marginal note on ch. 5. 42

---

lowed the death of Stephen had a twofold effect: (1) the dispersed disciples preached Christ and established churches within Palestine; (2) churches were established beyond Palestine, "Phoenicia" was a district, about a hundred twenty miles long and fifteen miles broad, which lay to the north of Palestine on the shores of the Mediterranean, and on the slopes of Lebanon; its chief cities were Tyre, Sidon, and Tripolis; it formed a part of the Roman province of Syria. The gospel was preached and churches were established in Phoenicia. (Acts 21: 1-4; 27: 3.) "Cyprus" was a large and fertile island nearly opposite Antioch, while Antioch was the capital of the Roman province of Syria; it was situated on the Orontes River, about sixteen miles from the sea, with Seleucia for its seaport.

20 **But there were some of them, men of Cyprus and Cyrene,**—Here we have a contrast with those who preached the gospel "to none save only to Jews," as there were "some of them" who were scattered abroad, "who, when they were come to Antioch, spake unto the Greeks also." The best authorities consider "the Greeks" here as meaning the Gentiles; however, some authorities understand it to mean "Grecian Jews." (Acts 6: 1.) These men from "Cyprus and Cyrene" were "Hellenists," Greek-speaking Jews, who, having lived abroad, had learned to speak the Grecian language; however, they spoke "unto the Greeks." "Hellenists" is used to mean those Jews who had been abroad and spoke the Grecian language; but "Hellenes" means the Gentiles who did not become Jewish proselytes. Hence, the contrast and the new departure lie in the fact that before this the disciples sought to convert to Jesus only the Jews, including the Grecians who were Jews, but now they began to preach to the Gentiles as such. This was after the conversion of Cornelius, and probably in the year A.D. 42.

21 **And the hand of the Lord was with them:**—"The hand of the Lord" is an Old Testament phrase (Ex. 9: 3; Isa. 59: 1) and

the Lord was with them: and a great number that believed turned unto the

---

is used frequently by Luke (Luke 1: 66; Acts 4: 28, 30; 13: 11).
This was proof that the Lord was with them in preaching the gospel to Gentiles; it also confirmed the word which was preached to
them. As a result of this "a great number that believed turned
unto the Lord." Turn to the Lord is a common expression for
Gentiles who believed on Christ. (Acts 14: 15; 15: 19; 26: 18,
20; 1 Thess. 1: 9.) "A great number" of Gentiles were converted; we do not know how many, but we do know that a church
was established in Antioch. Antioch now is to become the center
from which the gospel is spread throughout the Gentile world, as
Jerusalem was the center of preaching the gospel to the Jews.

13. BARNABAS COMES TO ANTIOCH
11: 22-24

Lord. 22 And the report concerning them came to the ears of the church
which was in Jerusalem: and they sent forth Barnabas as far as Antioch: 23

---

22 And the report concerning them—The church had been
established at Antioch and was composed largely of Gentile Christians. The conversion of Cornelius and the discussion which followed his conversion prepared the apostles and the church at Jerusalem for the good news of the young but fast-growing church at
Antioch. News did not travel fast at that time, but the church in
Jerusalem heard of the establishment of the church at Antioch, and
"sent forth Barnabas as far as Antioch." The first mention we have
of Barnabas was a very favorable one. (Acts 4: 36, 37.) Here
he sold his field and "brought the money and laid it at the apostles'
feet" for distribution in helping those in need. The next mention
that we have of him is when he introduced and commended the
new convert Saul to the apostles at Jerusalem. (Acts 9: 27.)
Now we have the church at Jerusalem sending him to Antioch.
Barnabas belonged to Cyprus; he was sent to Antioch as Peter and
John had been sent to Samaria. (Acts 8: 14.) Barnabas was a
good man, judicious, broadminded, and generous. He was of the
tribe of Levi, spoke Greek, and was well qualified to mix with the

who, when he was come, and had seen the grace of God, was glad; and he
exhorted them all, [4]that with purpose of heart they would cleave unto the
Lord: 24 for he was a good man, and full of the Holy Spirit and of faith:
and much people was added unto the Lord. 25 And he went forth to Tarsus

[4]Some ancient authorities read *that they would cleave unto the purpose of their
heart in the Lord*

people of Antioch; they could trust him to give wise counsel and to
bring an accurate report to Jerusalem.

23 **who, when he was come,**—Barnabas was full of the Holy
Spirit; he was possibly acquainted with those who had gone to Antioch and first preached the gospel there; as he was a Grecian Jew,
he would be in sympathy with the Gentile converts, and would be
welcomed by the Christians in Antioch of both Jews and Gentiles.
When Barnabas saw "the grace of God" he was glad. He "exhorted them all." His first name was Joseph, but the apostles surnamed him Barnabas, "which is, being interpreted, Son of exhortation." (Acts 4: 36.) Barnabas had a special gift for work of this
kind; he exhorted these Christians with one purpose of heart to
"cleave unto the Lord." "Cleave" here is from the original "pros-
menein," and means "to keep on remaining loyal" to the Lord; he
exhorted them to be persistent; this was needed in such a pagan
city as Antioch.

24 **for he was a good man,**—Very few times in the Bible is
one called "a good man"; Barnabas came in this class. He was
good and full of the Holy Spirit. This explains his conduct. Besides being really good, he was full of the Holy Spirit and faith.
As a result of his labors "much people was added unto the Lord."
These people were added to the Lord when they were added to the
church, they were added to the church when they heard the gospel, believed it, repented of their sins, and were baptized into
Christ. This is the way people were added to the Lord. It should
be noticed how prominent "the Lord" is made here. Christ is
called "the Lord Jesus" (verse 20); the "hand of the Lord" was
with them (verse 21); and the believers turned "unto the Lord"
(verse 21); Barnabas encouraged the people to cleave "unto the
Lord" (verse 23); and much people was added "unto the Lord"
(verse 24). The result of Barnabas' visit to Antioch was that
"much people was added unto the Lord"; that is, literally, a great

multitude was added to the Lord. We now have a large congregation of disciples in Antioch.

14. PAUL BROUGHT TO ANTIOCH
11: 25, 26

to seek for Saul; 26 and when he had found him, he brought him unto Antioch. And it came to pass, that even for a whole year they were gathered
together [5]with the church, and taught much people; and that the disciples
were called Christians first in Antioch.

---

[5]Gr. *in*

---

25 **And he went forth to Tarsus to seek for Saul;**—After
Saul's conversion he went into Arabia and returned to Damascus;
next we find him in Jerusalem; he did but little work in Jerusalem; Barnabas had commended him to the apostles and the church
there, but it was thought best for Saul to go to another field; so
when it was found that the Jews were seeking to kill him, the
brethren "brought him down to Caesarea, and sent him forth to
Tarsus." (Acts 9: 30.) It seems that he did not remain idle in
Cilicia (Gal. 1: 21), but preached the gospel in Cilicia and Syria
(Acts 15: 41). The work was too heavy for Barnabas in Antioch,
so he went to Tarsus, about eighty miles away, to find Saul.
"Seek" is from the original "anazetesai," and means "to seek or
hunt up"; the word suggests that Barnabas had some difficulty in
finding Saul. The Holy Spirit guided Barnabas in his search, and
Barnabas had full confidence in Saul as being the right person to
help in the great work at Antioch.

26 **and when he had found him,**—After finding Saul and reporting to him of the great work that had been done at Antioch,
Saul accepted the invitation to join Barnabas in the work of the
Lord in that field. They labored together "for a whole year" "with
the church" at Antioch. This is the second time Barnabas introduces Saul; Barnabas here and for more than a year later appears
as the leader, and not Saul. (Acts 13: 1, 2.) Barnabas leads in
the first great work that is done with Saul. They not only
preached the gospel to the unsaved, but they edified the church:
they "taught much people."

**and that the disciples were called Christians first in An-
tioch.**—Up to this time believers in Christ had been called "believers," "disciples," "saints," "brethren," "those of the Way"; but

now they receive a new name. Much discussion has been had as
to who called them "Christians." "Were called" shows that they
not only called themselves by that name, but that others called
them by that name. "Were called" is from the original "chremati-
sai," and has the force of divine command. (Matt. 2: 12, 22;
Luke 2: 26; Acts 10: 22.) However, some claim that the word
does not have that meaning here, but that it has the same meaning
as Rom. 7: 3, and means to be called or named by someone else
from one's business. Some contend that the name was given by
their enemies as a name of contempt. It matters but little as to
who first coined the name and applied it to the disciples of Christ,
since we have the name divinely approved by Peter in 1 Pet. 4: 16.
Here Peter, speaking or writing by the Holy Spirit, says: "If a
man suffer as a Christian, let him not be ashamed; but let him glorify God in this name." The other instance in divine record where
the name is used is in Acts 26: 28, where Agrippa acknowledges
that Paul is persuading him to be a Christian. "Christians" is
from the Greek "Christianous"; this termination was frequent in
Latin in the early days; whether this name was derived from the
Latin or not, the termination became common enough in Greek,
and therefore there is no necessity to ascribe the name "Christianos" to a Roman origin. Later "Christianos" was modified to
"Chrestianos" (both words being pronounced alike). Each of the
three languages has contributed to the formation of this word.
The *thought* is Jewish, denoting the Anointed One; the *root*,
Christ, is Greek; the *termination,* ianoi, is Latin. So in the providence of God, the same three nations whose differing dialects proclaimed above the cross, "Jesus the King of the Jews," now unite
in forming a word which for all time shall be applied to those who
follow Christ. Antioch, the center from which the gospel radiated
among the Gentiles, has given us the common name, Christian.

15. THE FAMINE AND RELIEF
11 : 27-30

27 Now in these days there came down prophets from Jerusalem unto

---

27 **Now in these days there came down prophets**—"In these
days" means the time while the church at Antioch was being in-

Antioch. 28 And there stood up one of them named Agabus, and signified
by the Spirit that there should be a great famine over all ⁶the world: which
came to pass in the days of Claudius. 29 And the disciples, every man according to his ability, determined to send ⁷relief unto the brethren that dwelt

⁶Gr. *the inhabited earth*
⁷Gr. *for ministry.* Comp. ch. 6. 1

creased with a great multitude of Gentile converts during the
year's residence there of Barnabas and Saul. "Prophets" came
down "from Jerusalem unto Antioch." Many think of a prophet
as one who foretells future events; this is included in the term, but
does not cover its meaning entirely. The word is a compound
Greek word, "pro," which means "before, in front of"; and
"phemi," which means "to speak"; hence, "prophet" means to
speak before, in front of, or speak beforehand, in behalf of, instead
of one; hence, it means one who speaks for God; hence, a teacher.
Judas and Silas are called prophets. (Acts 15: 32.) They were not
just "foretellers," but they were "forthtellers." These teachers
came from Jerusalem to Antioch to instruct further the disciples in
Antioch.

28 **And there stood up one of them named Agabus,**—This
Agabus is mentioned again in Acts 21: 10; he was from Judea,
and by a very simple object lesson he foretold the imprisonment of
Paul at Jerusalem. At this time Agabus "signified by the spirit"
that there should "be a great famine over all the world." Luke,
the historian, records that this took place during "the days of Claudius." The date of this severe famine was A.D. 45. "Agabus"
means "locust," he predicted this great famine literally over all the
inhabited earth which occurred during the reign of Claudius Caesar. His reign was from A.D. 41 to A.D. 54, and this famine in
A.D. 45. Some authorities put it at other dates as A.D. 44, 46,
and 48; some claim that this great famine continued from A.D. 44
to A.D. 48.

29 **And the disciples, every man**—The Gentile Christians volunteered to send help to the Christians in Judea; this was an act of
Christian charity on their part to help their Jewish brethren. We
are not told how much relief was sent, but "every man according
to his ability" purposed to send relief. The prophecy of this famine was made in order to give the disciples time to collect money
and food in advance of the need; the disciples believed Agabus and

in Judaea : 30 which also they did, sending it to the elders by the hand of Barnabas and Saul.

proceeded at once to prepare for the relief. The warning of Agabus stirred the Christians in Antioch so that they determined to do what they could for those in distress.

30 which also they did,—When the time came that the relief was needed, the church at Antioch selected Barnabas and Saul to take the relief to those who were suffering in Judea. After the famine began and after the persecution by Herod, and Herod's death in A.D. 44, most of the Christians at Jerusalem were probably poor. Barnabas and Saul carried the relief "to the elders." This is the first mention of "the elders" of the church. The word "elders" here comes from the Greek "presbuterous," from which we get our word "presbyters." In Acts 20: 17 and verse 28 "elders" and "bishops" are used interchangeably, as in Tit. 1: 5, 7. It is probable that the visit of Barnabas and Saul to Jerusalem took place after the events recorded in Acts 12: 1-23. This visit is omitted in Gal. 1: 18 and 2: 1. Jerusalem is not mentioned here, but Judea is mentioned; this has caused some to think that the relief was not sent to the elders of the church at Jerusalem. Barnabas was especially suited to carry this relief to the suffering because he had come down from Jerusalem.

16. MARTYRDOM OF JAMES
12: 1, 2

1 Now about that time Herod the king put forth his hands to afflict cer-

1 Now about that time Herod—"About that time" was A.D. 44, as Herod's death occurred in this year; Barnabas and Saul came from Antioch to Jerusalem after the persecution by Herod near the close of A.D. 44 or the beginning of A.D. 45. "Herod the king," this was Herod Agrippa I, the grandson of Herod the Great; he was ruler over Palestine from A.D. 42 to A.D. 44; he was the son of Aristobulus, the nephew of Herod Antipas, the brother of Herodias, and the father of Herod Agrippa II. He went to Rome at an early age, was educated at the court of Tiber-

tain of the church. 2 And he killed James the brother of John with the

ius, and had become a companion of Caligula. He determined "to afflict certain of the church." It had been probably more than eight years since the persecution over the death of Stephen ceased with the conversion of Saul; but the disciples were not popular in Jerusalem with either Sadducees or Pharisees.

2 **And he killed James**—This James was the brother of John and was closely associated with Peter during the personal ministry of Jesus. Peter, James and John formed the inner circle of the apostles. He was the son of Zebedee, and was one of the first disciples of Jesus. At one time James and John were ambitious to be nearest Jesus in his kingdom, and James felt sure that he could drink of the same cup of suffering as Jesus (Matt. 20: 20-25), and his death shows that he stood the test. James was the first of the apostles to die, and his brother John was the last. The martyrdom of James showed the early disciples that God did not always mean to interpose to deliver the apostles, and also taught them that they were to be partakers of the sufferings of Christ. It is thought that James was killed about the close of A.D. 43. He was killed "with the sword." There were four modes of capital punishment in use among the Jews, namely; (1) stoning; (2) burning; (3) decapitation; (4) strangling. "Stoning" was authorized by the law of Moses; crucifixion was a Roman punishment, and was not practiced save under Roman governors.

17. IMPRISONMENT AND DELIVERANCE OF PETER
12: 3-19

sword. 3 And when he saw that it pleased the Jews, he proceeded to seize

3 **And when he saw that it pleased the Jews,**—It is likely that Herod had pleased both the rulers of the Jews and the people, because James, one of the leaders of the disciples, had been killed; this encouraged Herod to attempt to destroy other leaders among the Christians; hence, "he proceeded to seize Peter also." The Pharisees had always hated the disciples because they taught the resurrection of the dead; the Pharisees, no doubt, had heard of Peter's making common with the Gentiles; hence, they would be eager to have Peter destroyed. Luke, the historian, here indirectly

Peter also. And *those* were the days of unleavened bread. 4 And when he
had taken him, he put him in prison, and delivered him to four quaternions
of soldiers to guard him; intending after the Passover to bring him forth to
the people. 5 Peter therefore was kept in the prison: but prayer was made

locates the time of the year when Peter was arrested; those were
the days of unleavened bread. The Feast of the Passover came on
the fourteenth day of the first month, Abib, or Nisan; the feast of
"unleavened bread" followed the Passover and continued seven
days. (Ex. 12: 12, 13, 29, 30; Lev. 23: 5-8; Deut. 16: 1-8.)
Since the feast of unleavened bread followed the Passover so
closely, the same name was applied to both feasts; the Passover
was sometimes called the feast of unleavened bread, and the feast
of unleavened bread was called the Passover; both came in the first
month of the Jewish year, Abib, or Nisan, and correspond to our
latter part of March and the first of April. (See Luke 22: 1.)

4 **And when he had taken him,**—It seems that there was some
delay in the arrest of Peter; we know not the cause of the delay,
but when he was found he was put in prison and they "delivered
him to four quaternions of soldiers to guard him"; that is, he was
given to a band of four soldiers on guard at one time, two within,
one on each side of Peter, bound one to each of his arms with
chains, a third posted outside the door, and a fourth in the passage
leading to the outside gate. It was customary to relieve the soldiers from duty every three hours, at each of the watches night and
day; hence, sixteen soldiers were responsible for him. In addition
to this, the prison doors were fastened and a great iron gate helped
to make secure the prisoner. Escape from the prison was humanly
impossible. Perhaps Peter was so imprisoned and held secure because they remembered that he at one time escaped from prison
(Acts 5: 19), and they did not intend that he should get away this
time. He was kept in prison until after "the Passover," and then
he was to be killed. Here we have this feast called "the Passover," and in verse 3 it is called "the days of unleavened bread."
Herod would not execute Peter during the Passover festival, because that would offend the Jews whom he wished to please.
"Bring him forth to the people" is similar to the description of the
trial of Jesus. (Luke 22: 66.) Herod intended to execute Peter

earnestly of the church unto God for him. 6 And when Herod was about to bring him forth, the same night Peter was sleeping between two soldiers, bound with two chains: and guards before the door kept the prison. 7 And behold, an angel of the Lord stood by him, and a light shined in the cell: and

within a week or ten days, but he did not know that his own death was nearer than that of Peter.

5 Peter therefore was kept in the prison:—Peter was in the inner prison or lower ward and would be led to the judgment seat where Herod Agrippa would sit so soon as the festal days were ended. (John 19: 13.) There is an emphatic contrast here. Peter was kept in prison, but "prayer was made earnestly of the church unto God for him." Here was a battle between the church and the world, the world attempting to destroy Peter and the church praying for him. We have King Herod, soldiers, prison, chains, iron gates on the one side, and a company of Christians praying on the other side; what will be the outcome? The prayers were made "earnestly," without ceasing. (Luke 22: 44.) It was a trying time with the church at Jerusalem; the apostle James had been killed and Peter was to be the next victim) hence, the disciples prayed "earnestly." This word comes from the Greek "ektenes," which means "strained," and from "ekteino," which means "to stretch"; it is the same word as used with respect to the prayer of Jesus (Luke 22: 44), and is the same Greek word translated "fervently" in 1 Pet. 1: 22.

6 And when Herod was about to bring him forth,—When the time arrived, or the festal days were ended, Herod had in mind to execute Peter the following day; but "the same night Peter was sleeping between two soldiers"; and was bound "with two chains." It should be noted that although the time of execution was near, yet Peter "was sleeping"; he was not disturbed about his condition. The two soldiers were chained to Peter and Peter was between them. The guards were on duty and standing "before the door" of the prison; hence, the two guards outside were keeping the door and the two soldiers within were chained to Peter with two chains. Perhaps Peter may have remembered what Jesus had said to him about his death, that he should live to be an old man. (John 21: 18.)

7 And behold, an angel of the Lord stood by him,—"An angel of the Lord" is here introduced by Luke with the same phra-

he smote Peter on the side, and awoke him, saying, Rise up quickly. And his chains fell off from his hands. 8 And the angel said unto him, Gird thyself, and bind on thy sandals. And he did so. And he saith unto him, Cast thy garment about thee, and follow me. 9 And he went out, and followed; and he knew not that it was true which was done ¹by the angel, but thought he saw a vision. 10 And when they were past the first and the second

---

¹Gr. *through*

---

seology as Luke used with respect to the visit of the angel to the shepherds. (Luke 2: 9.) This angel stood by Peter while he was asleep; "a light shined in the cell" with splendor and attended the presence of the angel; this light did not awaken Peter, so the angel "smote Peter on the side, and awoke him." When he was awake the angel said: "Rise up quickly." The angel roused Peter, he did not help him to arise, but commanded him to get up. "His chains fell off from his hands." The soldier who was appointed to guard a prisoner had the chain fastened to the wrist of his left hand, while the right hand remained at liberty to punish the prisoner if he attempted to escape; but Peter had chains around both hands as he was bound to two soldiers with two chains.

8 **And the angel said unto him,**—The angel gave further instruction to Peter and told him to gird himself and put on his sandals. For convenience Peter had unbound his girdle, unfastened his sandals, and was sleeping with his garment loosely over him; when he arose at the angel's touch it would fall loosely at his feet, so he would need to gird himself. Peter would need to be clad as he was about to make a journey from the prison; he obeyed at once and the angel commanded him to cast his garment about him and follow him The sandals worn at that time covered only the soles of the feet and were bound on the foot with a strap.

9 **And he went out, and followed;**—Perhaps the angel had caused a deep sleep to come upon the soldiers, so they were harmless as Peter escaped; Peter went out and followed the angel. The angel was in the form of a man and Peter "knew not that it was true which was done by the angel"; he thought that he "saw a vision." Peter was puzzled and did not know that the reality of escape was being made; he had had a vision in Joppa (Acts 10: 10) which Luke described as an ecstasy. Peter was so surprised that he scarcely knew whether he was asleep or awake.

guard, they came unto the iron gate that leadeth into the city; which opened to them of its own accord: and they went out, and passed on through one street; and straightway the angel departed from him. 11 And when Peter was come to himself, he said, Now I know of a truth, that the Lord hath sent forth his angel and delivered me out of the hand of Herod, and from all the expectation of the people of the Jews. 12 And when he had considered *the thing,* he came to the house of Mary the mother of John whose surname

10 **And when they were past the first and the second guard,** —The outer guards were stationed one nearer to the inner door of the prison and the other at some greater distance away; so when the angel had led Peter past these guards, "they came unto the iron gate that leadeth into the city." This description, with the words which immediately follow about the street into which they came, indicate that the prison in which Peter was kept was in the midst of the city. When they came to the iron gate it opened "of its own accord" to them and "they went out" and "passed on through one street" and immediately the angel left Peter. The angel had delivered Peter and now Peter could make his way alone. We have no means of knowing just where in Jerusalem this prison was located.

11 **And when Peter was come to himself,**—"Come to himself" is from the Greek "heautoi genomenos," which means "becoming at himself"; it is the same expression used in Luke 15: 17 where the prodigal son "came to himself," and means that he came to himself, as if he had been on a trip away from himself. Peter came out of his semidazed condition, and had all of his senses under control. He knew what had occurred—that the Lord had sent his angel and delivered him out of the hands of Herod and "from all the expectation of the people of the Jews." The Jews were expecting Herod to put Peter to death; they were anxious for him to do that so that Christianity would be checked.

12 **And when he had considered the thing,**—When Peter came to himself and realized that God had preserved him from death, "he came to the house of Mary the mother of John whose surname was Mark." It is probable that the disciples were accustomed to meeting at the house of Mary, so Peter's mind worked rapidly and he decided to go and find protection and companionship there. There are six Marys mentioned in the New Testament;

was Mark; where many were gathered together and were praying. 13 And when he knocked at the door of the gate, a maid came to answer, named Rhoda. 14 And when she knew Peter's voice, she opened not the gate for joy, but ran in, and told that Peter stood before the gate. 15 And they said unto her, Thou art mad. But she confidently affirmed that it was even so.

---

they are as follows: (1) Mary of Cleophas (John 19: 25); (2) Mary Magdalene (Luke 8: 2); (3) Mary the mother of Mark (Acts 12: 12); (4) Mary, sister of Lazarus (Luke 10: 42); (5) Mary, a Roman Christian (Rom. 16: 6); (6) Mary the mother of Jesus (Luke 1: 30). When Peter arrived at the house of Mary he found "many were gathered together and were praying." It seems that the praying had been going on all night, and a large number of the disciples were there. At another time the disciples gathered to pray (Acts 4: 31) after Peter had told the disciples of the threats of the Sanhedrin. "The supplication of a righteous man availeth much in its working." (James 5: 16.)

13 **And when he knocked at the door**—It is not strange that the door at the house of Mary would be fastened, as it was night and great fear was upon the disciples. Peter came to the door and knocked; this was the outer door, as there was a passage leading from the street to the inner court; just inside was a small room, like a porter's lodge, and a door admitting into the room from the court. A damsel by the name of Rhoda came to answer the knock. "Rhoda" means "rose." It was customary to name the daughters of the house after the most beautiful objects, as "Esther" which means a star; "Hadassah" which means "myrtle"; "Dorcas" which means "antelope"; "Margarita" which means "pearl"; "Susannah" which means "lily"; "Deborah" which means "bee"; and "Tamar" which means "palm tree." "Damsel" was used of a young female slave, as well as of a young girl; the narrative implies that she was more than a servant.

14 **And when she knew Peter's voice,**—Peter must have been a frequent visitor to Mary's house, and a frequent speaker to the disciples, as his voice was familiar even to the damsel. In her excitement and haste, when she recognized Peter's voice, she ran back into the house without opening the gate for Peter; she reported to the company that Peter was without and that he stood "before the gate."

15 **And they said unto her,**—The company within did not be-

And they said, It is his angel. 16 But Peter continued knocking: and when they had opened, they saw him, and were amazed. 17 But he, beckoning unto them with the hand to hold their peace, declared unto them how the Lord had brought him forth out of the prison. And he said, Tell these things unto James, and to the brethren. And he departed, and went to an-

---

lieve Rhoda; they saw she was excited and said to her: "Thou art mad." However, the damsel "confidently affirmed that it was even so." She seems to have been so earnest and so sincere that the company was convinced that something had occurred to her; hence, they were ready to say: "It is his angel." The Jews believed in the guardian angel, and they thought that Peter's "angel" had assumed the voice of Peter. (Matt. 18: 10.) These disciples perhaps thought that Peter's angel had come to make known to them something about Peter.

16 **But Peter continued knocking:**—The maiden had left the gate unopened and reported in excitement that Peter was at the gate; while she was gone Peter continued to knock for entrance, and when the gate was opened, "they saw him, and were amazed." It seems that all heard the knocking and several must have gone to the gate, and when it was opened, they were amazed to find Peter standing there. Surely they were not praying for Peter's delivery, or else they would not have been so amazed at an answer to their prayer; they were praying for him, but we do not know the petitions of their prayer.

17 **But he, beckoning unto them**—The company seems to have been as much excited as the maiden who first heard his voice; however, Peter motioned with his hand for them to keep silent. "Beckoning" with the hand is from the Greek "kataseisas tei cheiri," and literally means "shake down with the hand"; the speaker indicated by a downward movement of the hand his desire for silence; Peter was anxious for every precaution to be taken that no noise be made to attract attention to him. While the Lord had protected him from Herod by releasing him from prison, yet Peter does all that he can in righteousness to remain out of the hands of Herod. He told the little company "how the Lord had brought him forth out of the prison." It seems that James and others of the brethren were not present; there was no place in Jerusalem where all the disciples could meet. It is evident that this James was the Lord's brother, and he is now one of the leading

other place. 18 Now as soon as it was day, there was no small stir among
the soldiers, what was become of Peter. 19 And when Herod had sought for
him, and found him not, he examined the guards, and commanded that they
should be ²put to death. And he went down from Judaea to Caesarea, and
tarried there.

²Gr. *led away to death*

---

men of the church at Jerusalem. (Gal. 1: 19.) James is here recognized by Peter as a man of great influence. James was present
in Jerusalem when the question of circumcision was decided.
(Acts 15: 13.) After informing the group at the house of Mary
as to how he was released from prison and giving orders to report
his release to James and the other brethren, Peter departed "and
went to another place." We are not told where he went; he may
have left Jerusalem. Mary's house was too well known for him to
remain there if he would escape from Herod. Peter must use all
precaution and means of escape, so he may have left Jerusalem.
(Matt. 10: 23.)

18 **Now as soon as it was day,**—Early next morning the soldiers discovered that Peter had escaped, and "there was no small
stir among the soldiers." "Stir" is from the Greek "tarachos,"
and means "to agitate;" it is used only twice in the New Testament, here and in Acts 19: 23. Very likely the sixteen soldiers, or
"four quaternions" of soldiers were greatly disturbed over the escape of Peter; they were responsible for the prisoner with their
lives. (Acts 16: 27; 27: 42.)

19 **And when Herod had sought for him,**—The next morning, which was the day of execution, Herod sought for Peter, but
could not find him. We know not what report the soldiers gave to
Herod; Herod, following a custom or law in Rome, "examined the
guards, and commanded that they should be put to death."
"Examined" is from the Greek "anakrinas," which means "to sift
up and down, to question thoroughly." (Luke 23: 14; Acts 4: 9;
28: 18.) The soldiers were ordered to be put to death; this was
the ordinary Roman routine and not a proof of special cruelty on
the part of Herod Agrippa. After this Herod went from Judea to
Caesarea and remained there for a time; Herod, like the Roman
governor, though his principal residence was at Jerusalem, yet had
also a palace at Caesarea; he spent his time in either city as circumstances required.

18. DEATH OF HEROD AGRIPPA I
12: 20-23

20 Now he was highly displeased with them of Tyre and Sidon: and they came with one accord to him, and, having made Blastus the king's chamberlain their friend, they asked for peace, because their country was fed from the king's country. 21 And upon a set day Herod arrayed himself in royal apparel, and sat on the ³throne, and made an oration unto them. 22 And the

³Or, *judgment-seat*. See Mt. 27. 19

20 **Now he was highly displeased with them**—Herod was greatly "displeased with them of Tyre and Sidon." Tyre and Sidon were on the Mediterranean coast in Phoenicia; we are not informed here why he was so displeased with these cities. Tyre and Sidon were trading seaports, and much of the goods shipped at these ports passed through Galilee; Herod could divert a great deal of it to Caesarea or Joppa. Phoenicia was so populous that it depended on its neighbors for food, and much of that came from Galilee. Herod was in position to do much harm to these cities. However, agreement was reached with each other and they came to Herod. It seems that Tyre and Sidon had made "Blastus the king's chamberlain their friend"; hence, through him they asked for peace "because their country was fed from the king's country." The hostility between the Phoenicians and Herod was not an open war, but the representatives of Tyre and Sidon, together with Blastus, prevailed upon Herod to let the supplies be brought to these cities. Blastus had charge of his master's sleeping apartment and, to some extent, of his person. He had the duty of introducing visitors to him and remained in an adjoining room so that he would be ready when the king wanted him.

21 **And upon a set day Herod arrayed himself in royal apparel,**—The day was one appointed for holding a festival on which to make vows for Caesar's safety; Herod arrayed himself in his royal apparel and "sat on the throne, and made an oration unto them." We are told a vast multitude assembled to see the festival and games, and before these, the king, in all the pride of high state, appeared on the second day in a robe "made wholly of silver, and of a contexture truly wonderful, and came into the theatre early in the morning; at which time the silver of his garment, being illuminated by the fresh reflection of the sun's rays upon it, shone out

people shouted, *saying,* The voice of a god, and not of a man. 23 And immediately an angel of the Lord smote him, because he gave not God the glory: and he was eaten of worms, and gave up the ghost.

after a surprising manner, and was so resplendent as to spread a terror over those that looked intently upon him." (Josephus, Antiquities, 19: 8.)

22 And the people shouted,—When Herod made his speech, the people shouted his praise and said: "The voice of a god, and not of a man." They attributed to him the honor of a god, and their praise was tantamount to worship. The crowd repeated their flattering adulation to gain Herod's favor; their worship of him was pleasing to his vanity. This flattery was highly acceptable to Herod as he sat on his throne in the presence of a vast assembly of ambassadors who had come to him as a distinguished ruler with the special purpose of removing his displeasure toward the cities of Tyre and Sidon.

23 And immediately an angel of the Lord smote him,—Luke does not tell us that this angel was visible; his record does imply that Herod's death was a judgment from God; he had failed to give God praise; he received the honor which belonged to God; hence, his punishment was considered as divine judgment. "He was eaten of worms" and died. "Worm" is from the Greek "skolex," and was used of "intestinal worms"; there are several cases recorded in ancient history of such deaths. Josephus says that Herod Agrippa lingered for five days, and says that the rotting of his flesh produced worms; this is in harmony with Luke's description. It is recorded that Herod died in August, A.D. 44. Herod died a most revolting death, and much more shocking than a sudden stroke of death.

19. RETURN OF SAUL AND BARNABAS
12: 24, 25

24 But the word of God grew and multiplied.

24 But the word of God grew and multiplied.—This statement is given to show the contrast between what man was attempting to do to stop the growth of the church and what God was doing for it. "Grew and multiplied" is from the Greek "euxanen kai eplethuneto," and means "a very rapid increase;" persecutions

25 And Barnabas and Saul returned [4]from Jerusalem, when they had fulfilled their ministration, taking with them John whose surname was Mark.

[4]Many ancient authorities read *to Jerusalem*

did not stop the growth of the disciples, neither did it check the number of converts; in fact, the more bitter and severe the persecution the more rapidly did the church increase. The cause of Christ cannot be destroyed by persecution. The history of the church as revealed in Acts shows that the church multiplied more rapidly under persecution than at other times.

25 **And Barnabas and Saul returned**—Agabus had come from Jerusalem to Antioch and had prophesied of a "great famine over all the world" (Acts 11: 27, 28), and the disciples at Antioch determined to send relief to the Jewish brethren in Judea; they did this and sent their contribution by Barnabas and Saul; hence, Barnabas and Saul went to Jerusalem. We left them there as chapter 11 closed. When they had "fulfilled their ministration" they returned to Antioch and brought with them "John whose surname was Mark." Mark was the son of Mary into whose house Peter had gone after his escape from prison. Mark was a cousin of Barnabas. (Col. 4: 10.)

So far the historian, Luke, has narrated the facts of the beginning of the church on Pentecost; then its extension among the Jews and Samaritans. He has touched upon the extension of the church among the devout Gentiles, and the conversion of Saul of Tarsus. Some attention has been given to the persecution of the early church. Peter has been the central figure in the history of the spread of the church among the Jews; he was the apostle of the circumcision. Now the historian turns attention to the labors of Paul as the apostle to the uncircumcised or Gentiles; Antioch becomes the center from which the gospel is extended among the Gentiles "unto the uttermost part of the earth." (Acts 1: 8.)

PART TWO

HISTORY OF THE CHURCH: PAUL AS THE CHIEF ACTOR

SECTION ONE
PAUL'S FIRST MISSIONARY JOURNEY
13: 1 to 14: 28

1. PAUL AND BARNABAS IN CYPRUS
13: 1-12

1 Now there were at Antioch, in the church that was *there*, prophets and teachers, Barnabas, and Symeon that was called Niger, and Lucius of Cyrene, and Manean the foster-brother of Herod the tetrarch, and Saul. 2 And

---

1 **Now there were at Antioch, in the church**—"Antioch" was the capital of the Greek kingdom of Syria, and afterward became the residence of the Roman governor of the province. It was situated on the Orontes River, about sixteen miles from its mouth; its seaport was Seleucia. At Antioch was established the first church among the Gentiles, of which we have a record (Acts 11: 20, 21); here the disciples of Jesus were first called "Christians" (Acts 11: 26); here Paul exercised, so far as is distinctly recorded, his first systematic work (Acts 11: 22-26; 14: 26-28; 15: 35; 18: 22, 23); here he started on the beginning of his first missionary journey (Acts 13: 1-3); and to Antioch he came on his return from his missionary journey (Acts 14: 26). Paul began and ended his second missionary journey at this place. (Acts 15: 36; 18: 22.) Antioch was also the starting point of the third missionary journey, which was brought to an end by his imprisonment at Jerusalem and Caesarea.

prophets and teachers,—Some distinction is to be made between these terms; all prophets were teachers, but not all teachers were prophets; as all judges are lawyers, but not all lawyers are judges. A prophet had a higher or greater measure of the Holy Spirit. It seems that Barnabas, Symeon, and Lucius were prophets and Manaen and Saul were teachers—three prophets and two teachers. Barnabas heads the list (Acts 11: 22), and Saul comes last; Symeon is thought by some to be "Simon of Cyrene,"

as they ministered to the Lord, and fasted, the Holy Spirit said, Separate me
Barnabas and Saul for the work whereunto I have called them.   3 Then,
when they had fasted and prayed and laid their hands on them, they sent
them away.

---

who carried the cross for Jesus. (Mark 15: 21.) Lucius of Cyrene was probably one of the original evangelists. (Acts 11: 20.)
The name is another form of "Luke," but it is certainly not "Luke,
the beloved physician." Manaen shows how the gospel had
reached some of the higher classes, as he was foster brother of
Herod the tetrarch. This was Herod Antipas; "foster-brother" is
from the Greek "suntrophos," and means "one nourished with or
brought up with one." Saul is the last mentioned, but soon to be
placed first. (Verses 9-13.)

2 **And as thy ministered to the Lord,**—The work that
Barnabas and Saul were doing is called "ministered to the Lord";
hence, to preach the gospel to the unsaved and to edify the saints is
to minister to the Lord. (Matt. 25: 31-46.) While they were
fasting the Holy Spirit commanded the other "prophets and teachers" to "separate me Barnabas and Saul" for the work which they
had been called to do. Jewish Christians were keeping up the
Jewish fast. (Luke 18: 12.) We note that fasting was practiced
in the selection of elders of the church. (Acts 14: 23.) Fasting
was a voluntary act on the part of Christians. "Separate me" is
from the Greek "aphorisate de moi"; this separation was for a special purpose and should be obeyed at once. Barnabas and Saul had
both been called for this work sometime ago, but now they are to
be set apart in a special way to do in a larger sense the work for
which they were now prepared and to which they had been called.
Here Barnabas is mentioned before Saul again, showing that he is
still regarded as the leader. We do not know how the Holy Spirit
spoke to these, but very likely through one of the other prophets
and teachers.

3 **Then, when they had fasted and prayed**—It may be that
when they had finished the fast mentioned in verse 2 they prayed
for the Lord to guide them further, and to bless Barnabas and Saul
as they go into the field. Hands were laid upon them and they
were sent away. The subject of prayer, fasting, and laying on of
hands has provoked much discussion to but little profit. Some
have contended that such a procedure was essential to the "ordina-

4 So they, being sent forth by the Holy Spirit, went down to Seleucia; and from thence they sailed to Cyprus. 5 And when they were at Salamis, they proclaimed the word of God in the synagogues of the Jews: and they

---

tion" of elders, preachers, and evangelists; it has been claimed that such a procedure should be followed today. Others have claimed that hands were laid upon others by a superior, and to confer some spiritual gift; hence, when spiritual gifts ceased, this procedure ceased. Still others have contended that this was merely a solemn way of impressing upon one the serious and important duties that one should perform. We know what was done here, but we do not know that God intended it to be a precedent for inducting anyone into an office of the church or setting one apart to any special work.

4 **So they, being sent forth by the Holy Spirit,**—Luke again refers to the Holy Spirit as the authority for sending forth Barnabas and Saul to the preaching of the gospel; he does not intimate that there was any "church authority," or any ecclesiastical authority connected with this work. The Holy Spirit directed in this affair, and the church at Antioch is not even mentioned. Barnabas and Saul left Antioch and went about sixteen miles down the Orontes River to Seleucia, the seaport of Antioch; from Seleucia they "sailed to Cyprus," a distance of eighty to one hundred miles in a southwestern direction. Several reasons are assigned for their going to Cyprus; Barnabas was a native of this island and was acquainted with conditions there; again, it was on the way to Asia Minor by sea; then Paul was a native of Cilicia, just north of Cyprus; again, some of the disciples driven from Jerusalem by persecution had preached the gospel in Cyprus. (Acts 11: 19.)

5 **And when they were at Salamis,**—Salamis was on the eastern extremity of Cyprus, and the nearest port to Antioch. This seems to be the first place that they "proclaimed the word of God"; here they went into "the synagogues of the Jews," and preached the gospel. It was the invariable rule of Paul to preach to the Jews first and then to the Gentiles. (Rom. 1: 16.) There was a large number of Jews on this island; hence, there was a plurality of synagogues. They had as their attendant John Mark, the cousin of Barnabas, and the author of the Gospel according to Mark, and son of Mary of Jerusalem. (Acts 12: 12, 25.)

had also John as their attendant. 6 And when they had gone through the whole island unto Paphos, they found a certain ¹sorcerer, a false prophet, a Jew, whose name was Bar-Jesus; 7 who was with the proconsul, Sergius Paulus, a man of understanding. The same called unto him Barnabas and Saul, and sought to hear the word of God. 8 But Elymas the ¹sorcerer (for so is his name by interpretation) withstood them, seeking to turn aside the proconsul from the faith. 9 But Saul, who is also *called* Paul, filled with the

¹Gr. *Magus*: as in Mt. 2, 1, 7, 16

6-8 **And when they had gone through the whole island**—Cyprus is about one hundred fifty miles long and sixty miles wide, extending in length northeast and southwest. It is probable that they preached and taught at other places as they did at Salamis. Paphos was the capital of Cyprus, and was situated on the western coast of the island; the Roman governor lived here. They "found a certain sorcerer" living at Paphos; he was a Jew and a false prophet by the name of "Bar-Jesus." "Sorcerer" here comes from the Greek "magon," but does not always yield to this translation; it means one who is a magician. It is clear that he was ascribing his magical tricks to God and wanted his speech and prophetic statements to be taken at full face value. "Bar-Jesus" means the son of a man named Jesus. He is called "Elymas," which means "a wise man"; it is an Arabic name given to this Jew. He withstood Barnabas and Saul, attempting to turn aside "the proconsul from the faith." Elymas saw that his influence and power were gone if Sergius Paulus believed; hence, he sought with all of his influence to keep Sergius Paulus from believing what Barnabas and Saul preached.

9 **But Saul, who is also called Paul,**—The apostle to the Gentiles is called by two names. In the history of his life and work among the Jews he is called by his Jewish name Saul; but now that he is beginning his labors among the Roman Gentiles, his Roman name is used from this time on. Luke presents this new name in a remarkable way; the "also" does not mean that the name "Paul" was given now for the first time, but that he had always had it. Saul was a common name among the Jews; but now Luke uses "Paul" except when there is reference to his previous life. (Acts 22: 7; 26: 14.) Paul's work was chiefly among the Gentiles; he belonged to the tribe of Benjamin and wore the Jew-

Holy Spirit, fastened his eyes on him, 10 and said, O full of all guile and all villany, thou son of the devil, thou enemy of all righteousness, wilt thou not cease to pervert the right ways of the Lord? 11 And now, behold, the hand of the Lord is upon thee, and thou shalt be blind, not seeing the sun [2]for a season. And immediately there fell on him a mist and a darkness; and he

[2]Or, *until*

ish name of the first king of Israel. (Phil. 3: 5.) "Filled with the Holy Spirit" means that a fuller measure of the Holy Spirit came upon him in this case of emergency, so that he could with power rebuke the sorcerer miraculously. The Holy Spirit may also have enabled Paul to have an insight into the character of this wicked man. Some think that the phrase "fastened his eyes on him" shows that Paul's eyes were weak and that he had to strain himself to see Elymas; however, there is no evidence of this.

10 and said, O full of all guile and all villany,—Paul denounced Elymas with the severest terms that we have recorded in the New Testament. He used four of the strongest terms in denouncing the sorcerer: (1) "full of all guile"; (2) full of "all villany"; (3) "son of the devil"; (4) "enemy of all righteousness." "Guile" is from the Greek "delo," which means "to catch with bait"; hence Paul denounces Elymas as a trickster. "Villany" comes from "rhaidiourgias," and means "one who does something adroitly and with ease"; with deadly accuracy Paul pictured this deceiver. "Son of the devil" is from the Greek "diabolou," and means "a slanderer like the devil." (John 8: 44.) It is strange that Elymas, or Bar-Jesus, "son of Jesus," should be more appropriately called "son of the devil." "Enemy of all righteousness" means personal enemy to all justice, and seems to sum up the meaning of the other terms. Paul emphatically and interrogatively commanded him to cease perverting "the right ways of the Lord." Elymas, the false prophet, was making the right ways of the Lord crooked.

11 And now, behold, the hand of the Lord is upon thee,— Not only did Paul denounce Elymas in the most scathing terms, but he cursed him with blindness for a time; this curse was by "the hand of the Lord." He sought someone to guide him. The blindness was to be "for a season" (Luke 4: 13), if it should please God to restore his sight. We know not how long the sorcerer re-

went about seeking some to lead him by the hand. 12 Then the proconsul,
when he saw what was done, believed, being astonished at the teaching of the
Lord.

---

mained blind, neither do we know whether he ever repented.
Elymas should have been brought to repentance, since he should
know that his blindness was brought upon him for perverting the
gospel which Paul preached. "The hand of the Lord" frequently
meant a condemnation. (Ex. 9: 3; Judges 2: 15.)

12 **Then the pronconsul, when he saw**—When the proconsul
saw Elymas smitten with blindness he believed what Paul
preached; he saw that the Lord was with Paul and enabled him to
perform this miracle; hence, he was with him in what he was
teaching. Very likely the pronconsul was perplexed by the teaching of Barnabas and Paul and that of Elymas, but this miracle
helped him to see which taught the truth. He was astonished at
the manner of teaching and the confirmation of the teaching by this
miracle.

2. PAUL AND BARNABAS IN PERGA AND ANTIOCH IN PISIDIA
13: 13, 14

13 Now Paul and his company set sail from Paphos, and came to Perga
in Pamphylia: and John departed from them and returned to Jerusalem. 14
But they, passing through from Perga, came to Antioch of Pisidia; and they

---

13 **Now Paul and his company**—Up to this point Luke has
"Barnabas and Saul," but from now on it is "Paul and Barnabas";
frequently the events cluster around just Paul. Paul is mentioned
first with three exceptions (Acts 14: 12; 15: 12, 25); so completely does Paul get the attention from Luke that Barnabas and
Mark are called "his company." They "set sail from Paphos, and
came to Perga in Pamphylia." Paphos was on the west end of Cyprus, and they sailed in a northwestern direction to Perga, a town
on the mainland. Perga was about one hundred fifty miles from
Paphos. Mark, for some cause, left Paul and Barnabas at Perga
and returned to Jerusalem. So far Paul and Barnabas have visited
Cyprus, the native land of Barnabas, and close to Cilicia, the
homeland of Paul.

14 **But they, passing through from Perga,**—Paul and Barn-
bas did not remain long in Perga; Luke does not record that they

went into the synagogue on the sabbath day and sat down. 15 And after the

---

even preached the gospel in Perga on this visit, yet Perga was the capital of Pamphylia. Leaving Perga they traveled north about a hundred miles to "Antioch of Pisidia." Modern scholars have placed this Antioch in Phrygia, but Luke locates it in Pisidia. This Antioch was at the foot of the Taurus Mountains; it was reached by a difficult road over the mountains infested by robbers; here they found a synagogue and attended services there on the Sabbath. The Jews who had not become Christians still met in their synagogues on the Sabbath. When Paul and Barnabas entered the synagogue they "sat down" as any worshiper would. It would seem that there was but one synagogue of the Jews in Antioch, as "they went into the synagogue on the sabbath."

3. PAUL'S FIRST RECORDED SERMON
13: 15-43

reading of the law and the prophets the rulers of the synagogue sent unto them, saying, Brethren, if ye have any word of exhortation for the people,

---

15 **And after the reading of the law and the prophets**—The "synagogue," in its derivation, means "congregation"; it came into use during the exile in Babylon; however, some think that it had a much earlier origin. It is true that it reached its development after the return from Babylonian captivity. Wherever there were as many as ten Jews in a town or a city, a synagogue was built. Among the items of worship was "the reading of the law and the prophets." The law was first read in the synagogue till 163 B.C., when Antiochus Epiphanes prohibited it; then the reading of the prophets was substituted for the reading of the law. However, the Maccabees restored the reading of the law, but the reading of the prophets was continued. "The rulers of the synagogue" had the responsibility of selecting the readers and the speakers for the service. (Mark 5: 22, 35-38; Luke 8: 49; 13: 14; Acts 18: 8, 17.) After the usual reading, according to custom, the ruler of the synagogue called on anyone who was known to be competent to teach to interpret the word or make a religious address to the congregation. It may be that this ruler knew that Paul and Barnabas were men

say on. 16 And Paul stood up, and beckoning with the hand said,
Men of Israel, and ye that fear God, hearken: 17 The God of this people
Israel chose our fathers, and exalted the people when they sojourned in the
land of Egypt, and with a high arm led he them forth out of it. 18
And for about the time of forty years [a]as a nursing-father bare he

---

[a]Many ancient authorities read *suffered he their manners in the wilderness.* See
Deut. 9. 7

---

giving their lives to teaching, and coming from Jerusalem they
would receive a special invitation. So the ruler very courteously
invited them to speak. Paul took advantage of the occasion and
made the address which follows.

16 **And Paul stood up,**—It was the custom of the Jews to sit
while speaking (Luke 4: 20), but the Greeks and Romans stood
while speaking (Acts 17: 22). It is generally understood that
Paul on this occasion arose from his seat and stepped upon the
platform and then took his seat as he began to speak; or he may
have followed the Roman custom and stood during his entire address. Paul is the recognized leader now and the more gifted
speaker (Acts 14: 12) so that he responds to the invitation of the
ruler. Paul "beckoning with the hand" to get the attention of the
audience, and to begin in a formal way his address. This was a
dramatic gesture for quiet and order. (Acts 12: 17; 21: 40.)
After his gesture for silence Paul addressed them as "men of Israel" who feared God. This was a very dignified and solemn way
of beginning this most important address to the worshipers in the
synagogue at this hour.

17 **The God of this people Israel**—Here we have Paul's first
recorded address; he begins as did Stephen (Acts 7: 2-53) with
the history of the Jewish race and reciting many events in their
history. It is probable that Paul was present and heard Stephen's
speech and remembered it; then Paul was familiar with the history
of his own race. God had chosen Abraham, the father of the Jewish race, and had multiplied his seed in Egypt until they became a
mighty race there; he then by the hand of Moses or "with a high
arm led he them forth" out of Egypt. The phrase, "chose our fathers," refers to the call of Abraham and Isaac and Jacob.

18 **And for about the time of forty years**—The children of Israel were led out of Egyptian bondage, across the Red Sea, into

them in the wilderness. 19 And when he had destroyed seven nations in the
land of Canaan, he gave *them* their land for an inheritance, for about four
hundred and fifty years: 20 and after these things he gave *them* judges until

the wilderness and down to Mount Sinai; here the law was given
to them; they built the tabernacle and sojourned in their wanderings forty years in the wilderness. God fed them with the manna
(Ex. 16: 35; Duet. 8: 16), and cared for them in the wilderness
"as a nursing-father." God endured, bore with them continually
during the forty years as a father bears with a wayward son, using
every loving means to reclaim him and prepare him for a noble and
useful life.

19, 20 **And when he had destroyed seven nations**—After the
sojourn of forty years in the wilderness, and after the death of
Moses, Joshua led the children of Israel across the Jordan into the
land of Canaan. This land had been promised to Abraham.
(Gen. 12: 7; 13: 15; 15: 18; Gal. 3: 16.) Canaan was inhabited
by seven nations—Hittites, Girgashites, Amorites, Canaanites, Per-
izzites, Hivites, and Jebusites. (Deut. 7: 1.) These seven nations were mightier than the children of Israel, yet God gave "their
land for an inheritance" to the seed of Abraham. "For about four
hundred and fifty years" is an expression that has caused much
trouble with commentators. It is difficult to harmonize the chronological dates. It is not clear when the four hundred fifty years
begin or when they end; this complicates the interpretation of the
"four hundred and fifty years." In 1 Kings 6: 1 it is stated that
Solomon began building the temple in the four hundred eightieth
year after the exodus from Egypt. Paul here reckons the time as
follows: wanderings in the wilderness (verse 18), forty years;
under the judges (verse 20), four hundred fifty years; reign of
Saul (verse 21), forty years; total, five hundred fifty years. To
this total we must add the entire reign of David (forty years) and
the first three years of the reign of Solomon to get to the time
when the building of the temple was begun. Therefore, adding
these forty-three years, the entire period of time amounts to five
hundred seventy-three years. There is a discrepancy between the
five hundred seventy-three years based on Paul's reckoning and
the four hundred eighty years referred to in Kings—a difference of
ninety-three years. However, this is accounted for by the fact that

Samuel the prophet. 21 And afterward they asked for a king: and God gave
unto them Saul the son of Kish, a man of the tribe of Benjamin, for the
space of forty years. 22 And when he had removed him, he raised up David
to be their king; to whom also he bare witness and said, ⁴I have found David
the son of Jesse, a man after my heart, who shall do all my ⁵will. 23 Of this
man's seed hath God according to promise brought unto Israel a Saviour,
Jesus; 24 when John had first preached ⁶before his coming the baptism of repentance to all the people of Israel. 25 And as John was fulfilling his

⁴1 S. 13. 14; Ps. 89. 20
⁵Gr. *wills*
⁶Gr. *before the face of his entering in*

ninety-three years must be subtracted, as there are ninety-three
blank years as recorded in the book of Judges. In Num. 6: 12
the Nazirite lost time if he did not comply with the law, so Israel
when not ruled by the judges was ruled by foreign nations.
(Judges 3: 8, 14; 4: 3; 6: 1; 13: 1.)   This amounts to ninety-
three years, which makes the calculation correspond to the figures
as given by other writers.

21 **And afterward they asked for a king:**—The people rebelled against God's order of government and demanded a king;
so God gave them Saul of the tribe of Benjamin who reigned forty
years. The Old Testament does not state the length of Saul's reign.
It is a striking coincidence that the speaker Saul or Paul refers to
the ancient Saul as belonging to the tribe of Benjamin, his own
tribe.

22 **And when he had removed him,**—Saul was killed in battle
(1 Sam. 31: 4), or he fell upon his own sword and died; Jehovah
had rejected Saul and had made plans for another to take his place
(1 Sam. 15: 23).   David, of the tribe of Judah, was next selected
to take Saul's place; here he is described as a man after God's own
heart. (1 Sam. 13: 14; Psalm 89: 20.)   The quotations given by
Paul here are not literal, but the sense of the text is quoted; Paul
quotes in such a way that the Bible explains itself, and David is
seen to be a type of Christ.

23, 24 **Of this man's seed hath God**—The Messiah was to
come from the descendants of David according to the promise.
The promise is repeated frequently in Old Testament scripture.
(2 Sam. 7: 12; Psalm 132: 11; Isa. 11: 1, 10; Jer. 23: 5, 6; Zech.
3: 8.)   Paul tells his audience that God has fulfilled this promise
to David, and that the Messiah has come who was a Savior, and
that John was the first to preach that the kingdom of heaven was

course, he said, What suppose ye that I am? I am not *he*. But behold, there cometh one after me the shoes of whose feet I am not worthy to unloose! 26 Brethren, children of the stock of Abraham, and those among you that fear God, to us is the word of this salvation sent forth. 27 For they that dwell in Jerusalem, and their rulers, because they knew him not, nor the voices of the prophets which are read every sabbath, fulfilled *them* by con-

---

at hand. John "first preached before his coming the baptism of repentance to all the people of Israel." (Mark 1: 4; Luke 3: 3.) Paul simply shows here that John had come and had made ready the people prepared for the Lord; that John was the messenger who came before the Lord.

25 **And as John was fulfilling his course,**—Some thought that John was the Messiah, but John corrected their false conception and pointed them to Jesus; he said that he was not even worthy to unloose the shoes of the Messiah. The people thought that John was a prophet and a great character, but John declares that the Christ was so much greater than he as the master is greater than the servant that did the most menial service.

26 **Brethren, children of the stock of Abraham,**—All Jews gloried in the fact that they were descendants of Abraham. Paul addresses these Jews and honors them as among those who feared God. Paul not only addressed those who were of the lineage of Abraham, but all who "among you that fear God"; that is, to all proselytes and strangers with you, if they fear God, "the word of this salvation" is "sent forth." Jesus used similar language in speaking to the woman at the well. (John 4: 22.) Here Paul presents Jesus to them as the fulfillment of the prophecies and as the Savior of the world.

27 **For they that dwell in Jerusalem,**—Paul here in a very tactful way presents the crucifixion of Jesus. He includes that portion of the Jewish race that dwelt in Jerusalem "and their rulers" as the ones who had crucified Jesus; he very delicately states that they did it because they did not know Jesus, "nor the voices of the prophets which are read every sabbath." They fulfilled the prophecies in condemning Jesus. The implication is that these Jews at Jerusalem and their rulers would not have condemned him had they known him. Peter had said that it was done in ignorance. (Acts 3: 17.) Later, Paul wrote to Timothy that his persecution was done in ignorance, and that he obtained forgiveness

demning *him.* 28 And though they found no cause of death *in him,* yet asked they of Pilate that he should be slain. 29 And when they had fulfilled all things that were written of him, they took him down from the tree, and laid him in a tomb. 30 But God raised him from the dead: 31 and he was seen

because he was ignorant of what he was doing. (1 Tim. 1: 13.) The ignorance of the people and rulers mitigated the degree of their guilt, but it did not remove it; the fact still remains that they could have known that Jesus was the Messiah. Hence, it was willing ignorance and prejudice that caused them to condemn Jesus. "The voices of the prophets" is used here because the "voices" were heard as they were read aloud each Sabbath in the synagogue. In their ignorance they condemned Jesus and fulfilled the prophecies concerning his sufferings.

28 **And though they found no cause of death**—The Sanhedrin charged Jesus with blasphemy, but could not prove it. (Matt. 26: 65; 27: 24; Luke 23: 22.) At the time that Paul was speaking no part of the New Testament was written, but Paul knew that Jesus was innocent. Although the Jews and rulers could not prove their charges against Jesus, and also Pilate knew that their charges were not true, "yet asked they of Pilate that he should be slain." This was the most serious charge that Paul had made; he proceeds without fear to press the claims of Jesus as the Messiah and Savior of the world. Paul's words here are equivalent to a charge of causeless murder against the leaders of Judaism. This ought to have smitten with horror all who heard for the first time these charges. Pilate yielded to the clamor of the Jews and gave his consent for Jesus to be crucified. (Luke 23: 14, 22-24.)

29 **And when they had fulfilled all things**—Paul follows closely the details of the crucifixion of Jesus. When the Jews and Roman authorities had done all that they could to Jesus, they had fulfilled the prophecies. Joseph of Arimathea and Nicodemus took the body of Jesus from the cross and buried it in Joseph's new tomb. (Matt. 27: 57-60; John 19: 38, 39.) However, Paul gives the outline of the course followed, and may have had in mind that the Jews asked Pilate to have the bones of Jesus broken that his body should not remain on the cross during the Sabbath. (John 19: 31.) Paul does not distinguish the details here. The cross is spoken of as "the tree"; the original Greek is "xulou," and means

for many days of them that came up with him from Galilee to Jerusalem, who are now his witnesses unto the people. 32 And we bring you good tidings of the promise made unto the fathers, 33 that God hath fulfilled the same unto our children, in that he raised up Jesus; as also it is written in the second psalm, ¹Thou art my Son, this day have I begotten thee. 34 And as concerning that he raised him up from the dead, now no more to return to

¹Ps. 2. 7

---

not only "tree," but "wood." (Acts 5: 30; 10: 39; Gal. 3: 13.)

30, 31 **But God raised him from the dead:**—Again what man did to Jesus is brought in contrast with what God did for him; man crucified him, but God "raised him from the dead." Jesus was seen "for many days" after he was raised from the dead before he ascended back to God. "For many days" means forty days in all. (Acts 1: 3.) He was seen by many as Paul enumerates in 1 Cor. 15: 5-8. Those who had seen Jesus after his resurrection were made witnesses for him. The apostles were nearly all from Galilee; hence, they had followed Jesus from Galilee to Jerusalem and they were made his witnesses. This is the point that Peter used in his argument with such powerful effect on the day of Pentecost, and at another time. (Acts 2: 32; 3: 15.) The special work of the apostles was to witness for Christ. (Acts 1: 8, 22; 2: 32; 3: 15; 5: 32; 10: 41.) Paul enforces his argument by making the resurrection a proof that Jesus is the Son of God. (Rom. 1: 4; 1 Cor. 15: 3-8.)

32, 33 **And we bring you good tidings of the promise**—Paul here includes Barnabas as bringing to them the gospel which was promised to the fathers; God had fulfilled his promise in raising up Jesus from the dead. This promise was not only made to David, but was also made by Isaiah. (Isa. 55: 3.) Paul further quotes from Psalm 16: 10, which is a repetition of the promise. The promise received its fulfillment by the resurrection of Jesus; not his being raised up as the seed of David, but his being raised from the dead. "Thou art my Son" is the same as acknowledging himself as the Father; hence, God is his Father; he is the Son of God. The quotation which is here given not only refers to the birth of Jesus, but to his entire ministry on earth.

34 **And as concerning that he raised him up**—The resurrection of Jesus was distinguished from all other instances which had

corruption, he hath spoken on this wise, [2]I will give you the holy and sure *blessings* of David. 35 Because he saith also in another *psalm,* [3]Thou wilt not give thy Holy One to see corruption. 36 For David, after he had [4]in his own generation served the counsel of God, fell asleep, and was laid unto his fathers, and saw corruption: 37 but he whom God raised up [5]saw no corrup-

[2]Is. 55. 3
[3]Ps. 16. 10
[4]Or, *served his own generation by the counsel of God, fell asleep.* Or, *served his own generation, fell asleep by the counsel of God*

before taken place in that he was henceforward beyond the power of death. Lazarus and others who had been raised from the dead died again and returned to corruption, but not so with Jesus. He was raised to see corruption no more; hence, he was the first fruits of the resurrection; the first fruits of them that slept. (Rom. 6: 9: 1 Cor. 15: 20, 23.) "I will give you the holy and sure blessings of David" is a quotation from Isa. 55: 3. This means that they were promised the mercies which had been promised to David. The chief point in the promises was the coming of the Savior through David's posterity, and this Savior, who was to be the spiritual king of the Lord's people, was to have an uninterrupted dominion. (Luke 1: 33.) In order that this dominion should be an unbroken, uninterrupted one, it was necessary that when Jesus was raised up from the dead his resurrection should be an entire and final triumph over death; death must have no more power over him. This quotation from Isaiah shows that God had promised to David that the Messiah would come through his descendants, and that he would conquer death; hence, when Jesus was raised from the dead, ascended to heaven, entirely and forever beyond the reach of death, he began his reign over his kingdom, and is now upon David's throne.

35-37 **Because he saith also in another psalm,**—Again Paul quotes from the Psalms; this time Psalm 16: 10. Paul makes an application of this to Christ. He reasoned and showed that it could not apply to David, for David had lived his life and "served the counsel of God," and died and was buried, and his flesh decayed or saw corruption, so this could not apply to David. "But he whom God raised up saw no corruption." Paul quoted some of the Psalm that Peter used on the day of Pentecost. (Acts 2: 25-31.) Paul argued as Peter did that David died and underwent corruption, but Christ was raised and saw no corruption; hence,

tion. 38 Be it known unto you therefore, brethren, that through this man is proclaimed unto you remission of sins: 39 and by him every one that believeth is justified from all things, from which ye could not be justified by the law of Moses. 40 Beware therefore, lest that come upon you which is spoken in the prophets: 41 ⁵Behold, ye despisers, and wonder, and ⁶perish;

For I work a work in your days,

A work which ye shall in no wise believe, if one declare it unto you.

---

⁵Hab. 1. 5
⁶Or, *vanish away.* Jas. 4. 14

---

these prophecies were fulfilled in Christ. Paul had now presented evidence that Jesus was the Messiah; he had quoted and interwoven in his speech the prophecies that pertained to the Christ and showed their fulfillment in him. The scriptures had been fulfilled in the persecution, trials, crucifixion, burial, resurrection, and ascension of Jesus.

38, 39 **Be it known unto you therefore,**—Again Paul reasoned as did Peter on Pentecost. (Acts 2: 36.) This very man whom the Jews had crucified and whom God had raised from the dead was the one that Paul preached as the Savior of man, and the one through whom they could have remission of sins. "Remission of sins" is from the Greek "aphesis hamartion," and is used frequently by Luke. The keynote of Paul's message was the remission of sins through Christ; this was the message that Peter preached on Pentecost, and on other occasions. (Acts 2: 38; 5: 31; 10: 43.) This salvation came through Jesus Christ, but they must believe on him, for it is through faith in him that all are to be justified. Paul not only shows that Jesus is the Messiah, and Son of God, and that salvation is through him, but he further shows that the law of Moses was too weak to give redemption; they could not be justified by the law of Moses from their sins; hence, the need of a Savior. The law of Moses required perfect obedience; the sacrifices under the law did not justify the disobedience. "The righteous shall live by his faith." (Hab. 2: 4.) This faith is open to all, and whosoever believeth in Jesus shall be justified.

40, 41 **Beware therefore, lest that come upon you**—After proving that Jesus was the Christ, the Son of God, the Savior of men, Paul concludes his address with a solemn warning based upon the predictions of the prophets. The only way that they

42 And as they went out, they besought that these words might be spoken
to them the next sabbath. 3 Now when the synagogue broke up, many of
the Jews and of the devout proselytes followed Paul and Barnabas; who,
speaking to them, urged them to continue in the grace of God.

could escape the condemnation pronounced by the prophets was to
accept Christ. The general warnings contained in that part of the
Old Testament are called "the prophets"; the fearful condemnation
predicted by the prophets were as sure to be fulfilled on those who
rejected Christ as they were fulfilled in the coming of Christ. God's
predictions of punishment and condemnation are as sure to be fulfilled as his predictions of blessings. Whatever Jehovah has
predicted through his prophets will be fulfilled. While Paul uses
"prophets" in the plural, he cites a quotation from only one.
(Hab. 1: 5.) The sin which he warned Israel against was the deliberate rejection of the long-promised Messiah; and the punishment in which the despisers of Jesus would perish was carried out
to its bitter end only a few years after Paul's words were spoken in
the synagogue at Antioch; the destruction of Jerusalem and the
complete disintegration of the Jewish nation took place about A.D.
70.

42 **And as they went out,**—They listened intently to Paul's
address; this was the first time that they had heard of the Christ.
It seems that they were not ready to accept him, neither were they
ready to reject him; hence, they asked that Paul and Barnabas
speak to them again on the same subject the next Sabbath.
Perhaps the invitation came from the rulers of the synagogue.

43 **Now when the synagogue broke up,**—As the people dispersed from the synagogue "many of the Jews and of the devout
proselytes followed Paul and Barnabas." Two classes are mentioned here—Jews and "devout proselytes." "Devout proselytes"
means "worshiping proselytes," as described in verses 16 and 25,
as "ye that fear God." "Proselyte" is from "proseluton," and here
is understood to mean "the uncircumcised Gentiles" who attended
the synagogue worship; however, the Greek "proselutoi" usually
means those who had become circumcised, or "proselytes of righteousness"; it is also used to apply to "proselytes of the gate" who
had not yet become circumcised; it may have this meaning here.

"Proselutoi" occurs only four times in the New Testament, here and in Matt. 23: 15; Acts 2: 10; 6: 5. Paul and Barnabas encouraged those who followed them to further study these matters and exhorted them urgently "to continue in the grace of God." It seems from these words that some were inclined to believe them, possibly may have believed. Barnabas means "Son of exhortation," and he was given this name, it seems, because of his special gift along this line. (Acts 4: 36, 37.) When he came to Antioch the first time he exhorted the church there. (Acts 11: 23.)

Summing up the points emphasized in Paul's first recorded address, it is as follows:

Subject: JESUS IS THE MESSIAH

I. Proof from History.
   1. God chose and exalted a people (verse 17).
   2. He delivered them from Egypt (verse 17).
   3. He gave them a country (verses 18, 19).
   4. He provided judges for them (verse 20).
   5. At their request he gave them a king (verse 21).
   6. Removed Saul and raised up David (verse 22).
   7. From David's seed came Jesus (verse 23).

II. Proved Jesus to Be a Deliverer.
   1. By the testimony of John (verses 24, 25).
   2. By his rejection, which prophecy foretold (verses 26-29).
   3. By his resurrection, a fact attested.
     a. By eyewitnesses (verses 30-32).
     b. By scriptures (verses 33-37).

III. His Appeal and Warning.
   1. Encouragement to believe (verses 38, 39).
   2. Warnings from the prophets (verses 40, 41).

4. THE SECOND SPEECH AT ANTIOCH
13: 44-52

44 And the next sabbath almost the whole city was gathered together to

---

44 **And the next sabbath almost the whole city**—It is very likely that Paul and Barnabas spent a busy week in Antioch of

hear the word of [7]God. 45 But when the Jews saw the multitudes, they were filled with jealousy, and contradicted the things which were spoken by

---

[7]Many ancient authorities read *the Lord*

Pisidia and preached Christ to everyone as opportunity presented itself. This would create an interest in the appointment that he had for the following Sabbath. (The Jews still met on the Sabbath in their synagogues.) So the following Sabbath a very large attendance assembled, "almost the whole city was gathered together to hear the word of God." It is not probable that "almost the whole city" could assemble in the synagogue, but Paul could speak to the multitude from the synagogue and Barnabas could speak to those who assembled and could not gain entrance to the synagogue. Not only Jews and proselytes, but heathens or Gentiles assembled; even those who were not accustomed to meeting with the Jews came together "to hear the word of God." This shows that Paul and Barnabas during the week had not only preached the gospel to the Jews and "devout proselytes," but they had also preached to Gentiles.

45 **But when the Jews saw the multitudes,**—When the Jews saw this mixed multitude, "they were filled with jealousy"; they were not willing to share the blessings and salvation of the God of Abraham with the Gentiles; no such crowds came to the synagogue when they were speakers; hence, they were jealous of these new preachers from Antioch and Jerusalem. "Jealousy" is from the Greek "zelou," which means "to boil"; so these rabbis boiled with envy when they saw the crowds gathered to hear Paul and Barnabas. Jealousy must find an outlet, so they "contradicted" what Paul and Barnabas preached. "Contradicted" is from the Greek "antelegon," and means "to speak against, to say a word in opposition to"; they interrupted the service and publicly opposed Paul and Barnabas. They "blasphemed." "Blasphemed" is from the Greek "blasphemountes," and means "to speak against"; Paul and Barnabas spoke by inspiration, and when these Jews contradicted what they preached, they were contradicting the Holy Spirit; they were blaspheming God. This shows the extreme to which one will go when filled with envy and jealousy. Here again the prophecies were being fulfilled. (Deut. 32: 21; Rom. 10: 19.)

Paul, and [8]blasphemed. 46 And Paul and Barnabas spake out boldly, and said, It was necessary that the word of God should first be spoken to you. Seeing ye thrust it from you, and judge yourselves unworthy of eternal life, lo, we turn to the Gentiles. 47 For so hath the Lord commanded us, *saying,* [9]I have set thee for a light of the Gentiles. That thou shouldst be for salvation unto the uttermost part of the earth.

[8]Or, *railed*
[9]Is. 49. 6

It frequently occurs that those who begin by contradicting end by blaspheming.

46 **And Paul and Barnabas spake out boldly,**—Paul is not the only speaker here, as Barnabas is also speaking; they accepted the challenge of the rabbis; they would leave their synagogue, but not without a word of explanation; hence, they said: "It was necessary that the word of God should first be spoken to you." (See Rom. 1: 16.) The effect of this rejection of the preaching of the gospel by the Jews was to give occasion to preach to the Gentiles. "Now if their fall is the riches of the world, and their loss the riches of the Gentiles" (Rom. 11: 12), the Gentiles should now rejoice in the hearing of the gospel. They judged themselves unworthy of eternal life by rejecting the gospel. They thrust it from them; they blasphemed Paul and Barnabas who brought to them the word of God; by so doing they judged themselves "unworthy of eternal life." They had taken a definite stand against the gospel and judged themselves not worthy of the love of God and the salvation in Christ; hence, Paul and Barnabas turned to the Gentiles.

47 **For so hath the Lord commanded us,**—In declaring that he would "turn to the Gentiles," Paul quoted Isa. 49: 6, showing that he was fulfilling the prophecy in turning to the Gentiles with the gospel. Paul used their own prophets and scriptures to justify his preaching the gospel to the Gentiles. He also showed that the Messiah was not to be confined in his redemption of man to the Jews. The aged Simeon who, though waiting for the "consolation of Israel," yet saluted the rising of the same glorious light over the darkened Gentile land. (Luke 2: 25-32.) This also is in keeping with the program that Jesus had given his disciples just before he made his ascension; they were to be his witnesses "unto the uttermost part of the earth." (Acts 1: 8.)

48 And as the Gentiles heard this, they were glad, and glorified the word of
⁷God: and as many as were ordained to eternal life believed.   49 And the

---

48 **And as the Gentiles heard this,**—When the Gentiles heard
that they were included, even in the Jewish prophecies, and understood that the Savior of the world had come, "they were glad, and
glorified the word of God." They rejoiced in the opportunity that
they had for believing in the Christ. "And as many as were ordained to eternal life believed"; the Greek is "hosoi esan tetagmenoi eis zoen anionion." The word "tetagmenoi," or "ordained," is
considered by many as not being the best translation.
"Appointed" seems to be a better translation; hence, it would
mean that as many as were "appointed" to eternal life believed.
This translation has been interpreted to mean those who were foreordained to eternal life believed. If this be true, then all the rest
were doomed to eternal destruction, and there was no use for Paul
to preach the gospel to them. The root in the Greek is "tasso,"
and its primary meaning is "to set in order, to place in a certain
order." The word occurs eight times in the New Testament, and
is translated "ordained" only in this instance. Some have suggested that it is a better translation to say that as many as were
disposed to eternal life believed. Still another translation is that
"as many as were determined for eternal life believed." All who
believe in Christ, repent of their sins, and are baptized into him are
"ordained," "diposed," "determined," or "destined" to eternal life.
It does not matter which translation one accepts, the meaning is
that those who accept Christ may enjoy redemption in him.
Accepting Christ is an act of one's own will.

49 **And the word of the Lord was spread abroad**—Paul and
Barnabas met with great success in preaching the gospel to the
Gentiles. Although the Jews rejected it here, yet many of the
Gentiles accepted it. This indicates that Paul and Barnabas remained some time in the regions of Antioch; Antioch in Pisidia
would thus naturally become a center for preaching the gospel in
this section. The gospel spread beyond the town, and in the
neighboring villages the citizens had an opportunity to hear the
gospel and be saved.

word of the Lord was spread abroad throughout all the region, 50 But the Jews urged on the devout women of honorable estate, and the chief men of the city, and stirred up a persecution against Paul and Barnabas, and cast them out of their borders. 51 But they shook off the dust of their feet against them, and came unto Iconium. 52 And the disciples were filled with joy and with the Holy Spirit.

50 **But the Jews urged on the devout women**—"The Jews" did not remain idle; their persecuting zeal led them to enlist the help of "the devout women of honorable estate." It seems that the Jews were not so numerous in Antioch as they had only one synagogue, but they had influence with people of prominence. "The devout women of honorable estate" means the women among the proselytes of high station; the Jews influenced these Gentile women who had been worshiping according to the law of Moses. (Acts 17: 4.) The prominence of women in public life here at Antioch is in accord with what is known of conditions in the cities of Asia Minor. "The chief men of the city" are probably the officials or other prominent men in the city. These Jews were tactful enough to influence these men through the women who were proselytes of distinction. Now Paul and Barnabas and the young converts have three classes of enemies—the rulers of the Jews with other Jews, "the devout women of honorable estate," and "the chief men of the city." Paul refers to this persecution in his second letter to Timothy. (2 Tim. 3: 11.) They "cast them out of their borders." The persecution may have been a tumultuous outbreak.

51 **But they shook off the dust of their feet**—Paul and Barnabas as they left followed the command which Jesus gave to his disciples when he sent them out on their limited commission. (Luke 9: 5.) This was a tendency against those who received not the truth. When they left Antioch they traveled in a southeast direction, about sixty miles to Iconium. Iconium was a large city in Lycaonia.

52 **And the disciples were filled with joy**—Paul and Barnabas and all the Gentile Christians in Antioch of Pisidia rejoiced in the salvation in Christ. The persecution of the Jews had the opposite effect to that which they intended, for the disciples were "filled with joy and with the Holy Spirit"; this occurred frequently in the

early days of the church. (Acts 4: 8, 31; 9: 17; 13: 9.) The
blood of the martyrs is still the seed of the kingdom.

5. PAUL AND BARNABAS AT ICONIUM
14: 1-7

1 And it came to pass in Iconium that they entered together into the synagogue of the Jews, and so spake that a great multitude both of Jews and of
Greeks believed. 2 But the Jews that were disobedient stirred up the souls
of the Gentiles, and made them evil affected against the brethren. 3 Long

1 **And it came to pass in Iconium**—Paul and Barnabas were
successful in preaching the gospel in Iconium; when they arrived
there Paul and Barnabas both "together" went into the synagogue
of the Jews. They took advantage of the assembling of the Jews
to preach the gospel to them. As has been indicated Paul first
went to the Jews with the gospel and then to the Gentiles. (Rom.
1: 16.) Paul had an advantage in that he knew the scriptures and
was speaking by the Holy Spirit. By going into the synagogue he
would not only reach the Jews, but would also reach the pious
"proselytes," and through them could contact other Gentiles. It is
very likely that they went into the synagogue often, and "so spake"
the word of God that "a great multitude both of Jews and of
Greeks believed." They "so spake" the truth in Christ; that is,
spoke with such humility and conviction, with such earnestness
and interest, that "a great multitude" of Jews and "Greeks" were
converted. "Greeks" here may include both proselyte Greeks and
heathen Greeks; it may include all others except Jews.

2 **But the Jews that were disobedient**—The Jews who disbelieved were the "disobedient" Jews who "stirred up the souls of
the Gentiles" against Paul and Barnabas. To disbelieve is to diso-
bey, and to believe usually means to obey. "Disobedient" comes
from the Greek "apeithesantes," and means "to be unwilling to be
persuaded," or to withhold belief, and then also to withhold obedience; they refused to allow themselves to be persuaded by the
truth preached by Paul and Barnabas. They used their influence
on the Gentiles against Paul and Barnabas; through these disbelieving and disobedient Jews the Gentiles were disposed not to
hear the gospel, but to help persecute the preachers of the gospel.

time therefore they tarried *there* speaking boldly in the Lord, who bare witness unto the word of his grace, granting signs and wonders to be done by their hands. 4 But the multitude of the city was divided; and part held with the Jews, and part with the apostles. 5 And when there was made an onset

---

3 **Long time therefore they tarried there**—The "long time" here may include several months; Paul and Barnabas spoke boldly "in the Lord," or without fear they preached the gospel; though they had been threatened and knew that their preaching would provoke persecution, yet they did not yield to the opposition. God bore witness to the truth of the gospel by enabling them to perform miracles. The miracles which Paul and Barnabas were able to perform were God's testimony to the truth that they had preached. Though the Jews stirred up the Gentiles against Paul and Barnabas, yet many were converted, even "a great multitude both of Jews and of Greeks believed." (Verse 1.)

4 **But the multitude of the city was divided;**—When the gospel was preached some accepted and some rejected it; some were kindly disposed toward Paul and Barnabas, while others were bitterly opposed to them; the "multitude of the city was divided." The very things which produced strong conviction in some stirred bitterness in others; the earnest man always stimulates others to earnestness, either of agreement or enmity. Here Barnabas is included "with the apostles," though he was not an apostle in the sense that Peter, John, and Paul were. This is the first instance in the Acts that Paul is called an apostle. "Apostle" comes from the Greek "apostolos," and means "one who is sent out." Luke applies the word elsewhere in the Acts only to the twelve. Paul claimed to be an apostle, and equal with the other apostles. (Gal. 1: 1, 16-18.) The common use of "apostolos" is found in John 13: 16 and 2 Cor. 8: 23. Paul used the word and applied it to James the Lord's brother Gal. 1: 19) ; to Epaphroditus (Phil. 2: 25) as the messenger of the church in Philippi; to Silvanus and Timothy (1 Thess. 2: 6; Acts 18: 5) ; and to Andronicus and Junias (Rom. 16: 6, 7.) He even calls the Judaizing teachers "false apostles." (2 Cor. 11: 13.) The two parties here were Christians and non-Christians; it is likely that the Christians were in the minority.

both of the Gentiles and of the Jews with their rulers, to treat them shamefully and to stone them, 6 they became aware of it, and fled unto the cities of
Lycaonia, Lystra and Derbe, and the region round about: 7 and there they
¹preached the gospel.

¹See marginal note on ch. 5. 42

5-7 And when there was made an onset—Both Jews and
Gentiles made an attack on Paul and Barnabas. "Onset" is from
the Greek "horme," and means "a rush or impulse"; the word is
used only twice in the New Testament, here and in James 3: 4. It
is probable that no assault was actually made, but one was planned,
and they were eager to carry it out. The rulers of the Jews and the
magistrates of the city could not have participated in mob violence,
and the plot to stone Paul and Barnabas seems to point to Jewish
instigation for enforcing the punishment of blasphemy. Paul and
Barnabas learned of the plot to stone them and went to Lystra and
Derbe in Lycaonia; they preached the gospel in these cities and in
other regions. Lystra was about eighteen miles south from Iconium, and Derbe was about twenty miles east of Lystra. This was
a wild and desolate country; it was a region that was barren of
trees; Lystra was the chief city. In these rural towns it seems
that there were no synagogues, and Paul and Barnabas preached to
the scattered Jews and to the heathen population.

6. PAUL AND BARNABAS AT LYSTRA AND DERBE
14: 8-20

8 And at Lystra there sat a certain man, impotent in his feet, a cripple
from his mother's womb, who never had walked. 9 The same heard Paul

8 And at Lystra there sat a certain man,—While Paul was
speaking to some group, he observed "a certain man" who was
crippled in his feet; he never had walked. It seemed that he was
seated on the ground, but he was no beggar; he was one whose
history from his infancy was known to the greater number who
heard Paul speak. This case is very much like the lame man that
Peter and John healed. (Acts 3: 1-11.) Luke, the physician,
gives a good description of the condition of this man. It would
take a miracle to heal this man.

9, 10 The same heard Paul speaking:—As there was no synagogue in Lystra, possibly Paul and Barnabas were speaking in an

speaking: who, fastening his eyes upon him, and seeing that he had faith to be made whole, 10 said with a loud voice, Stand upright on thy feet. And he leaped up and walked. 11 And when the multitude saw what Paul had done, they lifted up their voice, saying in the speech of Lycaonia, The gods are come down to us in the likeness of men. 12 And they called Barnabas, ²Jupi-

---

²Gr. *Zeus*

---

open-air meeting; this crippled man was in the audience and heard Paul speaking. Paul observed him and saw that he had sufficient faith to be cured. Here again we note that Paul, "fastening his eyes upon him" (see Acts 13: 9), said "with a loud voice, Stand upright on thy feet." Paul raised his voice so that everyone in the audience who was listening to him heard what was said; he attracted the attention of his hearers to this crippled man. It was a strange command to these heathen people to command one who had never walked to stand upon his feet. The man obeyed immediately and "leaped up and walked"; the Greek is "helato kai periepatei," which means "he leaped up with a single bound and began to walk." The sudden leaping up and walking shows that Paul had power to cure the man; his healing was not gradual or continuous, but was immediate or instantaneous. He walked as a demonstration of the miracle of his healing.

11 **And when the multitude saw what Paul had done,**—The multitude was astonished when they saw this lame man leap up and walk, and "they lifted up their voice" and began to shout the praises of Paul and Barnabas in the "speech of Lycaonia." It seems that Paul had been speaking in the Greek language, and now they spoke in their own language. It seems that neither Paul nor Barnabas understood this language, for it was not until the oxen and garlands were brought that they saw what the people meant; yet they understood Paul and Barnabas. "The speech of Lycaonia" was a dialect peculiar to Lycaonia. This shows that the gift of tongues did not give the apostles power to speak or to understand all dialects. The Lycaonians saw the healing; they recognized it as supernatural; so they exclaimed: "The gods are come down to us in the likeness of men." This shows that the natives were simple and idolatrous.

12 **And they called Barnabas, Jupiter;**—They called Barnabas, Jupiter, and Paul, Mercury; Luke assigns the reason for this

ter; and Paul, ³Mercury, because he was the chief speaker. 13 And the priest of Jupiter whose *temple* was before the city, brought oxen and garlands unto the gates, and would have done sacrifice with the multitudes. 14 But when the apostles, Barnabas and Paul, heard of it, they rent their garments, and sprang forth among the multitude, crying out 15 and saying, Sirs,

---

³Gr. *Hermes*

---

that Paul was the "chief speaker." Here Barnabas is mentioned before Paul. "Mercury" was the god of eloquence; the heathen mythologies abound with appearances of their deities in human shape; they said that Jupiter and Mercury wandered through the neighboring country of Phrygia. "Hermes" is the Greek name for Mercury, and "Zeus" is the Greek name for Jupiter. "Zeus," the king of the gods, was of stately and commanding presence; there may be some hints as to Paul's appearance in this incident.

13 **And the priest of Jupiter**—The statue, or the temple containing the statue, was outside the city gates; the statue of Zeus, or Jupiter, stood beside the approach to the city without the wall; the double gates leading into the city adjoined this temple. It seems that the procession came to the porch or outer door with the "oxen and garlands" in order to make sacrifice unto Paul and Barnabas. The "garlands" were placed on the oxen before they were slain; it was common with these heathen people to sacrifice bullocks to Jupiter and Mercury. The way the sacrifice was made was to cut the throats of the oxen and receive the blood in a vessel, and take the blood and pour it on the altar, and make a feast and eat the flesh.

14-16 **But when the apostles, Barnabas and Paul,**—Here Barnabas is mentioned first, and is called an apostle. It seems that on this occasion Barnabas received from the people the chief honor; hence, Luke places his name first; he is also called an apostle; though he was not an apostle in the sense that the twelve were, or even as was Paul, yet he was an apostle in the sense that he was sent out by the church at Antioch. When Paul and Barnabas heard and learned what the natives were about to do, they "rent their garments, and sprang forth among the multitude" and stopped their wild and heathenish custom. Paul and Barnabas were astonished that these natives should attempt to pay such hom-

why do ye these things? We also are men of like ⁴passions with you, and
bring you good tidings, that ye should turn from these vain things unto a
living God, who made the heaven and the earth and the sea, and all that in
them is; 16 who in the generations gone by suffered all the ⁵ nations to walk

⁴Or, *nature*
⁵Or, *Gentiles.* See ch. 4. 25

age and worship to them. However, it gave them a splendid occasion to direct the worship to the true and "living God." As they
were worshiping, or about to worship, it becomes a fitting occasion
to instruct them in the true worship. This Paul and Barnabas attempted to do. They declared unto them that they were just men,
not gods, with "like passions" as other men. "Passion" comes
from the Greek "pascho," and means "to experience." It is used
here and in James 5: 17; it means "of like nature" more exactly
and affected by like sensations. After clearing their minds on this
point, Paul and Barnabas began preaching Christ to them; they
brought "good tidings," or the gospel, to them. "Good tidings"
comes from the Greek "euaggelizomenoi," and means the same as
"gospelizing" or "evangelizing." We now have Paul's preaching
to the Gentiles free from any Jewish environment, and he makes
the same line of argument seen in Acts 17: 21-32 and Rom. 1:
18-23. "Living God" is put in contrast to idols or gods made of
wood or stone; these idols are dumb and inactive, but the living
God is active, for he "made the heaven and the earth and the sea,
and all that in them is." What a contrast between the God who
created the heavens and the earth and the god that these heathens
worshiped! God had been merciful to the people before Christ
came, but now he wants all to know Christ; he permitted the people "to walk in their own ways," but now they must follow the
Christ who is the Savior of the world. For wise reasons God permitted men to see what they could and would do, and in this way
become better prepared to receive newer light. Paul makes the
same argument in Acts 17: 30 in his speech at Athens. He also
makes the same argument in Rom. 1, 2, and 11. The ignorance
and the sins of the Gentile world had been allowed to run their
course, as the law of Moses had been allowed to do its partial and
imperfect work among the Jews. Now they are to hear the gospel
and be saved by it.

in their own ways. 17 And yet he left not himself without witness in that he did good and gave you from heaven rains and fruitful seasons, filling your hearts with food and gladness. 18 And with these sayings scarce restrained they the multitudes from doing sacrifice unto them.

19 But there came Jews thither from Antioch and Iconium: and having persuaded the multitudes, they stoned Paul, and dragged him out of the city,

---

17 And yet he left not himself without witness,—Here again we have the outline of what is presented in Rom. 1 : 19, 20. God gave rains and fruitful seasons and blessed them through the natural laws; Paul recognizes God in the operation of natural laws. We should be able to see the hand of God in nature; "the heavens declare the glory of God; and the firmament showeth his handiwork." (Psalm 19: 1.) The "living God" was not like Jupiter, but during all this time attracted men by his graciousness toward them; the goodness of God was still attracting them to see his larger and richer goodness in the gospel of Christ.

18 And with these sayings scarce restrained they—We have only a brief outline of the speech that Paul made; he had a difficult task in keeping these natives from making their sacrifices; it had been a hard thing to do, but finally Paul and Barnabas won and the natives left off their worship which they had planned to give Paul and Barnabas. No mention is made here of the success that Paul and Barnabas had at Lystra. Among the more conspicuous converts were the devout Jewesses, Lois and her daughter Eunice, and the young Timothy. (2 Tim. 1: 5.)

19 But there came Jews thither from Antioch and Iconium: —These enemies of Paul and Barnabas came a distance from eighty to a hundred miles; this shows how determined they were to persecute Paul and Barnabas and to keep people from accepting the truth. The opposition aroused against a man or a cause is sometimes proof of his power or the power of the truth. The intense opposition here bears evidence of the force of the truth as preached by Paul and Barnabas. Men do not stone dead trees for their fruit, or arm themselves against weak cowards, or grow excited over a weak opponent. These Jews came and "persuaded the multitudes" to stone Paul. What a contrast! At one time they are about to worship Paul and Barnabas as gods, but at another time they are ready to stone them to death. Popular feelings can-

supposing that he was dead. 20 But as the disciples stood round about him, he rose up, and entered into the city: and on the morrow he went forth with Barnabas to Derbe. 21 And when they had ⁶preached the gospel to that

⁶Gr. *brought the good tidings.* Comp. ch. 5. 42

not be relied upon. The sudden change of feeling here is as startling as that which transformed the "Hosannas" of the multitude at Jerusalem into the cry of "Crucify him." (Matt. 21: 9; 27: 22.) They fell upon Paul and stoned him and "dragged him out of the city, supposing that he was dead." The manner of punishment, stoning, shows that the punishment was planned by the Jews; they were eager to satisfy themselves that they were inflicting punishment on a blasphemer; stoning him to death, and casting him out to be buried with the burial of lower animals, or his flesh to be consumed by dogs and vultures. It was an instance in Paul's life that he mentioned later. (2 Cor. 11: 25.) The sufferings endured at Lystra stand out at the close of his life, in the vista of past years, with a marvelous distinctness. (2 Tim. 3: 11.)

20 **But as the disciples stood round about him,**—The disciples followed the mob as it dragged the body of Paul out of the city. Perhaps they were going to give his body a decent burial. It may be that Lois, Eunice, and Timothy were all present weeping over the supposed dead body of Paul, but as they stood around Paul rose up "and entered into the city." We do not know how Barnabas escaped being stoned; he may not have been present when they attacked Paul. But the next day Paul and Barnabas left Lystra and went to Derbe. This was a distance of about twenty miles southeast from Lystra. This journey must have occupied several hours, and was a difficult journey for Paul in his present condition.

7. THEIR RETURN TO ANTIOCH IN SYRIA
14: 21-28

city, and had made many disciples, they returned to Lystra, and to Iconium,

21 **And when they had preached the gospel to that city,**— Derbe was not so large a city as Lystra, and after Paul and Barnabas had evangelized in that city, they were ready to return or go

and to Antioch, 22 confirming the souls of the disciples, exhorting them to
continue in the faith, and that through many tribulations we must enter into
the kingdom of God. 23 And when they had appointed for them elders in
every church, and had prayed with fasting, they commended them to the

---

elsewhere. It seems that they were not disturbed by the Jews at
Derbe; neither do we know how long they remained in Derbe.
They are now at the end of their first missionary tour and are
ready to return. Derbe was the frontier city of the Roman Empire; the shortest route from Derbe to Antioch in Syria would
have been to have gone by land through Cilicia and visited Tarsus,
Paul's native city, and on through the kingdom of Antiochus to
Antioch, but they chose to return and visit the churches that they
had established. So they "returned to Lystra, and to Iconium, and
to Antioch" in Pisidia.

22 **confirming the souls of the disciples,**—"Confirming" is
from the Greek "episterizontes"; it is used here and in Acts 15:
32, 41. Each time the word is used in Acts it has reference to the
churches. It means to make more firm, to give additional
strength. The churches were encouraged "to continue in the
faith," which means that they were to remain steadfast. "The
faith," as used here, comes from the Greek "tei pistei," and means
more than trust or belief; it may have the meaning of the entire
gospel. These new converts were from heathenism, and were persecuted; some family ties had been broken, social ties severed, and
they were in need of encouragement. So Paul exhorted them that
"we" must endure great tribulations in order to enter "into the
kingdom of God." The new converts were thus warned of the
persecution and tribulation that would befall them. Paul here recognizes that "the kingdom of God" had been established and that
these Christians were in it.

23 **And when they had appointed for them elders in every
church,**—Here it seems that Paul and Barnabas had established
churches at the different places where they had preached.
"Church," as used here, means the local congregation. The con-
gregations needed some form of organization; hence, elders were
appointed. The rulers in these little groups of disciples were "elders" or "bishops." "Elders" here is from the Greek "presbuterous." It means here men of age and dignity; these leaders were

Lord, on whom they had believed. 24 And they passed through Pisidia, and came to Pamphylia. 25 And when they had spoken the word in Perga, they

selected from the elderly men who presided over the assemblies, and managed the affairs of the church. "Elders" is the term used in speaking of Jewish communities, while "bishops" is the term applied in speaking of Gentile communities. The solemn duties and responsibilities were impressed upon them by prayer and fasting; in this way they were commended "to the Lord, on whom they had believed." It seems that this was done in the public assembly where the prayers were offered. To be "commended" to the Lord was to be entrusted with the responsibilities of carrying on the work of the church, which was the work of the Lord. They had trusted the Lord in becoming disciples, and now they are entrusted with the Lord's work. It should be noted that the "elders" were appointed in "every church." There was a plurality of elders in each church; this is the New Testament order. Nothing is said about the mode of "appointing" the elders. The word "appointed" is from the Greek "cheirotoneo," and originally means to "extend the hand"; "cheir" means hand, and "teino" means "to stretch"; hence, the original meaning was to stretch forth the hand, to vote by show of the hands; finally it came to mean to appoint with the approval of an assembly, and then to appoint without regard to choice. Various interpretations have been given to this; writers and commentators who favored the Episcopal form of church government have said that it meant the imposition of hands to set the persons apart for the office of elders; those who favored the Presbyterian form of government have said that it meant to select and set apart men that may have been previously elected or chosen by the members; those who favored the Congregational form of church government have held that it implied a selection of officers by the members. Since the New Testament does not tell us how the elders were appointed, it seems that any method which promotes unity and does not violate a principle may be used.

24-26 **And they passed through Pisidia,**—It seems that they returned by the same route that they had traveled in reaching these points. Antioch was in Pisidia. After leaving Antioch on their return, they passed through Pisidia and into Pamphylia. They went down to Attalia; 26 and thence they sailed to Antioch, from whence they had been committed to the grace of God for the work which they had fulfilled. 27 And when they were come, and had gathered the church together, they rehearsed all things that God had done with them, and that he had opened a door of faith unto the Gentiles. 28 And they tarried no little time with the disciples.

---

preached in Perga; they retraced their steps until they came to Perga; here they halted. It was the place where John Mark had left them, and on their first visit we are not told that they preached in Perga. We are not told what success they had in Perga at this time. On their return journey, instead of taking ship at Perga, they crossed by land to Attalia; this was a seaport of Pamphylia, and from here they sailed to Antioch in Syria, "from whence they had been committed to the grace of God for the work which they had fulfilled." Luke, the historian, does not record any of the events that took place from the time that they set sail from Attalia until they arrived at Antioch in Syria. They had accomplished the work to which they had been consecrated; they are now back at their starting point and ready to give a report of their work.

27, 28 **And when they were come, and had gathered the church together,**—When they returned to Antioch the church was gathered together; that is, the church assembled to hear the report that Paul and Barnabas had to make. They had many experiences to rehearse; Paul could tell them about the persecution and suffering that he had had to endure. In the report they gave God praise for all that had been done; "they rehearsed all things that God had done with them, and that he had opened a door of faith unto the Gentiles." After reporting what God had done with them in converting the Gentiles, "they tarried no little time with the disciples" at Antioch. We do not know how long they remained at Antioch. It seems that they left Antioch about A.D. 44 or 45, and it is estimated that they were gone on the first tour two or three years. We know that they were back in Jerusalem in A.D. 50; hence, they must have remained in Antioch "no little time," or about two years.

Summary of Paul's First Journey

Distance from Antioch in Syria to Seleucia, sixteen miles by land; Seleucia to Salamis, ninety miles by water; Salamis to Paphos, one hundred fifty miles by land; Paphos to Perga, one hundred fifty miles by water; Perga to Antioch in Pisidia, one hundred miles by land; Antioch in Pisidia to Iconium, sixty miles by land; Iconium to Lystra, eighteen miles by land; Lystra to Derbe, twenty miles by land; total distance, six hundred four miles.

Of the six hundred four miles from Antioch in Syria to Derbe two hundred forty miles were made by water. The return journey was about the same distance, which would make twelve hundred eight miles; this was a long journey at that time with the ancient modes of travel. Paul and Barnabas had traveled the twelve hundred eight miles and had established more than half a dozen churches within the two or three years that they were gone on this journey.

SECTION TWO

DISPUTE ABOUT CIRCUMCISION SETTLED
15:1-35.

1. QUESTION RAISED AT ANTIOCH IN SYRIA
15:1

1 And certain men came down from Judaea and taught the brethren, *saying*, Except ye be circumcised after the custom of Moses, ye cannot be saved.

---

1 **And certain men came down from Judaea**—Paul and Barnabas had just reported "all things" that God had done for the Gentiles through them, and that he had "opened a door of faith unto the Gentiles." (Acts 14:27.) Now certain ones came down "from Judaea," or Jerusalem, claiming to have been sent by the apostles at Jerusalem. (Verse 24.) They attempted to close the door that opened to the Gentiles. These brethren from Jerusalem came to Antioch with Jewish prejudice and exclusive narrowness. They claimed that the Gentile Christians could not be saved without circumcision. Thus they made the Jewish rite of circumcision a condition of Gentile salvation; they claimed that the church at Jerusalem authorized them to so teach. The church at Antioch was composed of Jew and Gentile converts. (Acts 11:19, 20.) This was the place where such a question would be raised; the Jews and Gentiles had not been accustomed to meeting together for worship, except as the Gentiles became proselytes to the Jewish religion. But now in the early church Gentiles who were not proselytes and Jews were brought together in the church. We do not know to what extent this question disturbed the church at Antioch, but from what follows it seems that it involved great issues. Now when these teachers came from Jerusalem and began to teach that the Gentile Christians must be "circumcised" according to "the custom of Moses" or they could not be saved, such teaching would arouse both the Jewish and Gentile portion of the church at Antioch. Hence, the teaching of those from Jerusalem would likely cause dissension.

2. PAUL AND BARNABAS SENT TO JERUSALEM
15: 2-5

2 And when Paul and Barnabas had no small dissension and questioning with them, *the brethren* appointed that Paul and Barnabas, and certain other of them, should go up to Jerusalem unto the apostles and elders about this question. 3 They therefore, being brought on their way by the church,

---

2 And when Paul and Barnabas had no small dissension— Paul and Barnabas "tarried no little time" with the church at Antioch; during this time these brethren came down from Jerusalem and insisted that the Gentile Christians be circumcised; Paul and Barnabas opposed them and "had no small dissension and questioning with them." There seems to have been a very heated argument. "Dissension" comes from the Greek "staseos," which literally means "strife," a standing against it; it means an established order or opinion; a strife, one party holding to the established custom, and the other opposing them. "Questioning" comes from "zeteseos," and means "a seeking" or "examining together, a mutual questioning and discussion." Finally the church appointed "Paul and Barnabas, and certain other of them" to go to Jerusalem "unto the apostles and elders about this question." Paul gives an account of this in Gal. 2: 1-10. It seems that Paul suggested their going to Jerusalem. (Gal. 2: 1.) It seems that these teachers from Jerusalem had reported that they were contending for circumcision of the Gentiles because the church at Jerusalem had so instructed them. Paul knew that it was best then to go to Jerusalem and to settle the matter, not for himself, but for those who did not know any better. We are told in Gal. 2: 1 that Paul took Titus with him. It is usually reckoned that this journey of Paul's to Jerusalem was his third visit to that city since his conversion, and that it occurred about A.D. 50.

3 They therefore, being brought on their way by the church,—The church at Antioch not only, at Paul's suggestion, requested these brethren to go to Jerusalem, but it assisted them in making the journey by helping to defray expenses and by their prayers and encouragement; they were thus "brought on their way by the church." They passed through Phoenicia and Samaria by land. It was a journey of about three hundred miles southward

passed through both Phoenicia and Samaria, declaring the conversion of the
Gentiles : and they caused great joy unto all the brethren.   4 And when they
were come to Jerusalem, they were received of the church and the apostles
and the elders, and they rehearsed all things that God had done with them.
5 But there rose up certain of the sect of the Pharisees who believed, saying,
It is needful to circumcise them, and to charge them to keep the law of
Moses.

---

along the coast of the Mediterranean Sea, through Tyre and
Sidon, cities of Phoenicia, and on through Samaria, probably
where Philip had preached the gospel, and on to Jerusalem. As
they went along the way, and as they had opportunity, they declared "the conversion of the Gentiles," which "caused great joy
unto all the brethren." The great joy caused to the brethren of
Phoenicia and Samaria by the recital of the conversion of the Gentiles shows the general sympathy with Paul and Barnabas.

4 **And when they were come to Jerusalem,**—They left Antioch for Jerusalem to take the matter to "the apostles and the elders," so when they came to Jerusalem "they were received of the
church and the apostles and the elders." The entire church was interested in the question. We know not how many of the apostles
were present, neither do we know how many elders were in the
church at Jerusalem. It should be noticed that though the apostles
were there with all their apostolic authority, yet they recognized
the "elders" of the church there, and took them into consultation
with them. It seems that when they arrived they received a hearty
welcome and that they lost no time in rehearsing "all things that
God had done with them." Paul and Barnabas implied in their rehearsal that what they had done, it was God doing it through them ;
therefore, God had accepted the Gentiles without circumcision,
and that the Jewish brethren ought to accept them.

5 **But there rose up certain of the sect of the Pharisees—**
These Pharisees believed ; they were Christians, but had been converted from the "sect of the Pharisees" to Christianity. The teachers at Antioch who had come down from Jerusalem are not described as Pharisees. Here for the first time we learn that some of
the Pharisees had become Christians, and it is fair to imply that
those who went out from Jerusalem to Antioch were from among
these converted Pharisees. They were bold in their declaration

and clear in the statement of the issue. They said: "It is needful to circumcise them, and to charge them to keep the law of Moses." This brings the issue to the fore; it is whether the Gentile Christians should be circumcised.

3. APOSTLES AND ELDERS IN COUNCIL
15: 6-29

6 And the apostles and the elders were gathered together to consider of this matter. 7 And when there had been much questioning, Peter rose up, and said unto them,
Brethren, ye know that [1]a good while ago God made choice among you, that by my mouth the Gentiles should hear the word of the [2]gospel, and be-

[1]Gr. *from early days*
[2]Or, *good tidings*

---

6 **And the apostles and the elders were gathered together**— Luke does not mention the "church" as he did in verse 4, but "the apostles and the elders" are mentioned; we know that the church is included here as we learn from verses 12 and 22. The "whole church" was called together to consider this matter with "the apostles and the elders." The apostles, with their authority, no doubt, took the lead, and thus the church with its elders was trained under the guidance of the apostles. The importance of the matter was recognized and was given due consideration.

7 **And when there had been much questioning,**—It seems that a very full and free discussion was had; both sides were heard without partiality; this is the only fair way to discuss any matter over which there is a diversity of sentiment. "Questioning" is from the Greek "zeteseos," and is the same word as used in verse 2. Here it means "debating," as that is what was had. Some contended for the affirmative, the Gentile Christians should be circumcised, and keep the law of Moses. Paul and Barnabas with others took the negative of this proposition. After much discussion "Peter rose up" and expressed himself. He referred to the case of Cornelius; he was a Gentile and was converted to Christ by the preaching of the gospel by Peter. God had accepted the entire household of Cornelius as Christians; even the church at Jerusalem (Acts 11) had also accepted the Gentiles as Christians without requiring them to be circumcised. Peter reminds the church of this and refreshes their memory, for he says it had been "a good while

lieve. 8 And God, who knoweth the heart, bare them witness, giving them
the Holy Spirit, even as he did unto us; 9 and he made no distinction between us and them, cleansing their hearts by faith. 10 Now therefore why
make ye trial of God, that ye should put a yoke upon the neck of the disci-

---

ago." According to the best chronology, it had been at least ten
years since the conversion of Cornelius, and it had been about
twenty years since Pentecost, so the church at this time was about
twenty years old. It was fitting for Peter to speak at this time; he
had waited until both sides had been heard and now it is his time
as an apostle, and with the experience that he had had at the house
of Cornelius and the church at Jerusalem, to speak as he did.

8, 9 **And God, who knoweth the heart,**—God had given the
Holy Spirit to the household of Cornelius (Acts 10: 44, 45); this
shows that God, who knoweth all things, had accepted the Gentiles
without circumcision; Peter had related the incident to the church
at Jerusalem and the church had accepted the Gentiles as Christians without circumcision (Acts 11: 18.) God had made no distinction between the Jew and Gentile, and man should make no
distinction. Peter seemed to be somewhat surprised that there
should be no difference, but God had made none, and he had to accept that fact. Peter gives an additional thought that both Jews and
Gentile were accepted by God on the basis of their faith in Christ;
neither Jew nor Gentile was to be accepted as Christians by keeping
the law of Moses. Their hearts were purified by faith; anyone
who believed in idolatry had an impure heart, and those who believed in Christ, in the sense of accepting Christ, had a pure
heart. Both Jew and Gentile had to hear the same gospel, believe
the same gospel, repent of their sins, and be buried with Christ in
baptism and raised to walk in a new life, in order to become Christians; no distinction so far as the terms of remission of sins are
concerned; no distinction so far as acceptance to God.

10 **Now therefore why make ye trial of God,**—Peter puts the
matter in an interrogative form and asks, "Why make ye trial of
God?" as though God had made a mistake when he gave the Holy
Spirit to the household of Cornelius and accepted them without
circumcision. They were refusing to accept that which God had
accepted, or they were rejecting those whom God had accepted.

ples which neither our fathers nor we were able to bear? 11 But we believe that we shall be saved through the grace of the Lord Jesus, in like manner as they.

12 And all the multitude kept silence; and they hearkened unto Barnabas

---

They were laying down conditions that God had not imposed on the Gentiles, and placing a yoke upon the Gentiles that even the Jews were not able to bear. No Jew ever kept the law of Moses perfectly; even those who were now insisting on the circumcision of the Gentile Christians had not kept faithfully the law, yet they wanted to place that yoke upon the Gentile Christians. Peter shows here that they not only opposed God, but they were inconsistent with themselves. The figure of "a yoke" is used here, and is the same that Paul used in Gal. 5: 1. Peter had been slow to see this point, as it took a miracle to convince him of the truth of it at Joppa and Caesarea. Peter has made four points that stand out distinctly: (1) he was directed by God to receive the Gentiles, as in the case of Cornelius; (2) God endorsed the reception of the Gentiles by giving them the Holy Spirit; (3) faith produced precisely the same effect in both Jew and Gentile; (4) the Jews have no right to put on the Gentiles a yoke which God had not put on them.

11 **But we believe that we shall be saved**—The salvation which both Jew and Gentile could enjoy came through the grace of God. "Grace" means the unmerited favor of God; the free grace of God was expressed by his sending Jesus to earth to die for the sins of the world. The conditions of remission are faith in the Lord Jesus Christ and obedience to his commands. Salvation was not to come through the law of Moses, but through Christ. We have in this verse the last recorded words of Peter in the Acts.

12 **And all the multitude kept silence;**—The church had assembled with its elders and the apostles; now "the multitude kept silence"; the multitude became silent after Peter's speech; he had profoundly impressed the multitude and had presented such clear and forcible arguments that there was nothing that could be said with profit. Again, the church had learned to respect the apostles when they spoke. Paul and Barnabas now spoke. Here again Barnabas is mentioned before Paul, because he was better known

and Paul rehearsing what signs and wonders God had wrought among the Gentiles through them. 13 And after they had held their peace, James answered, saying,

Brethren, hearken unto me: 14 Symeon hath rehearsed how first God visited the *Gentiles, to take out of them a people for his name. 15 And to this

---

*See marginal note on ch. 4. 25

---

at Jerusalem than Paul. Paul and Barnabas rehearsed "what signs and wonders God had wrought among the Gentiles through them." Again, Paul and Barnabas give God the praise and honor for all that had been done among the Gentiles. Three times (Acts 14: 27; 15: 4, 12) Paul is described as telling the facts about the work that was done among the Gentiles; the rehearsal of the facts was more powerful than mere argument. God had done wonderful things among the Gentiles, and had accepted the Gentiles without circumcision. The Jewish Christians put themselves in opposition to God when they insisted on the circumcision of the Gentile Christians. Paul and Barnabas merely testified to the facts and left the Jewish Christians to make application of them and to draw their own conclusions; there was only one conclusion to draw, and it was in favor of Paul and Barnabas.

13, 14 **And after they had held their peace,**—There had been a general discussion in which all who wished took part; then Peter made a speech and presented invincible arguments; then Paul and Barnabas briefly rehearsed what God had done for the Gentiles through them, with the clear conclusion that God had accepted the Gentiles without circumcision; now James makes the final speech. This James has been called "James the Just," and he was considered a representative of the Jewish Christians. The Judaizing teachers possibly counted on him as a champion of their views, for they later made the wrong use of his name against Peter at Antioch. (Gal. 2: 12.) This is the James who was the author of the epistle of James; he was not one of the twelve apostles, but after the death of James (Acts 12: 2), the brother of John, he became a leader in the church at Jerusalem. James reviewed the argument made by Peter as to how "God visited the Gentiles" to preach the gospel to them, and "take out of them a people for his name." James here has reference to Cornelius and his household; they had

agree the words of the prophets; as it is written, 16 ⁴After these things I
will return.
>   And I will build again the tabernacle of David, which is fallen;
>   And I will build again the ruins thereof,
>   And I will set it up:
> 17 That the residue of men may seek after the Lord,
>   And all the ⁵Gentiles, upon whom my name is called,
> 18 Saith the Lord, who maketh these things known from of old. 19 Where-

---

⁴Am. 9. 11, 12
⁵Or, *who doeth these things which were known &c.*

---

been called out from among the heathen to be God's chosen just as
Israel was.   James clearly sees the hand of God in Peter's course
at Caesarea, and in what Paul and Barnabas had done among the
Gentiles.

15-18 **And to this agree the words of the prophets;**—It was
startling to the Jewish Christians that God would extend the privileges of the gospel to the Gentiles; however, they should have
known that the Messiah was to be a universal Savior. The prophets of Israel had foretold of the acceptance of the Gentiles. The
prophet Amos is quoted here (Amos 9: 11, 12) by James, but the
quotation is not a literal quotation from the Old Testament; some
of the words are changed, but James, by the Holy Spirit, is giving
the meaning of the prophecies. While James quotes only one
prophet, Amos, yet he uses "prophets" in the plural. Other prophets had foretold the acceptance of the Gentiles. (Isa. 2: 2-4; 49: 6;
Mic. 4: 1-4.) The interpretation of the quotation given by James
is that "the tabernacle of David" had been wrecked, but that it
would be rebuilt and that the Gentiles would be admitted into it.
The prophecy from Amos speaks first of the fall of the Jewish
race, next the promise that God would build a new church on the
ruins of the old and gather the Gentiles into it, and finally those
who were saved would enjoy salvation only through the Messiah.
The picture here is the wrecked tent or tabernacle which was
erected was boughs of trees at the Feast of Tabernacles, and which
was rebuilt annually. "Tabernacle of David" is from the Greek
"skenen Daueid," and is a poetical figure of the throne of David.
(2 Sam. 7: 12.)   In the rebuilding of the spiritual house of David,
believers are to come from all nations of the earth.   By the figure
of a place falling to ruins, the devastated state of the kingdom is

fore my judgment is, that we trouble not them that from among the Gentiles turn to God; 20 but that we ⁶write unto them, that they abstain from the pollutions of idols, and from fornication, and from what is strangled, and

⁶Or, *enjoin them*

represented; the prosperity to be bestowed was to come in the days of the Messiah, and would consist of spiritual blessings, and a kingdom of righteousness would be established by the Messiah and the Gentiles would seek the Lord and become his people.

19, 20 **Wherefore my judgment is,**—James now, speaking by the Holy Spirit, gives his judgment in the matter. It seems that James was acting as chairman of the meeting, and that it was left to him to sum up and conclude the whole matter. He is now ready to do this. The conclusion that James expresses is "that we trouble not them that from among the Gentiles turn to God." This decision coincided with the decision that Paul and Barnabas had already reached and had preached. It was against the Judaizing teachers. James' decision, as expressed, was somewhat in the form of a motion; the question had been discussed and now James moved that the entire church coincide with Paul and Barnabas, and that they write. James agrees with Peter in his support of Paul and Barnabas in their contention for the freedom of the Gentiles from the law of Moses. A further admonition of James is that "we write unto them" and give them such help and encouragement as they may need. In this letter James suggests that they "abstain from the pollutions of idols, and from fornication, and from what is strangled, and from blood." Four things are here mentioned: (1) pollution of idols; (2) fornication; (3) what is strangled; (4) abstain from blood. The words which James uses here denote formal decision sent by special messengers to the Gentile Christians. "Pollutions of idols" means the worship of idols, and especially eating the meats offered unto idols; one who in any form worships an idol is said to be unclean; hence, they should refrain from the pollution of idols. Idolatry, fornication, and murder were common sins among the heathen; these Gentile Christians had left all of these things when they became Christians, and are now exhorted not to return to them. The law of Moses enjoined certain restrictions about the eating of blood and respecting the life of animals; the Gentile Christians are not to be controlled by the

from blood. 21 For Moses from generations of old hath in every city them that preach him, being read in the synagogues every sabbath.

22 Then it seemed good to the apostles and the elders, with the whole church, to choose men out of their company, and send them to Antioch with

---

law of Moses; they are to observe the general principles of righteousness and holiness.

21 **For Moses from generations of old**—The law of Moses was read in every synagogue on the Sabbath; there was usually a teacher that interpreted or gave the meaning of the law. Hence, to "preach" Moses was to preach and interpret the law of Moses; so to "preach" Christ is to preach the gospel, or to preach the law of Christ. Wherever there was a synagogue Moses was preached on the Sabbath. There have been different views as to why James made this statement. Some think that James here answers an objection that the Jewish Christians might advance; that is, if such freedom were granted to the Gentiles, the law of Moses would decline in authority; others think that it was not necessary to write these things to Jewish Christians, for they had the law of Moses; a third view regards these words as spoken in the interest of peace and harmony between the Gentile and Jewish Christians. It seems that James had reference in a general way to the general practice of the Jews, and it was not necessary to place the burden of the law upon the Gentiles. The Jews had for a long time been taught to respect the law of Moses; they did not have to lose any respect for Moses or for the law, but they were to see that salvation came through Christ, and not through the keeping of the law.

22 **Then it seemed good to the apostles and the elders,**—A unanimous decision was reached, since "the apostles and the elders, with the whole church," decided to select some brethren to accompany Paul and Barnabas to Antioch and there give the decision reached by the church at Jerusalem. We are not told how they reached the decision, whether all the members were consulted, or whether the membership expressed agreement with the apostles and the elders. The apostles and elders led in the agreement as they did in the discussion. This was a great victory for Paul and Barnabas and for the truth. However, James was practical, and did not stop with just the speeches and the decision; it must be

Paul and Barnabas; *namely,* Judas called Barsabbas, and Silas, chief men among the brethren: 23 and they wrote *thus* by them, [7]The apostles and the elders, brethren, unto the brethren who are of the Gentiles in Antioch and Syria and Cilicia, greeting: 24 Forasmuch as we have heard that certain [8]who went out from us have troubled you with words, subverting your

---

[7]Or, *The apostles and the elder brethren*
[8]Some ancient authorities omit *who went out*

---

conveyed to the church at Antioch. While they trusted Paul and Barnabas, yet they followed the wise course in selecting some brethren to accompany Paul and Barnabas to Antioch and bear the decision as a message to the church at Antioch. So they selected "Judas called Barsabbas, and Silas, chief men among the brethren." Some have thought "Judas called Barsabbas" was a brother of Barnabas, but there is no evidence to this effect. Silas is probably the abbreviated form of Silvanus, who later became one of Paul's companions in traveling. (1 Pet. 5: 12.) Judas and Silas were "chief men among the brethren." Such men would carry weight with the church at Antioch.

23 **and they wrote thus by them,**—The letter written was brief, yet it was clear and emphatic. The form of the letter shows that "the apostles and the elders" and brethren include "the whole church"; hence, it is a letter from the church at Jerusalem to the church at Antioch. The importance of this letter is enhanced in value by the fact that the Jerusalem church was the center of Christianity among the Jews, and the church at Antioch was the center among the Gentiles; this will help to bring together the Jewish and Gentile Christians. The letter is addressed to the Gentile Christians in "Antioch and Syria and Cilicia." The decision reached affected all Gentile Christians in every country, but only Syria and Cilicia are mentioned. This geographical notice of the Gentile Christians gives some idea as to the effect of the preaching of Paul and Barnabas; the harvest had been great. This also shows the activity of the church at Antioch in preaching the gospel to the regions round about.

24 **Forasmuch as we have heard that certain who went out from us**—Recognition is given here of those Judaizing teachers who had gone from Jerusalem to Antioch, claiming to have been sent out by the church at Jerusalem; condemnation or denial is made of their being sent by the church at Jerusalem. Hence, they

souls; to whom we gave no commandment; 25 it seemed good unto us, having come to one accord, to choose out men and send them unto you with our beloved Barnabas and Paul, 26 men that have hazarded their lives for the

---

had no apostolic authority for insisting that the Gentile Christians should be circumcised; neither did the church at Jerusalem endorse them. The church at Jerusalem felt in some measure to be responsible for the trouble these teachers had caused the church at Antioch, but now they are repudiated and a correction of their teachings is made. Hence, these teachers went of their own accord and on their own responsibility, and did not represent the church at Jerusalem. Their teaching had subverted the souls of the Gentile Christians. "Subverting" comes from the Greek "anaskeuazo," and means "to pack up baggage, to plunder, to ravage"; this is a vivid picture of the havoc wrought by the Judaizers among the simple-minded Greek Christians in Antioch.

25, 26 **it seemed good unto us, having come to one accord,** —So there was a unanimous decision reached. The apostles, elders, and the "whole church" had come to "one accord" about this matter. "Having come to one accord" is from the Greek "genomenois homothumadon," and clearly means that the final unity was the result of the private and public talks or discussion which was had on the subject. We are not told whether the Christians from "the sect of the Pharisees" (verse 5), who at first contended that "it is needful to circumcise them, and to charge them to keep the law of Moses," had been convinced, or had withdrawn from the assembly; however, it seems clear that all were convinced. Here again we have the order: "Barnabas and Paul," instead of "Paul and Barnabas." This is the order that was used before Paul's first missionary journey, when he became the more prominent of the two. (Acts 11: 30; 13: 2.) Barnabas in this official letter stands before Paul, because Paul had spent but little time in Jerusalem, while Barnabas among the Christians there had for some time been a well-known character and honored leader. The church at Jerusalem recognized the great danger that Paul and Barnabas had suffered, as they are described in this letter as "men that have hazarded their lives for the name of our Lord Jesus Christ." They recognized the courage and heroism of Paul and Barnabas; this fact also proved the sincerity of Paul and Barnabas.

name of our Lord Jesus Christ. 27 We have sent therefore Judas and Silas, who themselves also shall tell you the same things by word of mouth. 28 For it seemed good to the Holy Spirit, and to us, to lay upon you no greater burden than these necessary things: 29 that ye abstain from things sacrificed to idols, and from blood, and from things strangled, and from fornication; from

27 **We have sent therefore Judas and Silas,**—Judas and Silas would confirm by word of mouth that which was written in the letter. Here we see another reason for sending Judas and Silas along with Paul and Barnabas. Nothing is said in the entire account of Luke of the presence of Titus who went along with Paul and Barnabas. (Gal. 2: 1-3.) Judas and Silas could not only confirm what was written, but they could represent the church at Jerusalem. They would testify to the genuineness of the letter and would strengthen the decision that had been reached; their presence and testimony would have a good effect also on the Gentile Christians.

28 **For it seemed good to the Holy Spirit, and to us,**—Here the authority of the Holy Spirit accompanies the decision written in the letter. This showed that the decision reached was the will of God, and that those who so expressed themselves were expressing the will of God. The decision was not merely man's decision or opinion, but was the inspired will of God. No burden was to be placed upon the Gentile Christians other than what the Holy Spirit placed upon them. Only such "necessary things" were required by the Holy Spirit. The restrictions named did constitute some burden, but it was necessary for their salvation. Some think that these "necessary things" were only "necessary" for the times in which they lived, but are not necessary for Christians today; however, it seems that these things are as necessary today as they were at that time.

29 **that ye abstain from things sacrificed to idols,**—James had mentioned these things in his speech. (Verse 20.) They now write them in the letter which is to be sent. In his speech James stated that they should "abstain from the pollutions of idols," but now it is written that they should "abstain from things sacrificed to idols." Some discussion has been had as to the meaning of abstaining "from blood." Some think that it means to abstain from murder; others, to abstain from the eating of blood as forbidden by

which if ye keep yourselves, it shall be well with you. Fare ye well.

---

the law of Moses. It seems clear here that "the blood" is the blood of animals and that it should not be eaten. (Lev. 17: 10-15.) The heathen caught the blood of the animal in a vessel when the animal was slain and ate it as food; this was not allowed to the Jew for the reasons assigned in Lev. 17: 13, 14 and Deut. 12: 16, 23. God had forbidden Noah and his descendants to eat blood. (Gen. 9: 4.) Then it was incorporated in the law of Moses, and seems to be forbidden of Christians today. "Things strangled" means that they were to refrain from eating the flesh of animals that had been strangled. "Strangled" comes from the Greek "pniktou," and means "life taken without shedding the blood"; hence, animals strangled had the blood left in the body, and in eating the flesh one would eat the blood. They were to keep themselves from fornication, or live chaste lives. The letter concludes that if the Gentile Christians would observe these things it would be well with them, and then concludes with "fare ye well." This comes from the Greek "valete," and means "be ye strong." This was a common way of closing a letter.

4. DECISION RECEIVED AT ANTIOCH
15: 30-35

30 So they, when they were dismissed, came down to Antioch; and having gathered the multitude together, they delivered the epistle. 31 And when

---

30 **So they, when they were dismissed,**—It seems that there was some formal dismissal or sending of Paul and Barnabas, Judas and Silas, away from Jerusalem. We are not told how they journeyed from Jerusalem to Antioch, but they probably went through Phoenicia and Samaria and comforted the disciples on the way by telling them of the decision at Jerusalem. This would encourage other Christians to preach the gospel to the Gentiles, and it would encourage the Gentiles to accept the gospel. When they arrived at Antioch, they "gathered the multitude together," or the church was assembled, and "they delivered the epistle." It should be noted that the message is not called "a judgment," "a sentence," "an order," or "a decree"; it is simply called "the epistle." This

they had read it, they rejoiced for the [1]consolation. *32* And Judas and Silas, being themselves also prophets, [2]exhorted the brethren with many words, and confirmed them. *33* And after they had spent some time *there,* they were dismissed in peace from the brethren unto those that had sent them forth.[3]

[1]Or, *exhortation*
[2]Or, *comforted*
[3]Some ancient authorities insert, with variations, ver. 34 *But it seemed good unto Silas to abide there*

was the first or beginning of the New Testament scripture, the first of the epistles; it was addressed to Christians in Antioch, in Syria, and Cilicia; later other epistles were written. Since this one has been incorporated in the book of Acts, emphasis has not been given to it that probably would have been given had it been separate and independent from the history in Acts.

31 And when they had read it,—There was a formal sending away from the church at Jerusalem and a formal reception of these brethren at Antioch. It seems that there was no delay in gathering the church together at Antioch and reading the epistle. It gave great consolation to the church at Antioch. "Consolation" comes from the Greek "paraklesei," which means "encouragement"; consolation and exhortation are very close akin. There was great rejoicing at Antioch, and especially among the Gentile Christians there.

32 And Judas and Silas, being themselves also prophets,— The first mention of Judas and Silas (verse 22) classes them as "chief men among the brethren"; now they are spoken of as "prophets." "Prophetai" is the same word used for Paul and Barnabas and Agabus (Acts 11: 27-30); it means "for speakers for Christ." These brethren were useful while at Antioch, for they exhorted the brethren and confirmed them in the faith. It was a happy time with the church at Antioch to have this question settled, for it had given much trouble.

33 And after they had spent some time there,—We do not know how long Judas and Silas remained at Antioch, but long enough to encourage the church there. It seems that they were dismissed in a formal way as they were received in a formal way. "Dismissed in peace" was a formal dismissal. (Mark 5: 34; Luke 7: 50; 8: 48; Acts 16: 36.) Probably Judas and Silas returned to Jerusalem to give an account to the church there, but Silas soon returned to Antioch and he and Paul became fellow workers.

35 But Paul and Barnabas tarried in Antioch, teaching and *preaching the word of the Lord, with many others also.

*Comp. marginal note on ch. 5. 42

(34 **But it seemed good unto Silas to abide there.**)—This verse has been omitted by the revisers because it is not found in the older manuscripts and in many of the chief versions. It was evidently a marginal insertion to explain how Silas was conveniently at hand (verse 40) for Paul to choose him as a companion in travel.

35 **But Paul and Barnabas tarried in Antioch,**—Judas and Silas returned to Jerusalem, but Paul and Barnabas remained in Antioch. As they tarried in Antioch they taught and preached "the word of the Lord." During the sojourn of Paul and Barnabas in Antioch the dispute took place between Paul and Peter as related in Gal. 2: 11-16. Luke omits this episode, but relates the dispute between Paul and Barnabas. (Verse 39.) "Teaching" means to instruct; hence, they instructed the church. While "preaching" means the proclamation of the gospel, it is sometimes applied to evangelists who proclaim the gospel to aliens. "Teaching" is expounding the word of the Lord, while "preaching" is evangelizing or proclaiming the gospel. There were many other teachers and preachers in Antioch.

SECTION THREE

PAUL'S SECOND MISSIONARY JOURNEY
15: 36 to 18: 22

1. PAUL SELECTS SILAS
15: 36-41

36 And after some days Paul said unto Barnabas, Let us return now and visit the brethren in every city wherein we proclaimed the word of the Lord, *and see* how they fare. 37 And Barnabas was minded to take with them John also, who was called Mark. 38 But Paul thought not good to take with them him who withdrew from them from Pamphylia, and went not with

---

36 **And after some days Paul said unto Barnabas,**—Paul takes the initiative as the leader; he had publicly rebuked Peter (Gal. 2: 11-21) and is anxious to go back to the fields where he has planted churches. He desired to return and "visit the brethren in every city" where he and Barnabas had preached "the word of the Lord." He was anxious to see how the young churches were getting along, and to give them any further instructions that they might need. We must know that the "some days" and the "some time" that expired while the church was busy in the development of leaders and teachers kept up the zeal of the church. A commonly accepted chronology of Acts makes the interval between the visit of Paul and Barnabas to Jerusalem and the beginning of Paul's second missionary journey somewhat more than a year.

37 **And Barnabas was minded to take with them John**—Barnabas wished and willed to take along with them John Mark, his cousin. Mark had started with them on the first tour, but had turned around at Perga (Acts 13: 13) and returned to Jerusalem. It was to the house of Mary the mother of Mark that Peter went after his release from prison (Acts 12: 12).

38 **But Paul thought not good to take with them him**—Barnabas had resolved to take Mark with him, and may have spoken to him and arranged with him to go, but Paul thought it was not best to take Mark since he "withdrew from them from Pamphylia," and did not continue with them on their first journey. Here was a difference in judgment; we are not to understand that the Holy Spirit guided either one of these good men, as it was a mere

them to the work. 39 And there arose a sharp contention, so that they parted asunder one from the other, and Barnabas took Mark with him, and sailed away unto Cyprus: 40 but Paul chose Silas, and went forth, being

difference in human judgment as to what was expedient in the matter. Since Mark had turned back on the first journey, Paul was not willing to risk taking with them as a helper one who had left them in the midst of the work on their first journey.

39 **And there arose a sharp contention,**—"Contention" here comes from the Greek "paroxusmos," and is our word for "paroxysm" in English; it means to sharpen as of a blade, and of the spirit. It seems that the "Son of consolation," Barnabas, lost his temper in a dispute over his cousin, and Paul uses sharp words toward his benefactor and friend. It is frequently the case that little irritations of life give occasion for violent explosions. Some think that the incident between Paul and Peter (Gal. 2: 11-21) was known to Mark, and that Mark took sides with Peter; hence, Paul was not so kindly disposed to take Mark with them; he would have been a hindrance to the progress of the gospel among the Gentiles had he gone with them and held to the view that the Gentiles should be circumcised. However, we do not know any more than is recorded here. The result of the contention determined Paul and Barnabas to separate and each follow his own independent course. We know that Paul held no malice toward Barnabas and Mark. Barnabas is not mentioned again in Acts, but both Barnabas and Mark are mentioned by Paul in a way that showed confidence had been restored, for Paul speaks of them in warm commendation in his letters to Corinth, Colosse, and Timothy. (1 Cor. 9: 6; Col. 4: 10, 11; 2 Tim. 4: 11.) "Barnabas took Mark with him, and sailed away unto Cyprus." Cyprus was the home of Barnabas; this was the first place visited by Paul and Barnabas on their first tour. Paul's mention of Barnabas in 1 Cor. 9: 6 shows that Barnabas was busy in the work of the ministry, and the later mentions of Mark show that Paul had confidence in him and commended him very highly.

40 **but Paul chose Silas, and went forth,**—Silas had returned to Jerusalem with Judas after his visit to Antioch, but now we find

commended by the brethren to the grace of the Lord.   41 And he went
through Syria and Cilicia, confirming the churches.

him back in Antioch. Paul was commended by the brethren to the
grace of God which shows that his selection of Silas was approved
by the church at Antioch.   It seems that the sympathy of the
church at Antioch was with Paul rather than with Barnabas in the
contention between Paul and Barnabas. Silas was a suitable companion for Paul; he had influence in the church in Jerusalem
(verse 22) and was apparently a Roman citizen also. (Acts 16:
37.) Silas, or Silvanus, is mentioned in the epistles by Paul and
Peter. (1 Thess. 1: 1; 2 Thess. 1: 1; 2 Cor. 1: 19; 1 Pet. 5: 12.)
It is remarkable that Peter mentions both Mark and Silas as with
him at the same time. (1 Pet. 5: 12, 13.)

41 **And he went through Syria and Cilicia,**—Paul and Silas
went forth on Paul's second missionary tour to confirm the
churches and to establish other churches. They are to further the
cause of Christ especially among the Gentiles. It is interesting to
know that Barnabas went to his native Cyprus, and Paul went to
his native Cilicia, each to regions familiar from childhood. Paul
and Silas would have to go through a part of Syria in order to
reach Cilicia if they traveled by land. The letter from the church
at Jerusalem to the Gentile Christians would be of special interest
to the churches in Syria and Cilicia, as it was addressed to the
Christians in these provinces. (Acts 15: 23.)   The reading of
this letter would confirm the churches in these sections, but the
presence of Paul and Silas would have great influence on the
churches.

2. PAUL REVISITS THE CHURCHES: TIMOTHY
16: 1-5

1 And he came also to Derbe and to Lystra: and behold, a certain disci-

1 **And he came also to Derbe and to Lystra:**—The journey
of Paul on the second missionary tour appears to have been by
land northward from Antioch around the northeastern point of the
Mediterranean Sea and thence westward to Tarsus. Derbe was
the last point that Paul and Barnabas had visited on their first mis-

ple was there, named Timothy, the son of a Jewess that believed; but his father was a Greek. 2 The same was well reported of by the brethren that were at Lystra and Iconium. 3 Him would Paul have to go forth with him;

---

sionary tour; Lystra was the place where they had stoned Paul and "dragged him out of the city, supposing that he was dead." (Acts 14: 19.) Paul and Barnabas had left Lystra and gone to Derbe, but Paul is not afraid to return to Lystra. Lystra and Derbe were cities of Lycaonia. Timothy, or Timotheus, one of Paul's earliest converts (1 Tim. 1: 2), was the son of a Jewess and a Greek (2 Tim. 1: 5), who had been trained by his mother, Eunice, and his grandmother, Lois, in the Old Testament scriptures (2 Tim. 3: 15). Timothy had been converted at Lystra and had been pressed into the service by the Christians there. (1 Tim. 1: 18.) He had been given a gift by the elders of the church at Lystra and was now invited by Paul to accompany him on this tour. (1 Tim. 4: 14.) Paul's work took him among Jews as well as Gentiles, and the Jews would have looked upon Timothy as an apostate had he not been circumcised, so Paul, to avoid offense, circumcised the young man. Timothy afterward worked with Paul (Rom. 16: 21), and was his messenger to the Corinthian church (1 Cor. 4: 17) and to the church at Thessalonica (1 Thess. 3: 2-6.) He was at Rome with Paul. (Phil. 1: 1; 2: 19; Col. 1: 1; Phile. 1.) Timothy suffered much for the truth with Paul. (Heb. 13: 23.)

2 **The same was well reported of**—"Well reported of" is from the Greek "emartureito," and means "a continuous witness"; Timothy had good witness of his Christian life in his hometown of Lystra and also in Derbe; he had exercised his gifts and graces for the ministry and had been commended by the brethren. The phrase used here to describe Timothy is the same as that used to describe Cornelius (Acts 10: 22) and Ananias (Acts 22: 12). Timothy had been silently preparing himself for his work in the world by his work at Lystra and Iconium. Probably four or five years had elapsed since Paul had preached the gospel in these cities.

3 **Him would Paul have to go forth with him;**—Paul saw that Timothy would be not only a good gospel preacher and a great help to him, but that he would be a help to Timothy. The

and he took and circumcised him because of the Jews that were in those parts: for they all knew that his father was a Greek. 4 And as they went on their way through the cities, they delivered them the decrees to keep which

---

apostles desired to train younger men who could carry on the work after they had passed away; the elders and older ones in the church today should train the young men to carry on the work of the Lord. Later Paul wrote to Timothy and said: "The things which thou hast heard from me among many witnesses, the same commit thou to faithful men, who shall be able to teach others also." (2 Tim. 2: 2.)   Silas had taken the place of Barnabas, and Timothy is to take the place of Mark. Paul took Timothy and circumcised him; anyone could perform this rite.   Paul did not do this as a Christian act, for he had contended that it was not necessary to circumcise either Jew or Gentile in order to become a Christian.   The decision at Jerusalem had made it clear that the Gentile could become a Christian without circumcision, and that a Jew did not have to cease practicing circumcision in order to be a Christian; circumcision had nothing to do with becoming a Christian or with living the Christian life.   Timothy's father was a Greek or a Gentile, and while his mother and grandmother were faithful in teaching him the Old Testament, yet he had not been circumcised.   He had now been a Christian for four or five years, but had not been circumcised.   The conduct of Paul here was an instance of his accommodation to Jewish prejudices, and did not involve any departure from his previous views of Christian duty and Christian liberty.

4 **And as they went on their way through the cities,**— Wherever Paul and Silas went they delivered "the decrees" which had been "ordained of the apostles and elders that were at Jerusalem." This shows Paul's loyalty to the church at Jerusalem and to the other apostles. However, Paul did this because it was the will of God that it should be done. The word "decrees" here is from the Greek "dogmata," and that is from the Greek verb "dokeo," which means "to give an opinion."   It is used of public decrees of rulers (Luke 2: 1; Acts 17: 7), and of the requirements of the Mosaic law (Col. 2: 14).   Here it is used to designate the regulations or conclusions reached at Jerusalem. These "decrees" would

had been ordained of the apostles and elders that were at Jerusalem. 5 For the churches were strengthened ⁵in the faith, and increased in number daily.

⁵Or, *in faith*

encourage Gentile Christians, or encourage Gentiles to accept the gospel; they would also instruct the Jews as to the will of God on this question. Some claim that the word implies that Paul left copies of these "decrees" wherever he went.

5 **So the churches were strengthened in the faith,—** "Strengthened" is from the Greek "esterounto," and means "to make firm and solid." It is used here and in Acts 3: 7, 16—only three times in the New Testament. The blessings of God rested upon the work of Paul, Silas, and Timothy, and the churches increased "in number daily." The number of churches and of members was increased, for both ideas may be contained in this verse. The results of the work of Paul and his company were that the churches were confirmed in the faith, established in the truth of the gospel, and the number of churches and members were daily increased.

3. PAUL ENTERS EUROPE
16: 6-12

6 And they went through ⁶the region of Phrygia and Galatia, having been forbidden of the Holy Spirit to speak the word in Asia; 7 and when they

⁶Or, *Phrygia and the region of Galatia*

6 **And they went through the region of Phrygia and Galatia,—** "Phrygia" at this time was a broken portion of Asia Minor, under the jurisdiction of three or four distinct governors; it was west of Antioch in Pisidia; its chief cities mentioned in the New Testament are Colosse, Laodicea, and Hierapolis. "Galatia" was a great midland district of Asia Minor, east of Phrygia, inhabited by the descendants of the Gauls, who invaded Greece and Asia in the third century B.C. It became a formal province of Rome in A.D. 26. Paul laid the foundation of the Galatian churches, to which he wrote his epistle to the Galatians on this missionary tour. While he was in Galatia he was attacked by sickness. (Gal. 4: 13, 14.) He was not permitted by the Holy Spirit to speak the word or

were come over against Mysia, they assayed to go into Bithynia; and the
Spirit of Jesus suffered them not; 8 and passing by Mysia, they came down
to Troas.   9 And a vision appeared to Paul in the night: There was a man
of Macedonia standing, beseeching him, and saying, Come over into Mace-

preach in Asia on this trip. "Asia" represents the provinces of
Lydia, Mysia, and Caria.

7, 8 and when they were come over against Mysia,—The
territories or provinces then were not very well defined or outlined; hence, it is difficult to set the boundaries of these provinces.
Luke here says that Paul had been hindered by the Holy Spirit
from going west into Asia, but went northward so as to come in
front of Bithynia; this journey would take him directly through
Phrygia and the north Galatian country. "Bithynia" was a district
on the Black Sea; Paul was not allowed to deviate from the course
that led directly to Europe. It should be noticed that the Holy
Spirit led Paul away from the scene of his former labors and into
new fields. He had been warned not to preach in Asia, and he had
taken this as a sign to continue in the peninsuala and to return to
Galatia by Bithynia; he was checked again; he had now only one
way to travel, and that was westward to the seacoast; so he and
his companions went along the southern border of Mysia, and
passing by that region he came to Troas.

9 And a vision appeared to Paul in the night:—Troas bears
the name of the ancient Troy which was a seaport on the Helles-
point. This Troas was about four miles from the site of the ancient Troy. Paul and his company were led westward to this city,
and here the Lord caused Paul to have a vision one night, and in
this vision he saw a man of Macedonia, standing and "beseeching
him" by saying: "Come over into Macedonia, and help us."
"Vision" is from the Greek "horama," and includes something that
is seen. We are reminded here of the vision of Peter and Cornelius. Some think that this "man of Macedonia" was Luke; we
know that Luke joins Paul's company at Troas. Paul was miraculously granted this vision, as he had been divinely prohibited visiting other places; he is now divinely guided to go into Europe.
This vision does not come in the form of a command from Christ,
but it comes in the form of a petition from man. Paul understood

donia, and help us. 10 And when he had seen the vision, straightway we sought to go forth into Macedonia, concluding that God had called us to [7]preach the gospel unto them.

11 Setting sail therefore from Troas, we made a straight course to Samothrace, and the day following to Neapolis; 12 and from thence to Philippi, which is a city of Macedonia, the first of the district, a *Roman* colony: and

---

[7]Gr. *bring the good tidings.* See ch. 5. 42

---

the vision and at once made preparation to go into Europe.

10 **And when he had seen the vision,**—Paul "straightway," or immediately, "sought to go forth into Macedonia," for he concluded "that God had called us to preach the gospel unto them." Paul's answer to the call was earnest and instant; he was a man of action and was ready to obey the call at once. Luke introduces himself into the narrative by the pronoun "we"; he was a physician (Col. 4: 14) and a Gentile (Col. 4: 11, 14); it is possible that this means that Luke had been preaching the gospel in those regions and that he was happy to join the company with Paul. Luke accompanied Paul into Macedonia, and was with him at Samothrace, Neapolis, and Philippi. The way Luke introduces himself with the pronouns "we" and "us" shows that he was a preacher of the gospel as well as a physician. The clause, "that God had called us to preach the gospel," shows that he included himself with Paul, Silas, and Timothy as preachers of the gospel. Nothing is said here about their preaching the gospel in Troas, yet Paul makes reference to the church there in 2 Cor. 2: 12. Acts 20: 6 shows that there was a church at Troas.

11, 12 **Setting sail therefore from Troas,**—Samothrace was an island in the Aegean Sea on the Thracian coast, about sixty miles in a direct line from Troas. "Samothrace" is one of the most ancient names of the island of Samos, but in order to distinguish it from another Samos, in the sea, it was called by the compound name, "Samothrace," or "Samos of Trace," it being not far from the country of Thrace. "Neapolis" was a seaport in Macedonia. Luke was familiar with terms of travel by water. On this trip they had the wind in their favor and were able to take a straight course. They went from Neapolis to Philippi, a distance of about twelve miles inland. Philippi was a Roman colony, and was the capital or chief city of Macedonia. They tarried at this place certain days.

4. LYDIA CONVERTED
16: 13-15

we were in this city tarrying certain days. 13 And on the sabbath day we went forth without the gate by a river side, [8]where we supposed there was a place of prayer; and we sat down, and spake unto the women that were come together. 14 And a certain woman named Lydia, a seller of purple, of

---

[8]Many authorities read *where was wont to be &c.*

---

13 **And on the sabbath day we went forth**—Paul and his company wasted no time after arriving at Philippi; on the Sabbath day, the Jewish Sabbath, Paul's company went "without the gate by a river side" and found some women who were accustomed to meeting there for prayer. It seems that there was no synagogue in Philippi and that these women went to this accustomed place for worship. The little river Gangites or Gargites was one mile west of the town. Philippi was a military outpost of the Roman government, and but few Jews lived there. It may be that Paul and his company had located this place of prayer before this time; they probably saw it as they entered Philippi. The rule of the rabbis required ten men to constitute a synagogue, but here had gathered only a group of women. Where the Jews had no synagogue they sometimes had a building or an open-air place near the river or sea; they needed the water for ceremonial washings. While in Babylon "by the rivers" they sat down. (Psalm 137: 1; Ezra 8: 15, 21.) Claudius had banished the Jews from Rome, and therefore from colonies (Acts 18: 2), and it may be that this Roman city had obeyed that order. "We sat down, and spake unto the women" that gathered there. Sitting was the Jewish attitude for public speaking; it was not mere conversation, but more likely conversational preaching of an expository character. Luke uses the pronoun "we," including himself, Paul, Silas, and Timothy, but Paul was the chief speaker.

14 **And a certain woman named Lydia,**—"Lydia" was a common name among the Greeks and Romans; it was itself a province in Asia Minor; she was born in Thyatira which was in Lydia. Thyatira was one of the seven churches of Asia mentioned in Rev.

the city of Thyatira, one that worshipped God, heard us: whose heart the
Lord opened to give heed unto the things which were spoken by Paul. 15
And when she was baptized, and her household, she besought us, saying, If

---

2: 18; it was famous for its purple dyes. Lydia was a seller of
purple, either the coloring matter or the fabric already dyed. The
purple color was esteemed very highly by the ancients. There was
great demand for this fabric, as it was used on the official toga at
Rome and in Roman colonies. The term "royal purple" is still
used. (Luke 16: 19.) Lydia was a woman of some means to
carry on such an important business so far from her native city;
some think that she was a free-woman, since racial names were
often borne by slaves. Lydia "worshipped God"; she heard Paul
and his company preach the gospel. She was either a Jewess or a
proselyte to the Jewish religion. The Greek for "worshipped" is
"sebomene," and means "a God-fearer, or proselyte of the gate."
It may be that she had become a proselyte while in Philippi; she
was only a sojourner in Philippi, for Paul writes a letter to the
church at Philippi later, but does not mention Lydia, the first convert of the church there. "Whose heart the Lord opened" simply
means that her mind was enlightened by the preaching of the gospel. "Opened" is from the Greek "dienoixen," which means "to
open up wide or completely like a folding door." A person's heart
is said to be closed up against instruction when it is unwilling to
hear it or to obey it. Jesus opened the mind of the disciples to
understand the scriptures. (Luke 24: 45.) God had led Paul and
his company to Lydia, and they had preached the gospel by the
power of the Holy Spirit to her, and caused her to understand;
hence, in this way the Lord "opened" her heart. She gave "heed
unto the things which were spoken by Paul." Here Paul is made
the chief speaker. "To give heed" is from the Greek "prosechein,"
and means "to hold the mind on, or to keep the mind centered on"
the things which were spoken by Paul, whose words gripped her
attention.

15 **And when she was baptized, and her household,**—Both
Lydia and all who composed her family received the truth which
Paul presented; her household consisted of persons in her employ.
The Gangites River was near, as this prayer meeting was held "by

ye have judged me to be faithful to the Lord, come into my house, and abide *there*. And she constrained us.

---

a river"; so Lydia was baptized in the river. "Household" is from the Greek "oikos," and originally meant the building, and then it came to mean the inmates of the house. There is nothing here to show whether Lydia's "household" included any others than "the women" whom she had employed. There is no evidence that her household included any infants, as the household of Cornelius, the jailer, and Crispus evidently had no infants in them. There is no evidence that Lydia even was married or had a husband or had children. There is no evidence here of infant baptism. After her conversion she persuaded Paul and his company to sojourn with her for a while. Peter's reception at the house of Simon, the tanner, and the entertainment of Lydia are instances of the hospitality which was characteristic of early Christians.

5. PAUL AND SILAS IN PRISON
16: 16-24

16 And it came to pass, as we were going to the place of prayer, that a certain maid having [1]a spirit of divination met us, who brought her masters

---

[1]Gr. *a spirit, a Python*

---

16 And it came to pass, as we were going—Paul and his company continued to visit the place of prayer by the riverside in Philippi after the conversion of Lydia and her household for some days; we are not told just how long they continued to visit this place; they could get an audience there and hence preach the gospel to those who gathered there. One day while they were on their way to this place of prayer "a certain maid having a spirit of divination" met them; Luke is in the company, as he uses the pronoun "us." This maid was a slave, and she was possessed with "a spirit of divination"; the Greek is "pneuma puthona," which means the spirit of python. "Python" was the spirit that traditionally guarded Delphi. In Greek mythology Python was a dragon, which was slain by Apollo, who was called the Pythian Apollo; and as Apollo was the god of oracles, his priests were said to be inspired by him. This slave girl was owned by joint owners who used her

much gain by soothsaying. 17 The same following after Paul and us cried out, saying, These men are ²servants of the Most High God, who proclaim unto you ³the way of salvation. 18 And this she did for many days. But Paul, being sore troubled, turned and said to the spirit, I charge thee in the name of Jesus Christ to come out of her. And it came out that very hour. 19 But when her masters saw that the hope of their gain was ⁴gone, they

---

²Gr. *bondservants*
³Or, *a way*
⁴Gr. *come out*

---

powers as a source of revenue, and it appears that they made large sums of money from her unfortunate condition.

17 **The same following after Paul and us**—This maiden followed Paul, Silas, and Luke: Timothy may have been in the company. As she followed them she "cried out" to those who were in hearing distance that "these men are servants of the Most High God"; the heathen used this inscription for the Supreme Being; her testimony was like that borne by the demoniacs to Jesus as "Son of the Most High God." (Luke 8: 28.) Demons frequently bore testimony to the divinity of Jesus. (Matt. 8: 29; Mark 1: 24; 3: 11; Luke 4: 41.) This maiden may have heard Paul preach about Jesus as "the way of salvation." She knew the mission of Paul and his company; he preached Jesus to sinners as the way of salvation.

18 **And this she did for many days.**—She kept this testimony before the public by repeating her words for "many days." Paul was not willing to receive the testimony of this "spirit of divination"; he wanted the faith of people to be based upon the word of God, the testimony of the Holy Spirit, and not upon the testimony of demons. Paul, "being sore troubled" at the persistent testimony of this maiden, rebuked the spirit by saying: "I charge thee in the name of Jesus Christ to come out of her." Paul recognized the demon or evil spirit in her and spoke to it. He commanded the spirit "in the name of Jesus Christ," or by his authority, to come out of her. This was according to the promise of Jesus. (Mark 16: 17.) Paul did not want any evidence from this source, as he did not want the homage of the people of Lystra. (Acts 14: 14.) The evil spirit obeyed immediately and came out of her.

19 **But when her masters saw**—When those who jointly owned her saw that the hope of their gain was gone, they were

laid hold on Paul and Silas, and dragged them into the marketplace before the rulers, 20 and when they had brought them unto the ⁵magistrates, they said, These men, being Jews, do exceedingly trouble our city, 21 and set forth customs which it is not lawful for us to receive, or to observe, being Romans. 22 And the multitude rose up together against them: and the

⁵Gr. *proetors*: comp. ver. 22, 35, 36, 38

angry with Paul and Silas and seized them and "dragged them into the marketplace before the rulers." "The marketplace" was the Roman forum near which would be the courts of law as in our courthouse square. They were seeking for revenge; hence, they had Paul and Silas arrested and brought before the proper authorities for trial and punishment.

20, 21 **and when they had brought them unto the magistrates,**—"Magistrates" is from the Greek "strategois," and literally means "leader of an army, or general"; but in civic life it means a governor. "Strategois" is the Greek rendering of the Latin "praetores," or praetors; the Roman praetors were accompanied by "lictors," who bore rods with which to punish those who were convicted. The joint owners of this slave girl attempted to prejudice the court before any evidence was given; they said these men, "being Jews," caused trouble in the city. They caused the trouble by setting "forth customs" which, they said, they were not according to law to receive, "or to observe," as Roman citizens. There is a sharp contrast between Paul and his company, "being Jews," and those who were making the charge as Roman citizens. Roman magistrates would not pass sentence on abstract theological questions (Acts 18: 15), but if the peace was disturbed or a secret sect was organized, the magistrates would pass sentence on these things. The Roman law forbade Romans to introduce or practice any new religion; they were required to worship their own gods and no others. The Jews were permitted to practice their own religion, provided they did not attempt to proselyte Roman citizens. Hence, when Paul and Silas preached Jesus, they were preaching a new religion and were subject to prosecution and punishment according to the Roman law. The owners of this girl sought vengeance on Paul and Silas by thus bearing witness against them.

22 **And the multitude rose up together against them:—** There was no mob, as Paul and Silas were in the hands of officers,

⁵magistrates rent their garments off them, and commanded to beat them with rods. 23 And when they had laid many stripes upon them, they cast them into prison, charging the jailor to keep them safely: 24 who, having received such a charge, cast them into the inner prison, and made their feet fast in the

---

but a sudden and violent uprising of the people reinforced the charges that had been made against them; there was a strong appeal to race and national prejudice. This violent uprising had its influence on the "magistrates," and they "rent their garments off them," and commanded that Paul and Silas be beaten "with rods." The magistrates did not tear their own clothes off themselves, but did tear the clothes off Paul and Silas that the lictors might beat their bare backs with their rods. The magistrates gave the orders that Paul and Silas be beaten with rods. Paul later said: "Thrice was I beaten with rods." (2 Cor. 11: 25.) This may have been one of the times.

23 **And when they had laid many stripes upon them,**— "Many stripes" is from the Greek "pollas plegas" the Jewish law was forty stripes save one, or thirty-nine stripes. (2 Cor. 11: 24.) The Roman custom depended on the whims of the judge; it was a severe ordeal. It was the custom to inflict the stripes on the naked body. After Paul and Silas were beaten they were then put in prison and the jailer given strict orders to keep them safely. Luke does not include himself or Timothy in this punishment.

24 **who, having received such a charge,**—The jailer was given strict orders to put them in prison, and was given such strict orders that he thought he would put them in the safest place, so he "cast them into the inner prison, and made their feet fast in the stocks." "The inner prison" was the third compartment of the prison. In a Roman prison there were usually three distinct parts: (1) the communiora, or where the prisoners had light and fresh air; (2) the interiora, shut off by strong iron gates with bars and locks; (3) the tullianium, or dungeon, the place of execution or for one condemned to die. Not only were they put in the inner prison, but their feet were placed "in the stocks." Usually the "stocks" were fixed so that the arms and legs, and even necks of the prisoners were confined; but here only the feet were placed in the stocks. "Stocks" was an instrument of torture as well as con-

finement, consisting of heavy pieces of wood with holes, into which
the feet were placed in such a manner that they were stretched
widely apart so as to cause the sufferer great pain. Paul and Silas
were placed in such torture during this eventful night.

6. THE JAILER CONVERTED
16: 25-34

stocks. 25 But about midnight Paul and Silas were praying and singing
hymns unto God, and the prisoners were listening to them; 26 and suddenly
there was a great earthquake, so that the foundations of the prison-house
were shaken: and immediately all the doors were opened: and every one's

25 But about midnight Paul and Silas were praying—"Midnight" was one division of the watches. Paul and Silas were suffering from stripes, loss of blood, hunger, and the stocks in which
they were fastened. It seems that they had not slept any up to this
time, yet in the midst of their suffering and inconvenience of position, they could pray to God and sing his praises. They were
praying and singing simultaneously, and blending together their
petition and praise. Their wounds were undressed, filth and ver-
min that infested prisons of that day added to their pain, while
their position was one of torture, sleep was out of the question, but
they had the privilege and comfort of prayer. Other prisoners
heard their prayers and songs; they were "listening to them." It
was an unusual occurrence for prisoners to be praying and praising God; Paul and Silas sang the gospel, and men who would not
listen to a sermon heard the gospel in song. Other prisoners were
not the only ones who heard Paul and Silas; God and Christ, for
whom they were suffering, heard them.

26 and suddenly there was a great earthquake,—Luke and
Timothy were not in prison; we know not why they were not cast
into prison with Paul and Silas; hence, Luke regards this "earthquake," Greek "seismos," or shaking of the earth as an answer to
prayer. (Acts 4: 31.) This was a very violent earthquake, for it
even was felt down to the foundations of the prison walls and the
doors were broken open, and the staples of the chains fell out of
the walls. The opening of the doors and the loosening of the
chains by the earthquake is difficult to understand unless one understands the construction of the prisons of that time. The quak-

bands were loosed. 27 And the jailor, being roused out of sleep and seeing
the prison doors open, drew his sword and was about to kill himself, supposing that the prisoners had escaped. 28 But Paul cried with a loud voice,
saying, Do thyself no harm: for we are all here. 29 And he called for lights

ing of the earth forced the door posts apart from each other so
that the bar which fastened the door slipped from its hold, and the
door swung open. The chains and stocks were detached from the
wall which was shaken so that they were loose from the wall.

27 **And the jailor, being roused out of sleep**—Such an earthquake would naturally arouse the jailer and frighten all of the prisoners. It is noted that neither the groans nor singing of hymns
had kept the jailer from sleeping; nothing but the terror of an
earthquake could disturb him. When he saw that the prison doors
were open, he naturally supposed that the prisoners had all escaped
and, knowing that he would have to pay the penalty for their escape with his own life, he "was about to kill himself." By the
Roman law the jailer was subject to the same death as the escaped
prisoners would have suffered; suicide was preferred by many to
the death and torture that they would have to suffer. Sometimes
jailers were selected from the lowest class, and sometimes from the
criminal class (Acts 12: 19; 27: 42), and were punished by death
if the prisoners escaped. It appears that the prisoners were too
frightened to escape, or did not have time to escape before the
jailer made his appearance.

28 **But Paul cried with a loud voice, saying,**—Paul was master of the situation here as he frequently was at other times. He
saw what the jailer was about to do, and checked him by crying
with a "loud voice." "Do thyself no harm: for we are all here."
The earthquake had loosened the staples of the chains which were
fastened in the wall and then to the prisoners, and the bars of the
doors had been loosened and the doors opened, but no prisoner had
escaped; it may be that the chains were still on the prisoners and
prevented a hasty escape; at any rate, none of them had escaped.
Some have questioned the accuracy of Luke's account by saying
that Paul could not see what the jailer was about to do, as the
jailer could not see that the prisoners had not escaped; however,
there was enough light for Paul to see what was about to be done;

and sprang in, and, trembling for fear, fell down before Paul and Silas, 30 and brought them out and said, Sirs, what must I do to be saved? 31 And they said, Believe on the Lord Jesus, and thou shalt be saved, thou and thy

the jailer saw the prison doors open without any other light, and so Paul could and did see what the jailer was about to do.

29, 30 And he called for lights and sprang in,—When the jailer heard Paul's assuring command, he called for lights and made a hasty investigation and found that Paul had spoken the truth to him; he then, "trembling for fear, fell down before Paul and Silas." In some way he connected the earthquake and the safety of the prisoners with Paul and Silas. He may have known something of their miraculous power, and especially the cure of the slave girl for which Paul and Silas had been thrust into prison. It is very probable that the jailer first attended to his proper duties and secured all the prisoners before he came to Paul and Silas; his life was at stake, and he would promptly see that the prisoners were safe before he did anything else. It seems very unreasonable that he would neglect attention to the other prisoners and come and fall down at the feet of Paul and Silas. The jailer brought Paul and Silas out of the inner prison and probably into the court and asked: "Sirs, what must I do to be saved?" He left the other prisoners inside and realized that he must now deal with these men of whom he had heard something as servants of the "Most High God." The jailer did not ask what he should do to be saved from the wrath of his superiors; he had nothing to fear from them, since the prisoners were all safe. Neither did he ask what he should do to save himself from the anger of heathen gods, for his appeal would not be to Paul and Silas, as they did not worship these gods. The answer that Paul gave implies the meaning of his question; he is asking what he must do to be saved from his sins.

31 And they said, Believe on the Lord Jesus,—He had asked both Paul and Silas what he should do to be saved from his sins, and now both are included in the answer; "they said" is the expression that Luke uses. "Believe on the Lord Jesus" is the answer to this direct question. Faith in the Christ, personal trust in him as a Redeemer, is required. "And in none other is there salvation: for neither is there any other name under heaven, that is

house. 32 And they spake the word of ⁶the Lord unto him, with all that
were in his house. 33 And he took them the same hour of the night, and

⁶Some ancient authorities read *God*

given among men, wherein we must be saved." (Acts 4: 12.)
The answer is brief, simple, plain, and accurate; not only could he
be saved through faith in Christ, but his entire household could be
saved; in fact, everyone could be saved on the same terms of the
gospel.

32 **And they spake the word of the Lord unto him,**—The
answer was that the jailer should believe on the Lord Jesus Christ;
but he cannot believe in Jesus as the Savior of the world, as his
Savior, without evidence. "So belief cometh of hearing, and hearing by the word of Christ." (Rom. 10: 17.) He could not believe without first hearing the evidence of testimony concerning
the Christ; hence, "they spake the word of the Lord unto him" and
to all "that were in his house." Paul and Silas preached the gospel to them so that he could obey their command to believe on the
Lord Jesus Christ. Paul and Silas had sung the gospel to the prisoners, and they now preached it to the jailer and all that were in
his house. As a heathen the jailer was ignorant of both the truths
and commands of the gospel; these were taught him by Paul and
Silas; hence, his faith would have a true foundation. They spoke
the word of the Lord not only to the jailer, but to those who were
in his house; this shows that the jailer's household was composed
of those who were capable of hearing and understanding the gospel; hence, they were responsible if they did not hear and obey the
gospel.

33 **And he took them the same hour of the night,**—"He took
them" implies that he took them away from one place to that of
another; we are not informed as to where he took them, but we
know that he took them to a place where there was much water,
for he "washed their stripes." This shows that he not only believed the words that had been preached to him, but that he was
penitent of his sins, and was willing to do everything that he could
for the comfort and ease of Paul and Silas. He "was baptized, he
and all his, immediately." There was no delay in his doing what
he was commanded to do. In giving the commission Jesus had

washed their stripes; and was baptized, he and all his, immediately. 34 And
he brought them up into his house, and set ⁷food before them, and rejoiced
greatly, with all his house, ⁸having believed in God.

⁷Gr. *a table*
⁸Or, *having believed God*

said: "He that believeth and is baptized shall be saved; but he that
disbelieveth shall be condemned." (Mark 16: 16.) The jailer
had heard the gospel, he believed it, was penitent of his sins, and is
now baptized; on these conditions and obedience to them, he could
claim remission of sins. All who had heard the gospel in the
jailer's household, and all who believed it, were baptized. It is
worthy of note that there was no delay in their being baptized; no
one deferred baptism by the instruction of an inspired guide, but,
on the other hand, in every case of their hearing, believing, repenting of their sins, baptism was attended to immediately.

34 **And he brought them up into his house,**—The jailer now
does all that he can for Paul and Silas. As a jailer he was not
acting illegally, for while he was responsible for the prisoners, he
was under no obligations to fulfill this duty in any particular way.
Paul and Silas would not try to escape, and the jailer had confidence in them as servants of God. The jailer must be responsible
for the safekeeping of his prisoners, and he now feels safe about
Paul and Silas. After bringing them "up into his house" he "set
food before them, and rejoiced greatly." He had occasion to rejoice. We note the contrast between the jailer's joy and the dread
of the magistrates. (Verse 38.) A great change had taken place
within a short time in the jailer's house. It is very likely that the
trouble and arrest of Paul and Silas took place at the third hour of
the day, or nine o'clock in the morning, and they had probably
been fasting for nearly twenty-four hours. We do not know who
this jailer was, but some have suggested he was Stephanas. (1
Cor. 1: 16; 16: 15, 17.) Lydia and her household were the first
converts in Europe and at Philippi; the jailer and his household
were the next; hence, the nucleus of the church at Philippi was the
households of Lydia and the jailer. Later Paul wrote a letter to
this church.

7. PAUL AND SILAS RELEASED FROM PRISON
16: 35-40

35 But when it was day, the [9]magistrates sent the [10]serjeants, saying, Let those men go. 36 And the jailor reported the words to Paul, *saying,* The [9]magistrates have sent to let you go: now therefore come forth, and go in peace. 37 But Paul said unto them, They have beaten us publicly, uncondemned, men that are Romans, and have cast us into prison; and do they

[9]Gr. *proetors.* See ver. 20
[10]Gr. *lictors*

---

35 But when it was day, the magistrates sent—The magistrates or praetors and lictors knew nothing about what had taken place during the night, but they surely had learned something about the earthquake and its effects. All that Luke has related took place in the night, so the next morning early the authorities sent the lictors or sergeants and commanded them to "let those men go." There had been no further inquiry as to the charges against Paul and Silas, no regular trial, but the magistrates were uneasy. No reason is given for the change of mind of the magistrates; the jailer received orders to release Paul and Silas.

36 And the jailor reported the words to Paul,—No doubt the jailer received the words with joy, because he was now in sympathy with Paul and Silas and would be glad to see them go without further trial or punishment. He even invited Paul and Silas to "come forth, and go in peace." Paul and Silas had not taken advantage of the jailer simply because they were preachers of the gospel; although they had baptized the jailer and his household, yet they asked no favors of him that would involve him in any way with the authorities. Paul and Silas knew a better way, and did not obey the orders of the jailer.

37 But Paul said unto them, They have beaten us publicly, —The reply of Paul is very full of brevity and energy, and brings a serious charge against the magistrates. He charges the authorities with the following: (1) beating them publicly; (2) beating uncondemned men; (3) beating with rods men that are Roman citizens; (4) after beating them they had been cast into prison. These four charges were serious; Paul knew that they were, and he does not hesitate to prefer these charges. The magistrates had done so much publicly, and they now sought to release Paul and Silas privately; they attempted to evade the charges and escape

now cast us out privily? nay verily; but let them come themselves and bring us out. 38 And the ¹⁰serjeants reported these words unto the ⁹magistrates: and they feared when they heard that they were Romans; 39

any punishment that was due them. Paul rightly demanded vindication; he demanded that they acknowledge their mistakes and correct them. They were too eager to cast Paul and Silas into prison, and they are now too eager to dismiss them; they have prisoners on their hands with whom they must now reckon. If Paul and Silas had gone away secretly, a stain would have rested on their reputation, which would have reflected dishonor on the gospel they preached. Paul's reply was that they publicly declared them criminals by the treatment given them, and now they must publicly declare their innocence. They had violated the Roman law in beating Roman citizens before they were condemned; they had done this openly; that is, publicly; they had put them in prison without a fair trial; these were all serious charges.

38 **And the serjeants reported these words**—The "serjeants" were the lictors, whose duty it was to carry the rods and scourge those who were sentenced to punishment. The sergeants were sent by the magistrates to release or have released Paul and Silas. When the magistrates heard that Paul, and probably Silas, were Roman citizens, they "feared" because they had scourged and imprisoned Roman citizens without a fair trial. Paul submitted to scourging by his own countrymen five times (2 Cor. 11: 24), but never claimed the rights as a Roman citizen to the Jews. The magistrates did not know that Paul and Silas were Roman citizens, as Lysias did not know it. (Acts 22: 27.) No one challenged Paul's claim as a Roman citizen at any time; it was a grave offense to make a false claim to Roman citizenship. To violate the Roman law with respect to Roman citizenship subjected a magistrate to the danger of being summoned to Rome to answer for his offense; the punishment for this crime was death and confiscation of goods. This accounts for the fear that these magistrates had when they heard of Paul's Roman citizenship. Death was the penalty for making a claim to Roman citizenship when it was false; seldom did anyone make a false claim because of the severe penalty; hence, they believed Paul's statement.

and they came and besought them; and when they had brought them out, they asked them to go away from the city. 40 And they went out of the prison, and entered into *the house of* Lydia: and when they had seen the brethren, they [11]comforted them, and departed.

[11]Or, *exhorted*

39 **and they came and besought them;**—It is very probable that the magistrates made due amends for the wrongs they had done to Paul and Silas. They now urgently besought them to leave the city. "They asked" them to leave the city. "Asked" is from the Greek "eroton," and means that they kept on begging them to leave the city for fear of further trouble The magistrates had no right to command or demand that they leave the city, but they asked them as a favor and as a means of preventing any further trouble. Paul and Silas were willing to go, but not secretly; Paul would not desert the young converts nor bring a scandal on the name of Christ by a secret departure; they departed leisurely in such a way as to clear their own names of any blame or shame that might be attached to their imprisonment. Paul and Silas were vindicated, and they could now leave the city.

40 **And they went out of the prison,**—When they left the prison they went to the house of Lydia where the disciples assembled there to greet them. "The brethren" here include Luke and Timothy, the jailer and those who were baptized with him, and others who were converted in Philippi. Paul, Silas, Timothy, and Luke were all guests of Lydia before Paul and Silas' imprisonment. (Verse 15.) It is very likely that the church at Philippi first met in the house of Lydia. Paul and Silas "comforted" the brethren. Who needed comforting more than Paul and Silas? Yet they comforted others. After comforting the brethren Paul and Silas "departed"; Luke and Timothy did not accompany them, but remained at Philippi; some think that Luke remained until Paul returned to Philippi. From Luke's use of the pronouns "we" and "us," we learned that he was with Paul and Silas from Troas to Philippi. He uses a different mode of expression in this verse; namely, the use of the third person, "they"; this shows that the writer did not accompany Paul and Silas from Philippi; he continues to use the third person in his narrative until he comes to Acts

20: 5, where the use of the first person is resumed. By a study of these passages and of Acts 20: 6, it appears probable that Luke remained in Philippi until Paul returned to this city on his way to Asia Minor and to Jerusalem. Luke mentions Timothy in Acts 17: 14, and from that passage we learn that he was afterward at Berea with Paul and Silas. Paul left him there with Silas when he himself went to Athens; hence, we conclude that Timothy was left with Luke at Philippi, while Paul and Silas went through Amphipolis and Apollonia to Thessalonica.

8, PAUL AND SILAS AT THESSALONICA
17: 1-9

1 Now when they had passed through Amphipolis and Apollonia, they came to Thessalonica, where was a synagogue of the Jews: 2 and Paul, as his custom was, went in unto them, and for three ¹sabbath days reasoned with them from the scriptures, 3 opening and alleging that it behooved the

¹Or, *weeks*

1 **Now when they had passed through Amphipolis**—Paul and Silas left Philippi and "passed through Amphipolis and Apollonia." They journeyed southwest from Philippi about thirty-three miles and came to Amphipolis, which was a Roman military station; Apollonia was about thirty miles farther on, in the district of Macedonia known as Mygdonia, and was about thirty-seven miles from Thessalonica. It seems that Paul and his company did not stop very long in these cities; some think that it was not wise for them to remain so near Philippi as Apollonia. In neither city was there a synagogue as a center of worship; these cities could be evangelized better from Philippi and Thessalonica. Thessalonica was the largest city in Macedonia; the article before "synagogue" implies that this was the chief, if not the only, synagogue of the district; hence, it is concluded that the other towns passed through had no synagogues.

2, 3 **and Paul, as his custom was,**—Paul followed "his custom" of going to the Jews first. Later he wrote: "For I am not ashamed of the gospel: for it is the power of God unto salvation to every one that believeth; to the Jew first, and also to the Greek." (Rom. 1: 16.) Paul preached the gospel "to the Jew first" and then to the Gentiles. The Jews met in their synagogue and, since

Christ to suffer, and to rise again from the dead; and that this Jesus, whom, *said he,* I proclaim unto you, is the Christ. 4 And some of them were persuaded, and consorted with Paul and Silas; and of the devout Greeks a great multitude, and of the chief women not a few. 5 But the Jews, being moved with jealousy, took unto them certain vile fellows of the rabble, and gather-

---

Paul was a Jew, he had access to the synagogue and went there and preached Christ; he used the Jewish center of worship as a place from which to radiate the gospel to the Gentiles. Here he remained "for three sabbath days," and reasoned "from the scriptures," the Old Testament, and proclaimed Jesus as the Christ unto them. It is to be understood that Paul and his company were busy the other days of the week preaching from house to house the unsearchable riches of Christ. "Opening" and "alleging" mean that he made plain what was before announced and asserted with reasons for his assertion. He showed from the scriptures that it was necessary for Christ to suffer, to be crucified, buried, and raised from the dead; hence, it was no reproach on Christ that he had been crucified; the prophets had foretold this.

4 **And some of them were persuaded,**—Some of the Jews believed or were convinced by Paul's reasoning. It seems that Paul's teaching was by arguments which they were unable to refute. Those who believed "consorted with Paul and Silas." "Consorted" is from the Greek "proskleroo," which means "to assign by lot"; hence, those who believed were given to Paul and Silas by the grace of God. These believers cast in their lot with Paul and Silas and decided to be associated with them. A few of the Jews were convinced, but a great number "of the devout Greeks," proselytes of the gate, believed; these were heathen by birth who had embraced a part of the Jewish faith. They did not have the religious prejudices which clung so closely to the Jews. Many of "the chief women" also believed. Many women of the highest social standing became believers here as they did at Philippi and Berea. There seem to have been four classes who were converted at this place: (1) Jews; (2) Greek God-fearing proselytes; (3) other Greeks; (4) honorable women.

5 **But the Jews, being moved with jealousy,**—This means the unbelieving Jews. Our English words "zeal" and "jealousy" are from the same Greek word "zelos." These unbelieving Jews were

ing a crowd, set the city on an uproar; and assaulting the house of Jason, they sought to bring them forth to the people. 6 And when they found them not, they dragged Jason and certain brethren before the rulers of the city, crying, These that have turned [2]the world upside down are come hither also; 7 whom Jason hath received: and these all act contrary to the decrees of

[2]Gr. *the inhabited earth*

filled "with jealousy." They did not like to see so many drawn away from their own party; they were jealous of Paul and Silas as the Jews were jealous of the leadership of Christ. They knew how to raise a mob; they went to "certain vile fellows of the rabble" and raised a mob and "set the city on an uproar." It is strange that the Jewish rabbis would resort to such base methods of opposing the truth; it is also strange how such ones could excite the people so as to cause an uproar in the city. "Vile fellows of the rabble" mean those who had no calling, but lounged around the market place in the hope of picking up a chance living, and who were ready for anything bad or good that might present itself. There must have been many Jews in Thessalonica. This mob, excited by religious prejudice and jealousy, made an attack on the "house of Jason." It seems that he was the host of Paul and Silas; we know nothing more of him than is revealed here. The name is found in the list of those whom Paul speaks of as his "kinsmen," but this may be quite a different person. (Rom. 16: 21.) They sought to bring Jason and his guests out to the people who were infuriated and ready to do them violence.

6, 7 **And when they found them not,**—Paul and Silas were not found; it is not known where they were. They then seized Jason and "dragged" him and "certain brethren before the rulers." Their failure to find Paul and Silas augmented their anger, and they sought to take vengeance on Jason and any other Christians whom they could lay hands on. They brought them before the city officials; Thessalonica was a free city. During these three weeks Paul and Silas had made many disciples and a congregation or church had been formed. They preferred the charge against Paul and Silas that they had "turned the world upside down," or had disturbed the peace wherever they had gone. "The world" means the inhabited earth, and especially the whole Roman Empire, which embraced a very large portion of the known world.

Caesar, saying that there is another king, *one* Jesus. 8 And they troubled
the multitude and the rulers of the city, when they heard these things. 9
And when they had taken security from Jason and the rest, they let them go.

Perhaps their accusation was exaggerated, as men moved by the
spirit of jealousy do not correctly represent their enemies. They
furthermore charged Jason with having received these disturbers
of the peace. Jason was charged with aiding and plotting with
Paul and Silas as traitors. They specify before the rulers that
they were teaching and acting "contrary to the decrees of Caesar."
Paul in preaching Jesus preached him as a King; these grossly
prejudiced accusers did not understand the nature of his kingdom
or the sense in which Jesus was King. This was the same charge
with which the Pharisees and Herodians had attempted to catch
Jesus. (Mark 12: 14.) It is the same charge that the Sanhedrin
made against Jesus to Pilate. (Luke 23: 2.) The Jews here, as
before Pilate (John 19: 15), renounced their hope of a Messianic
King.

8, 9 **And they troubled the multitude**—These Jews, by bringing Jason and other Christians before the rulers, caused more disturbance than Paul and Silas had caused; they created confusion;
when the rulers heard the accusation they were disturbed. They
were ignorant of many of the facts, nevertheless they were troubled
about the matter. They would not let Jason and the brethren go
until they had put them under bond not to disturb the peace. The
exact point of this guarantee is not stated; however, it is implied
that they did not want preached that which had caused the disturbance; they may have requested that Paul and Silas leave the city.
The charge that they brought against the brethren was serious, but
the proof was meager, so all that could be done was to take security of the brethren.

9. AT BEREA
17: 10-14

10 And the brethren immediately sent away Paul and Silas by night unto

10 **And the brethren immediately sent away Paul and Silas**
—Berea was about fifty miles southwest of Thessalonica. Paul's

Beroea: who when they were come thither went into the synagogue of the Jews. 11 Now these were more noble than those in Thessalonica, in that they received the word with all readiness of mind, examining the scriptures daily, whether these things were so. 12 Many of them therefore believed; also of the Greek women of honorable estate, and of men, not a few. 13 But

labors had not been in vain in Thessalonica; he had established a church there. (1 Thess. 1: 7f; 2: 13, 20.) Two of the brethren, Aristarchus and Secundus, later accompanied Paul to Jerusalem (Acts 20: 4), and Aristarchus finally went with him to Rome (Acts 27: 2). The brethren immediately sent Paul and Silas from Thessalonica. They left at night, and Timothy either left with them or soon followed them, for we find him at Berea. (Verse 14.) Paul was not able to return to Thessalonica, but later sent Timothy back to the church there. (1 Thess. 3: 2.) Paul found a synagogue at Berea and immediately began preaching there. We are not told how long they were on the way coming to Berea.

11 **Now these were more noble than those in Thessalonica,** —This is a great commendation of the Jews at Berea. "More noble" is applied first to nobility of birth, but here it applies to character. They received Paul's preaching "with all readiness of mind," but they examined "the scriptures daily" to ascertain whether he was preaching the truth. Evidently Paul had used the Old Testament scriptures, and they were examining these to verify what Paul preached. It does not appear how long they continued searching the scriptures, but evidently long enough to satisfy their own minds as to the truth. It is refreshing to find that the people of Berea exercised greater candor, more openness of mind, and intelligence than those at Thessalonica. Paul expounded the scriptures daily in Thessalonica, but the Bereans, instead of resenting his interpretation, examined the scriptures for themselves.

12 **Many of them therefore believed;**—As a result of their fair-mindedness, their honesty of heart, and their faithful searching of the scriptures, many believed. Among the number that believed were some "Greek women of honorable estate." These were women of rank; they were influential, and may have been the wives of the chief citizens. The work of the apostles here as elsewhere extended beyond the synagogue.

13 **But when the Jews of Thessalonica**—The persecution that had begun at Thessalonica was now carried fifty miles away to

when the Jews of Thessalonica had knowledge that the word of God was proclaimed of Paul at Beroea also, they came thither likewise, stirring up and troubling the multitudes. 14 And then immediately the brethren sent forth Paul to go as far as to the sea: and Silas and Timothy abode there

Berea. When the Jews in Thessalonica heard that Paul and Silas had gone to Berea and had proclaimed the gospel there, they "came thither likewise, stirring up and troubling the multitudes." Paul and Silas had left Thessalonica by night, which implies that they secretly left Thessalonica, and the Jews did not know where they had gone; but as soon as they learned, they became active and went to Berea and caused trouble there. They "stirred," shaking the crowds like an earthquake, and "troubled" the multitude like a disturbing tornado. The Jews had been successful in Thessalonica, and this gave them courage to go to Berea and oppose Paul there. We do not know how long Paul had been in Berea when they came; he had been there long enough to establish a church. Progress was being made until these Jews came from Thessalonica; then a whirl of excitement disturbed the labors of Paul and Silas.

14 **And then immediately the brethren sent forth Paul**— They acted with haste and sent Paul away, while Silas and Timothy remained in Berea. We are not told what charges were preferred against Paul, but probably the same ones that were made at Thessalonica. Paul was to go "as far as to the sea," which means the Aegean Sea. This gives the impression that the movement was a feint in order to baffle the pursuers, while Paul went in another direction. Silas and Timothy were not exposed to the danger that Paul was; hence, they could abide in Berea. Paul was the leader and was in the greater danger; Silas and Timothy could bring the news to Paul when they left Berea to go to Paul.

10. PAUL'S ADDRESS AT ATHENS
17: 15-34

still. 15 But they that conducted Paul brought him as far as Athens: and

15 **But they that conducted Paul**—Some of the brethren accompanied Paul as a guide and for partial protection. He went as

receiving a commandment unto Silas and Timothy that they should come to him with all speed, they departed.

16 Now while Paul waited for them at Athens, his spirit was provoked within him as he beheld the city full of idols. 17 So he reasoned in the synagogue with the Jews and the devout persons, and in the marketplace every day with them that met him. 18 And certain also of the Epicurean

---

far as Athens. We do not know who escorted him; neither do we know whether he went by land or by sea. It is generally thought that he went by sea. The distance between Berea and Athens by land is about 250 Roman miles; this would take about twelve days to make the journey, whereas three days would have been sufficient for the voyage by sea; hence, the conclusion by many that he went by sea. After reaching Athens, Paul commanded his escorts to tell Silas and Timothy that they should come to him "with all speed." Without delay they departed. Paul was alone in Athens and would not be able to go about his work until they came. Later history shows that they were unable to reach him at Athens, but joined him at Corinth. (Acts 18: 5.)

16 **Now while Paul waited for them at Athens,**—Athens has a very interesting history; it has been called one of the most beautiful cities in the world; it was situated about five miles inland northeast of the Saronic Gulf, an arm of the Aegean Sea; four famous mountains lie around it, and four still more famous hills were within the city; the first one was Lycabettus, the Acropolis, the Areopagus, or Mars' Hill, the Pnyx, on which the assemblies of the people were held and Demosthenes spoke his oration. The name of Athens was synonymous with the most graceful conceptions of art and the profoundest study of philosophy. While Paul waited here, "his spirit was provoked within him" as he saw that the city was "full of idols." Athens was wholly given to idolatry. It is said that Athens had more idols or images than all the rest of Greece. Pretonius satirically said it was easier to find a god than a man in Athens; Xenophon calls the city one great altar, one great offering to the gods. This was enough to stir Paul to preach the gospel to them.

17 **So he reasoned in the synagogue**—While waiting for Silas and Timothy, Paul was busy. He went into the synagogue and there reasoned with the Jews and "the devout persons"; we must know that since Paul's spirit was "provoked within him" that he

and Stoic philosophers encountered him. And some said, What would this
babbler say? others, He seemeth to be a setter forth of ³strange ⁴gods:

³Or, *foreign divinities*
⁴Gr. *demons*

must have preached the gospel with great power. Such a mind as
Paul's, freighted with such a message as his, could not begin to
move in such an atmosphere without soon encountering opposition.
Wherever he could find people, in the synagogue, at idol worship,
in the market place, he preached Christ to them. Two classes are
found here—the native Jews and Gentile worshipers, whether proselytes or not, we do not know. He had access to the Gentile
world through these devout persons, while his first appeal was yet
to the Jews. "The marketplace" is generally supposed to designate the great place known as the ancient "forum," or old market
place. It was a famous place, because Socrates taught there, and
all the great philosophers taught or discoursed to the people there.

18 **And certain also of the Epicurean and Stoic**—In Paul's
day there were two systems of philosophy prominent throughout
the Roman world; they are regarded as conflicting, though in
many points they resemble each other. "Epicurean" is named
from its founder, Epicurus; he lived 342-270 B.C. His disciples
were known as the school of the "garden," from the garden in
Athens where the master instructed them, in distinction from the
disciples of the "porch" or the academy where the Stoics met.
Epicurus taught that the end of living was pleasure; he taught that
the enjoyment of tranquil pleasure was the highest end of human
existence. "Stoic" philosophers were the advocates of the theory
founded by Zeno. "Stoic" was derived from "Stoa," "a porch."
Zeno taught that God was the soul of the world, or the world was
God; that everything was governed by fate, to which God himself
was subject; they denied the immortality of the soul. The Stoic
philosophers taught that virtue was its own reward, and vice its
own punishment; that pleasure was no good, and pain no evil.
Both classes of philosophers were in Athens and encountered Paul.
They asked: "What would this babbler say?" "Babbler," as used
here, means a "seed picker"; it was applied to a bird that picks up
seeds as food; hence, Paul is called a "seed picker," or has picked

because he [5]preached Jesus and the resurrection. 19 And they took hold of
him, and brought him [6]unto [7]the Areopagus, saying, May we know what this
new teaching is, which is spoken by thee? 20 For thou bringest certain
strange things to our ears: we would know therefore what these things
mean. 21 (Now all the Athenians and the strangers sojourning there [8]spent

[5]See marginal note on ch. 5. 42
[6]Or, *before*
[7]Or, *the hill of Mars*
[8]Or, *had leisure for nothing else*

up some crumbs of knowledge. In contempt they compared him to
the small bird that fed on small seeds, and said that he preached a
strange religion, "because he preached Jesus and the resurrection."
Little did they understand what this meant at that time.

19, 20 **And they took hold of him, and brought him unto the
Areopagus,**—This does not mean that they used force or arrested
him; they constrained him, or escorted him to "the Areopagus";
this place also bears the name "Mars' Hill." Here had often assembled the noblest blood of Athens, the politicians of highest
rank, the best orators, and the most profound philosophers. It
was at this place that Socrates was arraigned and condemned.
"The Areopagus," as used here, was not the hill, but the council of
the Areopagus, which sat in some hall in the market place. We
are to think of Paul as being surrounded by philosophers and pro-
fessors of the Athens University, and lecturers who occupied
chairs in the university. They asked Paul concerning "this new
teaching" of which they had heard. They added that he had
brought "certain strange things" to their ears. Hence, they would
like to know more about these things. They make a polite request
of him that he tell them more about his "new teaching" or "strange
gods" which he set forth. They must be commended for their desire to know; they are different from the Jews and others at Thessalonica and Berea, who ran Paul out of the cities.

21 **(Now all the Athenians and the strangers)**—Luke, the
historian, has put in this historical explanation of the Athenians; it
shows why they were eager to hear Paul. These men of Athens
were so eager to hear or learn something new that they took Paul,
a stranger, to the great place of discussion to hear him. They were
ready to hear anything that was new. The natives of Athens and
the strangers who sojourned there alike were eager to hear the

their time in nothing else, but either to tell or to hear some new thing.)   22
And Paul stood in the midst of the Areopagus, and said,

Ye men of Athens, in all things I perceive that ye are [9]very religious. 23
For as I passed along, and observed the objects of your worship, I found

[9]Or, *somewhat superstitious*

new things. They spent their leisure time in nothing else but either to tell or to hear something "new," something later than the latest notion that they had learned. It seems that they had leisure time and they devoted or spent their time in hearing and telling what is new. Demosthenes in his first great Philippic orations says the same thing of them: "Tell me, do you, going round, still wish to ask in the market, is there any news? Can there be anything newer than that a Macedonian?" etc. Novelty was their life's pursuit; so without having any regard for the importance of the teaching, they were ready to listen because it was new.

22 **And Paul stood in the midst of the Areopagus,**—There was a crowd of spectators and philosophers present, and Paul seized the opportunity to preach Christ to this strange audience, as he did in Caesarea later before Herod Agrippa and the crowd of prominent people gathered by Festus. Paul did not speak as a man on trial, but as one attempting to get a hearing for the gospel of Christ. He "stood" that he might be heard by all. He addressed them according to their accustomed way of being addressed. "In all things I perceive that ye are very religious." The Authorized Version says "superstitious," but here we have "religious." The Greek is "hos deisidaimonesterous"; "Deisidaimon" is a neutral word from "deido," to fear, and "daimon," deity. The Greeks used it either in the good sense of pious or religious or the bad sense of superstitious. Thayer suggests that Paul used it "with kindly ambiguity"; while others think that Luke uses the word to represent the religious feeling of the Athenians which bordered on superstition. In Acts 25: 19 Festus uses the term "deisidaimonia" for "religion."

23 **For as I passed along, and observed**—Paul introduced his speech by an observation which he had made while sojourning in Athens and waiting for Silas and Timothy to come there. He had observed "the objects" of their worship; he had observed the idols

also an altar with this inscription, TO AN UNKNOWN GOD. What therefore ye worship in ignorance, this I set forth unto you. 24 The God that made the world and all things therein, he, being Lord of heaven and earth, dwelleth not in [10]temples made with hands; 25 neither is he served by

[10]Or, *sanctuaries*

which they worshiped, as well as their worshiping their idols. Paul has been described as standing on an elevated platform, surrounded by the learned and the wise of Athens, the multitude being perhaps on the steps and in the vale below. Paul had directly before him the far-famed Acropolis with its wonders of Grecian art, and beneath him on his left the majestic Theseum, the earliest and still most perfect of the Athenian structures, while all around other temples and altars filled the entire city. He had passed along the streets and had given attention to their devotion in prayer and worship; he had noticed their altars, images, and inscribed names of their gods. He had also observed their inscription, "To AN UNKNOWN GOD." Some think that Paul referred to Jehovah whom the Jews worshiped, and who was unknown to these Athenians. Others think that the inscription read "to the unknown gods." "Unknown" is from the Greek "agnostos." The Athenians acknowledged by their inscription that they did not know the God that Paul preached; hence, Paul's opportunity to declare unto them the God and Father of our Lord the Christ. They worshiped in ignorance, but Paul would have them know the true God.

24 **The God that made the world**—Jehovah God was not to be confused with any of their numerous gods save with this "Unknown God." Paul declares Jehovah God as the one who "made the world and all things therein." He is the creator of all things. He was no Epicurean god, who dwelt apart and in constant repose; nor was the world a thing of chance as the Athenian philosophers taught. He was the creator of the world and everything in it; he is also "Lord of heaven and earth," and being such a God, he dwells not in temples made by hands, but fills the earth.

25 **neither is he served by men's hands,**—Jehovah God is not served by human hands, as if he needed help like man; he was not made by the hands of men, and does not need the assistance of men

men's hands, as though he needed anything, seeing he himself giveth to all
life, and breath, and all things; 26 and he made of one every nation of men to
dwell on all the face of the earth, having determined *their* appointed seasons,
and the bounds of their habitation; 27 that they should seek God, if haply
they might feel after him and find him, though he is not far from each one of

to exist. He is the author of all life, and of all things. The heathen
clothed their gods with costly garments, overlaid them with silver
and gold, carried them in state, installed them at banquets, and
brought them costly offerings of food and drink. The God that
Paul served, and the one that he now declares or makes known to
these Athenians, gives life, sustains it, and gives every good thing
that man enjoys.

26 **and he made of one every nation of men**—God created
Adam and then formed Eve, and from this one pair has come all
the nations of earth. The nations and races of men have a common origin; God made them all, and hence is their creator. The
Greeks, like the Jews, thought themselves of finer nature, a superior race in origin, character and destiny. Paul instructs them of
the brotherhood of man; this was indeed strange to Greek ears;
they had an idea of different origins, different gods, different reli-
gions for different nations. Paul thus starts to reason with them
about one God, Creator of all, and deduces from it one religion,
one origin for all, one brotherhood, one salvation for the race.
God had fixed the limits of their territory as he had determined the
duration of their existence. It was this God who had given their
seasons, spring, summer, fall, and winter; he had ordained seed-
time and harvest and prepared the earth for man's habitation.

27 **that they should seek God,**—All things which God has
given to man should encourage man to seek to know his Creator,
and to know him as his great Benefactor. The gift of this bounti-
ful earth, with its teeming productions and supplies for human
need, coupled with its beautiful and wise adaptations to man's
well-being, should move man to seek after more and higher knowledge of the Giver of every good and perfect gift. Paul here pictures the blind groping of the darkened heathen mind after God to
"find him." "Feel after him" is a vivid picture of the darkened
and benighted condition of those who thought themselves to be

us: 28 for in him we live, and move, and have our being; as certain even of
your own poets have said,

For we are also his offspring.

29 Being then the offspring of God, we ought not to think that ¹the Godhead
is like unto gold, or silver, or stone, graven by art and device of man.   30

---

¹Or, *that which is divine*

---

wise. The evidences of God were round about them; yet they did
not know him. "He is not far from each one of us" in his blessings and gifts.

28 **for in him we live, and move,**—The proof of God's nearness, not Stoic pantheism, but real existence of God, was evident
and surrounded man, is that man is said to exist in God. This
shows how near God is to us, and how vitally and intimately we
are connected with him. We are entirely dependent upon him for
life and for everything that sustains life; there should be no difficulty in finding him if one is inclined in heart to know him. Paul
declares further that "for we are also his offspring." He is our
Creator; he is our origin; we exist in him; we are dependent upon
him; we must look to him for everything. Paul here quotes one of
their poets; his quotation is from Aratus of Soli in Cilicia; he lived
about 270 B.C., and was a Stoic philosopher. Cleanthes, a Stoic
philosopher, who lived 300 to 220 B.C., has the same words in his
"Hymn to Zeus." Possibly Cleanthes used the words first. The
passage reads: "For we all greatly need Jupiter, for we are his
offspring—full of grace, he grants men tokens of favor."

29 **Being then the offspring of God,**—Paul uses tact and skill
here. "We," including himself, ought not to have such a low conception of "the Godhead"; they had formed too low a conception,
and Paul would refine and elevate their conception of God.
"Godhead" literally means "the divine." It comes from the Greek,
"to theion," and means the divine nature like "theiotes" in Rom.
1: 20. Paul uses in Col. 2: 9 the Greek "theotes." Some think
that Paul used "to theion" here to get back behind all their notions
of various gods to the real nature of God. The divine nature of
God cannot be like "gold, or silver, or stone, graven by art and
device of man." The "Godhead" includes God the Creator, Christ

The times of ignorance therefore God overlooked; but now he ²commandeth men that they should all everywhere repent: 31 inasmuch as he hath appointed a day in which he will judge ³the world in righteousness ⁴by ⁵the man whom he hath ordained; whereof he hath given assurance unto all men, in that he hath raised him from the dead.

---

²Some ancient authorities read *declareth to men*
³Gr. *the inhabited earth*
⁴Gr. *in*
⁵Or, *a man*

---

the Savior, and the Holy Spirit; these cannot be represented by any material thing.

30 **The times of ignorance therefore God overlooked;**— "The times"; that is, before a revelation of God was given through Christ; this was a period of "ignorance," "agnoias." The past history of the heathen world was a history of idolatry, involving the grossest ignorance of God, and of all that was truly good. These Athenians confessed their ignorance by their inscription of an altar to "An Unknown God." These long times of heathen ignorance God overlooked, passed over, "winked at"; the time has now come when he will not overlook such ignorance, but "commandeth men that they should all everywhere repent." Things have changed now since Christ has come with a full knowledge of God and has revealed God's will to man. The command to repent implies their guilt of sin in their idolatry. The universal duty of repentance Paul enforces by the consideration of the judgment. All have sinned and all must repent; this is true not only of the Athenians, but of all men in every generation.

31 **inasmuch as he hath appointed a day**—This day of judgment had been appointed long ago, but through Christ it has been made known with greater clearness. All who know Christ now know that God has raised him from the dead; by his resurrection all are to know that they are to be judged by him. Paul's argument has advanced through different stages; he has spoken first of God as the Creator of the world and of man; then he argued that man should exalt God above all things that he has made; this should lead them to seek after him. Now the days of God's revelation through nature are at an end, and he has spoken through his Son whom he raised from the dead, to prove that he was the Son

32 Now when they heard of the resurrection of the dead, some mocked;
but others said, We will hear thee concerning this yet again. 33 Thus Paul
went out from among them. 34 But certain men clave unto him, and believed: among whom also was Dionysius the Areopagite, and a woman named
Damaris, and others with them.

---

of God. Now through him God will judge the world; hence, all
men should prepare themselves for the judgment by repentance.

32, 33 Now when they heard of the resurrection—It may be
that these Athenians who had brought Paul to the Areopagus to
hear him stopped his speech and would let him proceed no further.
Neither party among his hearers would have any sympathy with
the doctrine of the resurrection and the final judgment. "Some
mocked" just as did some men on the day of Pentecost. (Acts 2:
13.) The Epicureans believed that this life was all there was to
life; the Stoic teachers taught that all would finally be absorbed in
the Godhead; hence, they would not believe in the resurrection
from the dead. It seems most likely that the Epicureans would be
the ones who mocked Paul, and perhaps it was these "others" who
said: "We will hear thee concerning this yet again." This reminds one of Felix's decision. (Acts 24: 25.) Paul "went out
from among them." This shows that he was not on trial nor
under any judicial restraint. He had presented them the truth of
God; they had understood him; he had nothing more to offer
them; hence, he left them to seek others more favorably inclined to
hear the truth.

34 But certain men clave unto him,—There were three classes
among Paul's hearers: (1) the Epicureans who mocked the truth;
(2) those who procrastinated and promised to hear him again;
(3) those who believed him. Among those who believed was
"Dionysius the Areopagite." There were several men and at least
one woman of position who accepted his teaching. Dionysius was
a member of the great Athenian Council; his position, influence,
and learning caused his name to be mentioned here. It is thought
that Dionysius had some supervision of the entire public administration. The woman who believed was named "Damaris." We
are not told for what she was noted; she must have been a woman
of distinction and power since her name is given. Tradition has it

that a church was founded here later, and the Parthenon became a
Christian temple.

11. PAUL AT CORINTH
18: 1-18

1 After these things he departed from Athens, and came to Corinth. 2
And he found a certain Jew named Aquila, a man of Pontus by race, lately
come from Italy, with his wife Priscilla, because Claudius had commanded all

1 **After these things he departed from Athens,**—Paul left
Athens and went to Corinth; this city was between forty-five and
fifty miles from Athens, in a course west by a little south. Corinth
was the capital of Achaia, and the chief city of this province.
Corinth had been destroyed by Mummius in 146 B.C., and had
been restored by Julius Caesar in 46 B.C. Much of the sculpture
and fine arts that had adorned the old Corinth was destroyed.
Paul visited the new Corinth. The destruction of the old Corinth
was so complete that it passed into a proverb. The new Corinth
soon surpassed its former state in wealth and splendor, and became
a vast commercial center. The laxity of the morals of Corinth was
proverbial. Paul made reference to this in his letter to the church
later. (1 Cor. 5: 1; 6: 9, 10.) Paul went into the midst of this
city which had less promise, at first, than Athens, but, ultimately,
far more fruitful in results.

2 **And he found a certain Jew named Aquila,**—When Paul
came to Corinth, being a Jew, he would naturally seek some companion among the Jews; he may have gone to the synagogue and
met Aquila there. Luke calls him "a certain Jew" from "Pontus."
It is also significant to know that Paul "found" him. The Jews
had certain guilds by which they kept together whether in street or
synagogue. His birth in Pontus indicates that he belonged to the
dispersion of the Jews of that province (1 Pet. 1: 1) which lay
between Bithynia and Armenia. Here we meet first with "his wife
Priscilla." She was a prominent woman and stood high in social
position so that her name is sometimes placed before that of her
husband. (Verse 18; Rom. 16: 3; 2 Tim. 4: 19.) Some think
that Aquila and Priscilla were Christians when Paul met them;
others think that Paul converted them. We do not know, and no

the Jews to depart from Rome: and he came unto them; 3 and because he
was of the same trade, he abode with them, and they wrought; for by their
trade they were tentmakers. 4 And he reasoned in the synagogue every sabbath, and [6]persuaded Jews and Greeks.

[6]Gr. *sought to persuade*

history gives any record by which we may determine. They sojourned later with Paul during his long residence at Ephesus; and
once (Rom. 16: 3, 4), Paul tells us, they "laid down their own
necks" for him. If they were Christians when Paul met them,
they are the two most ancient known members of the primitive
church at Rome. They had been driven from Rome because of the
order which had been given by Claudius; this was about A.D. 49;
Claudius had ordered the Jews to leave Rome because of the constant tumult that they instigated. Jews were unpopular in Rome;
it has been estimated that there were twenty thousand Jews in
Rome at that time.

3 **and because he was of the same trade,**—This is the first
mention that we have of Paul's occupation or trade. Every Jewish
boy was carefully taught a trade; one rabbi among the Jews said
that a father had just as well teach his boy to steal as to fail to
teach him a trade. Aquila was a tentmaker; this was Paul's trade.
They had at least three things in common now—they were of the
same race, being Jews; of the same trade, tentmakers; and now of
the same faith, both Christians. Tentmaking was a common occupation in Paul's native Cilicia; these tents were made of rough
goat's hair; goats abounded in the hill country of Cilicia. This
tent cloth was generally known as "Cilicium." Paul alludes to the
toil of his hands. (Acts 20: 34.) He makes other allusions to
working with his own hands to support himself and others. (1 Cor.
4: 12; 1 Thess. 2: 9; 2 Thess. 3: 8.)

4 **And he reasoned in the synagogue every sabbath,**—This
was Paul's invariable rule; he preached the gospel "to the Jew
first" and then to Gentiles. He went to the synagogue on the Sabbath because the Jews met on the Sabbath. His going into the
synagogue on the Sabbath was in no sense endorsing the Jewish
Sabbath as a day to be observed by Christians. On these Sabbaths
Paul "reasoned" and "persuaded" both "Jews and Greeks" to ac-

5 But when Silas and Timothy came down from Macedonia, Paul was
constrained by the word, testifying to the Jews that Jesus was the Christ. 6
And when they opposed themselves and [7]blasphemed, he shook out his rai-

[7]Or, *railed*

cept Jesus as the Messiah and Savior of the world. He convinced
them by his reasoning that Jesus was the Christ, and persuaded
them to accept him as such. As the "Greeks" here are mentioned
with the Jews in the synagogue, it is to be understood that they
were proselytes.

5 **But when Silas and Timothy came**—Paul had left Silas and
Timothy at Berea (Acts 17: 14), and had given instruction to
those who had conducted him to Athens for Silas and Timothy to
come "to him with all speed" (Acts 17: 15). It seems they did not
get to Athens before Paul left; hence, they came to Corinth. The
coming of Silas and Timothy greatly encouraged Paul; they
brought gifts from Macedonia to him which relieved him for the
time being of tentmaking, so that he could give all of his time to
preaching the gospel. (2 Cor. 11: 9; Phil. 4: 15; 1 Thess. 3: 6.)
Paul "was constrained" to preach "to the Jews that Jesus was the
Christ." Being now free from the burden of working with his
hands, Paul gave his time to preaching and convincing the Jews of
the Messiahship of Jesus. "Constrained" is from the Greek "su-
neicheto" and was used once very solemnly by Christ. (Luke 12:
50.) It indicates an intense divine impulse, urging to a work
which would not be delayed or hindered by anything. The Authorized Version translates this as "pressed in the spirit," but the Revised Version gives a better translation. The meaning seems to be
that he was engrossed by the word, or engrossed by the preaching
of the gospel. He had been relieved of anxiety and toil by the arrival of Silas and Timothy with the gifts from Macedonia, and was
now giving all of his time to preaching the word.

6 **And when they opposed themselves and blasphemed,**—
We know not how long Paul had now been in Corinth; he had reasoned in the synagogue and persuaded his hearers to accept the
Christ as their Savior. Some of them refused to accept Jesus as
the Messiah and even indulged in reproachful and reviling language against Paul and the Christ. When they took this attitude

ment and said unto them, Your blood *be* upon your own heads; I am clean: from henceforth I will go unto the Gentiles. 7 And he departed thence, and went into the house of a certain man named Titus Justus, one that worshipped God, whose house joined hard to the synagogue. 8 And Crispus, the ruler of the synagogue, [8]believed in the Lord with all his house; and many of

---

[8]Gr. *believed the Lord*

Paul turned from them; he knew that he could do them no good by further reasoning and persuading them. "He shook out his raiment," and thus signified to the Jews his deep abhorrence of their conduct and his unwillingness to be associated with them intimately any longer. This is similar to the act of Paul and Barnabas at Antioch in Pisidia (Acts 13: 51), and the instruction Jesus gave his disciples (Matt. 10: 14). "Your blood be upon your own heads"; this was not a curse, but a solemn disclaimer of responsibility. (Ezek. 3: 18f.; 33: 4, 8f.; Acts 20: 26.) The Jews had used this expression in assuming responsibility for the crucifixion of Christ. (Matt. 27: 25; see also Matt. 23: 35.) Paul was not responsible any further; he had preached Christ to them and they had rejected him. Now he turns to the Gentiles.

7 **And he departed thence,**—Paul now left the synagogue and, probably by invitation, went into the house joining the synagogue; this was owned by "a certain man named Titus Justus." We do not know much about this Titus. He was evidently a Roman citizen, and was not the Titus who afterwards became a companion of Paul; however, some think that he was. Paul assembled the converts to Christianity in his house and taught them there. This "Titus Justus" "worshipped God." Evidently he was a proselyte; the phrase "worshipped God" is the one that is frequently used to designate a proselyte to the Jewish worship. Paul probably continued to lodge with Aquila and Priscilla, but taught all who would come to him in the house of Titus Justus.

8 **And Crispus, the ruler of the synagogue,**—Crispus is mentioned by Paul in 1 Cor. 1: 14. Paul baptized him. (1 Cor. 1: 14.) He was distinguished as a ruler of the synagogue; there may have been more than one synagogue in Corinth as we read in verse 17 of Sosthenes, the "ruler of the synagogue." However, Sosthenes may have been appointed immediately after Crispus was

the Corinthians hearing believed, and were baptized.   9 And the Lord said
unto Paul in the night by a vision, Be not afraid, but speak and hold not thy
peace: 10 for I am with thee, and no man shall set on thee to harm thee: for
I have much people in this city.   11 And he dwelt *there* a year and six
months, teaching the word of God among them.

---

converted. Luke sums up the results by saying that "many of the
Corinthians hearing believed, and were baptized." This was the
order and steps of the conversion of all. First the gospel is
preached, people hear the gospel, believe it, repent of their sins,
and are baptized; they are then in Christ and are called Christians.
Paul baptized, in addition to Crispus, Gaius and the household of
Stephanas. However, Silas and Timothy were now assisting him,
and would care for those who desired to be baptized.

9 **And the Lord said unto Paul in the night by a vision,—**
The Lord encouraged Paul in his work. "Be not afraid" literally
means "stop being afraid," and go on speaking, and do not become
silent. We know now why Paul should be afraid; he was threatened with danger and was becoming discouraged. Anyone discouraged needs encouragement; the Lord gave him a clear intimation of his will, either changing a purpose which was forming in
Paul's mind, or confirming his sense of duty to remain.

10 **for I am with thee, and no man shall set on thee**—These
are the words which the Lord used to encourage Paul; he had spoken to him at night in a vision. Jesus had promised to be with
those who preached his gospel. (Matt. 28: 20.) Here he is
promised that no man should harm him; this seems to imply that
someone was seeking or threatening to do Paul harm. The Lord
encourages him by saying that no one should so harm him.
Another reason why he should continue to preach in Corinth was
that "I have much people in this city." In a prospective sense
there were many in Corinth who would obey the gospel if they had
opportunity. They could become the people of God by hearing,
believing, repenting of their sins, and being baptized into Christ.
There were much people, not yet saved, but who would accept the
gospel when they heard it. This should have been encouragement
enough for Paul.

11 **And he dwelt there a year and six months,**—We do not
know how much time Paul spent in Corinth before this encourage-

12 But when Gallio was proconsul of Achaia, the Jews with one accord
rose up against Paul and brought him before the judgment-seat, 13 saying,
This man persuadeth men to worship God contrary to the law. 14 But when
Paul was about to open his mouth, Gallio said unto the Jews, If indeed it

---

ment was given to him. Some think that he was in Corinth about
two years in all; his work extended beyond the city (2 Cor. 11:
10), and there was a church in Cenchreae (Rom. 16: 1). We
cannot be certain as to the length of his stay in Corinth, as verse
18 speaks of his remaining there "yet many days," which may be
added to the "year and six months" of this verse. He taught "a
year and six months" undisturbed, until Gallio was appointed
"proconsul"; then trouble began, but Gallio refused to be disturbed with the charge.

12, 13 **But when Gallio was proconsul of Achaia,**—This Gallio was a brother of Seneca, who was a Stoic teacher and tutor of
Nero. He was a man of culture and refinement. Seneca said of
him: "No one of mortals is so pleasant to one person as he is to
all." The Jews "with one accord rose up against Paul." They
made an insurrection against Paul; they seized him and "brought
him before the judgment-seat." It was the custom of the provincial
governors of the Roman Empire to hold their courts on certain
days of the week; these were commonly held in the market place.
The "judgment-seat" was of two kinds: (1) fixed in some public
place; or (2) movable and taken about by the magistrate, to be
set up in whatever spot he might designate. They preferred the
charge against Paul that he persuaded "men to worship God contrary to the law." They did not mean by this that Paul was persuading people to worship God "contrary to the law" of Moses;
they meant the Roman law, or the law of the province of Achaia.
This is obvious since they brought Paul before Gallio and preferred the charge; he would have nothing to do about judging disputes contrary to the law of Moses. Their contention was that
though Jews had been banished from Rome as a measure of policy,
Judaism as such was still a legal religion to be tolerated and recognized by the Roman authority. Their charge was that he was
preaching a new religion that was not recognized by the laws of
Rome.

14 **But when Paul was about to open his mouth,**—Paul was
ready to answer the charge, but before he could speak, Gallio

were a matter of wrong or of wicked villany, O ye Jews, reason would that I should bear with you: 15 but if they are questions about words and names and your own law, look to it yourselves: I am not minded to be a judge of these matters. 16 And he drove them from the judgment-seat. 17 And they

---

ended the whole matter. It was not necessary for Paul to speak. The proconsul could hardly have resided in Achaia for eighteen months without hearing of the new covenant that Paul was promoting; he knew the Jews and probably knew something about Paul. In any case, from his standpoint, it was not a matter to be brought into his court. He said that if it was a matter of "wrong or of wicked villany" then he would attend to the matter and hear their accusation. If Paul had been guilty of doing wrong to anyone, or if he had violated any of the laws of the province, Gallio would hear them.

15 **but if they are questions about words and names**—Cases of injustice and open violence came properly under the authority of Gallio's court, but if the Jews were disturbed about "questions" on "words and names" of their own law, he had no interest in such. He was not interested in a parcel of questions about words and names; he did not care whether "Jesus" should also be called "Christ" or "Messiah"; Gallio knew that the Jews split hairs over words and names. He was not inclined to sit in judgment and settle disputes that arose among the Jews over their religious ritual. They should settle their own disputes; "look to it yourselves"; he turned the matter over to them with the statement that he was not willing to occupy his time with such small matters.

16, 17 **And he drove them from the judgment-seat.**—The Jews were confused at his abrupt dismissal of the charge that they brought against Paul. He drove them from his judgment seat; the words here imply a magisterial act; the order was given to his officers to clear the court, and the Jews who did not immediately retreat were exposed to the ignominy of blows from the officers. The Greeks then "laid hold on Sosthenes," who was the "ruler of the synagogue." They beat him in the presence of Gallio, and Gallio gave no attention to it. Had Paul been violating any of the Roman laws he would have condemned him. He looked upon the affair as being one of their own quarrels about some phase of their religion, and he let them have their way about it. The beating of

all laid hold on Sosthenes, the ruler of the synagogue, and beat him before
the judgment-seat.   And Gallio cared for none of these things.
   18 And Paul, having tarried after this yet many days, took his leave of
the brethren, and sailed thence for Syria, and with him Priscilla and Aquila:

Sosthenes was a small detail that belonged to the police court, and
not for the proconsul's judgment.   Sosthenes was, on this occasion, the chief object of their rage and ill-treatment; some think
that this is the Sosthenes mentioned by Paul as one of his companions.   (1 Cor. 1: 1.)   It has been a question of much dispute as to
why he was beaten by the Greeks; some have speculated in regard
to this that Sosthenes, being the leader, was defeated in his case
before Gallio, and hence needed to be punished for bringing such
trivial charges.   Some claim that it is not clear as to who beat Sosthenes; whether it was the infuriated Jews or whether the Gentiles; however, it seems clear that the Gentiles so punished Sosthenes.

   18 **And Paul, having tarried after this**—It is not certain
whether "tarried after this yet many days" means that Paul tarried
longer than the "year and six months," as mentioned in verse 11,
or that this time is included in the "year and six months."
However, the context seems to indicate that it was in addition to
the time mentioned in verse 11.   Paul was vindicated; there was
no reason for haste in leaving, and he usually left after such a crisis was past.   He took his leave of the church and "sailed thence
for Syria."   Antioch in Syria was his destination; he embarked
and sailed first to Ephesus.   He took Priscilla and Aquila with
him.   Cenchreae was a seaport of Corinth, and about ten miles
southeast from Corinth.   Priscilla here, as in Rom. 16: 3; 2 Tim.
4: 19, is named first on account of the prominent part she took in
the church.   A church had been planted at Cenchreae (Rom. 16:
1) probably by Paul during his residence at Corinth.   There is
some dispute about whether it was Aquila or Paul who had the
vow and had "shorn his head in Cenchreae."   Grotius, Wieseler,
Meyer, Howson, and others refer it to Aquila.   They claim that
this clause is parenthetic and belongs to Aquila.   The participle is
masculine; hence, cannot refer to Priscilla.   Since "Priscilla and
Aquila" are joined, and since the clause, "having shorn his head in

having shorn his head in Cenchreae; for he had a vow. 19 And they came

---

Cenchreae," is parenthetical, it cannot refer to Aquila. Hence, we conclude that it was Paul who had the vow and that he had shorn his head in Cenchreae. The other participles in this verse refer to Paul without any doubt; hence, we are justified in saying that it refers to Paul. We do not know what vow Paul had taken nor why he had made a vow; hence, we do not know why this reference to the vow. Paul, as a Jew, kept up his observance of the ceremonial law for some instances, but refused to impose it upon the Gentiles.

12. PAUL RETURNS TO ANTIOCH IN SYRIA
18: 19-22

to Ephesus, and he left them there: but he himself entered into the synagogue, and reasoned with the Jews. 20 And when they asked him to abide a longer time, he consented not; 21 but taking his leave of them, and saying, I will return again unto you if God will, he set sail from Ephesus.

---

19 **And they came to Ephesus,**—Ephesus was nearly due east from Cenchreae across the Aegean Sea; it could have been reached in two or three days under favorable sailing. Ephesus was the capital of the province of Asia; it was situated on the western shore of Asia Minor. Paul left Aquila and Priscilla at Ephesus. Before leaving Ephesus Paul entered into the synagogue and "reasoned with the Jews." "Reasoned" seems to be Luke's favorite word for Paul's discourses in the synagogue. (Acts 17: 2, 17; 18: 4; 19: 8, 9.)

20, 21 **And when they asked him to abide**—Frequently Paul has been run out of the synagogue by the Jews, but this is one time that he was asked "to abide a longer time," but he did not think it necessary to do so. He gave as his reason for not remaining, "I will return again unto you if God will," and set sail from Ephesus on his journey to Antioch. Paul was encouraged enough to make promise to return to them, "if the Lord will." (James 4: 13-15.) "If the Lord will" was a common expression among the early Christians. (Rom. 1: 10; 15: 32; 1 Cor. 4: 19; 16: 7; Heb. 6: 3.) Paul did return and Luke hastens to record the facts and results. (Acts 19: 1.) It would require about a month to sail from Ephe-

22 And when he had landed at Caesarea, he went up and saluted the church, and went down to Antioch. 23 And having spent some time *there,* he

sus to Caesarea. In chapters 20 and 21 it is a seven weeks' voyage; however, sojourns were made on the way.

22 And when he had landed at Caesarea,—Caesarea was on the eastern coast of the Mediterranean Sea; it was on the western border of the land of Canaan or Palestine. It was the Roman capital of Judea. Paul went from Caesarea "up" to Jerusalem and there "saluted the church," and then went "down" to Antioch. Geographically speaking, this was correct; the location of Jerusalem was much higher in elevation than Antioch in Syria. Paul saluted "the church"; this shows that the church at Jerusalem was still considered the "mother church" at the time Luke wrote. This was Paul's fourth visit to the church in Jerusalem after his conversion. When he came to Antioch, his second missionary journey was terminated. It had occupied about three years; during this time he had traveled through large districts of Asia Minor, visited the European cities of Philippi, Thessalonica, Berea, Athens, and Corinth; he had returned by way of Ephesus and the sea to Caesarea, Jerusalem, and to Antioch. The Jews had violently resisted him in nearly every place except Athens and Ephesus; however, churches were organized not only in Galatia, but also in Philippi, Thessalonica, and Corinth; perhaps churches were established in other places.

SECTION FOUR

PAUL'S THIRD MISSIONARY JOURNEY
18: 23 to 21: 16

1. PRISCILLA, AQUILA, AND APOLLOS AT EPHESUS
18: 23-28

departed, and went through the region of Galatia, and Phrygia, in order, establishing all the disciples.

24 Now a certain Jew named Apollos, an Alexandrian by race, [1]an eloquent man, came to Ephesus; and he was mighty in the scriptures. 25 This man had been [2]instructed in the way of the Lord; and being fervent in spirit,

---

[1]Or, *a learned man*
[2]Gr. *taught by word of mouth*

---

23 **And having spent some time there,**—Paul now remained at Antioch for some time; we cannot tell how long he sojourned there. It was now probably A.D. 54, and Paul begins his third great missionary journey. He left Antioch and probably went first to Tarsus; then he went in a northwest direction through Galatia, and then turning southwest journeyed through Phrygia and on to Ephesus. Probably this was the last time that Paul ever saw Antioch. Some place the visit of Peter to Antioch, to which Paul refers in Gal. 2: 11ff., at this time. Paul begins his third journey without a Barnabas or a Silas to help him.

24 **Now a certain Jew named Apollos,**—Apollos was born in Alexandria, which was a celebrated city and seaport of Egypt on the Mediterranean Sea, twelve miles from the mouth of the Nile River. It was named Alexandria in honor of Alexander the Great, who founded it, 332 B.C. Many Jews had gone to Alexandria, as it was a famous place of learning. The Alexandrian library was the greatest in the world. Apollos is described as "an eloquent man"; that is, a learned man. The Greek word "logios" can mean either a man of words or a man of ideas; Apollos was probably both learned and eloquent. He was especially "mighty in the scriptures." He knew well the Old Testament. Later Paul wrote that he planted and Apollos watered. (1 Cor. 3: 6.) Paul found Apollos at Ephesus on this visit.

25 **This man had been instructed in the way of the Lord;**—This is the same term used in Luke 1: 4. Apollos was instructed

he spake and taught accurately the things concerning Jesus, knowing only
the baptism of John: 26 and he began to speak boldly in the synagogue. But
when Priscilla and Aquila heard him, they took him unto them, and expounded unto him the way of God more accurately. 27 And when he was
minded to pass over into Achaia, the brethren encouraged him, and wrote to
the disciples to receive him: and when he was come, he ³helped them much

³Or, *helped much through grace them that had believed*

before he came to Ephesus. He had received only the instruction
as prepared by John the Baptist. (Matt. 3: 3; Mark 1: 3.) He
had been taught by John, or by some of John's disciples, as to the
Messiahship of Christ, and knew some of the facts of his life, doctrines, and miracles. He may not have heard of the death, burial,
and resurrection and ascension of Christ, neither did he know
about the descent of the Holy Spirit on Pentecost. He was zealous and "taught accurately the things concerning Jesus" so far as
he knew; however, he knew only the baptism of John. He did not
know of the baptism in water into the name of the Father and of
the Son and of the Holy Spirit. John's baptism was a "baptism of
repentance." (Mark 1: 4; Acts 13: 24; 19: 4.) John knew and
preached the coming of the Messiah, and had borne testimony that
Jesus was the Messiah.

26 **and he began to speak boldly in the synagogue.**—He entered the synagogue and taught boldly what he knew of the Christ.
He expounded to the Jews what he knew. Priscilla and Aquila,
who had accompanied Paul on his return from Cenchreae to
Ephesus, heard Apollos and saw that he knew so little about the
Christ. "They took him unto them, and expounded unto him the
way of God more accurately." They taught Apollos the gospel as
they had learned it from Paul. We are to understand that they
showed him that Christ had fulfilled the prophecies, and had done
just what John the Baptist predicted that he would do. Apollos
was an apt student and learned rapidly; he wanted to know the full
truth, and Aquila and Priscilla so taught him. Aquila and Priscilla "took him unto them," which means that they took him to
their home and into their hearts.

27 **And when he was minded to pass over into Achaia,**—
Apollos was at Ephesus, which was on the eastern coast of the Aegean Sea; Achaia was due west of Ephesus; it was the province
south of Macedonia; Achaia and Macedonia composed Greece.

that had believed through grace; 28 for he powerfully confuted the Jews,
[4]*and that* publicly, showing by the scriptures that Jesus was the Christ.

[4]Or, *showing publicly*

The brethren at Ephesus encouraged Apollos and "wrote to the
disciples to receive him." Since Apollos wanted to go into Achaia,
the brethren wrote a letter of introduction to the disciples in Corinth to receive him. Paul referred to this letter later (2 Cor. 3:
1), and pointed out that he himself needed no such letter of commendation. Priscilla and Aquila were well known in Corinth, and
their approval would carry much weight. Apollos was very useful
in Achaia, for he "helped them much" who had become Christians.
It was by the grace of God that they had learned of Jesus Christ
and had become Christians.

28 **for he powerfully confuted the Jews,**—Apollos was already "an eloquent man" and "mighty in the scriptures," and had
now been taught "the way of God more accurately," so he was
powerful in arguing with the Jews about the Christ. To confute
means to contest in rivalry; Apollos entered into a public debate
with the Jews showing that Jesus of Nazareth was the Christ.
Apollos was so popular in Corinth that later a party arose in the
church with the motto: "I am of Apollos." (1 Cor. 3: 4.) We
lose sight of Apollos here and get a last glimpse of him in Tit. 3:
13. He is in company with Zenas, the lawyer. It seems that he
had been laboring at Crete, and there also had gathered around
him a distinct company of disciples.

2. PAUL AT EPHESUS
19: 1-12

1 And it came to pass, that, while Apollos was at Corinth, Paul having
passed through the upper country came to Ephesus, and found certain disci-

1 **And it came to pass, that, while Apollos was at Corinth,**
—Luke, the writer of Acts, left the narrative of Paul's journey and
recorded the incidents about Apollos. While Apollos was at Corinth, Paul came to Ephesus; so Paul did not get to see Apollos
while he was at Ephesus. Paul passed through "the upper country" and came to Ephesus. The "upper," as used here, means that
part of the country to which men go up away from the sea; it is

ples: 2 and he said unto them, Did ye receive the Holy Spirit when ye believed? And they *said* unto him, Nay, we did not so much as hear whether [5]the Holy Spirit was *given*. 3 And he said, Into what then were ye baptized? And they said, Into John's baptism. 4 And Paul said, John baptized

---

[5]Or, *there is a Holy Spirit*

---

applied here to the more eastern parts of Asia Minor. Paul's journey was very likely through the districts of Lycaonia, Galatia, and Phrygia; he had visited these on his second missionary tour. He "came to Ephesus," according to the conditional promise which he had made when he left Ephesus. (Acts 18: 21.) When he arrived he "found certain disciples" there. These men are called "disciples" because they were, like Apollos, to a certain extent instructed concerning Jesus, and what they already knew drew them to listen to Paul who came to teach the disciples and preach the gospel.

2 **and he said unto them, Did ye receive the Holy Spirit**—In talking with them Paul learned that they were very deficient in their knowledge of the gospel. He asked them if they had received the Holy Spirit when they believed. Their reply showed how little they knew about the gospel. They answered: "Nay, we did not so much as hear whether the Holy Spirit was given." These "disciples" believed that Jesus was the promised Messiah, but they had not heard anything further than what John had preached. They had never heard of the gift at Pentecost; they had heard of the Holy Spirit, for John spoke of him. (Matt. 3: 11; John 1: 33.) So they had heard of the existence of the Holy Spirit, but not that he had come on Pentecost. It is difficult to understand why they knew so little about the Holy Spirit.

3 **And he said, Into what then were ye baptized?**—Paul suspects that they had not been baptized intelligently; hence, he asks: "Into what then were ye baptized?" He recognizes that they were baptized "into" something; he implies that scriptural baptism is "into" something; hence, his question. They very promptly answered: "Into John's baptism." This is the last mention in the New Testament of John the Baptist. These "disciples" had been baptized "into John's baptism," but they had not grasped the meaning of it. Evidently they had been baptized by some of

with the baptism of repentance, saying unto the people that they should believe on him that should come after him, that is, on Jesus. 5 And when they heard this, they were baptized into the name of the Lord Jesus. 6 And when Paul had laid his hands upon them, the Holy Spirit came on them; and they spake with tongues, and prophesied. 7 And they were in all about twelve men.

John's disciples after John's baptism had ceased; hence, their baptism was not valid. John's baptism was out of date; it was only in force during John's ministry, and was not to be continued.

4 **And Paul said, John baptized with the baptism of repentance,**—Here we have a fuller comment on the meaning of John's baptism. John's baptism is frequently described as a "baptism of repentance." John came to make ready a people prepared for the Lord. (Luke 1: 17.) Those who submitted to John's baptism pledged that they would receive the Christ when he came; John did not want to make disciples merely for himself; he wanted them to believe on "the one that cometh after me." (Matt. 3: 11; Mark 1: 7; Luke 3: 16; John 1: 15.) Evidently these disciples had been baptized, but had not accepted Christ. It seems clear that they had not accepted Christ because they did not know of him.

5 **And when they heard this,**—So soon as they learned from Paul of the Christ "they were baptized into the name of the Lord Jesus." We have no evidence that the apostles were rebaptized, neither others who were baptized by John; their baptism was accepted; but these were commanded to be baptized "into the name of the Lord Jesus." Their baptism was not accepted. Luke does not give a formula here for baptizing, but simply explains that these men were baptized in obedience to their faith in Christ. These disciples had never received such a baptism as Christ ordained; hence, they had to be baptized in order to enter Christ.

6, 7 **And when Paul had laid his hands upon them,**—This was not a baptism of the Holy Spirit; no human agency or administrator had any part in the baptism of the Holy Spirit. Hands were laid on the Samaritans by Peter and John (Acts 8: 16), and in Damascus in the case of Paul (Acts 9: 17). Here a supernatural or miraculous gift was bestowed upon these as "they spake with tongues, and prophesied." The speaking with tongues and prophesying was external and positive proof that the Holy Spirit

8 And he entered into the synagogue, and spake boldly for the space of
three months, reasoning and persuading *as to* the things concerning the kingdom of God.   9 But when some were hardened and disobedient, speaking evil
of the Way before the multitude, he departed from them, and separated the

had come on these twelve who were now fully obedient to the gospel and were ready for faithful service in his name.   There were
about twelve men in this number.   There is much discussion as to
why the inspired historian should use the word "about."   There is
no use to speculate as to why this term is used.

8 **And he entered into the synagogue,**—Since the incident of
John's disciples is mentioned before anything else, it seems proba-
ble that Paul had found them among the few Christian brethren in
Ephesus, and began teaching them before he visited the synagogue.
The Jews met in their synagogue for worship on the Sabbath, and
Paul went there and "spake boldly for the space of three months."
It seems that Christians held their religious services in the synagogue; he gave his Jewish brethren full opportunity to hear the
gospel in its fullness.   He may have just entered the synagogue on
their Sabbath, but it seems that he not only entered on the Sabbath
during this three months' sojourn, but on other occasions he
taught the people who assembled there.   Again we have Paul's
"reasoning and persuading"; he convinced them by his reasoning
and the scriptures that Jesus was the Christ, and he persuaded
them to accept him as their Savior.   He taught them "the things
concerning the kingdom of God."   Paul's idea of the "kingdom
of God" was that it was the church of God which had been purchased with the blood of Christ.   (Acts 20: 28.)   Paul understood
and taught that the kingdom had been established.

9 **But when some were hardened and disobedient,**—Paul
was permitted to speak longer in the synagogue here without interruption than any other place, unless it be Corinth.   Paul had the
same experience here that he had at other places; some believed
and some disbelieved.   Those who disbelieved hardened their heart
and began to speak "evil of the Way before the multitude."   Paul
was not a coward; he did not leave the synagogue simply because
some opposed him.   Evidently he saw the Jewish obstinacy and

disciples, reasoning daily in the school of Tyrannus. 10 And this continued for the space of two years; so that all they that dwelt in Asia heard the word of the Lord, both Jews and Greeks. 11 And God wrought special ⁶miracles by the hands of Paul: 12 insomuch that unto the sick were carried

⁶Gr. *powers*

---

turned away from them. He left the synagogue and took the disciples and reasoned "daily in the school of Tyrannus." The disbelieving Jews showed their hardness of heart by reviling Christ, his teaching, his disciples, and Christianity, "the Way." (Acts 9: 2.) Paul separated the disciples, and now the meeting place became the lecture room of Tyrannus. He had done the same thing at Corinth. (Acts 18: 7.) "School" is from the Greek "schole," and meant, originally, "to hold on, leisure," and then in later Greek, a "place where there is leisure." This is the only instance of its being used in the New Testament. The name "Tyrannus" is a common one, and means "tyrant." We know nothing about this Tyrannus; we do not know whether he was a heathen or a Jew.

10 **And this continued for the space of two years;**—Paul had been in Ephesus more than three months when he was forced to go to the lecture room of Tyrannus. He continued to preach the gospel here "for the space of two years." He continued edifying the saints and preaching to all who would come. He may have continued longer in Ephesus, and sojourning in the house of Aquila and Priscilla for some months. He remained here long enough for all who dwelt in that province to have opportunity to hear the gospel. Paul seems to have remained in Ephesus, but the gospel spread all over the province. Paul heard of the trouble that existed in the church at Corinth and wrote a letter to the church while at Ephesus; this letter seems to have been lost. (1 Cor. 5: 9.) He wrote the first Corinthian letter while at Ephesus.

11, 12 **And God wrought special miracles by the hands of Paul:**—Paul was endowed with miraculous gifts; he had the power to work miracles. He confirmed the word that he preached by working miracles. In Ephesus magicians and exorcists had claimed to work miracles; some superstitious people had believed in them. Paul had power to do even greater things than they even claimed. They even took handkerchiefs from Paul to the sick.

away from his body handkerchiefs or aprons, and the diseases departed from
them, and the evil spirits went out. 13 But certain also of the strolling Jews,

---

Paul did not have to visit the sick, but handkerchiefs and aprons
were carried from Paul and the diseases were healed and evil spirits cast out of those who possessed them. "Handkerchiefs" were
common in the eastern country to use to wipe perspiration from
the face. "Aprons" were the same as napkins. Paul did manual
work at Ephesus (Acts 20: 34) and so used handkerchiefs and
aprons. These special miracles would emphasize the work that
Paul was doing; the people could know that he was a teacher from
God, because God was with him in these great miracles.

3. THE SEVEN SONS OF SCEVA
19: 13-20

exorcists, took upon them to name over them that had the evil spirits the
name of the Lord Jesus, saying, I adjure you by Jesus whom Paul preacheth.
14 And there were seven sons of one Sceva, a Jew, a chief priest, who did
this. 15 And the evil spirit answered and said unto them, Jesus I ⁷know, and

---

⁷Or, *Recognize*

---

13 **But certain also of the strolling Jews,**—These "strolling
Jews" were "exorcists," who traveled from place to place and
practiced their spells of sorcery which was connected with the
name of Solomon. Jesus alluded to them in Palestine. (Matt. 12:
27; Luke 11: 19.) "Exorcists" comes from the Greek "exorkizo,"
which means "to exact an oath"; they used an oath as a spell or a
charm. These men regarded Paul as one of their own; they attempted to use the name of Christ as did Paul in performing his
miracles. They did not know Christ, but their formal oath was:
"I adjure you by Jesus whom Paul preacheth." This case is similar to that of Elymas the sorcerer (Acts 13: 8), and that of Simon
Magus (Acts 8: 21). They had not learned the difference between the real miracles that Paul performed and the pretended
ones of the exorcists.

14 **And there were seven sons of one Sceva,**—We do not
know who Sceva was; some think that he was a high priest.
Some think that the Greek here should be translated "ruler" in-

Paul I know; but who are ye? 16 And the man in whom the evil spirit was
leaped on them, and mastered both of them, and prevailed against them, so
that they fled out of that house naked and wounded.   17 And this became
known to all, both Jews and Greeks, that dwelt at Ephesus; and fear fell

---

stead of priest.   His name is of Latin origin.   "Chief priest"
means one who is at the head of one of the twenty-four courses of
the Levitical priesthood; hence, we cannot tell whether he had
been at the head of one of the twenty-four courses of priests of the
temple, or had once been the high priest at Jerusalem. He had
seven sons who were engaged in sorcery; they were exorcists.

15 And the evil spirit answered—These seven sons of Sceva
attempted to cast out an "evil spirit."   The evil spirit answered:
"Jesus I know, and Paul I know; but who are ye?"   The meaning
is, the Jesus whom you mention I recognize, and the Paul whom
you mention I know, but you, who are you?   The evil spirit did
not recognize in the sense of obeying the authority of these seven
sons.   "I know" is from "genosko," with respect to Jesus, and
from "epistomai," with respect to Paul; so the verbs are different,
and carry a different meaning.   The spirit here spoke through the
man as in Mark 3 : 11.

16 And the man in whom the evil spirit was—This shows
that the evil spirit spoke through the man who was afflicted.
Instead of this evil spirit obeying these exorcists, it leaped on
them.   "Both of them" seems to imply that only two of the seven
were attempting to practice upon this evil spirit; however, "both"
is from the Greek "amphoteron," and means "all" or more than
"two"; hence, here "amphoteroi" includes all seven; "both" in old
English was used foɪ moɪe than "two."   The defeat was so pronounced that the sons of Sceva "fled out of that house naked and
wounded."   The word "naked" here comes from the Greek "gum-
nous," and probably means only torn garments.   "Wounded" is
from the old verb "to wound."   It is used in the New Testament
only here and in Luke 20 : 12.   A similar case is found in Mark 5 :
3, 4, where no one could control the evil spirit.

17 And this became known to all,—This had a wonderful effect on the people of Ephesus; they learned of it, and all who had

upon them all, and the name of the Lord Jesus was magnified. 18 Many also of them that had believed came, confessing, and declaring their deeds. 19 And not a few of them that practised magical arts brought their books together and burned them in the sight of all; and they counted the price of

practiced hidden arts were so extensively known that fear fell upon them all when they learned what this evil spirit had done to the sons of Sceva. They thought that an undefined power resided in the sacred name of Jesus, and fear fell upon them as it did upon the church when Ananias and Sapphira were struck dead. (Acts 5: 5, 10.) It was a perilous thing for men to use the name of Jesus rashly; all people thought more of this name now than they had before. Hence, the name of Jesus was profoundly respected.

18 **Many also of them that had believed came,**—The fear of Jesus came upon the superstitious idolaters of Ephesus, and also upon the church. Luke is faithful to record the facts and does not hesitate to mention any shame that may have come upon the church. This was a humiliating confession and shows how many of the early converts were imperfect in their lives. Many of these early converts had kept some of the things which they had before their conversion; they practiced these things before their conversion and had not given them up, but now, since fear had come upon them, they were ready to destroy everything that pertained to this sorcery.

19 **And not a few of them that practised magical arts**—It seems that those who had been converted who had practiced the magical art, and even those who were not converted that practiced it, were ready now to quit the practice and destroy their books. They brought "their books together and burned them in the sight of all." These books were filled with incantations, recipes for love philters, formulas for casting out evil spirits, and such like. Ephesus swarmed with magicians and astrologers. The Christians brought their books and the others were led to renounce their evil practices; hence, they were ready to destroy their books. They burned them in the presence of all; this was a confession of the evils that they had practiced, and an open declaration to cease such evil works. "They counted the price of them, and found it fifty thousand pieces of silver." Ephesus was largely populated with

them, and found it fifty thousand pieces of silver. 20 So mightily grew the
word of the Lord and prevailed.

Greek citizens and probably the silver pieces were the Greek
"drachmae," or the Latin "denarius"; probably the total cost was
about ten thousand dollars. This was a great sacrifice. No doubt
that many of these books were rare and possessed a peculiar value
of their own from the precious secrets they were supposed to contain. The results of preaching the gospel to the Ephesians and the
confirmation of the word by miracles are thus seen in the effect
that it had on these people to cause them to suffer such a great
loss.

20 **So mightily grew the word**—While the people were in this
state of mind the word of God increased among them. Since they
had given up their magical arts, they were now ready to accept
something else; hence, the truth as preached by Paul found lodg-
ment in their hearts. The full meaning of the word rendered
"mightily" is "with overpowering force and strength, which nothing could resist." No wonder we find a large church at Ephesus.
"The word of the Lord" grew and "prevailed"; that is, it kept
growing and gaining strength; this was a day of triumph for
Christ in Ephesus; Ephesus for centuries after this was a center of
Christian power. Timothy came to Ephesus as also did John the
apostle.

4. THE MOB; SILVER SHRINES OF DIANA
19: 21-41

21 Now after these things were ended, Paul purposed in the spirit, when
he had passed through Macedonia and Achaia, to go to Jerusalem, saying,

21 **Now after these things were ended,**—After the burning of
the books on magical arts, Paul had it in heart to leave Ephesus.
Paul "passed through Macedonia and Achaia" on his way "to
Jerusalem." Paul had probably written the first Corinthian letter
while he was at Ephesus. He had a twofold object in this visit.
The first was to stir up the faith of the churches, and correct any
disorders which might be disturbing their development. The second was to bring to a close the collection for the poor saints at Jerusalem. (Rom. 15: 25; 1 Cor. 16: 1-3.) After he had com-

After I have been there, I must also see Rome. 22 And having sent into
Macedonia two of them that ministered unto him, Timothy and Erastus, he
himself stayed in Asia for a while.
23 And about that time there arose no small stir concerning the Way. 24

---

pleted his journey to Jerusalem he had it in heart to go to Rome.
He said: "I must also see Rome." This had been a long-cherished
plan of Paul's; he refers to it very distinctly in his letter to the
church at Rome. (Rom. 1: 13; see also Rom. 15: 23, 24, 28.)

22 **And having sent into Macedonia two of them**—Paul sent
Timothy and Erastus on to Macedonia while "he himself stayed in
Asia" for a longer time. He had sent Timothy to Corinth (1 Cor.
4: 17), and had requested the church to treat him with kindness;
he expected him to return, and he evidently had before Paul left
Ephesus; he then sent Titus to Corinth to finish what Timothy
had not quite succeeded in doing with instructions to meet him in
Troas. Now Timothy and Erastus (Rom. 16: 23; 2 Tim. 4: 20)
go on to Macedonia to prepare the way for Paul. For some reason Paul was delayed; he gives a reason for this in 1 Cor. 16: 8f.
There was a great opportunity for Paul to do more work in Ephesus; Pentecost came toward the end of May, and in this month the
festival of Artemis, or Diana, was held in Ephesus; a great multitude would come to the city, which would give Paul an opportunity to preach the gospel to a great number; however, Paul did not
remain till Pentecost.

23 **And about that time there arose**—Some trouble arose
about this time concerning "the Way." "The Way" is a very familiar term, and is used frequently by Luke as synonymous of the
disciples of Christ. (Acts 9: 2; 19: 9; 22: 4; 24: 14, 22.) This
term may have originated in the words which Christ had used of
himself when he said: "I am the way and the truth and the life:
no one cometh unto the Father, but by me." (John 14: 6.)
There had always been opposition to Christianity, but there seems
to have developed more opposition now than at some previous
time. The fight with wild beasts in 1 Cor. 15: 32, whatever it was,
was before that epistle was written, and so before this new uproar.
Paul as a Roman citizen could not be made to fight with wild

For a certain man named Demetrius, a silversmith, who made silver shrines of [1]Diana, brought no little business unto the craftsmen; 25 whom he gathered together, with the workmen of like occupation, and said, Sirs, ye know that by this business we have our wealth. 26 And ye see and hear, that not alone at Ephesus, but almost throughout all Asia, this Paul hath persuaded

[1]Gr. *Artemis*

beasts, but he so pictured the violent opponents of Christ in Ephesus.

24 **For a certain man named Demetrius,**—We do not know whether this Demetrius is the one spoken of in 3 John 12; however, he was from the neighborhood of Ephesus. Demetrius had something to do with this "no small stir" about the disciples of Christ. He was a silversmith and made images or shrines of Diana. He had a profitable business, and just at this time before the feast he would sell many of his shrines. A great multitude would come into the city to worship Diana, and they would want to take a shrine or image of Diana back home with them. Evidently Paul had condemned the practice of idolatry and this would hurt Demetrius' business; so many of the Ephesians had become Christians and had destroyed their idols that Demetrius was much concerned about his trade. We see that Demetrius was more concerned about making money than he was about becoming a Christian; he cared nothing about others becoming a Christian, but he did want to sell his shrines to them.

25 **whom he gathered together,**—Demetrius got busy; he gathered those who were of the same craft and persuaded them to join him in opposing Paul's preaching. Perhaps Demetrius was chief among those of his trade; trade unions or guilds were found among almost every kind of trade in the Roman Empire in apostolic times. This shows how easily the workman of the trade could be summoned to discuss anything relating to the trade, and how a disturbance could be had.

26 **And ye see and hear, that not alone at Ephesus,**—Here we have the argument that Demetrius makes to his fellow craftsmen to persuade them to join him in his opposition to the preaching of Paul. Not only in Ephesus, "but almost throughout all Asia," Paul had injured their trade by preaching Christ. Demetrius may have exaggerated some to excite his fellow crafts-

and turned away much people, saying that they are no gods, that are made with hands: 27 and not only is there danger that this our trade come into disrepute; but also that the temple of the great goddess ¹Diana be made of no account, and that she should even be deposed from her magnificence whom all Asia and ²the world worshippeth. 28 And when they heard this

²Gr. *the inhabited earth*

men to action. What Paul had preached had greatly disturbed his business. Demetrius does not mean the entire continent of Asia, but the province of Asia Minor. All the roads in Asia Minor centered in Ephesus; from its position it was almost as much a meeting place of eastern and western thought as was Alexandria. Pilgrims came from all parts of Asia Minor to visit the famous shrine of Diana. Demetrius not only exaggerated his statements to his fellow craftsmen, but he also exaggerated the effect of Paul's work. We know that Paul had established churches in Ephesus, Laodicea, and Colosse; John in Revelation speaks of the churches in Pergamum, Smyrna, Thyatira, Sardis, and Philadelphia. He correctly represented Paul's teaching when he said that he preached against their idolatrous worship.

27 **and not only is there danger that this our trade**—Demetrius in further arguing his case before his fellow craftsmen said that not only their trade was in danger, but that "the temple of the great goddess Diana" was in danger of being abandoned. Demetrius mentioned his business first, and then the destruction of the shrine next; he knew that they would feel more keenly the force of his argument if he mentioned their business first. Again, he mentions the magnificence of "the great goddess Diana" "whom all Asia and the world worshippeth." Here again he exaggerates; however, the temple of Diana was the most famous in the world, and a place of resort for people from all parts of Asia Minor and Greece. The temple of Diana was one of the wonders of the ancient world, and the glory and pride of all the Ephesians. If people followed the teachings of Paul they would give up their idolatry, and that would leave the temple desolate. Summing up Demetrius' argument he makes but two points: his trade would be injured and their religion would be in danger. He appealed to two of the strongest sentiments that rule the human heart—their finan-

they were filled with wrath, and cried out, saying, Great *is* [1]Diana of the Ephesians. 29 And the city was filled with the confusion: and they rushed with one accord into the theatre, having seized Gaius and Aristarchus, men of Macedonia, Paul's companions in travel. 30 And when Paul was minded

cial interests and their religion. Selfish interests and appeal to their prejudice caused a riot and the city was full of tumult.

28 And when they heard this—Demetrius' speech was very effective; he had made it probably in some open space near the place where the shrines were made. The people "were filled with wrath" and started an uproar. They shouted unanimously: "Great is Diana of the Ephesians." This was similar to the cry, "O Baal, hear us," by the priests of Baal on Mount Carmel in the days of Elijah. (1 Kings 18: 26.) The idol was enshrined in the temple; it was different from the Greek goddess, Diana, which was represented as fair and beautiful, standing with a bow in her hand and a stag at her side as a huntress. "Diana of the Ephesians" was a crude many-breasted female figure, ending below the breasts in a square pillar curiously carved with ancient symbols of bees, flowers, and corn. It was reputed to have fallen down from heaven.

29 And the city was filled with the confusion:—Lewin, in his "Saint Paul," describes this mob as follows: "The illiterate artisans, soured by reduced wages or want of employment, were roused into a state of frenzy, and full of rage they sallied forth into the streets to wreak vengeance on the object of their blind fury. The living mass rolled along, and the thousands of idlers, whom the games had attracted to Ephesus, swelled their numbers at every step, and the whole city was soon in a state of confusion." They "rushed with one accord into the theatre," but failing to find Paul, they then seized Gaius and Aristarchus, who had traveled with Paul from Macedonia. This Gaius is not mentioned anywhere else in the New Testament. He is not the one from Derbe (Acts 20: 4), nor the one from Corinth (Rom. 16: 23; 1 Cor. 1: 14), and probably not the one to whom John writes (3 John 1). Aristarchus was of Thessalonica (Acts 20: 4), and went with Paul to Rome (Acts 27: 2) and became of his own accord a sharer of Paul's exile and captivity (Col. 4: 10), and was Paul's fellow worker (Phile. 24). The mob rushed into the theatre, and being

to enter in unto the people, the disciples suffered him not. 31 And certain also of the [3]Asiarchs, being his friends, sent unto him and besought him not to adventure himself into the theatre. 32 Some therefore cried one thing, and some another: for the assembly was in confusion; and the more part knew not wherefore they were come together. 33 [4]And they brought Alex-

[3]That is, officers having charge of festivals &c. in the Roman province of Asia
[4]Or, *And* some *of the multitude instructed Alexander*

disappointed at not finding Paul, Gaius and Aristarchus were attacked.

30 And when Paul was minded to enter—Paul was no coward; he was ready to die for his Lord. He was loyal to his brethren and wanted to help them. It seems that he was out of reach of the mob when they seized Gaius and Aristarchus, and was anxious for their safety and zealous for the truth. The disciples would not permit him to risk his life with the mob. It is likely that he was dwelling with Aquila and Priscilla, who at this or some other time at Ephesus, "laid down their own necks" for his life. (Rom. 16: 4.) The brethren at Ephesus joined these two faithful disciples in restraining Paul from such danger.

31 And certain also of the Asiarchs,—"Asiarchs" were chief officials; there were ten in number who were chosen annually to superintend the games and festivals held in honor of the emperor and the gods. The games of Ephesus were held in the month of May in honor of Diana. Some of these officials were friends of Paul. It is interesting to observe that so many of those in high official position were friends of Paul. The apostle had great power in attracting honorable friends, such as Sergius Paulus, Gallio, Felix, and Festus, and the centurion on the voyage to Rome. It is remarkable that such leading and prominent men in this heathenish sport should have shown such a friendly and solicitous care for Paul. They used their influence on Paul to restrain him from going into the theatre where the infuriated mob had assembled.

32 Some therefore cried one thing, and some another:—The mob was greatly confused; some cried one thing, and some another; many of the mob did not know why they had assembled. Verse 32 is a further description of what is recorded in verse 29. The vast multitude had assembled with a vague idea that something was wrong; they did not know what; hence, they could not

ander out of the multitude, the Jews putting him forward. And Alexander
beckoned with the hand, and would have made a defence unto the people. 34
But when they perceived that he was a Jew, all with one voice about the
space of two hours cried out, Great is ¹Diana of the Ephesians. 35 And
when the townclerk had quieted the multitude, he saith, Ye men of Ephesus,

---

act intelligently on anything. It seems strange that Demetrius,
who was responsible for the mob, should remain in the background
and not inform the mob as to its purposes.

33 **And they brought Alexander out of the multitude,—**
Some think that this Alexander was the same as the coppersmith
of 2 Tim. 4: 14, whom Paul declared had done him much harm.
"Coppersmith" may be used in the general sense of "metalworker,"
and he may have been a fellow craftsman of Demetrius; this would
give him some influence. The Jews put Alexander forward, because they were afraid that they would be confused with Paul,
Gaius, and Aristarchus; the Jews opposed idolatry as did the
Christians. Alexander was put forward to defend the Jews; he
"beckoned with the hand"; that is, he rapidly waved his hand up
and down to quiet the people so that he could speak to them. It
seems that he was not permitted to speak.

34 **But when they perceived that he was a Jew,**—When
the angry mob learned that Alexander was a Jew, they gave no
heed to his request to speak to them. They knew that he was a
Jew by his features, speech, or manner of dress. The crowd now
became unanimous in their opposition to Alexander's speaking;
they would not hear him. The uproar continued for about "the
space of two hours"; they were wild with fury, excitement, and superstition; they continued shouting their slogan: "Great is Diana
of the Ephesians." Again they remind one of the procedure on the
part of the worshipers of Baal in the days of Elijah, who "called
on the name of Baal from morning even until noon, saying, O
Baal, hear us." (1 Kings 18: 26.)

35 **And when the townclerk had quieted the multitude,**—
Ephesus was a free city and elected its own officers; the recorder
or secretary was the chief magistrate of the city, though the proconsul of the province of Asia lived there. The functions of this
officer, in some respects, correspond to those fulfilled by the re-

what man is there who knoweth not that the city of the Ephesians is temple-keeper of the great [1]Diana, and of the *image* which fell down from [5]Jupiter? 36 Seeing then that these things cannot be gainsaid, ye ought to be quiet, and to do nothing rash.   37 For ye have brought *hither* these men, who are nei-

[5]Or, *heaven*

corder of modern times; among his duties were the guardianship and tabulation of the state papers, the archives of the city, and in drawing up the public records. He began to address the multitude by paying tribute to the city and referring to Ephesus as the "temple-keeper of the great Diana." He appealed to their superstition and to their civic pride. He meant to say, why imperil your cherished privileges granted by the Roman government by an unnecessary uproar about a question which no one would doubt? He appeals to their superstition and religion by referring to the fact that all knew that the image "fell down from Jupiter." Like other venerated idols, the statue of Diana was supposed to have fallen from the skies. He soothed the vanity of the crowd by his appeal to the world-wide fame of Ephesus and her image which fell down from heaven. The heavens were considered the home of Jupiter. Zeus, or Jupiter, was considered ruler of the sky or heavens.

36 **Seeing then that these things cannot be gainsaid,**—The town clerk called attention to some undeniable facts as he and they thought. The legends were accepted without any proof; the town clerk reasoned as if no one would deny them. Since no one could rob Ephesus of its glory or the statue of Diana of its honor, they need not be so disturbed; they ought to be quiet and not do anything rash. It was useless to be so excited about that from which no harm could come; this was the town clerk's first argument.

37 **For ye have brought hither these men,**—The town clerk here implies that they had acted rashly in precipitating the riot. The second argument that the town clerk makes is that Paul and his companions were not wicked men; they were "neither robbers of temples nor blasphemers of our goddess." They had done nothing to cause such an uproar. He reasoned that Paul and his companions have done nothing which would arouse their indignation. This statement shows how Paul had preached against error; he

ther robbers of temples nor blasphemers of our goddess. 38 If therefore Demetrius, and the craftsmen that are with him, have a matter against any
man, ⁶the courts are open, and there are proconsuls: let them accuse one
another. 39 But if ye seek anything about other matters, it shall be settled

⁶Or, *court* days *are kept*

seems to have preached positive truths rather than making a direct
attack on their error. He had hurt no religious prejudice by rude
invectives; he was no blasphemer of the gods of Greece and Rome,
but led men to the knowledge of truth by positive and kind representation of it. Paul had not shunned to preach the truth to them;
this truth opposed all of the errors to which they were wedded; but
he had preached the truth in such a way that they could not take
offense at him, if we take the statement of the town clerk at face
value. However, it may be that he was exaggerating and highly
complimenting Paul and his companions in order to appease the
anger of the crowd.

38 **If therefore Demetrius, and the craftsmen**—A third argument that the town clerk used called attention to the proper chan-
nels through which Demetrius and his fellow craftsmen could go
with any grievance that they may have. This is an appeal to them
to be law-abiding citizens, and let the proper authorities handle
any violation of a law. This argument condemns Demetrius and
his fellow craftsmen for causing such an uproar. The law was
open; the Roman officials held court at intervals in Ephesus. In
addition Ephesus was a free city, and had its local courts and magistrates. It may be that the court was in session at the time. The
town clerk here makes a definite appeal to the people to proceed
orderly and legally, and not resort to mob violence. The "proconsuls" were the governors and judges in these matters. In the time
of Paul, Asia was a senatorial province and was governed by a
proconsul; however, the term is used here in the plural, while only
one of these officials held office in the senatorial province. The
term seems to have been used in a general sense.

39 **But if ye seek anything about other matters,**—The town
clerk further argues the question that if they had any grievance
whatsoever there were well-established laws by which all these

in the regular assembly. 40 For indeed we are in danger to be ⁷accused concerning this day's riot, there being no cause *for it*: and as touching it we
shall not be able to give account of this concourse. 41 And when he had
thus spoken, he dismissed the assembly.

⁷Or, *accused of riot concerning this day*

---

matters could be settled. There was "the regular assembly"; this
was not a "regular assembly"; it was an *irregular* one; it was not a
legally organized assembly for settling disputes. Charges of illegal
conduct should be settled in the regular legal way; if they wished
to go further and pass resolutions about any matter, this could be
done in the regular way, and not rashly by an excited and infuriated assembly. The crowd of citizens that the town clerk was addressing was simply a mob gathering; their decisions could have
no weight, and such a meeting would only tend to damage the city
in the eyes of the Roman government. The term "assembly," as
used here, is from the Greek "ekklesiai," which is the same word
that is translated "church."

40 **For indeed we are in danger**—This is the concluding argument that the town clerk makes. The city was in danger by such a
procedure of losing some of its prestige as a "free city." Some of
the liberties were in danger by the conduct of this mob; these people were responsible for such illegal proceedings. They were responsible to their own city government; responsible to the officers
of the city; furthermore, they were responsible to the Roman government for such illegal assembly as was now convened. They
were in danger of being "accused concerning this day's riot," and
that too without any just cause for their proceedings. The highly
esteemed liberties which the city claimed might be forfeited by this
mob. There was a Roman law which made it a capital offense to
raise a riot. This mob was unable to defend itself if brought before the proper authorities.

41 **And when he had thus spoken,**—It seems that the town
clerk had great weight. The town clerk reasoned well; the offense
which they had committed was not likely to be passed over lightly
by the proconsuls; it would not be thought a legitimate excuse
that they had laid hold of two Jews whom they wanted to put to

death. After thus reasoning with them "he dismissed the assembly." Here he gives a noble name to the assembly, that of a recognized meeting, to shield them from any evil report of the meeting; he dismissed in a formal way the assembly. He gave a semblance of law and order to the mob by formally dismissing them; this would protect them against the charge to which they were liable.

5. PAUL REVISITS MACEDONIA

20: 1-6

1 And after the uproar ceased, Paul having sent for the disciples and exhorted them, took leave of them, and departed to go into Macedonia. 2 And when he had gone through those parts, and had given them much exhorta-

1 **And after the uproar ceased,**—There is no evidence that "the uproar" of the mob caused Paul to leave Ephesus; it might have hastened his departure. He had determined before that event to leave the city. (Acts 19: 21, 22.) Luke, the writer, is very brief here and passes over without a word an important period in Paul's life. We are able to fill up the gap in the narrative from scattered references in Paul's writings, especially from Second Corinthians. It seems that Paul left Ephesus by land and went by land to Troas; he waited there anxiously for Titus (2 Cor. 2: 13), whom he had sent to Corinth on a mission connected with the collection then being made by the Gentile churches for the relief of the poor saints in Jerusalem. For some cause Titus was delayed, and Paul sailed from Troas to Macedonia, where Titus met him with news from Corinth. (2 Cor. 7: 6.) Some think that Paul met Titus at Philippi, where he wrote the second Corinthian letter.

2 **And when he had gone through those parts,**—We do not know why Luke did not tell of Paul's sojourn in Troas (2 Cor. 2: 12f), nor of the meeting with Titus in Macedonia (2 Cor. 2: 13 to 7: 16), nor of Paul's visit to Illyricum (Rom. 15: 19f.), to give time for the second letter to Corinth to do its work. Paul finally came into Greece or Achaia and came to Corinth, whither he had at last come again after repeated attempts, delays, and pauses. Paul followed his usual custom of visiting and conferring with the churches already established. (Acts 15: 41; 18: 23.) We may know that Paul preached the gospel on his way to Corinth (2 Cor.

tion, he came into Greece. 3 And when he had spent three months *there,* and a plot was laid against him by the Jews as he was about to set sail for Syria, he determined to return through Macedonia. 4 And there accompanied him ¹as far as Asia, Sopater of Beroea, *the son* of Pyrrhus; and of the Thessalonians, Aristarchus and Secundus; and Gaius of Derbe, and Timothy; and of Asia, Tychicus and Trophimus. 5 But these ²had gone before,

¹Many ancient authorities omit *as far as Asia*
²Many ancient authorities read *came, and were waiting*

10: 16), and made excursions into the surrounding parts of Achaia, with Corinth as his headquarters.

3 And when he had spent three months there,—The historian Luke here briefly refers to Paul's second residence in Corinth. Some think that this was his third visit to Corinth. (2 Cor. 13: 1.) He may have made a short trip to Corinth during his three years' stay at Ephesus. He had been away from Corinth three years, and in that period many changes had taken place in the church. There were the disputes about the Lord's Supper, the divisions into different partisan groups, the immoral lives of some of the members, and many other evils that needed to be corrected. During the three months of his stay at Corinth, Paul wrote the great epistle to the Romans. (Rom. 15: 25; 16: 1.) The Galatian letter was possibly written at this time also. A plot was laid against Paul by the Jews while he was there, as he was about to "set sail for Syria." Paul, having heard of this plot, changed his course and, instead of sailing for Syria, he returned "through Macedonia." We do not know what this plot was, but we do know that it caused Paul to make a circuitous route through Macedonia.

4 And there accompanied him as far as Asia,—Seven brethren accompanied Paul: Sopater of Berea, Aristarchus and Secundus of Thessalonica, Gaius of Derbe, Timothy and Tychicus and Trophimus of Asia. We know nothing further of Sopater; Aristarchus has been mentioned before (Acts 19: 29); he was on the ship with Paul on the way to Rome (Acts 27: 2); and he is mentioned in Col. 4: 10 as Paul's fellow prisoner. We know nothing further of Secundus; Gaius was probably a friend of Timothy, who was from Lystra, a neighboring city to Derbe. Tychicus is mentioned four times in Paul's writings during his imprisonment at Rome. (Eph. 6: 21; Col. 4: 7; 2 Tim. 4: 12; Tit. 3: 12.)

and were waiting for us at Troas. 6 And we sailed away from Philippi after the days of unleavened bread, and came unto them to Troas in five days; where we tarried seven days.

Trophimus was with Paul in Jerusalem (Acts 21: 29), and is mentioned in 2 Tim. 4: 20. Paul was carrying a contribution contributed by the Gentile churches; hence, these brethren could assist him and serve as a bodyguard to him.

5 **But these had gone before,**—It is probable that only the last two went before and were waiting for the company at Troas. Here the language of the narrative suddenly changes from the third person to the first; Luke has now joined Paul's company. Paul and Luke were together from the time of the arrival of Paul at Troas (Acts 16: 8); they crossed over together into Europe, but when Paul left Philippi (Acts 16: 40), Luke was left behind, and, it has been supposed, made Philippi the center of his work for several years. Now again, after the lapse of five or six years, they meet. The remainder of the Acts is told by an eyewitness of the various events recorded; we conclude that from this time till Paul was entrusted to the charge of the soldiers at Rome Luke was continually with him. Many think that the seven brethren went before and waited for Paul and Luke to come to Troas.

6 **And we sailed away from Philippi**—Philippi was about ten or twelve miles from the seaport, Neapolis. They had come to Philippi by land. They remained there during "the days of unleavened bread." This was the Passover. The Passover proper lasted only one day, the fourteenth day of the first month, but there followed the Passover seven days, known as the Feast of Unleavened Bread; hence the two feasts were united and one name included the Passover and the Feast of Unleavened Bread, or the Feast of Unleavened Bread included the Passover. Paul was a Jew and Luke was a Gentile. The passover was to be eaten in Jerusalem; it may be that Paul remained here during this time to preach the gospel to Jews that might assemble. Again, the Feast of Unleavened Bread is mentioned as a chronological note of time; Paul did not tarry at Philippi to observe the Passover, but remained there that Luke might arrange and prepare for the journey. They set sail for Troas and arrived in "five days"; six years

before this Paul had made the voyage in the opposite direction in two days. (Acts 16: 11.) It may be that adverse winds delayed their sailing. They remained in Troas seven days.

6. PAUL AT TROAS
20: 7-12

7 And upon the first day of the week, when we were gathered together to break bread, Paul discoursed with them, intending to depart on the morrow; and prolonged his speech until midnight. 8 And there were many lights in the upper chamber where we were gathered together. 9 And there sat in the

7 **And upon the first day of the week,**—This is the first time that we have mentioned services "upon the first day of the week." Paul had written First Corinthians before this; in that letter he had designated that collections or contributions should be taken on the first day of the week. (1 Cor. 16: 2.) He tells us that he had given the same "order to the churches of Galatia." (1 Cor. 16: 1.) This shows that it had become a well-established custom for the early Christians to meet on the first day of the week; this custom is now a command, or rather, there is a command for this collection to be taken on the first day of the week. They had met at Troas or gathered "together to break bread" on "the first day of the week." "To break bread" is from the Greek "klasai arton," which is the same as in Acts 2: 42. This is used for the Lord's Supper; hence, we have here the purpose of their gathering together on the first day of the week. Paul was present and "discoursed with them," purposing to leave Troas on the following day. However, he "prolonged his speech until midnight." Paul's preaching was incidental, though instructive. Paul reasoned with them, and the conversation was used to solve doubts and clear away difficulties which might be in the way of some young Christians.

8 **And there were many lights in the upper chamber**—They were gathered in an "upper chamber" for the services. The upper room was used for devotional purposes; it was so located as to be retired and free from disturbance. It was located on the third story. The lights are mentioned by Luke to portray the scene, and it would at once be noticed if anyone absented himself from the audience.

window a certain young man named Eutychus, borne down with deep sleep; and as Paul discoursed yet longer, being borne down by his sleep he fell down from the third story, and was taken up dead. 10 And Paul went down, and fell on him, and embracing him said, Make ye no ado; for his life is in him. 11 And when he was gone up, and had broken the bread, and eaten, and had talked with them a long while, even till break of day, so he

---

9 **And there sat in the window a certain young man named Eutychus,**—Perhaps this young man sat on the window sill where the seats extended out over the street; the window was not of glass; hence, one could fall out the window very easily. This "certain young man" is called a "lad" in verse 12. Paul's discourse continued until midnight and the young man was "borne down with deep sleep," and while asleep, "he fell down from the third story, and was taken up dead." Eutychus was not merely taken up for dead, but "was taken up dead." This is recorded by Luke, the physician, who was present and knew all the particulars.

10 **And Paul went down, and fell on him,**—Paul went down the stairway, which was usually outside and led down to the street. Paul "fell on him" similar to what Elijah (1 Kings 17: 21) and Elisha (2 Kings 4: 34) did; Paul very likely placed his body upon the body of Eutychus as did Elijah and Elisha, and accompanied his action with prayer. Paul told the anxious ones who stood around that they should not make such ado, for the young man's life was in him. This is similar to what Christ said at the house of Jairus. (Luke 8: 52, 53.) Paul did not say that Eutychus had not been dead, but that after his efforts life was there. Some had attempted to prove that Eutychus was not dead, but the language clearly implies that he was dead, but now is alive.

11 **And when he was gone up, and had broken the bread,**— Commentators are not agreed as to whether the Lord's Supper was meant by "had broken the bread" or a common meal. If this was the Lord's Supper, and if they counted the day from midnight to midnight as we count it, then they ate the Lord's Supper on Monday; if they ate the Lord's Supper on Monday, they did not do what they met to do on the first day of the week; again, if this was the Lord's Supper, and if they began counting time from sunset to sunset, then they ate the Lord's Supper on the first day of the week. If this does not refer to the Lord's Supper, it refers to

departed. 12 And they brought the lad alive, and were not a little comforted.

---

a common meal; this would mean that they had already eaten the
Lord's Supper, and now, since there had been an interruption in
Paul's discourse by the falling of Eutychus out of the window,
Paul took nourishment and continued his speech. It seems better
to conclude that this was not the Lord's Supper, but that it was a
common meal which Paul ate in preparation for his expected departure. It is mentioned with particular reference to Paul, not to
the worshiping company; hence, we conclude that the Lord's Supper had been observed at an earlier period of the meeting, and
therefore, on the first day of the week, as they had met for that
purpose on that day.

12 **And they brought the lad alive,**—The young man was
brought into the assembly room in a normal condition; the word
"brought," not "carried," shows that he was in a normal condition.
The disciples were encouraged by Paul's speech and comforted by
the fact that the young man was alive and in a normal condition.
Paul and his company departed as they had intended, and left the
brethren further instructed and hopeful as the Lord's people.

7. AT MILETUS WITH THE ELDERS OF THE CHURCH
AT EPHESUS
20: 13-38

13 But we, going before to the ship, set sail for Assos, there intending to
take in Paul: for so had he appointed, intending himself to go [3]by land. 14
And when he met us at Assos, we took him in, and came to Mitylene. 15

[3]Or, *on foot*

---

13 **But we, going before to the ship,**—The company, including Luke, as the pronoun "we" shows, set sail from Troas for
Assos; this town was in Mysia on the north shore of the Gulf of
Adramyttium, about twenty miles from Troas by land, and about
thirty miles by sea. Paul had gone by land and had instructed his
company to meet him at Assos. Some think that Paul's company
had chartered a vessel and could make stops wherever ordered.

14 **And when he met us at Assos,**—The company came to
Assos, where Paul joined them, and then came to Mitylene.

And sailing from thence, we came the following day over against Chios; and the next day we touched at Samos; and ⁴the day after we came to Miletus. 16 For Paul had determined to sail past Ephesus, that he might not have to spend time in Asia; for he was hastening, if it were possible for him, to be at Jerusalem the day of Pentecost.

⁴Many ancient authorities insert *having tarried at Trogyllium*

Mitylene was the capital of Lesbos, and was about thirty miles from Assos. Mitylene was the birthplace of Sappho, the female poet, and the poet Alcaeus. It could be reached from Assos in one day's journey.

15 **And sailing from thence,**—It was a day's journey from Mitylene to Chios. The island of Chios is about five miles distant from the mainland; it was in the Aegean Sea. The next day the vessel "touched at Samos." The island of Samos lies off that part of the coast of Asia Minor, where the ancient Ionia joined on to Caria; it has been famous both in ancient Greek and modern European history. On the mainland opposite, at the termination of the ridge of Mycale, lay Trogyllium, for which the apostle's vessel made without stopping in Samos. The next day the vessel sailed to Miletus. Miletus had been a most famous seaport in earlier Greek history, but in the days of Paul its fame was eclipsed by Ephesus. It seems that they arrived at Miletus the fourth day after leaving Troas. Miletus was about twenty-eight miles south of Ephesus by land, and lay near the mouth of the Meander; it was one day's sail from Trogyllium.

16 **For Paul had determined to sail past Ephesus,**—Paul sought to evade stopping at Ephesus; at this time he did not wish to revisit the church there, lest the many friends and their pressing solicitations should delay his voyage. He did not have any time to spare, as he wanted to reach Jerusalem in time to be there at the Feast of Pentecost. If Paul could get to Jerusalem by Pentecost he could present the gifts of the Gentile churches in the presence of the great crowd of foreign Jews who would assemble in Jerusalem at the Pentecostal feast, and thus spread abroad in all lands the great fact that the Gentile Christians were one with their Jewish brethren; this would impress them that the disciples of the Lord were one body.

17 And from Miletus he sent to Ephesus, and called to him the ⁵elders of
the church. 18 And when they were come to him, he said unto them,
    Ye yourselves know, from the first day that I set foot in Asia, after what
manner I was with you all the time, 19 serving the Lord with all lowliness
of mind, and with tears, and with trials which befell me by the plots of the

⁵Or, *presbyters*

---

17 **And from Miletus he sent to Ephesus,**—Some think that
had the ship been entirely at Paul's disposal he would have asked
the elders at Ephesus to meet him at Trogyllium, which is very
near Ephesus. Had he gone to Ephesus he would probably have
been compelled to stay longer than he wished to stay. It would
take more than one day for Paul to send his messenger to Ephesus
and summon those whom he wished to see. If they came to him
on the next day that would be consumed in their conference, and
the voyage could hardly be begun again till the third day at the
earliest. He sent to Ephesus for the elders of the church to meet
him. The term "elders" here is from the Greek "presbuterous,"
from which we get our term "presbytor." The first term "elder"
applied to a disciple of Christ is found in Acts 11: 30, and then
again Acts 15: 4, 6, 22. The "elders" are not "apostles," but are
"bishops." (Phil. 1: 1.) The "elders" in this verse are called
"bishops" in verse 28. The duties of the elders are the ministration
of the affairs of the church, conducting public worship, preaching
the gospel to sinners, and edifying the membership.

18 **And when they were come to him,**—It is difficult to analyze Paul's address to the elders of the church of Ephesus at this
time; it is full of personality, instruction, and persuasion. He first
appealed to their knowledge of his manner of life among them; it
had been about four years since he began his work at Ephesus. In
fact, most of his work in Asia was done in Ephesus; these elders
knew his work at Ephesus and had heard of his labors elsewhere in
Asia. They knew Paul's manner of life and could vindicate him
against any of the reports circulated to his injury.

19 **serving the Lord with all lowliness of mind,**—Paul was
not puffed up; he did not boast of what he had done or what he
could do; he served the Lord with "all lowliness of mind." Paul

Jews; 20 how I shrank not from declaring unto you anything that was profitable, and teaching you publicly, and from house to house, 21 testifying both
to Jews and to Greeks repentance toward God, and faith toward our Lord

---

was clothed with humility and had a humble mind as he taught the
people and preached a crucified Lord. He preached with "tears."
He wrote to the church at Corinth "with many tears." (2 Cor. 2:
4.) In writing the church at Philippi he rehearsed some things to
the church there, and then said that he now told them "even weeping" at the time he wrote the Philippian letter. (Phil. 3: 18.)
This shows how earnestly and sincerely Paul engaged in the work
of the Lord. They knew the trials and plots that endangered
Paul's life. Though the Jews had at first desired him to return to
them, they soon fell into the same hostility of others. The Jews
who rejected the gospel became Paul's worst enemies.

20 **how I shrank not from declaring unto you anything**—
Amidst all the plots and hostilities to which Paul was subjected he
did not keep back "anything that was profitable" to them.
Everything that pertained to life and godliness had been declared
by Paul. He preached the gospel publicly in the synagogue of the
Jews and in the public assembly of the Gentiles; he preached the
gospel in private "from house to house"; he preached Christ publicly and in private circles, in the church or place of worship, and
in the dwellings. Paul, the great apostle to the Gentiles, set the example of teaching the word of God, both publicly and privately.

21 **testifying both to Jews and to Greeks repentance toward
God,**—Paul testified of all the things that were profitable to their
salvation; "testifying" is from the Greek "diamarturomenos," and
was used by Peter in Acts 2: 40, where Luke used the same word
to describe Peter's preaching. Again Luke uses "Jews and to
Greeks," thus including both as Paul did in Rom. 1: 16. He
preached "repentance toward God" and "faith toward our Lord
Jesus Christ." Repentance is required of Jews and Greeks, and
faith is needed by the Jews as well as the Greeks. Faith and repentance go together; to the alien they cannot be separated. John
the Baptist came to make ready a people prepared for Christ by
preaching repentance toward God; Christ preached repentance to-

Jesus [6]Christ. 22 And now, behold, I go bound in the spirit unto Jerusalem, not knowing the things that shall befall me there: 23 save that the Holy Spirit testifieth unto me in every city, saying that bonds and afflictions abide me. 24 But I hold not my life of any account as dear unto myself, [7]so that I may accomplish my course, and the ministry which I received from the Lord

[6]Many ancient authorities omit *Christ*
[7]Or, *in comparison of accomplishing my course*

ward God, and Paul, in preaching to the Athenians, first presented to them the true God, then called on them to repent of their idolatries which had dishonored God; after that he presented Christ as the crucified and risen Lord. (Acts 17: 29-31.)   All sin is against God; hence, repentance must be toward God. The writer here does not mean to say that repentance to the alien precedes faith. Such a position would teach that men repent toward God before they believe in God, and repent toward Christ before they believe in him.

22, 23 **And now, behold, I go bound in the spirit**—Here Paul mentions his journey to Jerusalem; he was now on his way and could not go to Ephesus and tarry there, as he was hastening on to Jerusalem. "Bound in the spirit" means that he was bound in his own spirit; it is the same as in Acts 19: 21, where he "purposed in the spirit." However, some have interpreted these words to mean that Paul was constrained by the Holy Spirit to make the journey to Jerusalem; the context seems to indicate that it is Paul's spirit. He did not know what would befall him; he was not concerned about the persecutions that would come upon him, as he was willing to die for Christ. The Holy Spirit testified that "bonds and afflictions" awaited him in every city where he went. The Holy Spirit had called Paul to the work (Acts 13: 2), and had moved the disciples (Acts 21: 4) and Agabus (Acts 21: 11) to warn Paul of the sufferings which were at hand. Perhaps many other warnings came to Paul that Luke does not record.

24 **But I hold not my life of any account as dear unto myself,**—Paul had given his life to Christ; it was not held as dear to himself, and he was willing to spend and be spent in order to further the cause of Christ. Paul glorified in tribulations (2 Cor. 12: 10f); he did not regard his life as valuable in comparison with his

Jesus, to testify the ⁸gospel of the grace of God. 25 And now, behold, I
know that ye all, among whom I went about preaching the kingdom, shall
see my face no more. 26 Wherefore I testify unto you this day, that I am
pure from the blood of all men. 27 For I shrank not from declaring unto

⁸Or, *good tidings*

---

joyfully completing his career and attaining the prize of the high
calling of God in Christ Jesus. Paul is determined to run the race
to the end and to preach the gospel of the grace of God to all who
would hear him. The race with Paul will last as long as life lasts;
he will not faint in the middle of sufferings which awaited him.
Later Paul said: "I have fought the good fight, I have finished the
course, I have kept the faith." (2 Tim. 4: 7.) The gospel is here
called "the gospel of the grace of God" because it was given by the
grace of God. Grace means the free favor of God.

25 **And now, behold, I know that ye all,**—We do not know
that Paul ever saw Ephesus again; it seems that Paul did not expect to see these elders again. Paul had preached "the kingdom"
at Ephesus. Daniel had prophesied (Dan. 2: 44) that God would
set up his kingdom; John the Baptist, Christ, and his apostles
before Pentecost preached that it was "at hand"; after Pentecost
the apostles preached that the kingdom was in existence and that
Christians were citizens in the kingdom; so here we find that Paul
went about preaching the kingdom.

26 **Wherefore I testify unto you this day,**—Paul is very personal; he is speaking face to face with the elders of the church at
Ephesus; he could call them to witness that he was stating the
truth to them. He had kept nothing back that pertained to the redemption of souls. He had taught them what to do to become
Christians, and had taught them how to live the Christian life, and
now he could declare "that I am pure from the blood of all men."
He had taught them the will of God and had warned them of the
doom of those who would not obey the gospel. As a watchman
standing on the wall, he had warned all; hence, he was not charge-
able with their destruction; his skirts were clear from the blood of
all, as he had faithfully warned all of their duty and of the coming
wrath. (Ezek. 3: 18-21.) Paul had declared the whole counsel
of God here as he had at Corinth. (Acts 18: 6.)

you the whole counsel of God. 28 Take heed unto yourselves, and to all the flock, in which the Holy Spirit hath made you ¹bishops, to feed the church of ²the Lord which he ³purchased with his own blood. 29 I know that after my

¹Or, *overseers*
²Some ancient authorities, including the two oldest manuscripts, read *God*
³Gr. *acquired*

27 **For I shrank not from declaring unto you**—He had not withheld anything from them that was needful for them to know or do for their own salvation. "The whole counsel of God" means all the counsel of God that concerned Paul's work as a preacher of the gospel and an apostle of Christ. Paul had not suppressed anything that pertained to the salvation of souls. The one who suppresses what he ought to declare is guilty of the blood of those who are lost. Paul had found great comfort in the Ephesian church, more power to declare the "mystery" of the gospel. (Eph. 3: 4.) God had revealed to Paul all things concerning Christ, salvation, the kingdom of God, and its relation to men; Paul had declared all that had been revealed unto him.

28 **Take heed unto yourselves, and to all the flock,**—The first duty belonging to elders is to take heed to themselves; they are to be "ensamples to the flock." (1 Pet. 5: 3.) They have the responsibility of setting an example before others; they must take heed that they are worthy examples. Another phase of their responsibility is to look after the flock. The church is here represented as "the flock." They are to look after "all the flock," not just a few of the members. "Flock" is from the Greek "poimnioi," which is contracted from "poimenion." (John 10: 16.) The Holy Spirit had made them bishops; the Holy Spirit had made them bishops by describing the qualifications and through the church had called them to be "bishops." "Bishops" here is from the Greek "episkopous," and is the same as "elders" in verse 17; hence, elders and bishops are just different terms applied to the same men. All who are elders today in a scriptural sense have been made elders by the Holy Spirit. "To feed the church" is a duty imposed upon the elders; as shepherds they are to see that the flock receives proper nourishment. The "elders" were to watch over the flocks as "bishops" and to tend and feed as "shepherds." Here the church is called "the church of the Lord," because the

departing grievous wolves shall enter in among you, not sparing the flock; 30
and from among your own selves shall men arise, speaking perverse things,
to draw away the disciples after them.   31 Wherefore watch ye, remember-
ing that by the space of three years I ceased not to admonish every one night

Lord had "purchased with his own blood" this institution. Every
member of the church has been brought with the price of the blood
of Christ (1 Cor. 6: 20) ; the church is composed of members;
hence, the church has been purchased with the blood of Christ.

29 **I know that after my departing**—Paul, with the Holy
Spirit, knew what would take place. After his departing, not his
death, but his leaving them, "grievous wolves" would "enter in
among" them, "not sparing the flock."   Paul keeps up the figure of
a flock, with shepherds, and ferocious wolves destroying the flock.
"Grievous wolves" means those that are savage, harsh, and rapa-
cious. Jesus had described false teachers as "ravening wolves."
(Matt. 7: 15.) These false teachers would destroy the faith of the
members; here Paul makes reference to teachers of dangerous doctrines, whether Judaizers or heathen theosophists such as the
Gnostics.

30 **and from among your own selves shall men arise,**—Paul
further predicts that false teachers should arise "from among your
own selves" who would disturb the church. False teachers
would arise among the elders of the church at Ephesus.   The
church at Ephesus became notorious in after days as a seat of a
great Gnostic heresy; even in the New Testament writings, not
fewer than six of the pioneers of these false teachers are mentioned
as belonging to Ephesus; they are: Hymenaeus and Alexander (1
Tim. 1: 20), Phygelus and Hermogenes (2 Tim. 1: 15), and Phi-
letus. In 3 John 9 we read of Diotrephes who lived at Ephesus.
The church at Ephesus is condemned for its false teachers later by
John. (Rev. 2: 2.)

31 **Wherefore watch ye,**—Paul not only warned these elders
and the church at Ephesus, but put them on their guard and asked
them to watch carefully. This was one phase of the duties of elders. He had held himself up as an example to them, and now he
warned them. He calls to their attention that "by the space of

and day with tears. 32 And now I commend you to ⁴God, and to the word
of his grace, which is able to build *you* up, and to give *you* the inheritance
among all them that are sanctified. 33 I coveted no man's silver, or gold, or

---

⁴Some ancient authorities read *the Lord*

---

three years I ceased not to admonish every one night and day with
tears." Paul did not cease admonishing them night and day with
all the earnestness of his soul to be on their guard and watch themselves and the flock over which they were to preside. Paul did not
mean to be exact as to time. It was about three years; two of these
he taught publicly in the school at Tyrannus (Acts 19: 10); three
months preceding he had taught in the Jewish synagogue (Acts
19: 8); and previously he had been in Ephesus with Aquila and
Priscilla (Acts 18: 19). It was usual among the Jews to reckon a
part of a day for a whole one, and so a part of a year might, in a
general statement, be reckoned for a whole year. He warned them
"with tears"; this shows how deep and tender was his solicitude
for the welfare of the church.

32 **And now I commend you to God,**—As he is about to leave
them he can do no better than to commend them to God; the apostle who had preached the gospel to them, and who had instructed
them in living the Christian life, now commends them to God who
is able to build them up and to give them an inheritance "among
all them that are sanctified." The precious truths of God are here
spoken of as the "word of his grace"; as grace and truth came
through Christ (John 1: 17), so the words that came through
Jesus may be called the words of grace. God's people today have
nothing else to guide them but "the word of his grace." Those
who are in Christ are sanctified; they have been sanctified by the
truth. (John 17: 17.) God alone can give an inheritance in
heaven; hence, he has promised all who are faithful to him the
crown of life. (Rev. 2: 10.)

33 **I coveted no man's silver,**—Paul did not preach for
money; he was conscious of having been actuated by no personal or
worldly considerations. He did not preach for the love of money,
nor display of talent, nor to gratify a selfish ambition; he had only
a simple and sincere desire to serve his Lord and his church. He

apparel. 34 Ye yourselves know that these hands ministered unto my necessities, and to them that were with me. 35 In all things I gave you an example, that so laboring ye ought to help the weak, and to remember the words of the Lord Jesus, that he himself said, It is more blessed to give than to receive.

here declares his solemn motives in preaching the gospel to them. One of the slanders against Paul was that he was raising the collection for himself and not for the poor. He includes "apparel" because much of the wealth in that eastern country consisted largely in fine apparel. (Gen. 24: 53; 2 Kings 5: 5; Psalm 45: 13f.)

34 **Ye yourselves know that these hands**—Paul needed no further proof or evidence; he could appeal to their own knowledge as to how he had worked with his hands and earned the necessities of life. He not only worked to support himself, but helped to support those who were with him. (1 Cor. 9: 12, 15.) Paul could hold up his hands in their sight as witnesses that he had worked and had honestly provided his own support. We have learned that Paul was a tentmaker, and that he frequently ministered to others. He said to the church at Corinth, while he was in Ephesus, that "we toil, working with our own hands." (1 Cor. 4: 12.)

35 **In all things I gave you an example,**—Not only did he give them an example as to how to live, but he gave them an example that they should work with their own hands to support themselves and to help support those that preach the gospel. He toiled not only for himself, but for others. Here he quotes one of the unwritten sayings of our Lord: "It is more blessed to give than to receive." These words were well known and quite familiar to his listeners, yet they are not found in any of the four writers of the gospel. They enforce with solemn distinctness the duty of liberality to the poor; they possess a far deeper meaning, for they assert as an eternal truth the higher blessedness of giving as compared with receiving. It may be that the full truth of this statement of our Lord in all its length and breadth and depth and height will never be fully understood by any but the redeemed, and not by them till they enter the city of the Lamb of God.

36 And when he had thus spoken, he kneeled down and prayed with them all. 37 And they all wept sore, and fell on Paul's neck and kissed him, 38 sorrowing most of all for the word which he had spoken, that they should behold his face no more. And they brought him on his way unto the ship.

---

36 And when he had thus spoken,—As he finished his address to these elders, Paul "kneeled down and prayed with them all." The early Christians were in the habit of "kneeling" in prayer on ordinary occasions. We read that Stephen, while they were stoning him to death, kneeled in prayer. (Acts 7 : 60.) Such a posture is a fitting attitude in prayer; this was the posture that Jesus took. (Luke 22 : 41.)

37 And they all wept sore,—Paul had a tender feeling for these brethren; he knew their weakness, and he knew their responsibilities. He wept with them. They "fell on Paul's neck and kissed him." "Kissed" is from the Greek "katephiloun," and means a repetition of the act; they kept on kissing or kissed repeatedly; some think that one after the other fell on his neck and kissed him by turns. They held Paul in high esteem, and had great affection for him.

38 sorrowing most of all for the word—The greatest cause of their grief was the thought that they would probably see Paul no more. He had said to them that they should see his "face no more" (verse 25), and this was the chief source of their sorrowing. Some think that Paul and the elders were wrong in this; they think that Paul revisited Ephesus after his first imprisonment in Rome; however, this is not clear. There is no statement that we can correctly interpret that he ever visited Ephesus again. His address had made a solemn impression on them, and his deep affection for them bound him to them, and their affection for Paul bound them to him.

8. PAUL RETURNS TO JERUSALEM
21: 1-16

1 And when it came to pass that we were parted from them and had set

---

1 And when it came to pass that we were parted—After the discourse to the elders of the church at Ephesus at Miletus, Paul

sail, we came with a straight course unto Cos, and the next day unto Rhodes, and from thence unto Patara: 2 and having found a ship crossing over unto Phoenicia, we went aboard, and set sail. 3 And when we had come in sight of Cyprus, leaving it on the left hand, we sailed unto Syria, and landed at Tyre; for there the ship was to unlade her burden. 4 And having found the

dismissed them and left Miletus and sailed southward to Cos, which was a small island about forty miles from Miletus; it seems that the vessel was under the direction of Paul, as he could sail as he pleased and make such stops as he wished. They could stay at a place as long as they pleased. It seems that the wind was favorable for sailing and they made the journey in one day. The next day they sailed from Cos to Rhodes, and from Rhodes to Patara. Rhodes is fifty miles southeast of Cos, and Patara is east of Rhodes.

2 and having found a ship crossing over—Paul sailed on the Mediterranean Sea southeast to Phoenicia. They changed vessels at Patara, as they "found a ship" going to Phoenicia. It was more than four hundred miles from Patara to Jerusalem; it seems that from Patara Paul and his company took a larger vessel, one that could sail across the open sea. Phoenicia is on the eastern coast of the Mediterranean Sea and northwest of Palestine.

3 And when we had come in sight of Cyprus,—Paul's company, now making the journey in a larger vessel than they first had, sailed a direct route to Phoenicia and left Cyprus to the left. They proceeded and landed at Tyre; the ship was to unload her burden at this place. "Syria" was the name given to the entire eastern coast of the Mediterranean Sea from Cilicia to Egypt. Paul was now on his way to Jerusalem; he could now easily find means of conveyance to that city. Tyre is the chief city of Phoenicia; it was about three hundred fifty miles from Patara, and under favorable conditions could be reached in four or five days' sailing. Tyre had been one of the most famous cities of the ancient world. Hiram, king of Tyre, aided Solomon in building the temple in about 1000 B.C. (1 Kings 15: 18.) Many prophets prophesied about Tyre. (Isa. 23; Ezek. 26 to 28; Amos 1: 9, 10.) Christ visited Tyre and its vicinity. (Matt. 15: 21; Mark 7: 24.)

disciples, we tarried there seven days: and these said to Paul through the Spirit, that he should not set foot in Jerusalem. 5 And when it came to pass that we had accomplished the days, we departed and went on our journey; and they all, with wives and children, brought us on our way till we were out of the city: and kneeling down on the beach, we prayed, and bade each other farewell; 6 and we went on board the ship, but they returned home again.

7 And when we had finished the voyage from Tyre, we arrived at Ptole-

---

4 **And having found the disciples,**—"Having found" indicates that some time and trouble were had in locating the disciples; "having found" is from the Greek "aneurontes," which means "to seek for, to find by searching." There was a church in Tyre, but the city was large, and the number of disciples may have been small. Paul had gone through Phoenicia on his way to Jerusalem at one time. (Acts 15: 3.) Paul and his companions "tarried there seven days." Among the disciples at Tyre were some who warned Paul of the dangers that awaited him at Jerusalem. The Holy Spirit had already told Paul that bonds and affliction awaited him at Jerusalem. (Acts 20: 23.) At this time Paul is warned by the disciples not to go to Jerusalem; they did not want Paul to suffer the persecutions that awaited him.

5, 6 **And when it came to pass that we had accomplished**— When Paul and his company had remained in Tyre seven days, they made preparation to proceed on their journey to Jerusalem. The disciples at Tyre, including the wives and children of the disciples, accompanied Paul to the outskirts of the city. They remained with him as long as they could. The entire company of disciples was so interested in him that they were ready to give him any assistance that he might need. They treated him as did the disciples at Miletus. (Acts 20: 37, 38.) This is the first mention of children in connection with the early church. Before parting, they kneeled down "on the beach," and prayed together; this was a fitting separation of these disciples who loved each other so much. After the prayer they "went on board the ship," but the disciples in Tyre returned home. Some think that this was the same ship on which they had sailed from Patara; others see no reason for concluding that it was the same.

7 **And when we had finished the voyage from Tyre,**—They sailed from Tyre, a distance of about thirty miles south, to Ptole-

mais; and we saluted the brethren, and abode with them one day. 8 And on the morrow we departed, and came unto Caesarea: and entering into the house of Philip the evangelist, who was one of the seven, we abode with him. 9 Now this man had four virgin daughters, who prophesied. 10 And as we

---

mais. There was a church at Ptolemais, and Paul and his company "saluted the brethren, and abode with them one day." Some think that the church here was founded by Philip, the evangelist, or some other disciples who were driven from Jerusalem by the persecution some twenty years previous to this. (Acts 11: 19.)

8 **And on the morrow we departed,**—The company left Ptolemais and continued south to Caesarea; it is not known whether this part of the trip was made by sea or by land. It was possible to make the journey by sea; however, some think that the verb seems rather to leave us to infer that it was a land journey; there was a good road between the two places. When they arrived at Caesarea, they entered "into the house of Philip the evangelist." This distinguishes him from the apostle Philip, one of the twelve. His evangelistic work followed the death of Stephen. The word "evangelizing" is from the Greek "eueggelizeto," and was used of Philip in Acts 8: 40. The earliest of the three New Testament examples of the word "evangelist" (Acts 21: 8; Eph. 4: 11; 2 Tim. 4: 5) is found here. This Philip was one of the seven. (Acts 6: 5.) He was selected with the others at Jerusalem to help serve tables. We find him busy after he left Jerusalem. (Acts 8: 5-13, 26-40.)

9 **Now this man had four virgin daughters,**—Philip's daughters were Christians; they were walking in their father's steps; they "prophesied," which meant more than to predict future events. Philip had the honor of having in his home four virgin daughters with a gift of prophecy; there was a certain phase of work in the early church that was done by women. Phoebe was a servant of the church at Cenchreae (Rom. 16: 1), and Philip's daughters had the gift of prophecy. These daughters of Philip had the power to interpret a divine message. God inspired women as well as men when they could be used in his service. They had a mission to proclaim the gospel in their own womanly way. (Acts 2: 17; 18: 26; Joel 2: 28, 29; 1 Cor. 11: 5; 14: 24.) These four

tarried there some days, there came down from Judaea a certain prophet, named Agabus. 11 And coming to us, and taking Paul's girdle, he bound his own feet and hands, and said, Thus saith the Holy Spirit, So shall the Jews at Jerusalem bind the man that owneth this girdle, and shall deliver him unto the hands of the Gentiles. 12 And when we heard these things, both we and they of that place besought him not to go up to Jerusalem. 13 Then Paul

---

daughters, being virgins, unmarried, could devote their whole time to the service of the church.

10 **And as we tarried there some days,**—We do not know how long they remained in Caesarea, or in the house of Philip; but during their sojourn a disciple by the name of Agabus, who had prophetic gift, came from Judea. This may have been the same Agabus mentioned in Acts 11: 28, who foretold the coming famine at Antioch, as the prophets mentioned on that occasion had recently come from Jerusalem; this name was somewhat unusual; hence, it is thought that this Agabus was the same. He was not prominent as was Barnabas. It seems that Paul had made the journey quicker than he had thought, and could remain in Caesarea "some days." This was Paul's third time to visit Caesarea. His first visit was on his journey from Jerusalem to Tarsus (Acts 9: 30); his second visit was on his return at the close of his second missionary tour (Acts 18: 22).

11 **And coming to us, and taking Paul's girdle,**—Agabus very vividly impressed his prophecy or prediction by an object lesson. He took Paul's girdle and bound "his own feet and hands" with it, and then said that the owner of this girdle should be bound and delivered into the hands of the Gentiles. He gave the Holy Spirit as authority, or rather spoke by the Holy Spirit. Old Testament prophets often employed symbolic deeds. (1 Kings 22: 11; Jer. 13: 1-7; Ezek. 4: 1-6.) Jesus used the symbolism of Peter's girding himself to impress a lesson. (John 21: 18.) Agabus was just from Jerusalem, and the Holy Spirit revealed to him what would be done to Paul when he arrived in Jerusalem.

12 **And when we heard these things,**—Luke and the others who had traveled with Paul joined the disciples at Caesarea in attempting to persuade Paul not to "go up to Jerusalem." This dramatic warning that Agabus gave was in addition to that which was given at Tyre. (Acts 21: 4.) This was the same as Paul had

answered, What do ye, weeping and breaking my heart? for I am ready not
to be bound only, but also to die at Jerusalem for the name of the Lord
Jesus.   14 And when he would not be persuaded, we ceased, saying, The will
of the Lord be done.

---

confessed at Miletus. (Acts 20. 23.) It seems strange that Luke
and the other messengers, together with Philip and his daughters,
joined in persuading Paul not to go to Jerusalem. It seems that
Paul was determined to go to Jerusalem, and that no one could dis-
suade him. This reminds one of the fixed determination of Martin
Luther to go to "the Diet of Worms"; Spalatin persuaded Luther
not to go, but he replied: "Though devils be as many in Worms as
tiles upon the roofs, yet thither will I go."   No one could prevent
Paul's going to Jerusalem at this time.

13 **Then Paul answered, What do ye,**—It was hard for Paul
to resist the earnest, pathetic, and forceful pleadings of his brethren and sisters; he had due respect for their judgment and their
interest in him; he knew as well as they that danger and persecution awaited him at Jerusalem. However, Paul was not one who
would shrink from duty because of danger, neither was he one who
would change his course to avoid persecution. Their weeping and
strong solicitations could not alter his determination. He was under a higher guidance than theirs, and was ready, if God willed
it, to die at Jerusalem; moreover, they could add to his burden by their weeping over him. Paul had had abundant warnings
of the dangers he must encounter as a Christian and as an apostle;
he had always expected them, and had made up his mind to meet
them without flinching. (Acts 9: 16; 20: 22, 23.) He was not to
be turned away from the path of duty, however hazardous it might
be. He would very gladly spend and be spent for the cause of
Christ. (2 Cor. 12: 15.)

14 **And when he would not be persuaded,**—When the company of disciples saw that Paul would not yield to their persuasion,
they ceased to persuade him and said: "The will of the Lord be
done."   Since Paul would not let them persuade him and have
their own way, they were willing for the Lord to have his way.
Many times we are resigned to the Lord's way because we cannot
have our own way. They seem, finally, to understand that Paul

15 And after these days we ⁵took up our baggage and went up to Jerusalem. 16 And there went with us also *certain* of the disciples from Caesarea, ¹bringing *with them* one Mnason of Cyprus, an early disciple, with whom we should lodge.

⁵Or, *made ready*
¹Or, *bringing* us to *one Mnason &c.*

had a higher leading than theirs in what he was doing. Painful events were seen by Paul's friends, but these sufferings appeared to Paul so evidently to lie in his path of duty that it would be wrong in him to avoid them by failing to go forward in that path.

15 **And after these days we took up our baggage**—Caesarea is about sixty-four miles north of Jerusalem. Some think that Paul and his companions put their baggage on pack horses and carried it to Jerusalem. However, we do not know. The English word now used always of the vehicle that carries was in common use at the time of the Authorized Version for the things carried. It is from the Greek "episkeuasamenoi," which originally meant the things necessary to pack up or saddle horses. They "went up to Jerusalem." Jerusalem was situated on a higher elevation than Caesarea ; hence, they would naturally go "up" to Jerusalem.

16 **And there went with us also certain of the disciples**— When the brethren could not persuade Paul to stay away from Jerusalem, it seems that some of them prepared to go with him. They would naturally go up to the Pentecost feast ; multitudes of the Jews would go to Jerusalem the last day before the feast began. The brethren would also like to be present to assist Paul and to witness the greetings of the church at Jerusalem extended to Paul. They took with them "one Mnason of Cyprus" ; he was an "early disciple," and the company would lodge with him. There has been some difficulty in translating this verse ; some think that it should be rendered that Paul and his company were brought to Mnason's house. This Mnason was originally from Cyprus ; he may have become a disciple on the day of Pentecost. Since Jerusalem would be filled with visitors, it would be difficult to find a lodging place ; but as Mnason was known to some of them, they would make sure of a lodging place with him.

This ends Paul's third missionary journey. He left Philippi and came to Miletus; next he came to Cos, then to Rhodes, then to Patara, and finally came to Tyre; they spent a week at Tyre; next they came to Ptolemais, then to Caesarea, and finally to Jerusalem. The narrative of this voyage is that of an eyewitness; Luke, the writer, includes himself. It seems that the ship left Troas on the first day of the week; four days were spent in the voyage to Miletus, and probably they remained there three days; three days were occupied in sailing thence to Patara, and probably four days in sailing to Tyre; seven days were spent in Tyre, and three days in coming to Caesarea. It is thought that Paul arrived at Caesarea about ten days before Pentecost; the journey had been made very rapidly, for the wind was favorable from Troas, and as the moon was full, the voyage from Patara to Tyre was made, not by coasting, but by running across the open sea.

SECTION FIVE

PAUL AT JERUSALEM
21 : 17 to 23 : 35

1. PAUL MOBBED IN THE TEMPLE
21 : 17-26

17 And when we were come to Jerusalem, the brethren received us gladly. 18 And the day following Paul went in with us unto James; and all the elders were present. 19 And when he had saluted them, he rehearsed one

17 And when we were come to Jerusalem,—Paul and his company made the journey from Caesarea to Jerusalem, sixty-four miles, in about two days. They were received by the brethren in Jerusalem, and especially those of Mnason's household with gladness. There are three sets of Christians at Jerusalem mentioned: (1) "the brethren," whom Paul met privately at the house of Mnason; (2) "the elders," or officers of the church in Jerusalem, who were present at his official reception; (3) "the multitude," or the entire number of Jewish Christians, both belonging to Jerusalem and those who were present at the Pentecost feast.

18 And the day following Paul went—Paul did not idle away any time; "the day following" his arrival in Jerusalem, he, with his companions in travel, went to see James; James the son of Zebedee had been killed by Herod previous to this time. (Acts 12: 2.) The James mentioned here is the same who is recognized as a leader in the church at Jerusalem. (Acts 12: 17; 15: 13.) This may have been "James the less." (Matt. 27: 56; Mark 15: 40.) There are five James mentioned in the New Testament—James, the son of Zebedee, and brother of John; James, the son of Alphaeus, one of the twelve apostles; James the less; James, the Lord's brother (Matt. 13: 55; Mark 6: 3); and James in Luke 6: 16, as the brother of Judas. "All the elders were present" at this meeting. It seems that there was a special interview which had been arranged for Paul with James and the elders of the church in Jerusalem. This was important, as many injurious reports had gained circulation respecting Paul's course.

by one the things which God had wrought among the Gentiles through his ministry.   20 And they, when they heard it, glorified God; and they said unto him, Thou seest, brother, how many ²thousands there are among the Jews of them that have believed; and they are all zealous for the law: 21

²Gr. *myriads*

19 **And when he had saluted them,**—At this official reception, it was thought important for "all the elders" to be present, and to hear a detailed report of Paul's work.   He gave a minute account of his work among the Gentiles; he would report that many Gentiles had forsaken their idols and were living faithful to God.   No doubt at this time he introduced Trophimus, with the others, who had brought the generous gifts from the Gentile churches to be distributed among the poor saints in Jerusalem and Judea.   This would show that he had taught the Gentile Christians to practice charity toward those who were in need.   It seems that Paul, in spite of the reports, won the favor of the church in Jerusalem.

20 **And they, when they heard it, glorified God;**—The Jewish Christians rejoiced in the fact that the Gentiles had been accepted by the Lord; they received with thanksgiving the offerings that Paul brought; however, they proceeded cautiously because there were "many thousands there" "among the Jews" who believed.   This shows that there were many Christians among the Jews in Jerusalem and surrounding country at this time.   The Greek, "posai muriades," literally means an indefinite number, and is the old word for "ten thousand" (Acts 19: 19) or "myriads" (Luke 12: 1; Acts 21: 20; Jude 14; Rev. 5: 11; 9: 16).   It is surprising to know that there were so many Christians in Jerusalem after the persecution which had scattered the early disciples. (Acts 8: 1-5.)   The number mentioned here may include the Christians from neighboring towns in Palestine and some foreign countries who had come to the Feast of Pentecost.   All these were "zealous for the law."   "Zealous" is from the Greek "zelotai," and means "to burn with zeal, to boil."   There was a party of "Zealots," a group of what would be called "extremists," or "hotheads."   One of this party was Simon Zelotes. (Acts 1: 13.)   James and the elders at Jerusalem attempt now to harmonize

and they have been informed concerning thee, that thou teachest all the Jews who are among the Gentiles to forsake Moses, telling them not to circumcise their children, neither to walk after the customs. 22 What is it therefore? they will certainly hear that thou art come. 23 Do therefore this that we say

---

Paul's work among the Gentiles and the Gentile converts with this great multitude of Jewish Christians who were zealous for the law.

21 **and they have been informed concerning thee,**—The report had reached Jerusalem that Paul had taught "all the Jews who are among the Gentiles to forsake Moses," and that they should not "circumcise their children, neither to walk after the customs." It seems that these Judaizers had brought trouble to Peter (Acts 11: 2) and also to Paul (Acts 15: 1, 5). The charge against Paul was not true; he had never taught that the Jews among the Gentiles should *not* circumcise their children; neither had he taught that they should *not* keep the ceremonial law of the Old Testament. Their charge against him was a malicious half-truth, for Paul had preached Christ, and that was more than advising the Jews to sink down to the level of Gentiles. Paul had never taught Jews that when they became Christians they were not to circumcise their children; he himself had circumcised Timothy. (Acts 16: 3.) Paul was a true follower of Christ and had taught that circumcision, the seal of the covenant which was superseded in Jesus Christ (Rom. 4: 11), had become of no effect in the relation between man and God (1 Cor. 7: 19; Gal. 5: 6; 6: 15; Eph. 2: 11-14). These Judaizing teachers saw what the end of such teaching was sure to be. "To walk after the customs" was to follow the ceremonial law. The charge was brought against Stephen (Acts 6: 14) that he would change "the customs which Moses delivered unto us." The charge against Paul with respect to the Mosaic rites was true only in the sense of his denying their necessity to the salvation of souls.

22 **What is it therefore?**—The question asked here simply means: Paul, what is to be done about this? James and the elders at Jerusalem do not believe the misrepresentations against Paul; however, many of the Jewish brethren do believe them. They would hear that Paul had come to Jerusalem; there was no effort to conceal that fact; they are ready to meet the issue in as tactful a way as possible. They know that the many Jewish Christians

to thee: We have four men that have a vow on them; 24 these take, and
purify thyself with them, and be at charges for them, that they may shave
their heads: and all shall know that there is no truth in the things whereof

---

would be anxious to see Paul and to hear the reports that he had
to make. By asking this question, James and the elders are re-
questing Paul to cooperate with them in satisfying the Jewish
Christians.

23 **Do therefore this that we say to thee:**—It seems that Paul
would not have opportunity to meet all the Jewish Christians and
explain the situation to them, but they advise Paul to do something
which the whole community would observe or hear about, and
which would show them and all men that Paul did reverence the
Mosaic law. Paul knew that the law was fulfilled in Christ; he
respected that law for that which it had done for the Jews, and because it came from God. It seems that after some deliberation the
elders thought out a plan of procedure by which Paul could set the
whole matter straight. They called to his attention that there were
"four men that have a vow on them." They propose to use this as
a matter to clear Paul of the false charges which were made
against him. This seems to be a temporary Nazirite vow. (Num.
6: 13-15.) Either Paul or Aquila had such a vow on leaving Cenchreae. (Acts 18: 18.)

24 **these take, and purify thyself with them,**—James and the
elders suggested that Paul take the four men who had a vow upon
them, and who evidently were Christians, and pay his and their expenses that they might fulfill their vow; this was to be done so that
the Jewish Christians would see that Paul had proper respect for
the law. James and the elders were attempting to offset the prejudice that some had against Paul. This has given commentators
generally much trouble; they have attempted to harmonize Paul's
conduct here with his teachings concerning the law. Confessedly,
it is a difficult task. Different comments have been offered as a
solution. They are as follows: (1) That Paul at this time did not
have a complete revelation of God's will; (2) that Paul did not
understand even what he had written by inspiration; (3) that Paul
dissembled, acted hypocritical; (4) that Paul did not do as James

they have been informed concerning thee; but that thou thyself also walkest
orderly, keeping the law. 25 But as touching the Gentiles that have believed,

and the elders suggested that he do; (5) that he compromised
principle for the sake of unity; (6) that he did from policy what
he would not have done by religious principle. No. 1 does not
seem to satisfy the conditions, as Paul had revelation enough of
God's will to know at this time what to do. No. 2 does not elimi-
nate the difficulty, and places Paul in a state of ignorance as to
what he had formerly taught; neither can we agree to the position
that Paul was hypocritical. No. 4 seems to contradict (verse 26).
No. 5 makes Paul a compromiser and surrenders in part that
which he knew to be the will of God; neither can we agree that
Paul acted merely from *policy*, which would make him a hypocrite.
It seems that Paul had not taught Jewish Christians to disrespect
the law of Moses. In fact, Paul and other faithful Christians
among the Jews were the only ones who properly respected the
law. Christ fulfilled the law; "for Christ is the end of the law unto
righteousness to every one that believeth." (Rom. 10: 4.) The
law was given by Jehovah until Christ should come; Paul understood this. He never thought that Christians had to keep the law
in order to be saved; neither did he at any time so act as though
the keeping of the law had anything to do with his salvation. Paul
said: "To the Jews I became as a Jew, that I might gain Jews; to
them that are under the law, as under the law, not being myself
under the law, that I might gain them that are under the law; to
them that are without law, as without law, not being without law to
God, but under law to Christ, that I might gain them that are
without law. To the weak I became weak, that I might gain the
weak: I am become all things to all men, that I may by all means
save some. And I do all things for the gospel's sake, that I may
be a joint partaker thereof." (1 Cor. 9: 20-23.) The above quotation describes the conduct of Paul here as elsewhere; he never
acted from mere *policy,* but was guided by *principle.* We are to
understand his conduct here in the light of the above. Since the
law of Moses contained some ceremonial rites, these could be observed for the sake of peace and harmony without violating a principle.

we ³wrote, giving judgment that they should keep themselves from things sacrificed to idols, and from blood, and from what is strangled, and from fornication. 26 Then Paul ⁴took the men, and the next day purifying himself with them went into the temple, declaring the fulfilment of the days of purification, until the offering was offered for every one of them.

³Or, *enjoined.* Many ancient authorities read *sent.*
⁴Or, *took the men the next day, and purifying himself &c.*

25 **But as touching the Gentiles that have believed,**—James and the elders are making further suggestions to Paul with explanations concerning the Gentile Christians. James was present in Jerusalem when the question of circumcision was discussed with Paul and Barnabas and others. (Acts 15: 13.) The decision reached there with James, Peter, and the elders of the church with Paul and Barnabas was that the law of Moses should not be imposed on the Gentiles. (Acts 15: 28, 29.) The four things mentioned in the letter that was written at that time are mentioned here; namely (1) abstain from things sacrificed to idols; (2) from blood; (3) from what is strangled; (4) from f o r n i c a t i o n. Everything settled in Jerusalem at that time and embodied in the letter is to remain exactly as it was. The liberty of the Gentile Christians was not to be touched by the law.

26 **Then Paul took the men,**—It was permitted for one man to bear the expense of another in keeping the Nazirite vow. Num. 6: 9-12 recites the law governing the Nazirite vow. The "charges" involved the payment (1) for the act of shaving the head for which there was a fixed fee to priest or Levite; (2) for the sacrifices which each Nazirite had to offer; namely, two doves or pigeons, a lamb, a ram, a basket of unleavened bread, a meat offering, and a drink offering. Paul agreed to pay for the expenses of the four in their fulfilling their vow. It seems that he appeared in the temple each day for the four. He thus kept his vow in fellowship with the four men, and when the period of his vow was ended and that of the others, the proper offerings were made for each one of them.

2. THE RIOT AND PAUL'S APPREHENSION
21 : 27-40

27 And when the seven days were almost completed, the Jews from Asia, when they saw him in the temple, stirred up all the multitude and laid hands on him, 28 crying out, Men of Israel, help: This is the man that teacheth all men everywere against the people, and the law, and this place; and moreover he brought Greeks also into the temple, and hath defiled this holy place. 29 For they had before seen with him in the city Trophimus the Ephesian,

27 **And when the seven days were almost completed,—** There is some discussion as to "the seven days" mentioned here; it is not known whether this has reference to the week of the Pentecost feast or the seven days required for keeping the vow and purification as required by law. Near the close of the seven days "Jews from Asia" caused trouble; in fact, there was an outburst of wild fury instigated by these Jews from Asia. Perhaps these were some of the Jews who had come "from Asia" to the Feast of Pentecost and who had heard Paul preach at Ephesus or in some other place of Asia; they had persecuted him in their own district and had stirred up the people in Jerusalem against him before he arrived. They saw Paul "in the temple"; he was probably in the court, along the inner wall of which there were small chambers in which the Nazirites used to live while fulfilling the last seven days of their vow. This court was separated with a wall from the court of the Gentiles. These infuriated Jews laid hands on Paul while he was there in the court of the temple.

28 **crying out, Men of Israel, help:**—They made an attack on Paul as though he had committed some crime; they called upon their fellow Jews to help them. Paul was seized with the marks of his Nazirite vow upon him. (Acts 24: 18.) They shouted their accusation against him which they had already spread among the people. (Acts 21: 21.) They had accused him of attempting to make Jews become as uncircumcised Gentiles, and that he had spoken against the law of Moses and had blasphemed the temple. They brought this same charge against Christ. (Mark 14: 58.) Also this charge was brought against Stephen where Paul was one of the number. (Acts 6: 13, 14.) They added to this charge that he had brought Gentiles "into the temple," and had "defiled this holy place." Their accusation was that he had defiled it by making

whom they supposed that Paul had brought into the temple. 30 And all the city was moved, and the people ran together; and they laid hold on Paul, and dragged him out of the temple: and straightway the doors were shut. 31 And as they were seeking to kill him, tidings came up to the ⁵chief captain of the ⁶band, that all Jerusalem was in confusion. 32 and forthwith he

⁵Or, *military tribune.* Gr. *chiliarch*
⁶Or, *cohort*

it common. The Jews hated Paul for his work, and were not careful about the charges which they brought against him.

29 **For they had before seen with him**—These "Jews from Asia" had seen Trophimus, a Gentile Ephesian, with Paul in the city, and they now saw some strange Jews with Paul in the court of the temple, and they hastily assumed that Paul had taken Trophimus into the temple with him. They were in error; they did not take time to investigate; they were so eager to prefer charges against Paul, and more anxious to find some cause for accusing him, that they did not take sufficient time. Perhaps they were honest, but honestly mistaken. They based their charges against Paul on a mere supposition, but their supposition was false; they did not care whether it was false or true, it served them well to make charges against Paul.

30 **And all the city was moved,**—These "Jews from Asia" were successful in stirring up a riot against Paul. The city was "moved"; that is, stirred with violent emotion. The same word is used by Tertullus in stirring up a riot against Paul later. (Acts 24: 5.) "The people ran together" in their excitement; they came from all quarters of the city when they heard the noise; the cry spread like wildfire over the city, and the people rushed pell-mell into the court of the temple. They laid hands on Paul, and "dragged him out of the temple." They were saving the temple by dragging Paul out of it. It seems clear that the ceremonies of Paul's vow were not yet accomplished, and if they did not violently lay hands on him he could flee to the altar for protection. The keepers of the temple closed the gates to prevent anyone disturbing further the worship in the temple.

31 **And as they were seeking to kill him,**—It seems that the intention of the mob was to kill Paul; that is, beat him to death in the crowd and no one could be charged with his murder; they

took soldiers and centurions, and ran down upon them: and they, when they saw the ⁵chief captain and the soldiers, left off beating Paul. 33 Then the ⁵chief captain came near, and laid hold on him, and commanded him to be

---

could accomplish their aim in killing Paul and avoid any individual responsibility for it. When the "chief captain" heard what was going on, he rushed to Paul's rescue. Herod the Great had built a strong fortress, the castle of Antonia, on a rock on the northwest corner of the temple area; it overlooked the temple, and was connected by two flights of stairs with the outermost courts of the temple on the northern and western sides. The Romans always kept this castle strongly garrisoned with troops to overawe Jerusalem. At festivals, when Jerusalem was filled with excitable crowds, the garrison consisted of a cohort or "band" of one thousand men. The "chief captain" of this number was called "Chiliarch." When the chief captain heard that all Jerusalem was in confusion, he hastened with his men to the scene of action.

32 **And forthwith he took soldiers**—The "chief captain" "took soldiers and centurions" and hastened "down upon them." The chief captain did not go with the view of protecting Paul, but to find out what was the matter, and seeing Paul in the hands of the mob, he arrested him, supposing that he had done something worthy of arrest. The mob "left off beating Paul" when the "chief captain and the soldiers" appeared on the scene. The mob probably thought that the Roman law would do justice, and if Paul were found by the chief captain to have been wrongfully treated they would be brought to an account. Furthermore, the chief captain with his soldiers could overpower the mob and make them let Paul go free.

33 **Then the chief captain came near,**—The Roman official came and formally arrested Paul, "laid hold on him," and commanded him to be "bound with two chains." Paul was bound with chains as though he were a violent and seditious person; probably they thought that he was the leader of a band of assassins. (Acts 21: 38.) Inquiry was made as to who Paul was, and what he had done. He had been arrested, and the one making the arrest did not know who he was or what accusation was brought against him.

bound with two chains; and inquired who he was, and what he had done. 34 And some shouted one thing, some another, among the crowd: and when he could not know the certainty for the uproar, he commanded him to be brought into the castle. 35 And when he came upon the stairs, so it was that he was borne of the soldiers for the violence of the crowd; 36 for the multitude of the people followed after, crying out, Away with him.

It seems that the chief captain asked Paul his name, and asked the crowd what he had done; naturally they were the ones to prefer the charges; he did not know Paul, and thinking him to be a criminal, he would not believe what Paul stated. Not many criminals will state accurately their own crimes.

34 **And some shouted one thing, some another,**—When inquiry was made as to the charges against Paul, no unanimous charge could be made; some preferred one charge and some another. Many of the mob knew neither Paul's name nor what he had done; hence, they could give no clear answer to the inquiry. The verb used here by Luke is the one he uses to express the confusion of the multitude which shouted against Jesus. (Luke 23: 21.) Luke is the only writer of the New Testament that uses this verb. The chief captain had made an honest effort to learn what charges were made against Paul, but could not learn from the mob; they did not know themselves; hence, he had Paul brought into the castle. "The castle" here signifies the barracks which the Romans had in the tower of Antonia; this was near the scene of action.

35, 36 **And when he came upon the stairs,**—Mob violence and uproar were common in Jerusalem during the feasts, and the Roman authorities attempted to keep order; the officers were severe on those who raised an insurrection or incited trouble. The castle in which the "chief captain" resided was near the temple; he rescued Paul from the mob, and when he could not learn from the mob, neither could he ascertain from Paul in the midst of such confusion, he sought to take him as a prisoner into his castle where he could make an investigation and ascertain the cause of the trouble. As the soldiers took Paul, the mob sought to take him away from the soldiers; they followed after Paul and shouted: "Away with him." It seems that the crowd pressed with more fury upon Paul when they saw that he was now to be taken out of their hands.

37 And as Paul was about to be brought into the castle, he saith unto the
⁵chief captain, May I say something unto thee?   And he said, Dost thou
know Greek?   38 Art thou not then the Egyptian, who before these days
stirred up to sedition and led out into the wilderness the four thousand men

Some of the soldiers had to lift Paul from his feet and carry him
up the stairs till he was out of reach of the mob.

37 And as Paul was about to be brought—As Paul was about
to be brought into the castle he asked the "chief captain" if he
might say something to the infuriated mob. The chief captain had
not yet learned anything about the character of the man that he
had suddenly rescued from death; his first supposition was entirely
erroneous. When Paul asked if he might speak to the mob, he
used the Greek language. This caused the chief captain to ask:
"Dost thou know Greek?" The officer had seized Paul as the best
means of quieting the riot; he thought his prisoner a Jewish desperado, and was greatly surprised to find him a cultured man who
could speak the Greek language.

38 Art thou not then the Egyptian,—The chief captain expected an affirmative answer; this Egyptian had given the Romans
much trouble; he had "stirred up to sedition" the people and had
"led out into the wilderness the four thousand men of the Assassins." It seems that the first thing which began to correct the false
impression of the chief captain was that Paul was a cultured man,
able to speak the cultural language, Greek. Then he inquired further if he were not the leader of that band who had caused so
much trouble to the Roman government. From this time the
Roman official seems to change his attitude toward Paul; he now
accepts what Paul states as the truth. The desperado that the
chief captain had in mind had led out "into the wilderness the four
thousand men" who were styled "the Assassins." He was a man of
much influence since he could lead out "four thousand men."
Josephus tells how this one was one of the many impostors of the
time. "Assassins" is from the Greek "sikarion," and is the same
as the Latin "sicarius," and means "one who carried a short
sword"; he carried this under his cloak and was a cutthroat.
These "Assassins" killed men by daylight in the midst of the city
of Jerusalem. They did not form a band of soldiers, but secretly

of the Assassins? 39 But Paul said, I am a Jew, of Tarsus in Cilicia, a citizen of no mean city: and I beseech thee, give me leave to speak unto the people. 40 And when he had given him leave, Paul, standing on the stairs, beckoned with the hand unto the people; and when there was made a great silence, he spake unto them in the Hebrew language, saying,

---

worked with their short daggers by going into the crowd at the feasts and wounding their adversaries, and when they had fallen the murderers mixed with the crowd and joined in the outcry against crime. They passed unsuspected for a long time.

39 **But Paul said, I am a Jew,—**Paul answered the chief captain and made his denial by stating simply who he was. He declared himself to be a Jew "of Tarsus in Cilicia." Tarsus was the metropolis of Cilicia, and a city remarkable for its culture and the zeal of its inhabitants for philosophic studies. It was "no mean city"; that is, it was a city of prominence. Tarsus was one of the great cities of the empire, and had a great university there. Paul was a citizen of this city, which was an honorable distinction. After briefly telling the chief captain who he was and that he was a citizen of the proud city of Tarsus, he asked the privilege "to speak unto the people." Paul desired to speak to his people, and in Jerusalem. That infuriated mob was as ignorant of the gospel as though the Christ had never come, suffered and died in that city. Surely, if anyone could, Paul could get them to see the truth by telling them how Jesus had revealed himself to him. He now had a chance. It seems that the chains were taken off of Paul and he was permitted to stand there and speak to his Jewish brethren.

40 **And when he had given him leave,—**They were still on the stairs; Paul was above them and out of their reach; they were beneath Paul and from his elevated position he could speak to them with ease if they would hear him. The chief captain promptly gave Paul permission to speak to the people. He "beckoned with the hand unto the people." He "beckoned with the hand," which meant that he demanded their attention. By his beckoning, the gesture gained an audience very readily, and a "great silence" was observed. Paul used tact in handling this mob; he now spoke in the native tongue of the Jews; he spoke in the Hebrew language. The

people of Jerusalem knew this language better than they knew the Greek; Paul could speak in either the Hebrew or the Greek language. It seems that Jesus used this language on special occasions. (Mark 5: 41; 14: 36; 15: 34.) Paul is given opportunity to make his first defense; he does so with courage and clearness.

3. PAUL'S DISCOURSE ON THE TEMPLE STAIRS
22: 1-30

1 Brethren and fathers, hear ye the defence which I now make unto you.
2 And when they heard that he spake unto them in the Hebrew language, they were the more quiet; and he saith,
3 I am a Jew, born in Tarsus of Cilicia, but brought up in this city, at

1 **Brethren and fathers, hear ye the defence**—We enter now upon a series of pleas made by Paul in his self-defense; this is the first of five pleas which are recorded in the following chapters. These pleas are made under different circumstances, and lead to the close of the book of Acts. This is Paul's first formal vindication of himself before his own people. He uses the same greeting that Stephen used. (Acts 7: 2.) "Fathers" here may include members of the Sanhedrin and rulers and doctors of the law. Paul here, like Stephen, mentions his ancestors; this is done by way of conciliation. "Defence" is from the Greek "apologia," and is the word from which we get "apology"; however, Paul is not making an "apology" in the sense that we use the term, but is using it in its original sense, which means "defence" without implying any wrong that he had done.

2 **And when they heard that he spake**—Paul spoke to them in his and their native tongue, the Hebrew language. By his speaking in the Hebrew he would show himself a Jew and familiar with their language and law. They may have expected him to speak in the Greek language. It had the desired effect, for when they heard him speak in the Hebrew language, the mob quieted down and was willing to listen to him.

3 **I am a Jew, born in Tarsus of Cilicia,**—Paul shows himself by birth and education to be a Jew; though of foreign birth, nevertheless, a Jew in the strictest sense. Perhaps Paul put the emphasis on "I," which means "I am indeed a Jew." Paul is not boasting, but he does set forth those things which distinguish him

the feet of Gamaliel, instructed according to the strict manner of the law of
our fathers, being zealous for God, even as ye all are this day: 4 and I persecuted this Way unto the death, binding and delivering into prisons both
men and women. 5 As also the high priest doth bear me witness, and all the
estate of the elders: from whom also I received letters unto the brethren,
and journeyed to Damascus to bring them also that were there unto Jerusa

---

as a Jew. Tarsus was a city of the province of Cilicia. Paul probably lived in Tarsus until he was eleven years of age, not later than
thirteen years of age, as the Jewish parents put their sons in training at the age of twelve. "Gamaliel" was an eminent Jewish
teacher at Jerusalem. The custom was for the teacher and student
to sit, the teacher on a higher level than the student. Hence, the
expression "at the feet of Gamaliel." Gamaliel was the grandson
of the famous rabbi Hillel, and so esteemed as a scribe that it was
said, "When Gamaliel died, the glory of the law ceased." Paul had
been "instructed according to the strict manner of the law" of the
Jews. Paul was "a Hebrew of Hebrews" (Phil. 3: 5), and as
touching the law, "a Pharisee" (Acts 26: 5). Paul had been
"zealous for God," even as these Jews were now. He had learned
better, and wished to teach them better.

4 and I persecuted this Way unto the death,—Paul had mentioned his former zeal for the law to let them know that at one time
he was as they now are; yet it was the deepest grief and shame to
him that he had been as they were now. (1 Cor. 15: 7-10.)
"This Way" is frequently used by Luke as a term for Christianity;
it was familiar to disciples or Christians. Paul had formerly pursued them unto death; he threw them into prison without regard
to sex; he showed his intense zeal for the law by his bitter persecution of Christians.

5 As also the high priest doth bear me witness.—The Gamaliel mentioned here by Paul is probably the same Gamaliel mentioned in Acts 5: 34. The high priest who had commissioned Paul
(Acts 9: 2, 14) was not in office at this time, but the documents of
his predecessor were in possession of the present high priest.
"Estate" has an old sense of the "assembly"; hence, "the estate of
the elders" means the assembly or council or Sanhedrin. Paul had
received authority by letters to go to Damascus "to bring them
also that were there unto Jerusalem in bonds to be punished."

lem in bonds to be punished. 6 And it came to pass, that, as I made my
journey, and drew nigh unto Damascus, about noon, suddenly there shone
from heaven a great light round about me. 7 And I fell unto the ground,
and heard a voice saying unto me, Saul, Saul, why persecutest thou me? 8
And I answered, Who art thou, Lord? And he said unto me, I am Jesus of
Nazareth, whom thou persecutest. 9 And they that were with me beheld indeed the light, but they heard not the voice of him that spake to me. 10 And

Paul was clothed with the highest authority that could be conferred upon him; he had authority from the highest priest and
from the Sanhedrin. At that time he was determined to stop the
spread of Christianity. (Acts 8: 1, 3; 26: 11.)

6 **And it came to pass, that, as I made my journey,**—There
are three accounts of Paul's conversion—one in chapter 9, another
in chapter 22, and the third in chapter 26. These separate accounts show only such minor variations as would naturally occur
when only the substantial facts are mentioned. "It came to pass";
that is, it occurred as Paul journeyed and approached Damascus.
Here he mentions that it was "about noon," which is not mentioned in chapter 9; in Acts 26: 13, in his defense before Agrippa,
Paul says it was at "midday." This "great light" "from heaven"
was very brilliant to exceed the brightness of the sun at midday.

7 **And I fell unto the ground,**—In Acts 9 Saul "fell upon the
earth" (verse 4), and "arose from the earth" (verse 8), but here
he "fell unto the ground"; no difference in meaning; in Acts 26:
14 it is related that they all fell "to the earth."

8 **And I answered, Who art thou, Lord?**—The answer
given to this question was: "I am Jesus of Nazareth, whom thou
persecutest." In chapter 9 Luke gives the answer as: "I am Jesus
whom thou persecutest." (Acts 9: 5.) In Acts 26: 15 the answer is: "I am Jesus whom thou persecutest."

9 **And they that were with me beheld**—In Acts 9: 7 Luke
says that the men who accompanied Paul "stood speechless, hearing the voice, but beholding no man," but here the record says that
"they heard not the voice of him that spake to me." In Acts 9 we
have Luke's record of the events, but here we have his record as
giving what Paul said; here he is quoting Paul. Some have
pointed out a contradiction in the record here and in Acts 9.

I said, What shall I do, Lord? And the Lord said unto me, Arise, and go into Damascus; and there it shall be told thee of all things which are appointed for thee to do. 11 And when I could not see for the glory of that light, being led by the hand of them that were with me I came into Damascus. 12 And one Ananias, a devout man according to the law, well reported of by all the Jews that dwelt there, 13 came unto me, and standing by me

There is no contradiction. Two different points of time in the event could be referred to; again, they heard but did not perceive; and again, they heard the voice or sound, but did not hear or distinguish the words. In Acts 26: 14 we learn that the voice was "in the Hebrew language." It may be that those who were with Paul did not understand the Hebrew language; hence, would hear the noise or sound, but would not understand. We are to understand that the attendants saw and heard enough to satisfy them of the miraculous appearing of Christ, but were not allowed to see his person or understand his words. We have here one of the evidences of the genuineness of this report of Paul's speech in that Luke did not try to avoid apparent discrepancies in details between the words of Paul and his own record already given.

10 **And I said, What shall I do, Lord?**—In answer to his question, the Lord told Saul to "arise, and go into Damascus." The Lord did not tell Saul further what to do; he did not forgive his sins or convert him here. Saul must hear the gospel, which is God's power unto salvation. Saul was directed to go into Damascus, and there he should receive fuller instruction about "all things which are appointed for thee to do." Paul was to meet Ananias in Damascus for further instruction. It should be noted that there were other things which Saul must do.

11 **And when I could not see for the glory of that light,**— The light was about the brightness of the Eastern noonday sun; it blinded Paul; some think that the glare of that light never quite left Paul, and that his eyes never recovered their full strength after this event. This supposition is based on Paul's expression: "Ye would have plucked out your eyes and given them to me." (Gal. 4: 15.) Paul was led by his traveling companions into Damascus where he was to meet Ananias.

12 **And one Ananias, a devout man according to the law,**— In Acts 9: 10 Luke calls Ananias a disciple. Here Paul speaks of

said unto me, Brother Saul, receive thy sight. And in that very hour I
[1]looked up on him. 14 And he said, The God of our fathers hath appointed
thee to know his will, and to see the Righteous One, and to hear a voice

[1]Or, *received my sight* and looked *upon him*

him as "a devout man according to the law." He was of good report among the Jews that dwelt in Damascus. This description
was suited to conciliate his audience in every lawful way. This
was consistent with the account which appears in Acts 21 : 20 in
the words of James as to "how many thousands there are among
the Jews of them that have believed." In this defense Paul is making it clear that his change was brought about by divine agencies.
He was at one time as they are now, but he has changed, and the
Lord is responsible for the change; hence, they should not blame
Paul.

13 **came unto me, and standing by me said unto me,**—Paul
now shows that Ananias came to him by divine authority.
Ananias was commissioned by the Lord to do what he did. He
addressed Paul with, "Brother Saul." This showed that Ananias
recognized Saul as a brother Jew; it does not show that Ananias
recognized Saul at this time as a Christian. Paul had addressed
these hostile Jews as "Brethren and fathers." (Acts 22: 1.) This
does not mean that Paul recognized these hostile Jews as Christians. Ananias restored sight to Paul; this showed Paul that Ananias was commissioned by the Lord; he had power to work miracles. Paul received his sight and looked upon Ananias.

14 **And he said, The God of our fathers**—Paul here quotes
what Ananias said to him in part. Ananias gives in substance
what was revealed to him about Saul's mission. Paul keeps constantly before his hearers that he is following divine instruction;
that the change that he has made was brought about by divine
agencies. Ananias is still loyal to the God of Israel, and speaks of
him as "the God of our fathers." Paul is to know the will of God
and "to see the Righteous One, and to hear a voice from his
mouth." This emphasizes that Paul was chosen of God to know
God's will and to see Christ. Paul was not only to know God's
will to save men, but he was to know his will about what he was to
do and to suffer in the service of God. Christ is frequently called

from his mouth. 15 For thou shalt be a witness for him unto all men of what thou hast seen and heard. 16 And now why tarriest thou? arise, and be baptized, and wash away thy sins, calling on his name. 17 And it came to

"the Righteous One." (Acts 3 · 14; 7: 52.) Paul was made an apostle by seeing Christ and being commissioned by him. (1 Cor. 9: 1; 15: 8; Gal. 1: 1, 11, 12.)

15 **For thou shalt be a witness**—Paul was to be a witness of the resurrection of Christ and to preach his gospel to the unsaved. He was called, as were the other apostles, and sent out as a witness. He was a chosen vessel of the Lord "to bear my name before the Gentiles and kings, and the children of Israel." (Acts 9: 15.) However, Paul does not mention "Gentiles" here, as it would arouse Jewish prejudice against his cause. He does say that he is to be a witness of Christ "unto all men" of all that he had seen and heard. Paul is very tactful in making this address. Paul in witnessing for Christ based his teachings on facts of knowledge and experience as did the other apostles.

16 **And now why tarriest thou?**—After instructing Paul as he was commissioned to do, Ananias encouraged him to do what the Lord commanded him to do; he was encouraged to do this *immediately;* he should not tarry or delay. He is now given more definite instruction as to what he should do. Paul was prostrate, or in a recumbent posture; hence, he is commanded to arise, and "be baptized." "Baptisai" is in the first aorist middle voice of the verb, not the passive form as in Acts 2: 38. It literally means "cause thyself to be baptized, or suffer someone to baptize thee." "And wash away thy sins" states the purpose of his baptism. "Apolousai" literally means "get washed off" as in 1 Cor. 6: 11. This signifies that baptism is in order to the remission of sins or the cleansing of sin. Paul's sins were not forgiven when he saw and heard the Lord on the way to Damascus. As Paul's body was to be washed in the act of baptism, so his sins were to be forgiven. "Calling on his name" means invoking the name of Christ in so doing. He was thus commanded to do all in the name of the Lord Jesus. Here baptism is clearly set forth as one of the conditions of the remission of sins, and not merely as a symbol of what had already been done.

pass, that, when I had returned to Jerusalem, and while I prayed in the temple, I fell into a trance, 18 and saw him saying unto me, Make haste, and get thee quickly out of Jerusalem; because they will not receive of thee testimony concerning me. 19 And I said, Lord, they themselves know that I imprisoned and beat in every synagogue them that believed on thee: 20 and when the blood of Stephen thy witness was shed, I also was standing by, and consenting, and keeping the garments of them that slew him. 21 And he said

---

17, 18 **And it came to pass, that, when I had returned to Jerusalem,**—It seems that it was after three years absence (Gal. 1: 18) that Paul returned to Jerusalem. Paul had left Jerusalem for Damascus with authority to persecute Christians; he was converted and ceased his persecution and went to preaching Christ, going into Arabia and then returning to Damascus, and after three years went to Jerusalem. When he came to Jerusalem this time he went into the temple to pray and fell into a trance. A mention of this showed that he still honored the temple as the house of God. This is a visit recorded in Acts 9: 29 when the Jews sought to kill Paul. This "trance," or state of ecstasy, was a special divine influence under which Paul was brought while praying. Peter fell into a trance while on the housetop. (Acts 10: 10.) Later he spoke of this trance as a vision. (Acts 10: 17.) In this trance Paul saw the Lord, and the Lord spoke to him and said: "Make haste, and get thee quickly out of Jerusalem." The reason assigned was because "they will not receive of thee testimony concerning me." Paul must leave Jerusalem, as they would not hear his testimony concerning Jesus; hence he goes and preaches to the Gentiles.

19 **And I said, Lord, they themselves know**—Paul here recounts the persecutions that he had brought against Christians. He seems to plead with the Lord that men cannot help receiving the testimony from one who had previously been such an enemy of Jesus of Nazareth. These words of Paul seemed to be now addressed to his hearers so that they may be impressed with strength of the testimony given by one who had imprisoned Christians. Paul had imprisoned and beaten Christians for believing on Christ.

20 **and when the blood of Stephen thy witness was shed,**—Paul seems further to argue his case by recounting the persecution that he brought upon the disciples of the Lord. He was present at

unto me, Depart: for I will send thee forth far hence unto the Gentiles.

22 And they gave him audience unto this word; and they lifted up their voice, and said, Away with such a fellow from the earth: for it is not fit that

the stoning of Stephen (Acts 7: 58); this was the first mention that we have of Paul. Paul stood by and encouraged those who stoned Stephen. He says that he was keeping the garments of them that slew him. Some think that Saul at this time was a member of the Sanhedrin, and that he was superintending the execution of Stephen. "Witness" is from the Greek "marturos," from which we get "martyr." The word was in its transition state at this time; hence, "Stephen thy witness," would mean "Stephen thy martyr."

21 **And he said unto me, Depart:**—The Lord did not discuss the matter with Paul. His answer was clear and emphatic; "depart"; that is, get out of Jerusalem. The words of the Lord were dignified but imperative. The Lord added that he would send Paul "far hence unto the Gentiles." This narration would impress the Jewish multitude that it was Paul's wish to labor among his own people, but that Christ had commanded him to go to the Gentiles. When they heard the word "Gentile" they were ready to destroy Paul. Paul's voice was drowned by the uproar of the multitude, and he was taken into the castle for safety and for further investigation and examination.

22 **And they gave him audience unto this word;**—"This word" does not mean the word "Gentile," but the Greek literally means this saying or this announcement that he was sent to the Gentiles. This reminds one very much of the ending of Stephen's speech as recorded in Acts 7. When Paul made his reference to Stephen the crowd may have been cut to the heart, and may have begun to gnash with their teeth. However, when the mention of the hated Gentiles was made, the old frenzy broke out, aggravated by the thought that Paul, standing on the stairway, was out of their reach. The crowd now shouted: "Away with such a fellow from the earth: for it is not fit that he should live." They could not conceive of their Messiah as having given such orders to such a base fellow as Paul. Paul's claim seemed so absurd and blasphemous to them that they would not hear him any longer.

he should live. 23 And as they cried out, and threw off their garments, and cast dust into the air, 24 the [2]chief captain commanded him to be brought into the castle, bidding that he should be examined by scourging, that he might know for what cause they so shouted against him. 25 And when they had tied him up [3]with the thongs, Paul said unto the centurion that stood by,

[2]Or, *military tribune.* Gr. *chiliarch*
[3]Or, *for*

23, 24 **And as they cried out, and threw off their garments,** —There are three acts mentioned here which express their great rage. Their loud and clamorous shouts, their throwing off their garments, and their casting dust into the air, all express their infuriated confusion, and their determination to destroy Paul if they could lay hands on him. Shouting with deafening cries, and tearing off garments, and hurling dust into the air are ways by which they showed their bitterness and furious anger. They thew off their outer robes or coverings to allow free gesticulation; they threw dust at Paul (2 Sam. 16: 13), and shouted incessantly. The chief captain or Roman officer saw that it was no use for Paul to talk longer; hence, he commanded Paul to be brought into the castle. He gave orders that Paul should "be examined by scourging." He commanded Paul to be tortured until he should confess to some crime. The "chief captain" could not understand Hebrew, and did not know what Paul had said; he only saw that Paul's speech had infuriated the mob again, and that in their opinion he was a criminal worthy of death. He thought that something must be done. "Scourging" was inflicted on a victim to extract the truth; the victim was put to torture, to compel him to confess his crime. Scourging is described as the mildest form of examination; a wooden post was erected in a slanting position, and the feet and hands were made fast to it with thongs, and blows applied with the scourge or whip, formed of three lashes or thongs made of leather or small cords, to which some iron points or sharp-cornered pieces of metal were fastened. Lysias did not care to see the torture applied, so he commanded others to scourge Paul.

25 **And when they had tied him up with the thongs,**—As they were making preparation to scourge Paul, he asked the centurion who was standing by: "Is it lawful for you to scourge a man that is a Roman, and uncondemned?" It seems that they had al-

Is it lawful for you to scourge a man that is a Roman, and uncondemned?
26 And when the centurion heard it, he went to the ²chief captain and told
him, saying, What art thou about to do? for this man is a Roman. 27 And
the ¹chief captain came and said unto him, Tell me, art thou a Roman? And
he said, Yea. 28 And the ¹chief captain answered, With a great sum obtained I this citizenship. And Paul said, I am *a Roman* born. 29 They then

¹Or, *military tribune.* Gr. *chiliarch*

---

ready tied Paul and had him ready to inflict the punishment, when
the centurion who was directing the punishment was astonished to
learn that Paul was a Roman citizen. Roman historians sometimes speak of centurions as presiding over punishment, and an officer of that rank seems to have had charge of the crucifixion of
Jesus. (Matt. 27: 54; Mark 15: 39; Luke 23: 47.) It was contrary to the Roman law to begin an examination of a Roman citizen by scourging. The chief captain had violated this law in or-
dering Paul to be scourged.

26 **And when the centurion heard it,**—When the centurion
learned that Paul was claiming the rights of a Roman citizen, he
reported at once to the chief captain and said: "What art thou
about to do? for this man is a Roman." Literally, the centurion
said: "What are you about to do? for this man is a Roman."
This was a warning to the chief captain not to go any further.
Paul did not mean that he was a "Roman" by birth or residence,
but in right and privilege, he was a Roman citizen. It was easy to
find out whether a prisoner was making a false claim to being a
Roman citizen; the punishment for such a claim was death. Both
the chief captain and the centurion admitted Paul's claim to be
true.

27 **And the chief captain came and said**—When the chief captain learned from the centurion that Paul was claiming the rights of
a Roman citizen, he went at once to Paul and put the question directly to him: "Art thou a Roman?" Paul answered emphatically;
"Yea," The chief captain was now satisfied that Paul's claim was
true; he was subject to penalty for commanding Paul to be
scourged.

28 **And the chief captain answered,**—It was difficult for the
chief captain to believe that Paul was a Roman citizen; hence, he
said: "With a great sum obtained I this citizenship." There were

that were about to examine him straightway departed from him: and the
¹chief captain also was afraid when he knew that he was a Roman, and because he had bound him.

---

usually three ways by which one enjoyed the rights of Roman citizenship; namely, by purchasing citizenship with a large sum of
money; next, by having citizenship conferred upon one because of
some great service to the Roman government; and third, by being
born a Roman. To be born a Roman citizen seems to have been
more honorable than to purchase the rights of citizenship. This
centurion enjoyed his rights of citizenship through purchase, but
Paul was "Roman born." We are not told how he obtained citizenship by birth. It was not because he was born in Tarsus, for
Tarsus was not a colony, but only a free city; birth in a free city
did not necessarily confer Roman citizenship. Paul's father or
grandfather had probably received the honor for some service to
the state; his father or grandfather might have even purchased
their Roman citizenship. It matters but little how he obtained
this; we are confronted with the fact that he was freeborn. Hence,
he stood in a more honorable relation to the Roman government
than did the chief captain.

29 **They then that were about to examine him**—Those who
had bound Paul quickly loosed him and departed from him. Even
the chief captain was afraid because he had commanded the Roman
citizen to be scourged. Lysias, the chief captain, knew the Roman
law, so he at once released Paul; he was about to commit a greater
crime than even Paul was accused of. Paul may have had some papers and abundant references in the city by which he was ready to
prove his claim to citizenship. The action of the chief captain
could be interpreted as taking sides with a Jewish mob; hence, he
is careful now to protect the safety of Paul. Paul had not only
been bound, but he was tied up to the whipping post. It was not
contrary to law to bind a Roman citizen in order to secure him for
trial, so Paul remained in chains, fastened to a soldier, while living in Rome awaiting his trial before Caesar. (Acts 28: 20.)
However, it was illegal to inflict the indignity of tying to the whipping post as slaves were accustomed to being tied.

30 But on the morrow, desiring to know the certainty wherefore he was accused of the Jews, he loosed him, and commanded the chief priests and all the council to come together, and brought Paul down and set him before them.

---

30 But on the morrow, desiring to know the certainty— Paul remained in the custody of the chief captain until the next day. The chief captain desired to know the reason for the Jews' accusation against Paul. He had failed in his attempt to find out from Paul; so his next course was to order the Sanhedrin to assemble and have Paul brought before it. It seems that he left Paul there for the council to examine and report on the case. He may have left the guard with Paul until after charges were ascertained. The chief captain commanded "the chief priests" and "all the council to come together." The "chief priests" are mentioned as the most important class; then the council as second class was mentioned. The chief captain seems to have left Paul before the council to examine and report on the case. Our next is a study of Paul before the council.

4. PAUL BEFORE THE SANHEDRIN
23: 1-10

1 And Paul, looking stedfastly on the council, said, Brethren, I have lived

---

1 And Paul, looking stedfastly on the council,—Paul fixed his eyes intently on the council; he had been brought before it to answer for his conduct. He was not a criminal—he had done nothing wrong. The Sanhedrin had discovered that Paul was accused of some religious offense; he was summoned before the council that they might find out what the accusations were; Paul himself did not know what the charges were. He had not been in the hall of the council since he had sat as a member of the court probably twenty-two years ago. He politely addressed the members of the council and declared his sincerity at once. He declared that he had lived "before God in all good conscience until this day." "Conscience" comes from the Greek "suneidesis," and means "joint knowledge." The Latin is "conscientia," from which our English "conscience" is derived. The Greek word for "lived"

before God in all good conscience until this day. 2 And the high priest Ananias commanded them that stood by him to smite him on the mouth. 3 Then said Paul unto him, God shall smite thee, thou whited wall: and sittest thou to judge me according to the law, and commandest me to be smitten contrary to the law? 4 And they that stood by said, Revilest thou God's high priest? 5 And Paul said, I knew not, brethren, that he was high

---

means "having a citizenship." This statement simply means that Paul had performed the duties of a citizen in a good conscience to God. (Phil. 3: 6, 20.) Paul declared that he had lived in such obedience to God's law that he had a clear conscience; it does not mean that he is claiming that he had not sinned. (1 Tim. 1: 15.)

2 **And the high priest Ananias**—The smiting on the mouth was a judicial and symbolic mode of silencing the speaker from saying what was improper or false. Ananias is not to be confused with Annas. (Acts 4: 6.) Ananias is thought to have been the son of Nebedaeus, and was appointed high priest by Herod in A.D. 48. History describes him as being violent, cruel, and gluttonous. It is recorded that he was assassinated about ten years later.

3 **Then said Paul unto him,**—Paul very boldly rebuked the high priest for his conduct. He said: "God shall smite thee, thou whited wall." "Whited wall" is the reflection of a stronger figure used by Christ, "whited sepulcher." (Matt. 23: 27.) Paul gives his reason for the injustice done to him. "Sittest thou to judge me according to the law, and commandest me to be smitten contrary to the law." The spirit of the law of Moses forbade one to be condemned without first being heard. Paul shows the inconsistency between theory and fact; Ananias should have upheld the dignity of the law by obeying it himself. His conduct is similar to mob violence today. The victim may need punishment, but for unconstituted authority to mete out the punishment is illegal. Paul here impeaches the high priest in the name of Christ.

4 **And they that stood by said,**—The attendants and servants of the high priest and the Sanhedrin rebuked Paul for his speech. The high priest was God's representative in spite of his bad character. (Deut. 17: 8f.) These attendants claim for Ananias all the dignity, sanctity, and prerogative of his office as God's high priest; this was against what Paul had already plainly intimated, that An-

priest: for it is written, ²Thou shalt not speak evil of a ruler of thy people.
6 But when Paul perceived that the one part were Sadducees and the other
Pharisees, he cried out in the council, Brethren, I am a Pharisee, a son of
Pharisees: touching the hope and resurrection of the dead I am called in
question. 7 And when he had so said, there arose a dissension between the

²Ex. 22. 28

anias was acting in direct opposition to God. Paul made reply to
these attendants which showed that he understood the situation.

5 And Paul said, I knew not, brethren,—This shows that
Paul did not know that it was the order of the high priest for him
to be smitten. Some take the view that Paul did not know that Ananias was the high priest. Surely, Paul, who had served as a
member of the Sanhedrin, and who was familiar with the proceedings of the council, would know the high priest. We cannot conceive of such ignorance on the part of Paul; hence, we must look
for another view of the matter. The Greek means that Paul did
not know that it was the high priest who gave the order to smite
his mouth. Some think that Paul's eyesight was not good, and that
he did not recognize Ananias as the high priest. It matters not
what interpretation may be given to Paul's language, he recognized, and so do we, that he was not treated justly. He quotes Ex.
22: 28, showing that he knew the law.

6 But when Paul perceived—Paul quickly saw the attitude of
the Sanhedrin toward him; he saw that he could not get a fair
hearing before the Sanhedrin. He further saw that there were two
parties in the council, the Sadducees and the Pharisees. He knew
the difference between these parties and tactfully brought them to
clash with each other. He declared that he was a Pharisee, and
the son of a Pharisee. He refers to this later in his letter to the
church at Philippi. (Phil. 3: 5.) He further declared that he was
called in question because of the resurrection of the dead. This is
not out of harmony with the statement that he did not know what
charges would be preferred against him. He mentions this point
at another time. (Acts 24: 21.) The chief point of difference between Pharisees and Sadducees was the resurrection; this was
Paul's chief point in preaching the gospel. If Christ had not been
raised from the dead, his preaching was false. (1 Cor. 15: 13,
14.)

Pharisees and Sadducees; and the assembly was divided. 8 For the Sadducees say that there is no resurrection, neither angel, nor spirit; but the Pharisees confess both.   9 And there arose a great clamor: and some of the
scribes of the Pharisees' part stood up, and strove, saying, We find no evil in

7 **And when he had so said,**—Paul's declaration started in the
Sanhedrin a discussion on the great question of the difference between the Pharisees and Sadducees.   The Pharisees were bitterly
opposed to the Sadducees on the question of the resurrection. The
party cries were at once heard, and Paul was prevented from going
on with his argument for the resurrection of the dead, the resurrection of Christ.   The difference between the Pharisees and
Sadducees had grown out of national differences dating from the
time of the captivity; they were partly social and partly religious.
The Sadducees were the Jewish aristocracy; they aimed at pre-
serving the temple service and the written regulations of the law of
Moses. Their theory or teaching limited man's existence to this
present life, and hence they denied a resurrection and a future life.
The Pharisees became the leaders of the people in the days of the
Persian and Greek rule; they were the unwavering champions of
the ceremonial separation under Roman authority.   The Pharisees
believed in the doctrine of the resurrection, and through that faith
Paul and many others had been brought to acknowledge the crucified and risen Lord.

8 **For the Sadducees say**—The Sadducees denied the resurrection, angels, and spirits.   These points constitute the chief
doctrinal differences between the Pharisees and Sadducees.   The
Sadducees believed in a negative doctrine; they denied three
things: (1) the resurrection, believing that the soul dies with the
body; (2) the existence of angels and (3) the existence of spirits.
The Sadducees cared very little for religion; they dropped out of
history soon after the first century of the Christian era.   The
Pharisees believed in a future life, the resurrection of the dead, and
the existence of both angels and spirits.

9 **And there arose a great clamor:**—The dissension grew
fiercer until there was a great clamor. The excitement was very
great and broke out in an uproar. The "scribes" belonged to the

this man: and what if a spirit hath spoken to him, or an angel? 10 And when there arose a great dissension, the [1]chief captain, fearing lest Paul should be torn in pieces by them, commanded the soldiers to go down and take him by force from among them, and bring him into the castle.

---

party of the Pharisees; they were the learned expounders of the law, and would naturally take the lead in such an argument. Hence, they took sides with Paul and defended him against the Sadducees, their enemies. They said: "We find no evil in this man." They were ready to take sides with Paul even before they had heard him; this shows their bias and prejudice. A few moments before this they were ready to condemn him, but now they are defending him. They "strove" with the Sadducees. "Strove" is from the Greek "diamachomai," and means "to fight it out," "to fight back and forth fiercely." In their defense of Paul they said: What does it matter "if a spirit hath spoken to him, or an angel"? They were willing to admit that perhaps a spirit or an angel had spoken to Paul; at least they were willing to admit this in their contention with the Sadducees.

10 **And when there arose a great dissension,**—The Sanhedrin was composed of about seventy to seventy-two men; we do not know what ratio of them belonged to the Pharisees. It seems that the Sadducees tried to seize and kill Paul, while the Pharisees attempted to rescue and protect him. The council itself became as bad as the mob that had tried to kill Paul the day before. The chief captain, Lysias, knew that Paul was a Roman citizen, and that he was held responsible for him; so he feared that Paul should be "torn in pieces by them"; therefore, he commanded his "soldiers to go down and take" Paul from the council and "bring him into the castle." Paul was hastily rescued from the Sanhedrin and delivered safely in the castle. Paul handled the situation very tactfully; he had been brought before a prejudiced court; he saw that the court could be divided, and that too over one of the things which he had preached; hence, he turned the two divisions against each other and put them to fighting each other, one party trying to protect him, and the other trying to kill him. The Roman authority then stepped in and brought him to safety.

5. PLOT TO KILL PAUL
23: 11-25

11 And the night following the Lord stood by him, and said, Be of good cheer: for as thou hast testified concerning me at Jerusalem, so must thou bear witness also at Rome.

12 And when it was day, the Jews banded together, and bound themselves under a curse, saying that they would neither eat nor drink till they had

---

11 **And the night following**—Paul was now a prisoner; the chief captain, Lysias, held him as a prisoner. Conditions were unfavorable to Paul; he is discouraged, cast down, full of gloomy doubts. There is no mention of any sympathy from the Jewish Christians in Jerusalem. At this time, when all seem to have forsaken him, "the Lord stood by him." He strengthened and encouraged Paul by saying, "Be of good cheer." Paul had desired to preach the gospel to his own people in Jerusalem; he had two opportunities, and twice he had to be rescued from those who sought to kill him. The first instance is recorded in Acts 9: 26-30, and the second is here. The Lord, who had appeared to him on the way to Damascus (Acts 9: 5), in the temple (Acts 22: 17, 18), and at Corinth (Acts 18: 9), now appeared to him and comforted him with the promise that he would be able to fulfill his desire to preach the gospel at Rome (Acts 19: 21; Rom. 1: 11-13; 15: 23). The promise was of further service to the Lord among the Gentiles, and especially at Rome.

12 **And when it was day,**—At the very time that the Lord was encouraging Paul, the Jews were plotting to kill him. These forty Jews who were planning to murder Paul were in the end to send him to Rome to preach the gospel there. We are not told whether these Jews were Pharisees or Sadducees; the inference is that they were in favor with the Sadducees who had so violently opposed Paul in the council. They bound themselves "under a curse" that they would "neither eat nor drink till they had killed Paul." These forty Jews "anathematized themselves." The Greek "anathematizo" means "to place one under a curse." King Saul took an "anathema" that imperiled the life of his son Jonathan. (1 Sam. 14: 24.) The Greek for "banded together" is "poiesantes sustrophen," and literally means "having made a con-

killed Paul. 13 And they were more than forty that made this conspiracy. 14 And they came to the chief priests and the elders, and said, We have bound ourselves under a great curse, to taste nothing until we have killed Paul. 15 Now therefore do ye with the council signify to the ¹chief captain that he bring him down unto you, as though ye would judge of his case more exactly: and we, before he comes near, are ready to slay him. 16 But Paul's

---

spiracy." This pledge not to eat nor drink was a very ancient form of oath or vow. (1 Sam. 14: 24; 2 Sam. 3: 35.)

13 **And they were more than forty**—Some think these forty were Assassins and of the Zealots, which was a wild and fanatical party of that time. The number "forty" shows how many enemies Paul had; it also shows how difficult it would be to keep the secret from Paul's friends. We do not know what curse they took upon themselves if they failed to carry out their desire.

14 **And they came to the chief priests**—These forty Jews who had bound themselves under an oath not to eat or drink until they had killed Paul came "to the chief priests and the elders" and reported their oath. David had divided the priests into twenty-four courses or classes. The head of each of these classes was called a "chief priest." The "elders" were the rulers of the cities; they may have included some members of the Sanhedrin. It seems clear that the chief priests and those of the elders here mentioned belonged to the party of the Sadducees. This band of assassins felt free to go to the Sanhedrin and make known their intentions; they knew that the Sanhedrin was in sympathy with their efforts to kill Paul. Jesus had predicted that "whosoever killeth you shall think that he offered service unto God." (John 16: 2.)

15 **Now therefore do ye with the council signify**—Paul was still in the hands of Lysias, the chief captain. This band of assassins told the Sanhedrin in detail their plan. The council was to call on the chief captain to send Paul to the council that Paul may be examined further; they were to call upon Paul and kill him before he came to the council. The council was to make a formal or legal request for a regular and legal investigation; it was assumed that Lysias would be disposed to grant the request. The forty men assured the council that they would do their part and would kill Paul before he came to the council. This would keep the council in the clear, as they thought. The conspirators had stated their case

sister's son heard of their lying in wait, ³and he came and entered into the
castle and told Paul.   17 And Paul called unto him one of the centurions,
and said, Bring this young man unto the ¹chief captain; for he hath something to tell him. 18 So he took him, and brought him to the ¹chief captain,
and said, Paul the prisoner called me unto him, and asked me to bring this

---

³Or, *having come in* upon them, *and he entered &c.*

clearly and had revealed the plot to the council which seemed
ready to cooperate with them in destroying Paul.

16 **But Paul's sister's son heard**—This is the only reference
that we have of Paul's family in the Acts. In his letter to the Romans Paul speaks of his "kinsmen" who lived in Rome. (Rom.
16: 7, 11.) His friends here, and afterwards at Caesarea (Acts
24: 23), appear to have been permitted to visit him, which shows
that the authorities did not think him to be a criminal. It is not
certain that Paul's sister resided in Jerusalem; neither is it certain
that the young man who informed Paul lived in Jerusalem. He
was granted permission to visit Paul. We do not know that Paul's
nephew was a Christian; neither do we know how he gained his
information. The fact that the young man "entered into the castle" and told Paul of the plot shows that Paul's friends had free
access to him.

17 **And Paul called unto him one of the centurions,**—Paul,
even as a prisoner, exercised some authority over others; he called
one of the "centurions" or officers to him, and requested this centurion to take "this young man" to "the chief captain." Paul did
not trust the centurion with the secret that had been brought to
him; he wanted the young man to tell the chief captain from his
own mouth the plot that had been laid for him. We gather here
that Paul's nephew was a "young man." Although Paul had been
assured of his safety by the Lord (Acts 23: 11), he used all precaution and proper means for his safety. God's promise does not
dispense with the legitimate means that we must use. This young
man had some important business with the chief captain, and Paul
desired that he be escorted to him by a centurion.

18 **So he took him, and brought him to the chief captain,**—
The centurion was kind enough to take Paul's nephew to the chief
captain. It is not known that the chief captain or the centurion

young man unto thee, who hath something to say to thee. 19 And the ¹chief captain took him by the hand, and going aside asked him privately, What is it that thou hast to tell me? 20 And he said, The Jews have agreed to ask thee to bring down Paul to-morrow unto the council, as though thou wouldest inquire somewhat more exactly concerning him. 21 Do not thou there-

---

knew that the young man was Paul's nephew. The centurion reported that Paul had called him and asked him to bring "this young man" to the chief captain, as he had "something" to say to him. The Roman officers now seem to be careful to treat Paul with kindness, since they know that he is a Roman citizen. Their previous treatment of him, when they thought he was only a Jew, exposed them to severe penalties of the law should Paul or his friends bring a complaint against them. It was a wise policy for the officers to give Paul as much freedom as possible and to grant his friends the privilege of communicating with him. This helps us to understand the willingness of the centurion to take the young man to Lysias, and the readiness of Lysias to grant a private interview with the young man.

19 **And the chief captain took him by the hand,**—In verse 18 the centurion refers to "Paul the prisoner"; Paul later, in writing some of his letters, refers to himself as a prisoner. (Eph. 4: 1.) The chief captain received the young man with courtesy; he "took him by the hand," which indicated an eager interest in what concerned the case of this prisoner; he showed the young man that he had confidence in him. He took the young man "aside" and "asked him privately" what matter he had to bring to him. This shows that the chief captain was eager to get all the information that he could. We do not know the age of this young man; the Greek "neanias" is the same word that is used with respect to Paul in Acts 7: 58; it is also the same word that is used for Eutychus in Acts 20: 9.

20 **And he said, The Jews have agreed**—The young man reported faithfully and accurately the plot that he had learned whereby the Jews had determined to kill Paul. This shows that the conspirators clearly represented the state of Jewish feeling toward Paul in Jerusalem. The young man was able to quote accurately the language of the conspirators. The young man reports that the Jews had agreed to ask Lysias to bring Paul before the

fore yield unto them: for there lie in wait for him of them more than forty men, who have bound themselves under a curse, neither to eat nor to drink till they have slain him: and now are they ready, looking for the promise from thee. 22 So the ¹chief captain let the young man go, charging him, Tell no man that thou hast signified these things to me. 23 And he called

¹Or, *military tribune.* Gr. *chiliarch*

council "as though thou wouldest inquire somewhat more exactly concerning him." But the conspirators had said to the council to bring Paul before the Sanhedrin so that the Sanhedrin might make further examination of Paul. There seems to be a slight discrepancy here. It may be that the inquiry was proposed to both parties, and the young man only refers to that by Lysias through courtesy to him.

21 **Do not thou therefore yield unto them:**—The young man now pleaded with Lysias not to yield or listen to the request from the Jews or the Council. The Greek here signifies "be not thou persuaded by them," or obey not their request. The young man gave the reason for Lysias' not yielding to their entreaty by saying that "there lie in wait for him of them more than forty men" who had determined not to eat nor to drink till they had killed Paul. He further urged that these Jews were now ready and "looking for the promise from thee" to bring Paul before the council. The Jews waited for the expected promise from the chief captain, and had made ready the ambuscade by which they hoped to get rid of Paul without the Sanhedrin having any apparent hand in the murder. The young man's language implies that the council had agreed to the base plot, or that he believed that they would do so. The haste which Lysias exercised in getting Paul out of the city implies that he and the other Roman officials believed the report of the young man.

22 **So the chief captain let the young man go,**—The chief captain was satisfied with the report, and believed that the young man had told the truth. He enjoined secrecy on the part of the young man that he should not let anyone know that he had reported the Jews to him. His sympathies were clearly with Paul. He cautioned the young man not to let anyone know what he had reported. He did this to avoid any interference with his own plans, or a new conspiracy; also to avoid danger to the young man

unto him two of the centurions, and said, Make ready two hundred soldiers to go as far as Caesarea, and horsemen threescore and ten, and spearmen two hundred, at the third hour of the night: 24 and *he bade them* provide beasts, and that they might set Paul thereon, and bring him safe unto Felix the governor. 25 And he wrote a letter after this form:

---

for revealing the secret; and again to avoid any explanation of his conduct to the Jewish leaders. He did not want the Jews to suspect that his action was based on any knowledge of their plot. He exercised his own rights in sending a prisoner under such circumstances to the governor at Caesarea.

23 **And he called unto him two of the centurions,**—Lysias acted with military promptitude; he ordered two centurions with two hundred soldiers or legionnaires and seventy cavalry and two hundred light armed troops to escort Paul to Caesarea. This was a large escort; he took every precaution to protect the safety of Paul and to deliver him to the Roman authorities at Caesarea. They left "at the third hour of the night." This was at nine P.M. It was early enough for them to travel a full night's journey under cover of the darkness. With a military guard of two hundred foot soldiers or heavy armed soldiers, seventy horsemen, and two hundred light armed footmen, four hundred seventy soldiers and their officers, Paul was safe from any mob force of conspirators who might try to seize him from the soldiers and kill him.

24 **and he bade them provide beasts,**—"Beasts" is from the Greek "ktene," and may mean asses or horses; it does not mean war horses. These beasts were for Paul and some soldier to ride. More than one would be needed for Paul's use, as he was chained to a soldier; one or more would be needed for baggage. Some have inferred that the entire force was to be mounted on "beasts"; but the order was to provide beasts that Paul might be set thereon. He was to be brought to "Felix the governor." Felix was a brother of Pallas, the notorious favorite of Claudius. He and his brothers had been slaves, but were now freedmen; Felix was made procurator of Judea by Claudius A.D. 52; he held this position until Festus succeeded him. He was married to Drusilla, the daughter of Herod Agrippa I, with the hope of winning the favor of the Jews. Felix was one of the most depraved men of his

time; Tacitus says of him that "with all cruelty and lust he exercised the power of a king with the spirit of a slave." The term "governor" means "leader," and was applied to leaders of all sorts.

25 **And he wrote a letter**—Lysias "wrote a letter" to Felix the governor. This was the formal and official explanation why Paul was sent to the higher officer for trial; it was called "elogium"; this letter was not an accusation against Paul, but rather a statement favorable to him. Some understand that Luke here gives only the substance of the letter and does not give a copy of it. A copy of the letter may have been given Paul after his appeal to Caesar; it was probably written in Latin. The letter was probably read in open court before Felix and its contents could be learned.

6. PAUL SENT TO CAESAREA
23: 26-35

26 Claudius Lysias unto the most excellent governor Felix, greeting. 27 This man was seized by the Jews, and was about to be slain of them, when I came upon them with the soldiers and rescued him, having learned that he

26 **Claudius Lysias unto the most excellent governor**—Paul was sent with a Roman escort of four hundred seventy soldiers from Jerusalem to Caesarea; this was a distance of about seventy miles. Felix was the governor, and Claudius Lysias was the chief captain. Felix was a higher official than Lysias; hence, the very courteous and formal salutation or greeting as given here. "Most excellent" is a term used by Luke in addressing Theophilus. (Luke 1: 3.) This salutation is usual in addressing men of high rank; it is similar to "most excellent" in Acts 24: 3. "Claudius Lysias" is a Latin name, and "Felix" is a Greek. Some think that the letter was written in Latin; others think that it was in Greek; we do not know in what language it was written.

27 **This man was seized by the Jews,**—Lysias here wishes to be understood that he interfered for Paul on account of learning that he was a Roman citizen; this would seem to gain him some favor for his loyalty. However, the truth was that he had unlawfully bound a Roman citizen. He concealed the injustice that he

was a Roman. 28 And desiring to know the cause wherefore they accused him, [2]I brought him down unto their council : 29 whom I found to be accused about questions of their law, but to have nothing laid to his charge worthy of death or of bonds. 30 And when it was shown to me that there would be a plot [3]against the man, I sent him to thee forthwith, charging his accusers also to speak against him before thee.[4]

---

[2]Some ancient authorities omit *I brought him down unto their council*
[3]Many ancient authorities read *against the man on their part, I sent him to thee, charging &c.*
[4]Many ancient authorities add *Farewell*

---

had done to Paul. We see here the difference between the simple truth of the history and the cunning artifice of the skeptical Lysias. This is what we would naturally expect from a clever worldly politician, who had more regard for the favor of his superiors than he had for the truth. Lysias did rescue Paul before he learned that Paul was a Roman citizen, but he had violated the Roman law before doing this.

28 **And desiring to know the cause**—Lysias proceeds to state the matter in such a way as to show his official acts were to be commended. Lysias, like Gallio, cared for none of those things which disturb the Jews, and regarded their religious affairs as of no consequence. Lysias intended to show that the prisoner had been treated illegally, and that he had done all that he could to learn the charges against Paul. He had taken Paul, he says, before the Jews' council. This was to ascertain the nature of his crime.

29 **whom I found to be accused**—Lysias further states that when he brought Paul before the Sanhedrin he found him accused of violating some of the laws of the Jews. The only accusation that he learned against Paul was that he had violated the law of Moses; this had nothing to do with the Roman law. This is a confession that he had not violated Roman law and was not worthy of death or bonds. Then why should Lysias send him to Felix ? Lysias proceeds to give his reason for sending Paul to Caesarea.

30 **And when it was shown to me**—Roman officers in reporting a prisoner to a higher official must give the charges. Lysias had no crime to charge against Paul, but the determined attempts on the part of the Jews to kill him seemed to demand further inquiry. He does not mention in this letter the fact that Paul was in

31 So the soldiers, as it was commanded them, took Paul and brought
him by night to Antipatris. 32 But on the morrow they left the horsemen
to go with him, and returned to the castle: 33 and they, when they came

---

danger of being torn into pieces before the council; he does declare
his knowledge of the plot to kill Paul. This was sufficient ground
for sending a Roman citizen where he might be expected to have a
fair trial according to Roman law. He states that he charged
Paul's accusers to go to Caesarea and make their charges known to
Felix. Lysias does not seem to state the facts as they are. There is
nothing in the record that shows that he commanded the accusers
to appear before Caesar's court. He may have done so; at least,
he says in this letter that he did. "Farewell" is added by many ancient authorities, but is omitted here. It will be observed that Lysias does not represent Paul as a convict, but as one who had been
rescued from a mob.

31 **So the soldiers, as it was commanded them,**—This letter
of Lysias is inserted by Luke, and breaks the continuity of the historical events. Verse 31 takes up the facts and continues them.
The soldiers obeyed the command and brought Paul by night to
Antipatris. This place was formerly called "Capharaba." It was
rebuilt by Herod the Great and called by him "Antipatris" in
memory of his father, Antipater. It was more than forty miles from
Jerusalem, and more than halfway from Caesarea. They journeyed all night and made good time. Paul was now out of reach
of his conspirators.

32 **But on the morrow they left the horsemen**—"On the
morrow" may mean the morning of the arrival at Antipatris, or it
may mean the day after they arrived there. It seems that some
time would be given for rest after journeying all night. It matters
but little as to whether it means the next day after leaving Jerusalem or the next day after arrival at Antipatris. "They left the
horsemen" to go on with Paul. The journey on to Caesarea was
through a hilly region where there was much danger. There were
four hundred seventy, and four hundred of them returned to Jerusalem, while the seventy horsemen continued with Paul. We are
not told why these four hundred turned back; they had orders to
go as far as Caesarea. (See verse 23.)

to Caesarea and delivered the letter to the governor, presented Paul also
before him. 34 And when he had read it, he asked of what province he was;
and when he understood that he was of Cilicia, 35 I will hear thee fully,

33 **and they, when they came to Caesarea**—Those who were
in charge of the cavalry went on with Paul to Caesarea and presented Paul with the letter from Lysias to Governor Felix. In this
way they executed their commission. It was probably a journey of
five or six hours from Antipatris to Caesarea. They waited further orders from the governor. Paul thus entered Caesarea with
the pomp of attendance very unlike the humble guise in which he
had left it. They entered Caesarea in daylight, and such a parade
would have attracted many curious eyes. Philip and other Christians of Caesarea must have been startled to recognize the rapid
fulfillment of prophecy concerning Paul's journey to Jerusalem.

34 **And when he had read it,**—When Felix read the letter
from Lysias, he inquired from what province Paul came. He was
informed by Paul or some other one that Paul was from Cilicia,
which was an imperial province. He did not inquire whether Paul
was a Roman citizen; that was stated in the letter of Lysias to
Felix. Felix probably inquired of his native province that he
might ascertain whether he had jurisdiction over him; it seems that
Felix would have gladly avoided trying Paul. There were laws
regulating provincial relations, and one government was not at liberty to rely entirely on another's letter, but must himself make
thorough investigation. This Felix did.

35 **I will hear thee fully,**—Since Cilicia was an imperial province, Felix had jurisdiction over the trial of Paul. He informed
Paul that he would hear him "fully" when his accusers came.
This meant that he would give Paul's case a formal examination,
and implied that he would give him a fair trial. Felix commanded
Paul to be "kept in Herod's palace." This was built by Herod the
Great; Judea was now a Roman province, and the palace of its
former kings had become the governor's official residence. It appears that Paul was dealt with kindly. It seems that Paul was
kept near the governor's place of residence. Paul was under hon-

said he, when thine accusers also are come: and he commanded him to be kept in Herod's [5]palace.

[5]Gr. *Proetorium*

orable restraint, "a Roman, and uncondemned." Paul was guarded or detained by soldiers, and had to wait the slow processes of a trial.

SECTION SIX

PAUL AT CAESAREA

24: 1 to 26: 32

1. PAUL'S ACCUSERS BEFORE FELIX

24: 1-9

1 And after five days the high priest Ananias came down with certain elders, and *with* an orator, one Tertullus; and they informed the governor against Paul. 2 And when he was called, Tertullus began to accuse him, saying,
Seeing that by thee we enjoy much peace, and that by thy providence evils are corrected for this nation, 3 we accept it in all ways and in all

---

1 **And after five days the high priest Ananias**—"After five days" may mean either after five days from Paul's departure from Jerusalem or his arrival in Caesarea; it is not clear as to the exact meaning; no one can determine from the context. Roman usage required that a case referred to a higher court should be tried as soon as possible. The high priest, Ananias, came down to Caesarea "with certain elders," probably of the Sadducean party. The fact that the high priest came with them indicates that the Sadducees considered this an important case; as one of their fundamental doctrines, the resurrection was at stake. It will be further noted that they "came down," as Jerusalem was on a higher elevation. Caesarea was about seventy miles from Jerusalem on the seacoast. They brought with them "an orator, one Tertullus." Tertullus was a Roman lawyer. There were many Roman lawyers in those days who went to the provinces to gain training in the practice of law that they might go to Rome and practice their profession. Tertullus "informed the governor against Paul"; that is, he made formal charges against Paul.

2, 3 **And when he was called, Tertullus began**—When the case was called and both sides were present. Tertullus began his formal charges against Paul. He began with exaggerated flattery of Felix, the Roman judge. He intended by his flattery to ingratiate himself into the good graces of Felix. Historians tell us that Felix had suppressed riots among the people and had been an officer of the peace, but Tertullus shrewdly does not mention any

places, most excellent Felix, with all thankfulness. 4 But, that I be not further tedious unto thee, I entreat thee to hear us of thy clemency a few
words. 5 For we have found this man a pestilent fellow, and a mover of
insurrections among all the Jews throughout [6]the world, and a ringleader of
the sect of the Nazarenes: 6 who moreover assayed to profane the temple:

---

[6]Gr. *the inhabited earth*

---

specific riot that he had quelled; he makes general statements to
flatter Felix. He acknowledged "with all thankfulness" the many
things that Felix had done for the peace and welfare of the nation.
He hails Felix as the reform governor; this pleased Felix.

4 But, that I be not further tedious unto thee,—Tertullus
proceeds with tact, and introduces his case in a very winning way.
He does not want to encroach upon the good deeds that Felix has
done; neither does he want to claim the time of Felix which could
be given to Felix's further good reforms. He is still flattering
Felix. He entreated Felix to hear the case of his "clemency."
"Clemency" is from the Greek "epieikes," and means "reasonable,
likely, fair"; it also may mean gentleness. The clemency of Felix
was an invention of Tertullus' flattery; Felix was well known as
an avaricious man; he was not a lover of righteousness.

5, 6 For we have found this man—Tertullus now presents in
a very logical way the charges that the Jews had against Paul. As
we analyze Tertullus' speech, we find that he made one general accusation against Paul; he was "a pestilent fellow." "Pestilent"
comes from the Greek "loimon," and it means "pest, plague, pesti-
lence." It is used only twice in the New Testament, here and in
Luke 21: 11. The greatest gospel preacher in the world was
charged with being a pest. In addition to this general charge, there
were three specific charges. He was "a mover of insurrections
among all the Jews throughout the world," which meant that he
was rebellious and excited sedition wherever he went. Probably
Tertullus could refer to the tumult at Thessalonica (Acts 17: 6)
and at Ephesus (Acts 19: 28). The second charge was that he
was "a ringleader of the sect of the Nazarenes"; this was a charge
of heresy, and was the chief offense that the Jews had against Paul.
However, here Tertullus makes it an offense against the laws of

on whom also we laid hold: ⁷8 from whom thou wilt be able, by examining him thyself, to take knowledge of all these things whereof we accuse him. 9 And the Jews also joined in the charge, affirming that these things were so.

⁷Some ancient authorities insert *and we would have judged him according to our law. 7 But the chief captain Lysias came, and with great violence took him away out of our hands, 8 commanding his accusers to come before thee*

the empire, as Paul was teaching a religion that was not licensed by the state; in this charge Paul is accused of introducing strange gods. "Sect of the Nazarenes" is used here with a sneer as applied to Jesus and his followers. "Sect" is from the Greek "hairesis," and is the word from which we get "heresy." The third charge was that he had profaned the temple. This was not true. Tertullus identifies himself in this speech with the Jews, as he is pleading their cause.

(7 This verse is omitted from the Standard Version. Some ancient authorities insert: "And we would have judged him according to our law. 7 But the chief captain Lysias came, and with great violence took him away out of our hands, 8 commanding his accusers to come before thee." This quotation includes part of verse 8. The Revised Version leaves out verse 7, and its translators regard verse 7 as an interpolation which was added clearly to prejudice Felix against Lysias. Some think that it was added as a clumsy attempt to complete the speech of Tertullus.)

8 **from whom thou wilt be able,**—Tertullus perpetrates another astute trick by saying that Felix would find Paul guilty of all that he had charged against him. He attempts to prejudice Felix against Paul before anything is said by Paul. He stated that Felix would learn the truth of these things after he had examined Paul. Some authorities think that Tertullus means that Felix would find these things true after an interview with Lysias; others think that he would find them true after examining Paul. This seems to be the meaning. "Examining" is from the Greek "anakrinas," and means to examine thoroughly up and down, as in Luke 23: 14. It does not mean to examine by torture.

9 **And the Jews also joined in the charge,**—Ananias and the elders who accompanied him endorsed the charges made by Tertullus, and testified that the accusations against Paul were true. We

are not told how they affirmed the truthfulness of the charges made by Tertullus; it may have been simply by gestures, or they may have been called upon by Felix to speak for themselves. It will be noted that Tertullus and the Jews kept back the fact that Paul was a Roman citizen; neither does it appear that Tertullus knew that Lysias had informed Felix that Paul was a Roman citizen.

2. PAUL'S DEFENSE BEFORE FELIX
24: 10-27

10 And when the governor had beckoned unto him to speak, Paul answered,
Forasmuch as I know that thou hast been of many years a judge unto this nation, I cheerfully make my defence: 11 seeing that thou canst take knowledge that it is not more than twelve days since I went up to worship at

10 **And when the governor had beckoned**—There is a wide contrast between Paul's defense and the accusation that Tertullus made against him. Tertullus had begun his speech with lying flatteries and distorted facts. Paul's tone was that of frankness and truthfulness. When the governor signified that Paul could speak, he began by courteously acknowledging the facts concerning Felix. Felix had now been judge for about six years; this was more than the average duration of a procuratorship. Hence, Paul's expression, "many years," was not an exaggeration. Felix, after having ruled for a short time with divided authority, had superseded Cumanus in A.D. 52 or 53. Paul did not stand before Felix as a criminal; he was glad of the opportunity to speak; he cheerfully made his defense.

11 **seeing that thou canst take knowledge**—Felix knew many of the facts and could ascertain the truthfulness of Paul's statements. He refuted the general charge of Tertullus by appealing to the facts which Felix knew. Paul had arrived in Jerusalem, had an interview with the elders of the church there, and had begun the seven days of purification. The seven days were almost ended when Paul was arrested; he was then brought before the Sanhedrin, and a conspiracy was formed against him and he was sent to Caesarea. He was now brought before Felix, and the trial seems to have taken place on the fifth day after he left Jerusalem. These "twelve days" may be reckoned as follows: first day, Paul arrived

Jerusalem: 12 and neither in the temple did they find me disputing with any man or stirring up a crowd, nor in the synagogues, nor in the city. 13 Neither can they prove to thee the things whereof they now accuse me. 14 But this I confess unto thee, that after the Way which they call a sect, so serve I

---

at Jerusalem and met with James (Acts 21: 15); second day, he had made his first visit to the temple as a Nazirite; third to seventh days, he performed the Nazirite ceremonies and was arrested by Claudius Lysias; eighth day, he was brought before the Sanhedrin; ninth day, he was informed of the assassination plot and left that night for Caesarea; tenth day, he arrived at Antipatris; eleventh day, he was delivered over to Felix in Caesarea; twelfth day, he was in the palace of Herod, thirteenth day, he appeared before Felix.

12 and neither in the temple did they find me—Paul here urged that the accusation of exciting sedition was incapable of proof; nowhere had he publicly disputed with the purpose of exciting a tumult; nor had he gone preaching and speaking up and down the streets of the city. Felix had been governor between six and seven years and was well acquainted with all the seditions, and from personal knowledge could say that Paul had not been engaged in any of the insurrections. He had only been in Palestine or in Jerusalem about twelve days, and five of these he had spent as a Roman prisoner; he simply had not had time, even if he had been so disposed, to engage in plots against the Roman government. On the contrary, he had come to Jerusalem to worship, and had not come to engage in discussion; neither had he gathered a crowd in the synagogue or the city. He did not belong to any mob; neither had he engaged in any plot.

13 Neither can they prove to thee—Paul flatly denies their charges by appealing to the facts which were known to Felix. The charges that Tertullus and the Jews had made were mere assertions; they did not have the proof of their charges; neither could they produce the proof, as the accusations were contrary to the well-known facts. Paul had no hired lawyer to plead for him, but the simple facts recited by him spoke eloquently for his freedom.

14 But this I confess unto thee,—Paul had nothing to keep back; he had nothing in his life as a Christian for which he was

the God of our fathers, believing all things which are according to the law, and which are written in the prophets; 15 having hope toward God, which these also themselves ¹look for, that there shall be a resurrection both of the just and unjust. 16 ²Herein I also exercise myself to have a conscience void

¹Or, *accept*
²Or, *On this account*

---

ashamed. But "this I confess unto thee"; Paul acknowledged that he was a Christian and that Tertullus and the Jews called Christianity "a sect." Paul did not call the church "a sect"; it was not a sect, but after the way which they called a sect he worshiped God. Christianity was never a "sect"; it is not a "sect" today. "Sect" means a division and a divergence. Tertullus had used the term in a bad sense (verse 4), of which the Nazarenes were a schismatic offshoot from the body of the Jewish worshipers. The word translated "heresy" is the same that is here translated "sect." Paul here claims Christianity to be the real, whole of Judaism, and not a "sect" of it. The essence of the law of Moses pointed to Christianity; the only use of the law of Moses was to bring the people to Christ. Christianity was the full, ripe fruit of Jerusalem. Paul believed in the law of Moses and in the prophets; he knew that Christianity was set forth both by the law and by the prophets.

15 **having hope toward God,**—Paul presented three reasons why his way of worship was not "a sect" or "heresy"; it was the only righteous and living way. First, he served the same God that "our fathers" served; this meant that Christianity was of God, as was the law of Moses. He had the same hope that the fathers and the prophets had, and this hope was to be realized through Christianity. The Jews were at that time looking for a Messiah; Paul pointed out that this Messiah had already come. The difference between Paul and the Jews was that they were looking for the Messiah, and Paul had already received him. Paul furthermore reaffirmed his belief in the resurrection "both of the just and unjust." He affirmed that belief in the resurrection was a cardinal teaching of the Jewish faith, from which he had never swerved. He was really more orthodox with respect to the law and the prophets than were the Sadducees who denied the resurrection.

of offence toward God and men always. 17 Now after some years I came to
bring alms to my nation, and offerings: 18 ³amidst which they found me
purified in the temple, with no crowd, nor yet with tumult: but *there were*

³Or, *in* presenting *which*

---

16 **Herein I also exercise myself**—"Herein" Paul exercised
himself in the belief as stated in verses 14 and 15. He had been
faithful in believing and practicing all that the law and the prophets taught; he had been conscientious in this, and had a clear
conscience "toward God and men." His belief in the resurrection
was the field in which he trained himself to live a becoming life in
God's presence with the expectation of judgment before God. The
fact of the resurrection was with Paul a stern solemnity and modified his whole life and conduct. Paul's words must have been bitter to Ananias; however, Paul was courageous enough to speak the
truth without fear or favor. Paul's rule of life was to keep himself
from sin, knowing that he should be judged according to the deeds
done in the body. A belief in the resurrection implied a belief in a
future life.

17 **Now after some years I came**—If Paul went up to Jerusalem in Acts 18: 22, which it seems that he did, it was some five
years ago. At least four years had elapsed since he had been to
Jerusalem. The alms which Paul here mentions were the sums of
money that he and his companions had collected in the churches of
Macedonia and Achaia for the relief of the church at Jerusalem.
This is the only mention in the Acts of Paul's generous work of
which we hear so much in Paul's epistles. (Rom. 15: 25; 1 Cor.
16: 1-4; 2 Cor. 8: 1-4.) Paul mentions this to show that he had
been interested and engaged in a good work of collecting sums of
money to disperse among the poor brethren, and was not what the
Sadducees represented him to be. Every statement that Paul
makes is a clear refutation of the charges made against him.

18 **amidst which they found me purified in the temple,**—
Paul here states the facts with respect to his visit to Jerusalem and
his manner of life while in the city. Paul was keeping his vow of a
Nazirite (Acts 21: 23-26) when he was arrested. In fact, he was
engaged in this service when they seized him. He had no crowd,
neither had he excited any tumult. Paul stated that there were

certain Jews from Asia—19 who ought to have been here before theé, and to
make accusation, if they had aught against me. 20 Or else let these men
themselves say what wrong-doing they found when I stood before the council, 21 except it be for this one voice, that I cried standing among them,
Touching the resurrection of the dead I am called in question before you this
day.

"certain Jews from Asia"; this either means that those who found
Paul in the temple were Jews from Asia Minor (Acts 21: 27), or
else it may be a more general statement.

19 **who ought to have been here**—It is to be observed that
none of those "forty" Jews who had banded themselves together
not to eat or drink until they had killed Paul were here to make
charges against him. Possibly Felix did not know of this plot
against Paul, but the high priest and other members of the Sanhedrin who were present before Felix did know of it. Those who
were present and preferring charges against Paul were not present when he did that of which they were assusing him. The present witnesses did not have firsthand evidence; those who had any
evidence at all were not present. These Asiatic Jews are not mentioned after the riot, though they almost succeeded in having Paul
put to death.

20 **Or else let these men themselves say**—Paul had stood before the council; the high priest and some members of the council
were present now before Felix.   Paul reminds them that no
charges were proved against him while he stood before the council. He challenges the high priest and other members of the Sanhedrin to state any charges that were proved against him in his trial
before the Sanhedrin.   His argument is that those who first preferred charges against him and caused him to be brought before
the Sanhedrin were not now present, but members of the Sanhedrin are present, and even these cannot state any charges that were
proved against him.

21 **except it be for this one voice,**—Paul here makes an ex-
ception to his statement above. He was charged by the Sadducees
as teaching the resurrection from the dead. It is noticeable how
often Paul refers to this point. Even in his legal defense Paul
drives the wedge between Pharisees and Sadducees; if he can by
any means show how near the truth the Pharisees are by their be-
life in the doctrine of the resurrection of the dead, he can more

22 But Felix, having more exact knowledge concerning the Way, deferred them, saying, When Lysias the *chief captain shall come down, I will
determine your matter. 23 And he gave order to the centurion that he
should be kept in charge, and should have indulgence; and not to forbid any
of his friends to minister unto him.

*Or, *military tribune.* Gr. *chiliarch*

---

easily bring them to believe in the Christ who has been crucified,
buried, and raised from the dead. Paul knew that some members
of the Sanhedrin, and many of the Jews, would sympathize with
him in his preaching the resurrection from the dead. His preaching the resurrection from the dead was the only thing that had
come directly under the notice of the Sanhedrin, and it had been
the cause of division in the Sanhedrin itself. Paul understood
clearly his case, and did not waste words; he presented his case
truly and accurately and briefly before Felix. Tertullus and the
Jews had no case at all.

22 **But Felix, having more exact knowledge**—Felix was not
ignorant of the teachings of Christ; during the years he had held
office in Judea and Samaria, at Jerusalem as well as Caesarea, he
had frequent opportunities to learn what Christians taught and how
they lived; even Philip, one of the seven (Acts 6: 5), lived at Caesarea. Felix had a more "exact knowledge" of Christianity than
the high priest and other Jews gave him credit of having. He
should have released Paul, and would have done so, had he not
sought to please the Jews. After hearing Paul's defense he knew
that he was innocent. However, he could not condemn Paul, but
he could compromise with the Jewish party by retaining Paul as a
prisoner. We do not know that "Lysias the chief captain" ever
came to Felix; we hear no more of him. This was Felix's way of
conciliating the Jews. Felix had another motive in retaining Paul
as a prisoner.

23 **And he gave order to the centurion**—While Felix retained
Paul as a prisoner, he gave orders to the centurion to show Paul
kindness, and to permit Paul's friends "to minister unto him."
There were three kinds of imprisonment among the Romans: (1)
the imprisonment in the common prison as Paul and Silas were
kept at Philippi; (2) the military arrest, when the prisoner was
chained to a soldier; this appears to have been the form of impris-

24 But after certain days, Felix came with Drusilla, [5]his wife, who was a Jewess, and sent for Paul, and heard him concerning the faith in Christ Jesus. 25 And as he reasoned of righteousness, and self-control, and the judgment to come, Felix was terrified, and answered, Go thy way for this

---

[5]Gr. *his own wife*

onment to which Paul was relegated during his Roman confinement; (3) the free custody in which the arrested party was usually released on bail. Paul speaks of his chains in Acts 28: 20, this shows the kind of imprisonment that Paul had. Indulgence was given Paul in respect to food, lodging, and friends, but this did not include removal of his chains.

24 **But after certain days,**—We do not know how long the "certain days" were. Some think that Felix had been away from Caesarea for a time, and when he returned he sent for Paul. He brought his wife, "Drusilla," "who was a Jewess." Under the influence of Felix she had left her former husband. She was one of three daughters of Herod Agrippa I; her sisters were Marianne and Bernice: her father murdered James; her great-uncle, Herod Antipas, beheaded John the Baptist; her great-grandfather, Herod the Great, had the babes of Bethlehem killed. It is said that Drusilla was gifted with great beauty. It is said that she perished at the eruption of Vesuvius in A.D. 79. Felix sent for Paul to hear him "concerning the faith in Christ Jesus." It may be that since he had his wife with him she was also eager to learn more of "the faith in Christ Jesus." It seems that Felix and Drusilla were in earnest in their inquiry about the Christ. We may know that Paul was glad of the opportunity to preach Christ to these wicked rulers.

25 **And as he reasoned of righteousness,**—Perhaps Felix and Drusilla did not hear just what they wanted to hear. After presenting Christ to them Paul reasoned of "righteousness." "Righteousness" is from the Greek "dikaiosmes," which meant upright conduct; this condemned Felix who had murdered a high priest, had been tyrannical, had taken bribes, and had been an unrighteous ruler. Paul also reasoned with him about "self-control." "Self-control" is from the Greek "egkrateias," which means temperance in this life, including especially continence and chastity.

time; and when I have a convenient season, I will call thee unto me. 26 He hoped withal that money would be given him of Paul: wherefore also he sent for him the oftener, and communed with him. 27 But when two years were fulfilled, Felix was succeeded by Porcius Festus; and desiring to gain favor with the Jews, Felix left Paul in bonds.

Drusilla in his presence was a witness of Felix's unbridled passions. Again, Paul reasoned to these unrighteous and intemperate rulers of "the judgment to come." He pointed out that certain judgments would overtake them, and that they would not escape punishment for their wickedness. Felix and Drusilla had lived as though they would never have to give an account for their deeds; Paul very forcibly brings them to face the consequences of their wicked deeds. Felix seems to have been brought under conviction, but Drusilla does not seem to have been affected. Felix knew himself to be a profligate, avaricious and mean; his conscience was awakened only to be stilled. He was "terrified," frightened, and dismissed Paul, saying that he would call for him at "a convenient season." That "season" never came. Felix becomes an example of the many millions who are lost by procrastination.

26 **He hoped withal that money would be given him**—Here we have another motive of Felix for keeping Paul in prison. Paul had mentioned in the presence of Felix that he had taken "alms" to the poor saints in Jerusalem. Felix evidently drew the idea that Paul or his friends would give him money to release him. This greed of gain in the very act of administering justice was the root evil of the weak and wicked character. Since Paul had money, or some of his friends were wealthy, why should not Felix get money from one or both of them? He sent for Paul often and "communed with him." Perhaps Felix would have passed sentence and released Paul, if it had not been that he hoped to get some money from Paul. Paul did not offer any bribe, and so Felix continued to have hope that he would buy his freedom.

27 **But when two years were fulfilled,**—Paul lingered in prison in Caesarea for two years; he was waiting for the second hearing under Felix which never came. Caesarea became the compulsory headquarters for Paul for two years. We know nothing of his history during this period; some think that Luke was with him, and that Paul and Luke had repeated conversations together; from

these conversations, guided by the Holy Spirit, Luke was enabled to write at least the latter portion of the book of Acts, which tells about Paul and his missionary labors. Felix was succeeded by Porcius Festus. Felix desired to gain favor with the Jews and left Paul a prisoner to be disposed of by Festus. The change of administration was caused by the complaints which the Jews brought against Felix, and which led Nero to recall him. This was about A.D. 60.

3. PAUL BEFORE FESTUS
25: 1-12

1 Festus therefore, [0]having come into the province, after three days went up to Jerusalem from Caesarea. 2 And the chief priests and the principal men of the Jews informed him against Paul; and they besought him, 3 asking a favor against him, that he would send for him to Jerusalem; laying a plot to kill him on the way. 4 Howbeit Festus answered, that Paul was kept

---

[0]Or, *having entered upon his province*

1 **Festus therefore, having come into the province,**—Festus was made governor by the emperor, Nero, in A.D. 60, and died two years afterward. He was a better man than Felix and there is a strong contrast between the honesty and straightforwardness of Festus and the wickedness of Felix. It seems that he rested one day in Caesarea and then went to Jerusalem. "After three days" means that he arrived in Caesarea one day, rested the next day, and the third day started for Jerusalem. This is the same language used of the resurrection of Christ, "after three days," which means "on the third day."

2, 3 **And the chief priests and the principal men**—When Festus arrived in Jerusalem the chief priests and important men among the Jews informed Festus against Paul. It seems that they placed formal charges against Paul before the governor and asked him to send Paul to Jerusalem to be tried there. They placed charges against Paul and then asked for themselves a favor; they had formed a plot to kill Paul on the way. These religious leaders, under the guise of seeking justice, were plotting to commit the greatest injustice to another. This plot was similar to the one that had been laid two years before. (Acts 23: 12.) They intended to conceal themselves along the way and seize Paul from the Roman guard and put him to death. Festus did not know of their plot.

in charge at Caesarea, and that he himself was about to depart *thither* shortly. 5 Let them therefore, saith he, that are of power among you go down with me, and if there is anything amiss in the man, let them accuse him.

6 And when he had tarried among them not more than eight or ten days, he went down unto Caesarea; and on the morrow he sat on the judgment-seat, and commanded Paul to be brought. 7 And when he was come, the

---

4 **Howbeit Festus answered, that Paul was kept**—Festus answered the Jews that Paul was a prisoner in Caesarea, and that he would soon return to Caesarea. This spoiled the plot that the Jews had laid to kill Paul. Festus denied their request. Some think that Festus had either been informed of the enmity on the part of the Jews against Paul, or that he wished to keep free from any of the troubles that arose at Jerusalem. Festus was a wise and firm official. He refused to alter judicial arrangements on private requests, and assured the Jews that the case would be taken in regular order as Felix had left it.

5 **Let them therefore, saith he,**—Since Paul was a prisoner in Caesarea, and since Festus was ready to return to Caesarea, he advised that some of the important or prominent Jews would go with him and make their accusations against Paul in Caesarea. The men "of power" among the Jews simply meant the members of the Sanhedrin. Luke changes from the indirect discourse in verse 4 to the direct in verse 5. Festus demanded that the charges against Paul should be supported by the leaders and representatives of the people, and not by a hired lawyer like Tertullus.

6 **And when he had tarried among them**—Festus remained in Jerusalem eight or ten days, and then went to Caesarea. Note again that "he went down unto Caesarea." This is true to the topography of the country. He lost no time; the next day after his arrival in Caesarea he called for Paul to be brought before him. This would give a formal presentation of his case. Some of the prominent Jews had gone "down" from Jerusalem to Caesarea as Festus had invited them. (See verse 5.) Festus "sat on the judgment-seat." The "judgment-seat" was an elevated throne or seat, reached probably by a step; sometimes it was fixed in some open place and was movable; it was the symbol of authority of a Roman judge, and is frequently mentioned in the New Testament. (Matt.

Jews that had come down from Jerusalem stood round about him, bringing against him many and grievous charges which they could not prove; 8 while Paul said in his defence, Neither against the law of the Jews, nor against the temple, nor against Caesar, have I sinned at all. 9 But Festus, desiring to gain favor with the Jews, answered Paul and said, Wilt thou go up to Jeru-

27: 19; John 19: 13; Acts 18: 12, 16, 17; 25: 6, 10, 17; Rom. 14: 10; 2 Cor. 5: 10.)

7 **And when he was come, the Jews,**—When Paul was brought before the judgment seat of Festus, the Jews who had come down from Jerusalem made many "grievous charges" against him; however, they were unable to prove any of their charges. The enemies of Paul were as prompt in preferring charges against him as was Festus in speeding up the trial. When Paul came into court the Jews "stood round about him"; that is, they took their stand as witnesses and accusers around him. It seems that they had no lawyer at this time, but appeared in mass and made their charges. Nothing is said as to the nature of the charges further than that they made many "grievous changes." Perhaps they were no more grievous than the charges made by Tertullus two years before. It is very likely that their charges were a repetition and reiteration of the former charges.

8 **while Paul said in his defence,**—It is likely that Paul also repeated his defense, which he made before Felix, and in reply to the charges preferred by Tertullus. Paul sums up the charges that they made against him, and puts them in three classes: (1) those against the law of the Jews; (2) those against the temple; (3) and those against Roman law. Festus was interested only in offenses committed against Roman law. We would infer that since Paul's defense indicated three counts of the indictment the Jews had made these three classes of charges. As the Jews alleged that he had broken the law of Israel, which Rome recognized as the religion of the province, he was therefore subject to the spiritual jurisdiction of the Sanhedrin. They made this charge, perhaps, that they might get Festus to send Paul to Jerusalem; if he did so, they could carry out their plot to kill him.

9 **But Festus, desiring to gain favor with the Jews,**—This is the charge that was brought against Felix. (Acts 24: 27.) For some cause Festus, like Felix, feared the Jews. Festus asked Paul

salem, and there be judged of these things before me? 10 But Paul said, I am standing before Caesar's judgment-seat, where I ought to be judged: to the Jews have I done no wrong, as thou also very well knowest. 11 If then I am a wrong-doer, and have committed anything worthy of death, I refuse not to die; but if none of those things is *true* whereof these accuse me, no man can ᵗgive me up unto them. I appeal unto Caesar. 12 Then Festus,

---

ᵗGr. *grant me by favor*

---

if he would be willing to go up to Jerusalem and there appear before him. If Festus was unwilling to give Paul justice in Caesarea, where his regular court was held, what assurance did Paul have that he would get justice before him in Jerusalem? Festus would have less courage to give justice in Jerusalem, where he was surrounded with influential Jews, than he had in Caesarea. Paul knew this. It is probable that Festus would have turned Paul over to the Jews in Jerusalem had he gone there for his trial. Festus' proposal was an informal statement that there was no case against Paul; that Paul had not committed any crime that Roman law could condemn.

10 **But Paul said, I am standing before Caesar's judgment-seat,**—Paul refused on just grounds to be taken to Jerusalem for trial. Paul's reply was emphatic and decisive. He had no hope of receiving justice from the Sanhedrin; he had no hope of receiving justice from Festus who feared the Jews. His only course was to appeal to Caesar. As a Roman citizen he had this right; no man or official could deny a Roman citizen of his right to appeal his case to the higher court. Festus had shown prejudice in favor of the Jews; this indicated that Paul would not receive justice in another trial before Festus. Paul declared his innocence as to any violation of Jewish law or Roman authority. He fearlessly confronted Festus with the fact that Festus knew that he was innocent of the charges brought against him.

11 **If then I am a wrong-doer,**—In further declaring his innocence Paul expressed willingness to suffer even death if he were guilty of a crime that demanded the death sentence. On the other hand, if he were not guilty of the things of which he was accused, he demanded, as a Roman citizen, the right to appeal his case to Caesar. Paul was a Roman citizen, and even Festus could not send Paul to Jerusalem to be tried by the Sanhedrin. Originally,

when he had conferred with the council, answered, Thou hast appealed unto
Caesar: unto Caesar shalt thou go.

---

the Roman law allowed an appeal from the magistrate to the people, but the emperor of Rome represented the people, and so the
appeal to Caesar was the right of every Roman citizen.   In his appeal to Caesar, Paul took his case out of the hands of Festus.
Perhaps Paul's long desire to see Rome (Acts 19: 21; Rom. 15:
22-28), and the promise of Jesus that he would see Rome (Acts
23: 11), may have helped Paul in deciding to make this emphatic
appeal to Caesar.

12 **Then Festus, when he had conferred with the council,**—
Festus advised "with the council."   "Council" comes from the
Greek "sumboulion."   This word in the New Testament usually
means "counsel," as in Matt. 12: 14, but here alone as an assembly
of counselors or "council."   Here it means the chief officers and advisers of the procurator or governor.   These local advisers were
necessary and helped the judge or governor, as he needed their experience and advice.   Such men were appointed in all provincial
courts to advise the procurator on matters of Roman law; they
formed his cabinet officers.   After Festus had advised with his
"council," he returned to his judgment seat and pronounced the
formal announcement of an appeal: "Thou hast appealed unto Caesar: unto Caesar shalt thou go."   The Roman Caesar at this time
was the notorious and wicked Nero.   Some think that Festus
meant to say that Paul had not bettered his case by making the
appeal.

4. FESTUS AND AGRIPPA
25: 13-27

13 Now when certain days were passed, Agrippa the king and Bernice
arrived at Caesarea, ¹and saluted Festus. 14 And as they tarried there many

¹Or, *having saluted*

---

13 **Now when certain days were passed,**—Each of the char-
acters before whom Paul was brought had a memorable history.
"Agrippa," as mentioned here, is King Herod Agrippa II; he was
the son of Agrippa I who died so miserably at Caesarea.   (Acts
12: 21-23.)   He was the great grandson of Herod the Great, and

days, Festus laid Paul's case before the king, saying, There is a certain man
left a prisoner by Felix; 15 about whom, when I was at Jerusalem, the chief
priests and the elders of the Jews informed *me*, asking for sentence against

---

was the last of the famous Herodian princes, who played so distinguished a part in the story of Israel during the last fifty years of
the existence of the Jews as a separate nation. Agrippa ruled over
a very small portion of his father's territory; the remainder had
been made into a Roman province of Judea. Agrippa II resided at
Caesarea Philippi; he died at an advanced age, having survived the
fall of Jerusalem many years; it is thought that he died in A.D. 99.
Bernice was a sister of Agrippa II; she was a sister also of Drusilla. Her beauty was famous. Her history reads like a terrible
romance. She married at an early age her uncle, Herod, king of
Chalcis; she was left a widow while young and went to reside with
her brother, Agrippa II. Polemo, king of Cilicia, adopted the
Jewish religion and made Bernice his wife; however, she soon deserted him, and again returned to her brother, Agrippa II, with
whom it is said she lived in illicit relationship. Later, she became the mistress of Titus, son of Vespasian, who took her
to Rome, but public indignation was so great that he did not
marry her. Festus had just recently been appointed governor
and Agrippa and Bernice came to Caesarea and congratulated
him on the honors which had been conferred upon him.

14, 15 **And as they tarried there many days,**—The time of
the sojourn of King Agrippa and Bernice was indefinite, "tarried
there many days"; the original may mean "more than one, or several days." There was sufficient time for Festus to discuss Paul's
case with King Agrippa. It would help confirm the friendship of
Agrippa and Bernice for Festus to advise with Agrippa about
Paul's case. Festus does not make any official report to Agrippa,
but engages him in an informal, personal talk about the case for his
advice. Agrippa was more familiar with Jewish affairs than Festus; he had greater experience as an official; hence, he would be of
service to Festus in advising him. We get from this conversation
that the Jews had asked the death sentence on Paul without a fair
trial. The Jews had evidently made two proposals to Festus: (1)
that he should condemn and punish Paul without trial; (2) that he
should bring Paul to Jerusalem for trial there, purposing to have

him. 16 To whom I answered, that it is not the custom of the Romans to
²give up any man, before that the accused have the accusers face to face, and
have had opportunity to make his defence concerning the matter laid against
him. 17 When therefore they were come together here, I made no delay, but
on the next day sat on the judgment-seat, and commanded the man to be
brought. 18 Concerning whom, when the accusers stood up, they brought
no charge of such evil things as I supposed; 19 but had certain questions

---

²Gr. *grant me by favor*

---

him killed on the road. Festus further informed Agrippa that
Paul had been left by Felix; hence, it was, perhaps, an old and dif-
ficult case. This would be a good reason for Festus advising with
Agrippa about it.

16 **To whom I answered, that it is not the custom**—It may
be that Festus did some boasting in the presence of Agrippa; the
record is not clear that he answered the Jews as he claimed that he
did. It may not be an accurate representation of the case by Festus. It may be that the Jews did ask for sentence against Paul,
and it may be that they did not. Roman officials were often unre-
liable; Festus had such a good opportunity to boast of his loyalty
to justice that he likely exaggerated in his own favor. Festus stated
a point of Roman law and the rights of a Roman citizen. The accused had a right to demand that his accusers meet him "face to
face" and make their charges, and give the accused the opportunity
of defending himself. Paul had told Festus exactly what Festus
says that he told the Jews. Those who accused Paul to Festus had
not met Paul face to face. Ishmael was then high priest in place of
Ananias.

17 **When therefore they were come together here,**—Festus
here relates accurately the facts. While he was in Jerusalem
Paul's accusers asked that Paul be brought to Jerusalem; Festus
refused to let him be brought to Jerusalem, but told them that he
would soon return to Caesarea and that they could come to Caesarea and prefer their charges against Paul. They did so, and Festus promptly demanded that Paul be brought before his judgment
seat the next day.

18 **Concerning whom, when the accusers stood up,**—Festus
continues his recitation of the details of the trial. When Paul's accusers bore witness against him and preferred their charges, and

against him of their own ³religion, and of one Jesus, who was dead, whom Paul affirmed to be alive. 20 And I, being perplexed how to inquire concerning these things, asked whether he would go to Jerusalem and there be judged of these matters. 21 But when Paul had appealed to be kept for the

³Or, *superstition*

Paul made his defense, Festus saw that there was no proof offered as he had expected. Perhaps Festus was influenced by Paul's accusers at Jerusalem, and supposed that Paul was guilty of sedition and disloyalty to the emperor. However, he discovered that the charges were nothing but the vaguest rumors which could not be proved.

19 **but had certain questions against him**—Festus discovered that the real point urged against Paul was connected with matters devoid of interest to a Roman; no Roman law had been violated by Paul. Festus, in speaking to Agrippa, a Jewish king, would not knowingly use an offensive term. Furthermore, he showed his ignorance of the entire matter when he said that the charges against Paul were of "their own religion, and of one Jesus, who was dead, whom Paul affirmed to be alive." Festus merely understood that Paul was affirming, with other Pharisees, not the general doctrine of a resurrection, but as bearing specific testimony that Jesus had been raised from the dead, while the others denied his affirmation. Festus was like Gallio at Corinth. (Acts 18: 17.) This remark shows that Luke gave only a short abstract of Paul's speech before the Sanhedrin and of his defense before Agrippa; we are not told that he even mentioned the name of Jesus; yet this name, and the fact of the resurrection of Jesus, had made the strongest impression on the mind of the Roman governor. "Religion," as used here, comes from the Greek "deisidaimonias," and is translated in the Authorized Version as "superstitious." The Greeks used this word to mean "pious," or "religious," or "superstitious." Paul used the word in Acts 17: 22.

20 **And I, being perplexed**—Festus had already determined what to do, and it was difficult for him to justify his conduct in not releasing Paul at once, and not put the government to the expense of an appeal to Caesar. He reports accurately that he had asked Paul if he would go to Jerusalem and be judged of these matters. Festus was ignorant as to how to conduct a judicial trial about

decision of ⁴the emperor, I commanded him to be kept till I should send him to Caesar. 22 And Agrippa *said* unto Festus, I also ⁵could wish to hear the man myself. To-morrow, saith he, thou shalt hear him.

23 So on the morrow, when Agrippa was come, and Bernice, with great

⁴Gr. *the Augustus*
⁵Or, *was wishing*

these matters of religion; to him they seemed to belong to a Jewish court; at least, this is what he says to Agrippa. This was his smooth excuse for proposing to deliver Paul over to the Jews, though it was contrary to Roman custom, as he had formerly stated. (Verse 16.) Festus stated before Agrippa not what he had formerly said, but what had since occurred to him upon reflecting.

21 **But when Paul had appealed**—When Paul made his appeal to Caesar, Festus had no further jurisdiction over him but to send him to Rome. There seems to be an undercurrent in Festus' conversation of his displeasure at the appeal to Caesar. He had to grant the appeal, but it was a reflection on Festus' fairness and justice that a Roman citizen should prefer the imperial tribunal at Rome to his own. Festus had proposed to remove the trial to Jerusalem; this had forced Paul to take the step of his appeal. The term "emperor," as used here, by many is translated "Augustus." The Greek is "Sebastos," and is a reverent title for the ruler of Rome.

22 **And Agrippa said unto Festus,**—After hearing Festus relate the details of the case, Agrippa became interested. Perhaps he had frequently heard of Paul and he desired to hear him. It may not have been a desire to satisfy his curiosity, but more to learn something about Christianity from its greatest advocate. Agrippa's courteous suggestion or request to Festus was promptly accepted, and Festus promised Agrippa that he should hear Paul the next day. This was as soon as arrangements could properly be made.

23 **So on the morrow, when Agrippa was come,**—According to promise, Festus made arrangements for Paul to be brought before Agrippa the next day. Luke's description is so vivid that one would think that he was an eyewitness to the parade. Much or "great pomp" was displayed on this occasion. King Agrippa,

pomp, and they were entered into the place of hearing with the °chief captains and the principal men of the city, at the command of Festus Paul was brought in. 24 And Festus saith, King Agrippa, and all men who are here

°Or, *military tribunes.* Gr. *chiliarchs*

Bernice, "the chief captains," or chiliarch, leader or captain of a thousand soldiers, and "the principal men of the city," together with Festus and his attendants—all these dressed in their royal garments and official robes—made a gorgeous display. The place of assembly was near Festus' court. After the procession had passed in and were seated, Paul, the prisoner, was brought in. The splendor of the procession and the glittering appearance of the court, Roman and Jewish guards, and the Sanhedrin officials, all made a very imposing scene, and showed an emphatic contrast to the humble prisoner in chains. About eighteen years before this event Herod, the father of Agrippa, was smitten by an angel of the Lord as punishment for his pride. (Acts 12: 23.) We have here one of the direct fulfillments of the prophecy of Jesus to his disciples when he said that they would be brought "before governors and kings" "for a testimony to them and to the Gentiles." (Matt. 10: 18.) Christ had said to Ananias, who was sent to Saul, that he would "bear my name before the Gentiles and kings, and the children of Israel." (Acts 9: 15.) We now have Paul standing before rulers and kings.

24 And Festus saith, King Agrippa, and all men—Festus now with equal pomp and dignity introduced the case to those who were assembled. Festus believed that the feeling against Paul among the Jews was general; he had come in contact only with Paul's enemies. Nothing new is stated in the introduction that Festus made except that the Jews of Caesarea had joined with those from Jerusalem in urging that Paul be put to death, and that they had asked Festus to pass such a sentence on him. Festus addressed Agrippa with a courteous title. It is very likely that the Sadducees from Jerusalem had been able in the course of two years to excite much animosity against Paul among their party in Caesarea; hence, when Festus came to Caesarea, these influential men joined the Sadducees from Jerusalem in demanding the death sentence upon Paul.

present with us, ye behold this man, about whom all the multitude of the
Jews made suit to me, both at Jerusalem and here, crying that he ought not
to live any longer. 25 But I found that he had committed nothing worthy of
death: and as he himself appealed to the ⁴emperor I determined to send him.
26 Of whom I have no certain thing to write unto my lord. Wherefore I
have brought him forth before you, and specially before thee, king Agrippa,
that, after examination had, I may have somewhat to write. 27 For it seemeth to me unreasonable, in sending a prisoner, not withal to signify the
charges against him.

---

25 But I found that he had committed—Festus is frank and
fair in stating that he had not found Paul "worthy of death."
These words were emphatic on the part of Festus; they admit that
Paul's accusers had failed to prove their charges. However, Festus was bound to send a formal report as to the matter, out of
which the case of appeal arose, and he was in doubt as to what he
should send to Caesar, and needed the advice and co-operation of
Agrippa. Perhaps Paul would have been set at liberty had it not
been for the persistent clamor of the Jews against him. However,
since Paul had made an appeal to Caesar, Festus must send him.
These points are mentioned to show the exact condition of the
case; Paul's appeal had stopped all judicial proceedings except at
Rome. This was not a judicial hearing, but only one for further
information, which Festus now declared.

26 Of whom I have no certain thing to write—It was the
rule or law when a case was appealed to the emperor to transmit a
detailed account of the crime charged, and also to give a full report
of the legal proceedings which had taken place in connection with
the case. It is clear that Festus must admit Paul's innocence, but
he reiterated that pressure from the Jews had caused him to retain
Paul. Festus referred to the emperor as "my lord." Augustus
and Tiberius had refused to let anyone address them with such a
title, but Caligula and Nero permitted such an address, and even
gloried in this title. Festus pleaded for help from the other
Roman officials, and especially from King Agrippa. He hoped
that from this examination of Paul he would be able to formulate
definitely what he should send to the emperor. This was a compli-
ment to his other officials, and especially an act of courtesy toward
King Agrippa.

27 For it seemeth to me unreasonable,—It seemed ridiculous
to Festus to send a prisoner who had appealed his case to Rome

without informing the higher court of the charges that were made
against him. Festus hoped that the interview before Agrippa
would bring out some fresh facts which had been kept in the background; at least, he thought that the Roman official, King
Agrippa, who was more familiar with Jewish religion, would help
him to formulate what he should send to Caesar. It is remarkable
how much trouble a single humble man gave to the Jews and the
Roman courts.

5. PAUL BEFORE AGRIPPA
26: 1-32

1 And Agrippa said unto Paul, Thou art permitted to speak for thyself.
Then Paul stretched forth his hand, and made his defence:
2 I think myself happy, king Agrippa, that I am to make my defence
before thee this day touching all the things whereof I am accused by the

---

1 **And Agrippa said unto Paul,**—After Festus had introduced
the case, Agrippa seems to assume the chairmanship of the meeting; so he addressed Paul and told him that he was permitted to
speak for himself. Agrippa as a king and guest presides at the
grandest place. No charges are preferred against Paul; Festus
had admitted that he had no proof of any charges. When Paul
was granted the privilege of speaking for himself, he "stretched
forth his hand." This was the usual gesture for silence. Paul
now stood before the assembly as a prisoner, with one arm, probably his left arm, chained to the soldier who guarded him. A wide
contrast in earthly pomp and glory between Paul, an innocent prisoner in chains, and the royal robed court is here seen.

2 **I think myself happy, king Agrippa,**—Paul now makes
"his defence." It is not a "defence" in the strictest sense of that
word; Paul is only being examined that Festus may learn more
about him. Paul did not flatter King Agrippa when he said, "I
think myself happy," but was speaking courteously to the king.
He was glad of the opportunity to preach Christ. The accusations
which were made against him involved the gospel. It is only another opportunity for Paul to preach the gospel. Agrippa could
understand Paul in all his references to Jewish beliefs and hopes.
Paul's beginning in his defense before Felix (Acts 24: 10) was
adorned with courteous language.

Jews: 3 ⁷especially because thou art expert in all customs and questions which are among the Jews: wherefore I beseech thee to hear me patiently. 4 My manner of life then from my youth up, which was from the beginning among mine own nation and at Jerusalem, know all the Jews; 5 having knowledge of me from the first, if they be willing to testify, that after the straitest sect of our religion I lived a Pharisee. 6 And now I stand *here* to be judged for the hope of the promise made of God unto our fathers; 7 unto which *promise* our twelve tribes, earnestly serving *God* night and day,

---

⁷Or, *because thou art especially expert*

3 **especially because thou art expert in all customs**—Agrippa knew the Jewish religion; he knew the sects of Pharisees and Sadducees; he knew their expectations of a Messiah, their ceremonial laws; hence, he could hear Paul with patience and understanding. Paul's defense is divided into two divisions: (1) his early life which was well known as a Pharisee (Acts 22: 3; Gal. 1: 14; Phil. 3: 5, 6), and (2) his life as a prisoner. Agrippa II was especially fitted to act as judge, for he was not merely a ruler of Jewish lands, and the appointed guardian of the temple, but he was also in religion, professedly at least, a Jew. His father, Agrippa I, was famous for his rigid observance of Jewish rites.

4, 5 **My manner of life then from my youth up,**—Paul's early life in Tarsus and in Jerusalem was open and known to all. Here Paul emphasizes his training and beliefs before his conversion. It is thought that Paul went as a youth to Jerusalem from Tarsus to get his education. Since all the Jews knew of his early life they could testify, if they would, that Paul belonged to the sect of the Pharisees, and was very jealous of all the tenets of faith and practice of the Pharisees. "After the straitest sect" comes from the Greek "akribestaten hairesin," which is a superlative expression. Paul was most rigid and precise in his life as a Pharisee. The word for "sect" is the same as that used in Acts 24: 5, and is sometimes translated "heresy." "Religion" is from the Greek "threskeias," and is the old word for religious worship or discipline. Paul knew the rules of the Pharisees, and he lived rigidly according to these rules.

6, 7 **And now I stand here to be judged**—Thus far Agrippa could bear testimony to the truthfulness of all that Paul had said. It was his belief in the fulfillment of an old national hope that had brought him to the place that he now stands as a prisoner before

hope to attain. And concerning this hope I am accused by the Jews, O king! 8 Why is it judged incredible with you, if God doth raise the dead? 9 I verily thought with myself that I ought to do many things contrary to the name of Jesus of Nazareth. 10 And this I also did in Jerusalem: and I both

---

Agrippa. The Pharisees had firmly and persistently hoped in the promises of God that a Messianic kingdom would be established, and Paul in preaching Christ was declaring that that hope had been realized. It was a strange paradox! Paul was now a prisoner for the very thing which the Jews emphasized so strongly and believed so confidently, and now he was made a prisoner by the Jews themselves! Paul had made the resurrection of Christ the basis of his gospel of the Messianic kingdom, and this had enraged the Jews. Paul declared that Jesus, who had been crucified and buried, was now raised from the dead, but the Jews denied this. (Acts 25 : 19.)

8 **Why is it judged incredible with you,**—Paul turned suddenly from Agrippa to the audience. "Incredible" means "unfaithful" (Luke 12: 46), "faithless" (John 20: 27), or "unbelievable." It is from the Greek "apiston." The Greek shows that Paul is not only addressing Agrippa, but his audience. If God can or does raise the dead, why should anyone not believe that he has raised Jesus? If he has raised Jesus, has not the crucified One become the Christ? All that Paul had done was to preach that Jesus of Nazareth was the Messiah; he had preached that this Jesus had been crucified, buried, and raised from the dead, and that he was now at the right hand of God, reigning over his Messianic kingdom. Why should Agrippa and others not believe in him?

9 **I verily thought with myself**—Here Paul in his defense makes a turn to his conversion. His words express sympathy for those who are now as he was before his conversion; he had been led from unbelief to faith; he will not become discouraged even in Agrippa in a like transition. (1 Tim. 1: 12-17.) Paul did not reason himself into Christianity by a chain of arguments, but he was brought into the highest degree of faith in it from the highest degree of prejudice. Paul is politely saying that he could excuse them more readily, because he was then sincerely doing the same kind of wrong to others which he was suffering then as a prisoner.

shut up many of the saints in prisons, having received authority from the
chief priests, and when they were put to death I gave my vote against them.
11 And punishing them oftentimes in all the synagogues, I strove to make
them blaspheme; and being exceedingly mad against them, I persecuted them

---

10 **And this I also did in Jerusalem:**—Paul here relates some
incidents of his persecution of Christians before he was converted.
He was an official persecutor of the saints under the direction of
the Sanhedrin. He mentions "the chief priests," who were Sadducees, though he himself was a Pharisee. Both Pharisees and Sadducees were then joined in persecuting Christians. When they
were put to death, he says: "I gave my vote against them." The
Greek "katenegka psephon" literally means "I cast down my peb-
ble." The ancient Greeks used white pebbles for acquittal (Rev.
2: 17) and black ones for conviction or condemnation. They literally cast the pebbles into the urn. Many think from this that Paul
was a member of the Sanhedrin, and if a member of it, that he was
married at that time, as no one was permitted to be a member of the
Sanhedrin who was unmarried. It is possible to take this language
figuratively as meaning that he gave his approval; hence, he would
not be necessarily a member of the Sanhedrin. It seems more
likely that he was a member. We know that he was not married
when he wrote 1 Cor. 7: 7f. It is possible that he was a widower
at the time he wrote First Corinthians.

11 **And punishing them oftentimes**—Paul had no mercy on
Christians at that time. Paul describes very accurately his zeal in
persecuting Christians. He went from one synagogue to another
in Jerusalem searching for Christians that he might bring them before the proper authorities and punish them. Sometimes the local
Sanhedrin sat in the synagogues and were judges under Jewish
law; punishment was administered in the presence of the judges
and in the synagogues. (Matt. 10: 17; 23: 34; Mark 13: 9.) "I
strove to make them blaspheme" indicates that he was not successful in making them "blaspheme." He attempted to make them
"blaspheme" because the sentence of death was passed upon the one
who blasphemed. In his mad efforts to cause them to blaspheme
he used every means available. To "blaspheme" means to speak

even unto foreign cities. 12 ¹Whereupon as I journeyed to Damascus with the authority and commission of the chief priest, 13 at midday, O king, I saw on the way a light from heaven, above the brightness of the sun, shining round about me and them that journeyed with me. 14 And when we were all fallen to the earth, I heard a voice saying unto me in the Hebrew language,

¹Or, *On which errand*

---

against God, Christ, or the Holy Spirit. Christians did not yield and maintained their integrity before God. "Being exceedingly mad against them" means that Paul not only acted in ignorance (1 Tim. 1: 13), but that he might plead the temporary insanity of madness. He even went into strange cities, or "foreign cities," which means that he went into cities outside Judea, perhaps in Galilee and Samaria, and especially Damascus.

12, 13 **Whereupon as I journeyed to Damascus**—Paul was clothed with his official authority as he journeyed to one of these "foreign cities," Damascus. This is the third account in Acts of Paul's conversion; the other two accounts are found in chapters 9 and 22. In this third account of Paul's conversion some new details are introduced; they are as follows: (1) it was at midday (verse 13); (2) the light was "above the brightness of the sun" (verse 13); (3) this light enveloped not only Paul, but those "that journeyed with me" (verse 13); (4) the whole company fell to the earth (verse 14); (5) Jesus spoke "in the Hebrew language" (verse 14); (6) he said, "It is hard for thee to kick against the goad" (verse 14); and (7) a much fuller account of what Jesus said to him, and in particular how he commissioned him to preach to the Gentiles (verses 16, 18). The variations noted in the three records of his conversion impress us with the truthfulness of the narrative, because they are so natural as to be a certain accompaniment of the same story told at different times.

14 **And when we were all fallen to the earth,**—Paul and the entire company traveling with him were smitten to the earth, and Paul heard the voice of the Christ speaking to him in the Hebrew language, and asking him why he persecuted Christ. The voice quoted a proverb: "It is hard for thee to kick against the goad." This is found as a proverb in both Greek and Latin literature; some think that there was a similar proverb among the Hebrews. A reference to this proverb by Paul at this time would impress

Saul, Saul, why persecutest thou me? it is hard for thee to kick against ²the goad. 15 And I said, Who art thou, Lord? And the Lord said, I am Jesus whom thou persecutest. 16 But arise, and stand upon thy feet: for to this end have I appeared unto thee, to appoint thee a minister and a witness both of the things ³wherein thou hast seen me, and of the things wherein I will appear unto thee; 17 delivering thee from the people, and from the Gentiles,

---

²Gr. *goads*
³Many ancient authorities read *which thou hast seen*

---

upon Festus and Agrippa Paul's culture and education. This throws some light on the state of Paul's mind before his conversion. Some think that Paul was already stifling conscientious doubts and scruples, and that he is warned against rebelling against God's will and wounding his conscience the more deeply. The "goad" was a stick six or eight feet long. The plow had but one handle and the plowman held the plow with one hand and the goad in the other; it was carried horizontally and used to prod the ox to make him go faster or obey the plowman. If the ox kicked when pricked with the goad he received a severer prod.

15 And I said, Who art thou, Lord?—Here the record is brief; Saul simply asks who spoke to him, or "Who art thou, Lord?" The record of the answer of Jesus is equally brief; he simply says, "I am Jesus whom thou persecutest." The word "persecute" is the Latin "persequor," which means "to follow through or after." Paul was following the disciples of Jesus and punishing them; to persecute a disciple of Jesus is to persecute him.

16 But arise, and stand upon thy feet:—Paul had been cast down; now he is to be raised up; he was smitten down and humbled before God that he might be exalted. There was no occasion for Paul to be afraid; he is summoned to a new and nobler work. He is to cease his persecution of Christ and go preach him as the Savior of man. He was to become a witness for Christ both in what he had already seen and heard and what he was yet to see and hear. Paul was an apostle because Jesus had appeared to him, taught him, and commissioned him. (1 Cor. 9: 1; 15: 8.) Paul had other visions besides the one on the road to Damascus. (Acts 18: 9; 23: 11; 2 Cor. 12: 2.) Paul is here given a twofold mission: (1) he is to be "a minister," which meant a servant; the service was to proclaim remission of sins and an inheritance among

unto whom I send thee, 18 to open their eyes, ⁴that they may turn from darkness to light and from the power of Satan unto God, that they may receive remission of sins and an inheritance among them that are sanctified by faith in me. 19 Wherefore O king Agrippa, I was not disobedient unto the

⁴Or, *to turn them*

---

the saints to the Gentiles; (2) furthermore, he was to be "a witness"; that is, he was to testify what he had seen and heard. The witness oftentimes must go further than verbal testimony: he must suffer and perhaps die for Christ. "Witness" and "martyr" are represented by the same word in the Greek, "martures."

17, 18 delivering thee from the people,—"Delivering" is from the Greek "exairoumenos," which means both "to choose out, to select" one from many and also "to rescue, to deliver." Some commentators hold to one meaning here and others to the latter sense; even some have given it both meanings. It seems that the American Standard revisers have given it the correct meaning. It must have been an encouragement to Paul to recall the assurance given him; he could face the trials and persecution with the assurance that the Lord would "deliver" him from the enemy. We have here condensed what Jesus said to Saul: (1) as he lay on the ground; (2) by the mouth of Ananias; (3) and in the vision in the temple. Paul was commissioned to convince, enlighten, and instruct. By enlightening the people they could see their lost condition; by instructing them they would know how to "turn from darkness to light," and be delivered "from the power of Satan unto God"; they would then be cleansed of their sins and receive a promise of "an inheritance among them that are sanctified by faith" in Christ. "Satan" is from the Greek "satana," and means "adversary," the inveterate adversary of God and all good; Satan is the head of the kingdom of evil, and of the whole hierarchy of evil spirits and evil influences. (2 Cor. 11: 14; Eph. 1: 21; 6: 12; Col. 2: 15; 2 Thess. 2: 9.) Paul's recitation of these words of Jesus to him justifies himself before this cultured audience for his response to the command of Jesus, which resulted in Paul's arrest and imprisonment.

19, 20 Wherefore, O king Agrippa, I was not disobedient— Paul here makes a direct address to Agrippa. He had made it

heavenly vision: 20 but declared both to them of Damascus first, and at Jerusalem, and throughout all the country of Judaea, and also to the Gentiles, that they should repent and turn to God, doing works worthy of ⁵repentance, 21 For this cause the Jews seized me in the temple, and assayed to kill me.

⁵Or, *their repentance*

clear that his command had come from God, his message was a "heavenly vision." He emphasized the divinity and authority by which he was commanded; he omitted the personal affliction of blindness and restoration to sight. The divine authority of his command is made clear to Agrippa; this would impress Agrippa more than the others. For Paul to be disobedient to this command from heaven would have been disobedience to God. How could any devout Jew refuse to obey the command? Next Paul began to recite what he did; he began to declare "both to them of Damascus first, and at Jerusalem, and throughout all the country of Judaea, and also to the Gentiles" the gospel of God. This included a demand of faith in the Lord Jesus Christ, repentance of sins, and obedience in baptism. This sketch of Paul's work showed to Agrippa that he began with his own people, and then went to the Gentiles. His service both to Jew and Gentile, according to his commission, was promptly rendered; he did not hesitate for a moment, but began at once. We know from the record that Luke has given that it is easy to trace Paul's preaching at Damascus and Jerusalem. Barnabas testified that he preached boldly at Damascus in the name of Jesus (Acts 9: 27), and that in Jerusalem he disputed against the Grecian Jews (Acts 9: 28, 29), but we have some difficulty in fixing the exact date of his preaching throughout all the country of Judea. "Works worthy of repentance" is an expression frequently used by John the Baptist. (Matt. 3: 8.) This meant the natural fruit of true repentance.

21 **For this cause the Jews seized me**—Paul here tells Agrippa why he was arrested or seized by the Jews; first, because he went about preaching the gospel, and especially because he delivered the message to the Gentiles, as well as to the Jews, thereby proclaiming that the kingdom of the Messiah made no distinction on account of nationality. Paul's unpardonable sin in the eyes of the Jews was his preaching the gospel to the Gentiles. Paul had

22 Having therefore obtained the help that is from God, I stand unto this day testifying both to small and great, saying nothing but what the prophets and Moses did say should come; 23 ⁶how that the Christ ⁷must suffer, *and* ⁶how that he first by the resurrection of the dead should proclaim light both to the people and to the Gentiles.

⁶Or, *if* Or, *whether*
⁷Or, *is subject to suffering*

been seized violently and illegally; he had been retained as a prisoner without cause; he now stood before Agrippa in chains as a prisoner for obeying God.

22 Having therefore obtained the help—Paul attributed the help that he had obtained from God as the source of his strength to continue suffering for Christ Jesus. The divine assistance enabled him to continue his work. The same source from which his commission had come was the source of his help. The memories of the stoning which he had received at Lystra, the persecutions of Philippi, Corinth, and Thessalonica, the danger in the theatre of Ephesus, and the later deadly perils at Jerusalem, all were endured by the help that was from Jehovah. Paul did not regard rank or age; he preached the gospel "both to small and great." He had preached the gospel to the poor, and now he was preaching it to King Agrippa and Governor Festus and the nobility of Caesarea. He had not gone beyond "what the prophets and Moses did say should come." He neither added to nor left off anything that had been said through Moses and the prophets.

23 how that the Christ must suffer,—The prophets had foretold the sufferings that Christ would endure; some give the interpretation of "must suffer" to mean that there was no escape of Christ from suffering, others give this the meaning of his nature as to how he may suffer; that is, the degree of sufferings that he could endure. When John the Baptist called Jesus "the Lamb of God," it was a new idea to those who had studied Isaiah and learned that the Messiah would be the suffering "servant" of God. Paul here showed two things: (1) that the Messiah was divinely destined to suffer; and (2) that the Messiah having suffered was the first fruits of the resurrection of the dead. Christ having been raised from the dead would proclaim light to the Jewish people and

24 And as he thus made his defence, Festus saith with a loud voice, Paul, thou art mad; thy much learning [8]is turning thee mad. 25 But Paul saith, I am not mad, most excellent Festus; but speak forth words of truth and soberness. 26 For the king knoweth of these things, unto whom also I speak freely: for I am persuaded that none of these things is hidden from him; for

[8]Gr. *turneth thee to madness*

---

to the Gentiles. "People" usually means God's people, Israel, as distinguished from the heathen.

24 And as he thus made his defence,—At this point Paul was rudely interrupted by Festus; it seems that he forgot the usual dignity of his office and burst out into a loud laugh of scorn and said: "Paul, thou art mad; thy much learning is turning thee mad." "Mad" is from the Greek "mainei," which means "raving." Festus did not understand Paul's enthusiasm and his speaking of visions and the resurrection of the dead. He thought that Paul's "much learning" was turning him to madness. "Much learning" literally means "many letters." (John 7: 15.) Our word "mania," or "maniac," comes from the Greek "manei." Paul had not displayed any high degree of learning, but what he had said was beyond the comprehension of Festus.

25 But Paul saith, I am not mad,—Paul was not "mad"; he was not a "maniac" as Festus declared, but spoke the truth. He spoke words of truth and not vain imaginations or fancies; he had no disease of the mind; his words were well chosen and expressed accurately what he had seen, heard, and experienced. Paul addressed Festus with his usual courtesy. He had not spoken words of fancy, but solid facts; not wild flight of the imagination, but literal and exact truth.

26 For the king knoweth of these things,—Festus did not understand, but King Agrippa understood. Agrippa was a Jew by practice, and knew about the hopes that the nation had in a coming Messiah; he knew something of the predictions of the prophets. He had heard much about Paul; hence, he understood Paul. Paul knew that his manner of life before his conversion and after his conversion was known to the public; furthermore, he knew that the crucifixion and burial and resurrection of Christ were public facts. Christians did not try to keep them secret, but published them to the world. The Jews had attempted to stop the preaching

this hath not been done in a corner. 27 King Agrippa, believest thou the prophets? I know that thou believest. 28 And Agrippa *said* unto Paul, ⁹With but little persuasion thou wouldest fain make me a Christian. 29 And

⁹Or, *In a little* time *thou &c.*

---

of these facts, but had failed to do so. Paul's experiences were not kept secret either; his vision on the road to Damascus, his coming to Jerusalem, and all that he had done had been published. Agrippa knew all these things. After answering Festus, Paul turned and continued his address to Agrippa.

27 **King Agrippa, believest thou the prophets?**—Paul had "cornered" Agrippa; he makes this direct appeal to Agrippa. As a professor of the Jewish religion Agrippa had accepted the prophets; hence, Paul's direct challenge to him. He must now reject the prophets or believe Paul. He must give up the Jewish religion or believe what Paul had preached. Paul probes the heart of Agrippa a little deeper when he added: "I know that thou believest." There was nothing left now for Agrippa but to believe what Paul had preached or to reject it. To reject it would be to reject the prophets and the Jewish religion. Agrippa might dispute Paul's interpretation of prophecy, but he could not as a Jew and in the presence of a Jew speak of Paul as Festus had.

28 **And Agrippa said unto Paul,**—Agrippa is forced to make reply; he could not evade; neither could he deny what Paul had said. Paul had not accused his enemies of any crime. His "defence" was the preaching of the gospel; he did not plead for himself, but reasoned and persuaded Agrippa to accept Christ. What a turn affairs had taken! The Authorized Version has Agrippa saying: "Almost thou persuadest me to be a Christian." "En oligio" does not mean "almost," but it is not clear as to what it does mean. Some think that it may refer to "time," "in little time," while others think that it means "with small effort you are trying to persuade me to be a Christian"; while still others think that Agrippa is speaking ironically, but not unpleasantly. He seems to push it aside for the time being, as if to say: "Do you think that you can make me become a Christian by your speech making?" Festus was contemptuously ignorant; King Agrippa was sadly indifferent. "Christian" is here used the second time by Luke. The

Paul *said,* I would to God, that [10]whether with little or with much, not thou only, but also all that hear me this day, might become such as I am, except these bonds.

30 And the king rose up, and the governor, and Bernice, and they that sat with them: 31 and when they had withdrawn, they spake one to another,

[10]Or, *both in little and in great,* i.e., in all respects

---

first time is in Acts 11: 26. There were many reasons for hindrances in the way of Agrippa's becoming a Christian. His wealth, his throne, his companion, his associations with Bernice and others, all were hindrances in becoming a Christian. Perhaps his nature was touched and he was, like Felix, made to tremble; but also like Felix, he procrastinated, with no intention ever to accept the Christ.

29 **And Paul said, I would to God,**—Paul makes a very happy response to Agrippa. We can gather some from Paul's answer as to what Agrippa meant. If Agrippa spoke ironically or sarcastically, Paul ignored his tone and responded courteously and sympathetically. "Whether with little or with much" may be translated "both in little and in great"; it may mean that Paul says: "I would pray to God, not as you put it, lightly, but as fully as I can," or "I would pray to God that whether persuaded with little evidence or much," or I would pray to God that "both in a little measure and in a great measure" Agrippa might become a Christian. He desired that Agrippa become as he was "except these bonds." He would have Agrippa and all others be Christians, but would have them free from the persecution and bonds which he had to endure. Paul had been brought before the assembly chained after the Roman fashion to a soldier or soldiers who kept guard over him. These chains had not been removed while Paul made his "defence." Paul was bound in chains, but Agrippa and the others were in the bonds of ignorance, bonds of sin, and bonds of imperfection.

30, 31 **And the king rose up, and the governor,**—The entire company led by King Agrippa "rose up" as if to dismiss Paul's address. The royal assembly had gathered with pomp; some of them may have been moved with curiosity; others to do honor to King Agrippa; but they withdrew—some of them hopelessly ignorant of what they had heard; others withdrew with indifference, and possibly tired of listening to Paul; still others with some conviction and a clearer understanding of Paul's case. When they had re-

saying, This man doeth nothing worthy of death or of bonds.   32 And
Agrippa said unto Festus, This man might have been set at liberty, if he had
not appealed unto Caesar.

---

tired, "they spake one to another," and expressed themselves as
being convinced that Paul had done "nothing worthy of death or of
bonds." They may have assembled with different motives and
viewpoints, but they are all agreed on this one thing; namely, Paul
is innocent.   Paul's words had made a favorable impression on
them.   However, they were all puzzled as to what disposition to
make of Paul's case.   Paul had won none of them to Christ, but he
had won their favor.   Festus was left by their confusion in the
same predicament that he was before Paul made his "defence."
Why did they not set him free?

32 **And Agrippa said unto Festus,**—This answers why Paul
had not been set free.   Agrippa told Festus that Paul could have
been set free "if he had not appealed unto Caesar."   Paul had appealed to Caesar *only* because Festus had tried to get him to go to
Jerusalem and be tried there.   Festus comes out with no honor in
the case.   Since Agrippa had some influence with Caesar, it may
be that Festus could write something favorable to Paul when sending him to Rome.   The authorities could not free themselves from
the responsibility for the safe custody of Paul, and by releasing
him, they would expose his life to the conspiracies of the Jews.   So
at least Paul gained that safe journey to Rome which he had for
many years been wishing to make.

SECTION SEVEN

PAUL'S VOYAGE TO ROME
27 : 1 to 28 : 10

1. FROM CAESAREA TO CRETE
27 : 1-12

1 And when it was determined that we should sail for Italy, they delivered Paul and certain other prisoners to a centurion named Julius, of the
Augustan [11]band. 2 And embarking in a ship of Adramyttium, which was
about to sail unto the places on the coast of Asia, we put to sea, Aristarchus,

---

[11]Or, *cohort*

---

1 **And when it was determined that we should sail for Italy,**
—We do not know how long Paul remained in Caesarea as a prisoner; it seems that there had been some doubt whether he was to
be sent to "Italy." The time for sailing was now fixed. Luke and
Aristarchus are now with Paul and are included in the "we" of this
verse. Some think that Luke was allowed to go as an attendant or
slave of Paul; this was permissible under Roman law. It is possible that Luke was not with Paul during his trials before Felix, Festus, and Agrippa. The details and minute accuracy of Luke's account of this voyage and shipwreck reveal more about the ancient
seafaring than may be read in other literature. "Other prisoners"
and "a centurion named Julius" were with Paul. It is to be noted
that Paul is classed with other prisoners. The Julian house, like
the Cornelian (Acts 10: 1), was an illustrious one in Italy.
Julius, like other centurions mentioned in the New Testament
(Matt. 8: 5; Mark 15: 39; Acts 10: 1), commands our respect.
"The Augustan band," or "cohort," is thought to have been a
corps of legionary centurions; the Augustan band may have been
an independent cohort assigned to that particular service, and
known as the Augustan or Imperial, because it corresponded in
some sense to the emperor's lifeguard at Rome.

2 **And embarking in a ship of Adramyttium,**—Paul's voyage
to Rome and the shipwreck as recorded in this chapter may be divided as follows :

a Macedonian of Thessalonica, being with us. 3 And the next day we touched at Sidon: and Julius treated Paul kindly, and gave him leave to go unto his friends and ¹refresh himself. 4 And putting to sea from thence, we

¹Gr. *receive attention*

---

(1) In the Ship of Adramyttium, verses 1-5.	The company on board. From Caesarea to Sidon. Along the coast of Cyprus. To Myra in Lycia.
(2) In the Ship of Alexandria, verses 6-12.	From Myra to Crete. To the port of Fair Havens in Crete. Paul's advice to the captain. They sail for the port of Phoenix in Crete.
(3) The Storm, verses 13-29.	The hurricane. Undergirding the ship. Lightening the ship. Paul's vision brings cheer to all. Nearing an unknown shore. Casting anchor. Night.
(4) The Shipwreck, verses 30-44.	The sailors attempt to desert the ship. Paul persuades the company to eat and be of good courage. They cast the wheat cargo overboard. Morning. They make for the shore. The wreck. All escape to the shore of Malta.

"Ship of Adramyttium" was a ship belonging to Adramyttium, a seaport of Mysia, on the western coast of Asia Minor, probably on its return journey from Caesarea. "Aristarchus, a Macedonian of Thessalonica," accompanied them. He is mentioned in Acts 19: 29; 20: 4; Col. 4: 10; Phile. 24.

3 **And the next day we touched at Sidon:**—This was probably in August A.D. 59 or 60. Sidon was sixty-seven miles from Caesarea; it was the rival of Tyre. The ship stopped here for trade. Julius was very kind to Paul and permitted him to leave the ship and visit for a while with "his friends and refresh himself." It may be that he had received orders from Festus and Agrippa to treat Paul courteously. At any rate, he was very kind to Paul and granted him favors that other prisoners did not receive. Paul had time to receive some personal comforts and clothing for the voyage. After two years in prison at Caesarea we may well believe that such things would be needed and acceptable to Paul.

sailed under the lee of Cyprus, because the winds were contrary. 5 And
when we had sailed across the sea which is off Cilicia and Pamphylia, we
came to Myra, *a city* of Lycia.   6 And there the centurion found a ship of
Alexandria sailing for Italy; and he put us therein. 7 And when we had

---

4 **And putting to sea from thence,**—The ship remained at
Sidon long enough to transact some business, which gave Paul
some time with his friends. They sailed from Sidon "under the lee
of Cyprus," which direction was northward along the coast, and by
the east side of Cyprus past the northeast point of that island.
Cyprus was thus on the left between the ship and the wind from
the northwest. The Estesian winds were blowing from the northwest so that they could not go straight across from Sidon to Patara with Cyprus on the right. "Lee" is the side sheltered from
the wind.

5 **And when we had sailed across the sea**—The winds seem
to have driven them farther north than the direct course which
they should have followed. They sailed across the sea "which is
off Cilicia and Pamphylia." The current runs westward along the
coast of Cilicia and Pamphylia and the land would protect them
from the wind. The ship came to Myra, "a city of Lycia." Myra
was about two and a half miles from the coast of Lycia; it was
near the mouth of the river Andriacus; Myra was at one time the
metropolis of Lycia. Lycia is a province joining Pamphylia on the
west. It is thought that the ship spent fifteen days struggling
along the Pamphylian coast.

6 **And there the centurion found a ship of Alexandria**—This
ship was from Alexandria in North Africa; it was bound directly
for Italy with a cargo of wheat on board and two hundred seventy-six passengers. It is thought to have been one of the fleet of
grain ships in use to carry wheat from Egypt to Italy. It must
have been driven out of its direct course by the wind. The Alexandrian ships were very large; the vessel was steered, not by a rud-
der, but by two broad oars, one on each side of the stern. The
rig consisted of one, or more than one, large square sail; flags
floated from the top of the mast, as in modern vessels. The ancients had no compass, and all charts and instruments were very
imperfect. This rig was specially favorable for running with the
wind, but they could sail within seven points of the wind; they

sailed slowly many days, and were come with difficulty over against Cnidus, the wind not [2]further suffering us, we sailed under the lee of Crete, over against Salmone; 8 and with difficulty coasting along it we came unto a certain place called Fair Havens; nigh whereunto was the city of Lasea.

9 And when much time was spent, and the voyage was now dangerous,

[2]Or, *suffering us to get there*

could make about seven knots an hour. A "knot" is a nautical mile, or 6,085 feet; hence, it would sail about 8.5 miles. These merchant ships were very large and could carry ten or eleven hundred tons; Josephus states that the ship in which he was wrecked had six hundred persons on board. The centurion transferred his prisoners to this ship.

7 **And when we had sailed slowly many days,**—The ship was large and heavy laden; the wind was contrary and they made very slow progress for many days. The prevailing wind was northwest, which was contrary to their course; hence, the ship worked slowly along from Myra to Cnidus. The distance from Myra to Cnidus is about one hundred thirty miles, but it seems that they were two or three weeks in making the journey on account of the strong westerly winds. The general direction of the coast till they reached Cnidus was westward. The ship was protected from the north by the land, but was open to head winds from the west, against which they struggled slowly on. The ship on leaving Cnidus seems to have turned southwest and "sailed under the lee of Crete, over against Salmone." Salmone was at the eastward end of the island of Crete; here they turned westward again and were protected from the northerly winds by the island of Crete; they sailed along the southern coast of Crete.

8 **and with difficulty coasting along**—They sailed along westward, protected by the island of Crete until they came to a place "called Fair Havens." "Fair Havens" is on the south coast of Crete; it lies a few miles east of Cape Matala, beyond which the coast suddenly trends to the north. "Lasea," the ruins of which were discovered in 1856, was about two hours' walk from Fair Havens. Fair Havens and Lasea are not mentioned by any writer except Luke.

9 **And when much time was spent,**—Much time was spent at Fair Havens waiting for favorable weather or making arrange-

because the Fast was now already gone by, Paul admonished them, 10 and said unto them, Sirs, I perceive that the voyage will be with injury and much loss, not only of the lading and the ship, but also of our lives. 11 But the centurion gave more heed to the master and to the owner of the ship, than to those things which were spoken by Paul. 12 And because the haven

---

ments for the continuation of the journey. "The voyage was now dangerous," and Luke adds, "because the Fast was now already gone by." The ancient considered navigation on the Mediterranean unsafe from early October until the middle of March; the most dangerous season was from the middle of September to the middle of November. Navigation on the open sea was discontinued during that season. In A.D. 59 the "Fast" occurred on October 5. The great Day of Atonement, as fixed by the law of Moses, occurred on the tenth day of Tisri (September-October). (Lev. 16: 29; 23: 27; Num. 29: 7.) It is not certain whether this was A.D. 59 or A.D. 60. In A.D. 60 the "Fast" occurred on September 23. Since Paul and his companions were accustomed to reckoning time from the Day of Atonement, it is natural for Luke, who traveled with Paul, to mention this "Fast." "Paul admonished them" of the great danger, but it seems that they did not heed his admonition.

10 **and said unto them, Sirs, I perceive**—Paul warned the captain and centurion and others that "the voyage" would not only be dangerous, but "with injury and much loss." Some think that a consultation was held whether they should remain in the harbor, which lay open to many winds, though sheltered from the northwest, or try to get to the safe harbor of Phoenix at the western end of the island. Paul had warned them that there would be much loss of property and lives if they continued at this time. It seems that they did not heed Paul's warning; the centurion was in charge of the soldiers.

11 **But the centurion gave more heed to the master**—It is natural that the centurion who had charge of the soldiers would give more heed to what the captain and owner of the ship would say than to what a prisoner would say. The centurion was responsible for the soldiers, the prisoner, and the cargo of wheat; it was thought that this was a government ship. "Master" is from the Greek "kubernetei," and means the steersman, pilot, sailing

was not commodious to winter in, the more part advised to put to sea from thence, if by any means they could reach Phoenix, and winter *there; which is* a haven of Crete, looking ³north-east and south-east. 13 And when the

³Gr. *down the south-west wind and down the north-west wind*

master. The centurion could not risk the criticism that would come upon him if he followed a prisoner's advice rather than those who controlled the vessel.

12 **And because the haven was not commodious**—It seems that a conference was held with those in control as to what should be done. Luke gives Paul's advice on the matter, and then states that there was division in judgment of the crew. The majority who advised the attempt to reach Phoenix were by no means sure that it would be successful—all were doubtful because of the present condition. Phoenix was a harbor in the south of Crete west from Fair Havens; it is said to be a safe harbor in winter, well closed in from the wind and from breakers; the harbor looked toward the east, or "looking north-east and south-east." There are two ways of interpreting the Greek; one is looking southwest and northwest, and the other is "looking north-east and south-east." It depends on the viewpoint from which one observed the harbor. If one is on the land and looks toward the harbor, the direction will be "north-east and south-east," but if one is in the harbor and looking toward the land, it will be southwest and northwest. The better interpretation is as the Revised Version has it.

2. THE STORM AND SHIPWRECK
27 : 13-44

south wind blew softly, supposing that they had obtained their purpose, they weighed anchor and sailed along Crete, close in shore. 14 But after no long

13 **And when the south wind blew softly,**—While in Fair Havens the stormy northwest wind ceased; a gentle breeze came from the south; they set sail for the harbor of Phoenix; they meant to keep close to the shore of Crete as it was safer. Phoenix was about forty miles west of Fair Havens on the southern shore of Crete. It was natural to hope that the south wind would continue long enough for them to sail the forty miles, as it would take but a few hours for the voyage. They were so sure that they did

time there beat down from it a tempestuous wind, which is called Euraquilo:
15 and when the ship was caught, and could not face the wind, we gave way
to it, and were driven. 16 And running under the lee of a small island called
⁴Cauda, we were able, with difficulty, to secure the boat: 17 and when they
had hoisted it up, they used helps, under-girding the ship; and, fearing lest

⁴Many ancient authorities read *Clauda*

not even take up the boat that they were towing behind the ship;
they took up anchor and sailed close to shore around Cape Matala,
a point on the south side of Crete a few miles west of Fair Havens.

14 **But after no long time**—In a short time after they set sail a
violent northeast wind came down on the ship from over the hills of
Crete and they could not face it, and had to go before it. This
"tempestuous wind" "is called Euraquilo." "Euraquilo" describes
the character of the wind; it comes from the Greek "Eurakulon,"
and is not found anywhere else in the New Testament; it has been
called a "hybrid" compounded of the Greek "euros," meaning
"east wind," and the Latin "aquilo," meaning "northeast." The
name here gives the direction of the wind.

15 **and when the ship was caught,**—The wind was so violent
that the ship was unable to face it and go further but had to yield
to the wind and be driven in its direction. The wind here is
represented as seizing the ship so that it was not able to look in the
eye of the wind; that is, to face it, and suddenly changed its course
to the direction that the gale was going; the ship scudded before
the wind.

16 **And running under the lee of a small island**—The ship
was forced to run "under the lee" for protection there; a small island named "Cauda," or "Clauda," furnished the protection.
Cauda was about twenty-three miles to the southwest of Crete.
The ancients towed a small vessel behind, and it was very difficult
to get this small vessel aboard. They were about to lose it. Luke
uses the pronoun "we" which indicates that the passengers as well
as the sailors were forced to work and help rescue the small boat;
it had to be lifted on board the ship. Their future safety depended
on their saving this boat.

17 **and when they had hoisted it up,**—An ancient ship with
sails was exposed to extreme dangers from such bursts of wind; the
straining of the great sail on a single mast was more than the hull

they should be cast upon the Syrtis, they lowered the gear, and so were driven. 18 And as we labored exceedingly with the storm, the next day they began to throw *the freight* overboard; 19 and the third day they cast out with their own hands the ⁵tackling of the ship. 20 And when neither sun nor stars shone upon *us* for many days, and no small tempest lay on *us,* all hope

---

⁵Or, *furniture*

---

could bear, and the ship was exposed to the storm and in danger of foundering in the open sea. Hence, "under-girding," with ropes or chains passing around the vessel, would help to hold the ship intact. Next they lowered all the sails, fearing that the gale might drive them southwest upon the "Syrtis," which meant the great African quicksands. The greater and lesser "Syrtis" were on the north coast of Africa; the one was west of Cyrene, and the other near Carthage; they were the dread of Mediterranean sailors in Roman times. This verse does not imply that the ship was then near the Syrtis; the greater Syrtis is here meant. After making this preparation by girding the ship and lowering the sail, they let the vessel drift.

18, 19 **And as we labored exceedingly with the storm,**—As the storm grew more furious the experienced sailors saw that the ship would not be able to weather it; hence, they put everyone to work. They labored with the storm the first day, and the second day they began to throw part of the cargo overboard. It is to be remembered that the ship was laden with wheat bound for Italy. The sailors and soldiers "with their own hands" on the third day threw overboard "the tackling of the ship." "Tackling" is from the Greek "skeuen," which means the furniture of the ship that could be spared. The danger was more imminent, and a part of the ship's gear would not have been thrown overboard without urgent necessity. The danger was great and increasing every moment; they had now disposed of the cargo of wheat and must suffer the loss of the furniture or equipment of the ship. The "tackling" which they threw overboard must refer to that furniture which would be useless in time of storm.

20 **And when neither sun nor stars shone**—The weather was so cloudy, and the storm so furious and continued so long that the danger increased hourly. It should be remembered that the great

that we should be saved was now taken away. 21 And when they had been long without food, then Paul stood forth in the midst of them and said, Sirs, ye should have hearkened unto me, and not have set sail from Crete, and have gotten this injury and loss. 22 And now I exhort you to be of good

reason which made ancient navigation perilous in winter was that the sky is then more overcast than at other seasons. They did not have efficient compass and were to large extent dependent upon the sun and stars for their bearings and steerings when the compass was not available. "All hope" of rescue was lost. Two stages in the progress of increasing fear have been mentioned; the third stage was absolute despair. It was at this psychological moment, when no escape through human agency was possible, that Paul interposed with divine encouragement. They did not know where they were drifting; no land was in sight; the ship was strained and possibly leaking; the tempest was high; and "all hope that we should be saved was now taken away."

21 **And when they had been long without food,**—Another thing which increased the hardship during this emergency was the lack of regular food. The fires were put out; the provisions were soaked with water; every effort that could be suggested for safety of the lives and ship was made. In the midst of the storm, when gloom and despair had settled heavily upon all, Paul stood in their midst and said: "Sirs, ye should have hearkened unto me, and not have set sail from Crete." He did not remind them of this in order to taunt them, but chiefly to impress them more forcibly with the counsel which he was now about to give. Paul interfered four times, twice unsuccessfully and twice successfully; he spoke twice from his own experience and good judgment; he spoke twice to tell his vision which promised them safety in the end. (See verses 10, 21-26, 31, 33-35.) Paul had advised them to winter in Fair Havens; his advice was discussed, but rejected. Paul was the only one who was calm and able to encourage the others by his message from God; he was the only one who could encourage them not to give way to despair, but keep up their strength for what was before them; Paul alone had the presence of mind to prevent the escape of the sailors.

cheer; for there shall be no loss of life among you, but *only* of the ship. 23
For there stood by me this night an angel of the God whose I am, whom
also I serve, 24 saying, Fear not, Paul; thou must stand before Caesar: and
lo, God hath granted thee all them that sail with thee. 25 Wherefore, sirs,
be of good cheer: for I believe God, that it shall be even so as it hath been

22 **And now I exhort you to be of good cheer;**—Paul, a prisoner, assumes authority to give advice and encourage the company.
No doubt Paul's look and tone of voice helped his words to give
encouragement to those in despair. It was unusual for a man,
even a prisoner, to stand in the midst of a scene of misery and
dejection with such calm confidence as Paul portrayed. Paul assured them that there would "be no loss of life among" them; he
added that the only loss that would be sustained was the ship. No
doubt that they were greatly encouraged when he gave the ground
or basis of his encouragement.

23 **For there stood by me this night an angel**—Paul gave
further reason for their taking courage; he recited his vision that
night. Paul was a servant of God; he had committed his life to
God and was in his care; hence, he was cheerful when others were
disturbed, trustful when others doubted. Paul had seen an angel
of God, and this angel had given courage to him. He now gives
God the honor for his courage and assurance; he did not take any
credit to himself as being wiser than others; he only pointed them
to the God whom he served as being able to take care of him and
others.

24 **saying, Fear not, Paul;**—This angel assured Paul that he
should "stand before Caesar." Paul had been praying, and the
angel came in answer to his prayer, and gave him the courage that
he now manifested. "God hath granted thee all them that sail with
thee" shows that Paul had been praying, not only for himself and
his Christian companions, but also for all on the ship. The lives of
those that sailed with Paul had been presented to him as a gift.
Since Paul was to stand before Caesar that meant that he would be
brought safely through the present danger. There is no assurance
here that all would become converted; only the safe arrival of all is
meant.

25, 26 **Wherefore, sirs, be of good cheer:**—The faith that
Paul had in God gave him an advantage over the others; he was

spoken unto me. 26 But we must be cast upon a certain island.
    27 But when the fourteenth night was come, as we were driven to and fro in the *sea of* Adria, about midnight the sailors surmised that they were drawing near to some country: 28 and they sounded, and found twenty fathoms; and after a little space, they sounded again, and found fifteen fathoms.

---

made both captain and pilot of the ship; his calmness and courage enabled him to take the place of the centurion in caring for the prisoners. The most useful man on board was Paul, because he believed in God and God took care of him. Paul spoke with assurance when he warned them that they should be "cast upon a certain island." It is very probable that Paul preached the gospel to all that were on the ship, and gave them his reason for believing in God. Since he predicted that they would be cast upon a certain island, it appears that some details of the manner of their preservation had been made known to Paul by the angel.

    27 **But when the fourteenth night was come,**—It is not clear as to the point of time that the "fourteenth night" is calculated; it is very probable that the time is reckoned from their leaving Fair Havens. The ship was driven "to and fro in the sea of Adria." "Adria" was a name given to the wide sweep of the Mediterranean lying between Greece, Italy, and Africa; this was not the Adriatic Sea as we now know it. "About midnight the sailors" thought that "they were drawing near to some country." Possibly the sound of the breakers, the white lines of foam seen through the darkness, were interpreted by the experienced sailors that they were drawing nigh to land. They did not know their location; hence, they did not know the country or land that they might be near; they were in total darkness and lost on the wild tempest of waters.

    28 **and they sounded, and found twenty fathoms;**— "Sounded" is from the Greek "bolisantes," and is apparently from "bolis," which means "a missile or dart," and hence to throw down the lead into the sea, to heave the lead, to take soundings. A "fathom" is reckoned as six feet; hence, the depth of the water at that point was one hundred twenty feet; however, "after a little space," or "a little later," they "sounded" again, and found the depth to be only "fifteen fathoms," or about ninety feet; this was

29 And fearing lest haply we should be cast ashore on rocky ground, they let go four anchors from the stern, and ¹wished for the day. 30 And as the sailors were seeking to flee out of the ship, and had lowered the boat into the sea, under color as though they would lay out anchors from the foreship, 31 Paul said to the centurion and to the soldiers, Except these abide in the ship,

---

¹Or, *prayed*

---

proof that a shore was near; they did not know what kind of shore, whether it was sandy or rocky; they feared that it was rocky.

29 And fearing lest haply we should be cast ashore—There was great fear that the ship would be cast upon a rocky shore; hence, "they let go four anchors from the stern." These "four anchors" should be sufficient to hold the ship in position; however, it was unusual to anchor the ship from the "stern." The usual way of anchoring a ship was from the bow. In this situation, had they anchored by the bow, the ship would have swung round from the wind and would have been more difficult to manage after the storm ceased. The harbor of St. Paul's Bay, in Malta, is still good for small ships. The ship had been drifting since it left Cauda. It is about four hundred seventy-six miles from Cauda to Malta. The only thing that they could do would be to wait for daylight. If the sailors had headed the ship toward the northwest to keep it from being driven upon the quicksands, it would have been beaten back by the northeast gale and would have drifted westward.

30 And as the sailors were seeking to flee—The hour of danger naturally aroused the instinct of self-preservation to the exclusion of better feelings. It was easy for the sailors to urge that the ship needed anchors fore as well as aft, and, while pretending to be occupied about this, to lower the boat which they had before hoisted on deck (verse 16), and so effect their escape. The boat, it might appear, was necessary to their purpose, as their aim was not merely to pass anchors from the bow, but to carry them out to the full tether of the cable's length. This was a treacherous act on the part of the sailors.

31 Paul said to the centurion and to the soldiers,—The shrewd observance of Paul detected what the sailors were doing, and he spoke to the centurion, and to the soldiers. He said: "Except these abide in the ship, ye cannot be saved." Paul had the

ye cannot be saved. 32 Then the soldiers cut away the ropes of the boat,
and let her fall off. 33 And while the day was coming on, Paul besought
them all to take some food, saying, This day is the fourteenth day that ye
wait and continue fasting, having taken nothing. 34 Wherefore I beseech

---

courage to rebuke their action and to warn them of the danger of
such a course. He had been assured of protection and safety by
the angel of the Lord, but he could not supinely lie down and leave
it all to God; he must do all that he could in order to be protected
by God. The soldiers and prisoners could not handle the large
ship under such critical conditions, so the presence and help of the
sailors were essential to the safety of others. All should have been
grateful to Paul for his thoughtful vigilance in these hours of darkness and danger.

32 **Then the soldiers cut away the ropes**—Apparently there
were four classes on board the ship; namely (1) the officials, including captain, pilot, and centurion; (2) sailors; (3) soldiers;
(4) prisoners. The sailors were attempting to flee, and when the
soldiers heard what Paul had said they cut the rope by which the
small ship had been lowered and let it fall off; this prevented the
sailors from escaping. The soldiers settled the question with military promptitude. The boat was left to drift off into the darkness
and perhaps was dashed to pieces on the rocks. God had promised
Paul that all should be saved; hence, he insists that all cooperate
harmoniously in order to fulfill that promise.

33 **And while the day was coming on,**—While they were
waiting for day to dawn, Paul again assumes the lead and takes
command and "besought them all to take some food." Nothing
could be done in the emergency until daylight; sleep was impossible; and anxiety and fear intense. Paul advised that since they
had been fasting about fourteen days some food be taken. He
knew that strength would be needed for hard work when morning
came; he also knew that if they would take nourishment they
would be encouraged for further duties. Soldiers and sailors would
need something that would draw them together after the incident
just mentioned; all were liable to be discouraged and irritable. It
is not clear whether the waiting means fourteen days of continuous
fasting, or only fourteen successive nights of eager watching without food. Paul probably means that they had taken no regular

you to take some food: for this is for your safety: for there shall not a hair perish from the head of any of you. 35 And when he had said this, and had taken bread, he gave thanks to God in the presence of all; and he brake it, and began to eat. 36 Then were they all of good cheer, and themselves also took

meals, and only bits of food now and then, as the word for "fasting" is not that which is commonly used in the New Testament to express entire abstinence from food.

34 **Wherefore I beseech you to take some food:**—Paul encouraged all of them "to take some food." Paul had promised them their lives, but they must work and cooperate with him for their safety. Paul, a captive going to judgment, yet what a leader of men he is! It was necessary that they take nourishment for their "safety." The Greek for "safety" is "soteria," which means personal or physical "safety," and not spiritual salvation. Paul meant that the preservation of his fellow passengers depended on their keeping up their strength. He reassures them that "not a hair" should "perish from the head of any of" them. This is a proverbial expression for safety. (1 Sam. 14: 45; 2 Sam. 14: 11; 1 Kings 1: 52; Luke 21: 18.)

35 **And when he had said this,**—Paul had given advice that they take some nourishment; he now sets the example by taking nourishment himself. Some have said that this was the Lord's Supper to Paul, Luke, and Aristarchus; however, it appears to be only a common meal, as Paul had encouraged all to take nourishment. The Lord's Supper was never intended to furnish physical nourishment to anyone. Paul "gave thanks to God" and then began to eat. "Thanks" is from the Greek "eucharistesen," and means giving thanks, as did our Lord on different occasions. (Luke 24: 30.)

36 **Then were they all of good cheer,**—Paul's words and example inspired cheerfulness and courage. It is wonderful how one calm, deliberate person can have such influence on others. The cheerfulness and hopefulness of Paul had spread to the entire company; they now looked to him as their friend and leader, and followed his example in eating. The giving of thanks to God called attention again of all to God, whom Paul served, and who had protected them and promised safety to them.

food. 37 And we were in all in the ship two hundred threescore and sixteen souls. 38 And when they had eaten enough, they lightened the ship, throwing out the wheat into the sea. 3 And when it was day, they knew not the land: but they perceived a certain bay with a beach, and they took counsel whether they could ²drive the ship upon it. 40 And casting off the anchors,

²Some ancient authorities read *bring the ship safe to shore*

37 **And we were in all in the ship**—The number is here given, either as a fact that had been omitted before, and was not without its interest, or probably because then for the first time, they were all gathered at their meal. Luke, the writer, had taken the trouble to count them. These two hundred seventy-six were under the influence now of Paul. This was a large company to be on this ship; however, the grain ships were large and frequently carried passengers. Some have interpreted the Greek to mean seventy-six, as this number is found in some ancient manuscript; these manuscripts are not of sufficient weight to change the text.

38 **And when they had eaten enough,**—"Eaten" is from the Greek "koresthentes," and means "to satisfy, to satiate." Hence, they were filled. The first effect of this was seen in renewed activity for work. They began now to lighten the ship. The "wheat" which they now cast out was a part of the cargo which had been reserved probably for provisions. It appears that they had only thrown overboard a part of the cargo as mentioned in verse 18. As they could no longer continue in the ship, it was not necessary to keep the ship burdened with this wheat. They hoped to keep the ship floating until they could reach the shore.

39 **And when it was day, they knew not the land:**—None of the sailors, neither the officers, recognized the land when daylight came. They perceived "a certain bay with a beach." It was such a sandy beach as would suit to run the ship ashore. The main coast was not safe for such an attempt. Some think that it was strange that they did not know the land, for Melita was a well-known island, having an admirable harbor, familiar to Alexandrian sailors; however, these sailors were not at this moment in the harbor, but on a part of the coast which they had never before seen. They held a consultation together to decide what to do; they decided to attempt to run ashore. This required the help of experienced

they left them in the sea, at the same time loosing the bands of the rudders; and hoisting up the foresail to the wind, they made for the beach. 41 But lighting upon a place where two seas met, they ran the vessel aground; and the foreship struck and remained unmoveable, but the stern began to break up by the violence *of the waves.* 42 And the soldiers' counsel was to kill the

sailors, and showed that Paul was right in having the sailors kept on board. (See verse 31.)

40 **And casting off the anchors,**—"Casting off" is from the Greek "perielontes," and literally means "having taken away from around"; that is, all four anchors from around the stern. These were left in the sea; they let the anchors go and the ropes fell down into the sea. They thought that they would have no further use for them. At the same time they loosed the bands of the rudders; the ancient ships were equipped with two rudders; these had been made fast and raised out of the water when the anchors were cast out. Since they now are to attempt to steer the ship toward the beach, they need to let down the rudders again into the water. Next, they hoisted "up the foresail to the wind." "Foresail" is from the Greek "artemona," and scholars have been puzzled as to which sail is indicated; the majority of scholars have agreed that it is "foresail." This does not mean what we understand as the "mainsail." "Wind," as used here, means a breeze, and the change of words seems to imply that there was a lull in the fury of the gale.

41 **But lighting upon a place where two seas met,**—Instead of landing on a smooth, sandy beach, the ship was run and grounded on a mudbank between the small island and the coast. Unexpectedly the ship stuck in this mud bar. The ship did not touch dry land, but stuck fast in the bank over which the water was too shallow to allow the ship to go further; they were still some distance from the shore. The waves swept through the channel behind the island and struck the stern of the ship sideways, and the ship began to break in pieces. Modern scholars who have attempted to trace the journey of Paul have found just such conditions as described here by Luke, showing the accuracy of his description. The front part of the ship was stuck in the mud, while the hind part was in deep water and exposed to the force of the two

prisoners, lest any *of them* should swim out, and escape. 43 But the centurion, desiring to save Paul, stayed them from their purpose; and commanded that they who could swim should cast themselves overboard, and get first to

currents; it seems that the hinder part of the ship was broken off and the entire crew and passengers crowded to the fore part.

42 And the soldiers' counsel was to kill the prisoners,—The soldiers were as cruel as the sailors. (Verse 30.) The sailors were willing to leave the soldiers and prisoners to perish, and now the soldiers want to kill the prisoners. Their excuse was to keep any of them from escaping. The soldiers were responsible for the lives of the prisoners. (Acts 12: 19.) The Roman law made the soldiers answerable with their own lives for the prisoners placed under their charge.

43 But the centurion, desiring to save Paul,—Paul had won the friendship of the centurion; he had been instrumental in saving the entire crew. The centurion was not without gratitude; hence, he would seek some way to save Paul. The centurion was in charge of the soldiers, and they must obey his command. He suggested as an alternative that the soldiers who could swim should "cast themselves overboard" and get to the land first; they could then take charge of the prisoners as they swam to land. The centurion was in full command of the soldiers; he had not in the confusion lost his thoughtfulness and presence of mind. By his suggestion there would be a body of soldiers ready on shore to help those who only could float thither by the aid of something to which they were clinging. We know that Paul had already been shipwrecked three times before this, and had been in the deep a night and a day. (2 Cor. 11: 15.) Hence, we may conclude that he was among those who swam to land. Many think that the centurion's suggestion included not only the soldiers who could swim, but even the prisoners who could swim were commanded to go to shore. It is probable that this suggestion came from Paul, as he had had experience in such trials.

44 and the rest, some on planks,—This strengthens the idea that all who could swim, both soldiers and prisoners, were commanded to do so. The others were to float on planks and such other things as could be had from the ship. It appears that there

the land; 44 and the rest, some on planks, and some on *other* things from the ship. And so it came to pass, that they all escaped safe to the land.

had been some broken pieces of timber from the bulwarks, loose spears, tables, stools, and other pieces of furniture, which could be used by those who could not swim. "All escaped safe to the land." This shows that Paul's prophecy (verse 24) was fulfilled; Paul, the prisoner, is the guide in the voyage, the hero in the shipwreck, and the example to all in calmness.

3. THREE MONTHS IN MELITA
28: 1-10

1 And when we were escaped, then we knew that the island was called ³Melita. 2 And the barbarians showed us no common kindness: for they kindled a fire, and received us all, because of the present rain, and because of

³Some ancient authorities read *Melitene*

1 **And when we were escaped,**—When the crew and all the passengers were safely on shore, they learned that the island was "called Melita." No doubt the sailors would have recognized the island had they approached it in the usual way. This island is now known as "Malta"; it is located about sixty-five or seventy miles south of Cilicia or Sicily; it is nine miles wide and seventeen miles long; it now belongs to Great Britain. At one time it was thought that the shipwreck was near the island of Meleda, but that view is no longer held. The island of Malta fits the description in every way, and was on the direct route to Syracuse and Rhegium.

2 **And the barbarians showed us no common kindness:**— "Barbarians" is from the Greek "barbaroi," and is a word used by the Greeks who called all men "Barbarians" who did not speak Greek (Rom. 1: 14), not "barbarians" as meaning rude or uncivilized; it simply meant "foreign folk." The term originally meant "uncouth repetition," Greek, "barbar," not understood by others. (1 Cor. 14: 11.) Paul used the term with "Scythian" in Col. 3: 11, and here it meant that they were not Christians. The inhabitants of the island showed "no common kindness" to the stranded crew and passengers. They were very kind to the strangers; "they kindled a fire," "received us all," made no distinction between the different classes represented in the company. It was

the cold. 3 But when Paul had gathered a bundle of sticks and laid them on the fire, a viper came out [4]by reason of the heat, and fastened on his hand. 4 And when the barbarians saw the *venomous* creature hanging from his hand, they said one to another, No doubt this man is a murderer, whom, though he hath escaped from the sea, yet Justice hath not suffered to live. 5

[4]Or, *from the heat*

cold, and the natives showed due consideration for the unfortunate ones who had been shipwrecked. The shipwrecked were wet from swimming to land, so the natives made a fire to warm and dry them.

3 **But when Paul had gathered a bundle of sticks**—We see Paul here making himself useful by helping as he had done along the journey before the shipwreck. It appears that he and other prisoners helped to throw overboard some of the cargo to lighten the ship. A poisonous serpent had hidden itself in the driftwood that Paul gathered, and when the wood was placed on the fire, this "viper," which was in a state of torpor because of the winter season, came out and "fastened" on Paul's hand. The serpent was warmed into activity by the heat and bit Paul. It is claimed by some that Luke's record is not true, since there are no poisonous reptiles there now. However, the fact that there are no poisonous vipers on Malta now does not prove that Luke's statements are false. The island now has a larger population than it had at that time. Such animals are driven away and destroyed by civilized man. Many sections of our own country were infested with dangerous animals and poisonous serpents at one time, but now the present-day civilization has driven them away, and many species have even become extinct.

4 **And when the barbarians saw the venomous creature**— The natives on the island were superstitious; they could see that Paul was a prisoner, and they naturally suspected that his crime was no small one; they concluded that he was a murderer, and though he had escaped death in the sea, "yet Justice hath not suffered to live." They personified "Justice," and expected Paul, as a condemned man, to fall down dead. They reasoned that Paul had fortunately escaped drowning in the sea, but now justice had overtaken him. They knew the bite of a viper would produce death.

Howbeit he shook off the creature into the fire, and took no harm. 6 But
they expected that he would have swollen, or fallen down dead suddenly: but
when they were long in expectation and beheld nothing amiss come to him,
they changed of their minds, and said that he was a god.
   7 Now in the neighborhood of that place were lands belonging to the
chief man of the island, named Publius; who received us, and entertained us

---

5 **Howbeit he shook off the creature**—There is nothing in the
Greek to represent "venomous" as used in verse 4, and the translators did not repeat it in verse 5. "Creature" is from the Greek
"therion," and the ancient medical writers applied the word to
"venomous serpent," and especially to vipers. The Greek "therion" has an interesting history. "Treacle" means "molasses," and
comes from "theriake," and means an antidote made from the flesh
of vipers. Paul shook off this viper into the fire and felt no harm
from its bite. Paul was not excited, but had perfect composure,
because he recalled the two promises: (1) that of Christ to his disciples concerning serpents (Mark 16: 18; Luke 10: 19); and (2)
the promise that he should preach the gospel in Rome; therefore,
he would not die before he reached that city.

   6 **But they expected that he would have swollen,**—In their
superstitious minds and the conclusion which they had erro-
neously reached, they expected Paul to fall down dead. As seen
above, they had concluded that he was some notorious criminal.
However, when Paul suffered no harm from the venomous viper,
they went to the other extreme in their reasoning, and "said that
he was a god." They waited long enough for the poison to take
effect, and when it did not, they easily jumped to the extreme position that he was "a god." They expected Paul's hand or body to
"have swollen"; this was the usual effect of the bite of a viper,
making itself apparent in a very short time. "Swollen" is from the
Greek verb "pimpremi," which means "to blow, to burn, to in-
flame, to cause to swell." They also expected Paul to fall down
dead. The two common results of the viper's bite were a swollen
body and death. Paul did not suffer either one, so "they changed
their minds."

   7 **Now in the neighborhood of that place**—Near the place
where the shipwrecked crew and passengers landed was "the chief
man of the island"; he was called "Publius." Publius is called

three days courteously. 8 And it was so, that the father of Publius lay sick of fever and dysentery: unto whom Paul entered in, and prayed, and laying his hands on him healed him. 9 And when this was done, the rest also that had diseases in the island came, and were cured: 10 who also honored us

---

"Protos," which was the official title of the ruler of the island. He received Paul and his companions, Luke and Aristarchus, and showed great favor to them by entertaining them. It is not known whether Julius, the centurion, or the other officials were invited. They were entertained for "three days courteously." Some think that the entire company was entertained by Publius; it is very likely that he would invite Julius, as Paul was in his charge as a prisoner.

8 **And it was so, that the father of Publius lay sick**—Publius' father lay sick of a fever. "Sick" is from the Greek "sunechomenon," which means "held together"; "fever" is from the Greek "puretois," and means intermittent attacks. "Dysentery" is from the Greek "dusenterioi," and is another medical term which Luke uses; these two diseases are commonly found together. Paul went into Publius' father and prayed, and laid his hands on him and healed him. Paul followed the same course as Peter in the case of Tabitha. (Acts 9: 36-43.) Paul was given miraculous power on this occasion to heal Publius' father. Luke, who was a physician, was with Paul, but nothing is said of his prescribing anything for the sick man. This is another fulfillment of the promise made by Jesus in Mark 16: 18.

9, 10 **And when this was done,**—The fact that Paul had cured Publius' father was speedily made known throughout the island. Nothing is said about Paul's preaching the gospel; that is taken for granted, and the miracles which he performed confirmed his words. His preaching and working miracles went together. As the people learned that there was one who could heal all these diseases, they brought the afflicted and diseased to Paul and he cured them. Naturally the ruler of the island and the people would bestow great honors on one who had such power as to heal instantly the disease. They showed their honors in a very substantial way, for when Paul and the others sailed from the island, "they put on board such things as we needed." It should be remembered that the shipwreck had lost everything in the sea; not only Paul and

with many honors; and when we sailed, they put on board such things as we needed.

---

other Christians received help from the natives, but all who needed help received clothing and provisions. These tokens of respect showed the kindness and appreciation of the natives. The good things which came to the soldiers and sailors came because of Paul. Naturally, the gospel would be commended to all, as Paul took no honor or credit to himself; he always gave his Lord honor and credit for what he taught and did.

SECTION EIGHT

PAUL AT ROME
28: 11-31

1. ARRIVAL AT ROME
28: 11-16

11 And after three months we set sail in a ship of Alexandria which had wintered in the island, whose sign was [1]The Twin Brothers. 12 And touching at Syracuse, we tarried there three days. 13 And from thence we [2]made a

[1]Gr. *Dioscuri*
[2]Some ancient authorities read *cast loose*

---

11 **And after three months we set sail**—It was now about February; the Day of Atonement or Fast occurred on the tenth of Tisri (September-October). (Lev. 16: 29; 23: 27; Num. 29: 7.) This day occurred in A.D. 59 on October 5, and in A.D. 60 it occurred on September 23. We do not know how long after the Day of Atonement before the ship left Fair Havens (Acts 27: 8); then there came the fourteen days of Acts 27: 27, bringing us near the end of October or the beginning of November. Three months from this would be the beginning of February. This was a little early for general navigation on the Mediterranean Sea at that time. The crew, of course, was anxious to sail at the earliest opportunity; they were anxious to reach their destination. There was another ship in the harbor from Alexandria; it had wintered "in the island," and since it probably belonged to the same company to which the stranded crew belonged, they prepared to sail on this vessel. Its sign was "The Twin Brothers," or Castor and Pollux. Castor and Pollux were deities of sailors whose figures were painted on one side of the ship; this sign was the name of the ship. Hence, Paul and his company board another grain ship of Alexandria bound for Rome.

12 **And touching at Syracuse,**—The ship left the island of Melita or Malta and sailed nearly due north to Syracuse; this was a direct course. The distance from Malta to Syracuse was about eighty miles; Syracuse was the principal place on the island of Sicily. They remained three days here, and Paul may have found some Christians with whom he could visit during this time. Ships

circuit, and arrived at Rhegium: and after one day a south wind sprang up, and on the second day we came to Puteoli; 14 where we found brethren, and were entreated to tarry with them seven days: and so we came to Rome. 15

from Alexandria to Italy usually stopped here; the stay there of three days was probably waiting for a favorable wind.

13 **And from thence we made a circuit,**—"Circuit" is from the Greek "perielthontes," and means "to go around," but here it appears to mean "casting loose"; the ship was not able to make a straight course to Rhegium; this was a town on the Italian side of the Straits of Messina. We are told that the ancient coins of Rhegium exhibit Castor and Pollux as twin brothers. After one day a south wind began, and on the second day they arrived at Puteoli. The distance from Rhegium to Puteoli was about one hundred eighty miles, and if the ship sailed seven knots, or seven nautical miles an hour, it would require about twenty-six hours to make the voyage. Puteoli was the customary port for the Alexandrian grain ships. "Puteoli" is derived from the springs "Putei," which abound there, or from the bad odor of the waters. It was the principal port south of Rome. Paul could look upon the well-known beauty of the Bay of Naples, and upon Vesuvius.

14 **where we found brethren,**—We know from the list of names recorded in Rom. 16 that the Christian brethren were at this time numerous in Rome. It appears that there were also Christians at Puteoli. This is the only mention of a congregation in Italy outside of Rome. Paul and his company tarried here seven days. Many have thought that he tarried there to spend the Lord's day with them as in Acts 20: 6, 7 at Troas and in Acts 21: 4 at Tyre. It appears that the centurion granted Paul much liberty. This is to be expected since Paul had proved himself to be an extraordinary prisoner, and had saved the lives of the centurion and others. After remaining there the seven days they came to Rome. This bare statement of the fact of their arrival is made by Luke to show the end of their journey. Luke, the historian, now turns aside in the next sentence to mention circumstances connected with their route from Puteoli. This is the climax of the book of Acts (Acts 19: 21; 23: 11), but it is not the close of Paul's career. Many scholars have contended that a new paragraph should begin

And from thence the brethren, when they heard of us, came to meet us as far as The Market of Appius and The Three Taverns; whom when Paul saw, he thanked God, and took courage.

16 And when we entered into Rome, [3]Paul was suffered to abide by himself with the soldier that guarded him.

[3]Some ancient authorities insert *the centurion delivered the prisoners to the Chief of the camp: but &c.*

with verse 15. Paul had now reached Rome, but not as he had at one time expected. (Rom. 15: 22-29.)

15 **And from thence the brethren,**—The news that Paul was on his way to Rome reached Rome or the church there before Paul arrived. It appears that the brethren from Puteoli forwarded the news to Rome, and the brethren from Rome came to meet Paul. Paul's meeting with the brethren refreshed him. (Acts 18: 5; Rom. 1: 11, 12; 15: 32; 2 Cor. 13; 7: 6.) Some of them came as far as "The Market of Appius," which was about forty-three miles from Rome. Others met him at "The Three Taverns," which was about thirty-three miles from Rome. It appears that there were two separate groups of brethren from Rome, one in advance of the other. Among these were possibly Aquila and Priscilla and others named in Rom. 16. We see here two very distinct charactersitics of Paul—the appreciation of help derived from the presence of friends and the gratitude which such services inspired in him. Paul saw that Christ was already at Rome; he was encouraged at the thought that Rome was receptive of the gospel.

16 **And when we entered into Rome,**—Luke is still with Paul; this is seen by the use of the pronoun "we." Paul was now in Rome, but a prisoner. Julius, the centurion, into whose hands Paul had been committed, now turned him over to the proper authorities. Some very ancient authorities insert in the text "the centurion delivered the prisoners to the Chief of the camp"; however, Paul was permitted "to abide by himself with the soldier that guarded him." It is not certain who was the chief officer to whom Paul was committed; some think that he was Burrus who was prefect of the Praetorian Guard from A.D. 51 to 62; others think that he was turned over to the captain of the peregrini. We may be sure that the centurion, Julius, recommended Paul very highly to the officer who took charge of him. The kind terms in which Festus

reported the case, and Paul's noble conduct and helpfulness on the voyage, would combine to influence the officer to grant to Paul every privilege and comfort within his power. Paul first retired to a friend's house (verse 23), and then rented an apartment for himself (verse 30). Wherever he was he was fastened by a chain to a soldier. Prisoners with light offenses charged against them were granted many favors. Paul tells us that he gradually became known to the greater number of the imperial bodyguard. (Phil. 1 : 12, 13.) Different soldiers relieved each other of this duty from time to time; this gave Paul an opportunity to preach the gospel to many of them.

2. INTERVIEW WITH THE JEWS
28 : 17-29

17 And it came to pass, that after three days he called together ⁴those that were the chief of the Jews: and when they were come together, he said unto them, I, brethren, though I had done nothing against the people, or the customs of our fathers, yet was delivered prisoner from Jerusalem into the

⁴Or, *those that were of the Jews first*

---

17 **And it came to pass, that after three days**—Probably the "three days" were spent in arranging a lodging for Paul and conferring with Christians who had long waited for him to visit them. Paul called together "those that were the chief of the Jews"; this by some is translated "those that were of the Jews first," and the prominent Gentiles later. However, it seems clear that it is better to regard the chiefs of the Jews, such as rulers and elders of the synagogue and heads of the principal Jewish families that had settled in Rome; it may have included also the scribes and some of the wealthier traders among the Jews. There were many Jews in Rome at this time. There were seven synagogues in Rome at this time. There was not room for Paul to receive all at the same time, and he would naturally invite those who were best informed and most influential. Paul being a prisoner and chained to a soldier could not go to any of their synagogues; hence, he must invite them to come to him. When they came together Paul made it clear that he had "nothing against the people, or the customs of our fathers." He had not come to Rome to prefer any charges against the Jews; he had appealed to Caesar in order to save his

hands of the Romans: 18 who, when they had examined me, desired to set me at liberty, because there was no cause of death in me. 19 But when the Jews spake against it, I was constrained to appeal unto Caesar; not that I had aught whereof to accuse my nation. 20 For this cause therefore did I ⁵entreat you to see and to speak with *me*: for because of the hope of Israel I

⁵Or, *call for you, to see and to speak with you*

own life. He had been delivered as a prisoner from Jerusalem and had been forced to make an appeal to Caesar.

18 **who, when they had examined me,**—Although Paul was a prisoner and under appeal to Caesar, he had done nothing to his people; the Romans, after examining him, had declared him innocent of any violation of Roman law or Jewish law; he had appealed to Caesar, not to accuse his own race, but to save his own life; he was a prisoner because he had accepted Jesus as the Messiah of his nation, and regarded his resurrection from the dead as evidence of the resurrection and of the Messiahship of Christ. How could Paul say that he had been delivered by the Jews into the Roman authorities? Lysias, the captain, had rescued Paul from a mob of Jews; he had been tried before Felix, then before Festus, and last before Agrippa. These Roman officials would have released Paul had it not been for the clamor of the Jews.

19 **But when the Jews spake against it,**—The verdict of the Roman authorities in each case was that Paul was not worthy of death or guilty of any crime. They wished to release Paul, but the Jews "spake against it," and Paul was forced to make his appeal to Caesar in order to save his own life. Paul speaks with kindness and courtesy about the opposition of the Jews to him. He uses conciliatory words and phrases such as "brethren," "the people," "our fathers," "the hope of Israel," and "not that I had aught whereof to accuse my nation." Paul did not wish to be an instrument in the hands of Roman tyranny; he knew the hardships his people had suffered in Rome, and that at different times they had been banished from Rome.

20 **For this cause therefore did I entreat you**—Here Paul gives his reason for sending for them or inviting them to come to him. He desired to speak to them and clear himself of whatever false reports may have been sent to Rome, or that Jews visiting

am bound with this chain. 21 And they said unto him, We neither received letters from Judaea concerning thee, nor did any of the brethren come hither and report or speak any harm of thee. 22 But we desire to hear of thee what thou thinkest: for as concerning this sect, it is known to us that everywhere it is spoken against.

Jerusalem from Rome may have heard in Jerusalem about him. Paul is a prisoner in chains; he must explain why he is a prisoner. He is forced to make his defense. He is a prisoner "because of the hope of Israel." The hope for which he suffered was twofold: (1) the expectation of the Messiah as bringing in the kingdom of heaven, which was cherished by every Israelite; (2) the hope of the resurrection from the dead, which he proclaimed as attested to by the resurrection, which proved that Jesus was the Christ, the Son of God.

21 **And they said unto him,**—After hearing Paul's explanation, some among them spoke and assured Paul that they had "neither received letters from Judaea" concerning Paul, nor "did any of the brethren" from Jerusalem make any report or "speak any harm" of him. "Letters" is from the Greek "grammata," which means an official document from the Sanhedrin containing charges against Paul. They do not mean to say that they had never heard of Paul, but that no official charges had been preferred against him in any way, either written or oral. The Jews in Judea had no definite reason to communicate with the Jews in Rome respecting Paul; they did not expect Paul to ever go to Rome; and since Paul's appeal to Caesar, it would have been almost impossible for them to have sent messengers who would arrive before Paul. Paul had sailed toward the very close of navigation for that season on the Mediterranean, and others could not have left Caesarea till the following spring. Again, it may be possible that after Paul's imprisonment of two years at Caesarea the enmity of the Jews had cooled off.

22 **But we desire to hear of thee**—They had heard something about this new "sect" which had risen among the Jews; it was everywhere spoken against. They had received no favorable report concerning it. They are to be commended in their fairness to hear Paul's side. "Sect" is from the Greek "haireseos," and is the same from which our word "heresy" comes. This would indicate that

---

23 And when they had appointed him a day, they came to him into his lodging in great number; to whom he expounded *the matter*, testifying the kingdom of God, and persuading them concerning Jesus, both from the law of Moses and from the prophets, from morning till evening. 24 And some

---

the number of Christians in Rome was small. If the edict of Claudius or the expulsion of the Jews from Rome (Acts 18: 2) was due to disturbance over Christ, then even in Rome the Jews had special reason for hostility toward Christians. Their language here indicates that there was a sharply drawn line of cleavage between Jews and Christians. Paul did not admit that Christianity was a "sect"; this is the way the Jews regarded it. Paul did not .egard Christianity as a new religion, nor as a substitute for the Jewish religion, but rather as a lawful and rightful successor of the Jewish religion; the old foretold the new; its hopes centered in the Messiah. Paul declared that the Messiah had come, and he would proclaim this flower and fruit of the old faith.

23 **And when they had appointed him a day,**—"Appointed" is from the Greek "taxamenoi," and means a formal arrangement, as in Matt. 28: 16, when Jesus appointed the mountain as the meeting place in Galilee; the Jews fixed a day, but Paul likely made suggestions. They came into Paul's lodging place, not his own hired house (verse 30), but to a house where he stayed as a guest. A larger number of Jews came at this time than had come at first. Paul had told them that for the sake of the Messianic hope of Israel he was bound with the chain that held him; he now expounded that this hope was from the Old Testament, and showed how at each stage it was fulfilled in the kingdom of Jesus the Christ. He spoke what Festus and Agrippa had refused to hear (Acts 26: 22-28); and his audience at this time, or at least part of it, was sympathetic, for they remained a long time with him. "Expounded" is from the Greek "exetitheto," and means "to set forth," as in Acts 11: 4 and 18: 26. Paul set forth the whole matter, testifying about the things of "the kingdom of God," and "persuading them concerning Jesus." How far his "persuading" was effective must be determined by the context, though the word itself sometimes means to convince. "Persuading" is from the Greek "peithon," and means "to persuade, to reason with, to con-

believed the things which were spoken, and some disbelieved. 25 And when they agreed not among themselves, they departed after that Paul had spoken one word, Well spake the Holy Spirit through Isaiah the prophet unto your fathers, 26 saying,

---

vince." This was a golden opportunity for Paul, and he drew his arguments from "the law of Moses" and "from the prophets." All believed the law and the prophets; there was common ground here; so Paul placed the prophecies of the kingdom of God, and of the Messiah to come, side by side with the life, death, and resurrection of Jesus; he showed the Jews how perfectly Jesus had fulfilled the law and the prophets.

24 And some believed the things which were spoken,—Here we have the results of Paul's preaching to this goodly company of Jews. They divide themselves into two companies: (1) those who believed his preaching; (2) those who disbelieved. We have no way of telling which was the larger company. "Believed," here, is from the Greek "epeithonto"; this is not the usual Greek word employed for "believed"; it leads to the same state of mind through a crisis of being convinced or persuaded. "Disbelieved" is from the Greek "epistoun," and means "to disbelieve, continue to disbelieve." Hearers usually divide themselves into the two classes—believers and disbelievers.

25 And when they agreed not among themselves,—"Agreed not" is from the Greek "asumphonoi ontes," which means "without symphony, out of harmony, dissonant, discordant." The figure is that they were like the various parts of a tune set to different keys; they were discordant, inharmonious. Who agreed not? It is difficult to determine whether those who disbelieved were in such discordant attitudes, or whether those who believed and those who disbelieved were so discordant. The context that follows leads us to infer that the disbelievers were inharmonious. Before the gathering was dismissed, Paul spoke and quoted the prophet Isaiah, and applied the prophecy to the disbelievers. The prophecy here quoted is from Isa. 6: 9, 10; no passage is quoted so often in the New Testament as this. It occurs five times in Matt. 13: 14; Mark 4: 12; Luke 8: 10; John 12: 40 and here. Jesus had used

⁶Go thou unto this people, and say,
By hearing ye shall hear, and shall in no wise understand;
And seeing ye shall see, and shall in no wise perceive:
27 For this people's heart is waxed gross,
And their ears are dull of hearing,
And their eyes they have closed;
Lest haply they should perceive with their eyes,
And hear with their ears,
And understand with their heart,
And should turn again,
And I should heal them.

⁶Is. 6. 9, 10

this quotation from Isaiah and applied it to the Jews; Paul now makes the same application of it.

26 **saying, Go thou unto this people,**—The quotation used by Paul here from Isaiah had been used by Christ as describing the spiritual state of the Jews of Palestine (Matt. 13: 13; Mark 4: 12; Luke 8: 10), while John (12: 40) reproduces them as giving the solution of the apparent failure of Christ's personal ministry. It appears that Paul was following Christ in the use of this quotation. They should hear words with the outward organ of hearing, but they would not understand the real meaning; their failure was due to a stubborn disposition of mind, and not a lack of mental ability. However, a stubborn heart led to deeper dullness of hearing, greater blindness, and obstinacy of mind; these were so great that they would not turn to God. Their willfull rejection of the Messiah brought to them a hardness of heart.

27 **For this people's heart is waxed gross,**—Literally, this means that their hearts had "become fat" as applied to the body; hence, they were dull, stupid, so that it was difficult to make an impression on them. They did not wish to see; they had closed their eyes. If they had seen, they would have had to give up their sinful pleasures, their selfish living, and their wicked ways. They would have had to separate themselves from friends and be persecuted, suffer, and perhaps die for the sake of Christ. If they should hear and see and understand, they would turn around and go back to God. If they should do this, God would heal them, cleanse them of their sin. Within about ten years from this time Jerusalem was completely destroyed, the temple broken down and

28 Be it known therefore unto you, that this salvation of God is sent unto the Gentiles: they will also hear.

---

[7]Some ancient authorities insert ver. 29 *And when he had said these words, the Jews departed, having much disputing among themselves*

---

obliterated, and the Jews were no longer a nation. They did not see the certain doom that awaited them for their rejection of the Messiah.

28 **Be it known therefore unto you,**—Here Paul sadly sounds a note of warning to these disbelieving Jews. Since they rejected the Messiah and the salvation that came through him, Paul, the apostle to the Gentiles, turned from them to the Gentiles. He had the assurance that the Gentiles would hear. Paul's words here are similar to the ones that he had spoken under like circumstances at Antioch in Pisidia. (Acts 13: 46.) Paul must preach the gospel; "woe is unto me, if I preach not the gospel." (1 Cor. 9: 16.) If the Jews will not hear him, he must turn to those who would hear him. The Jews could destroy themselves, but they could not destroy the kingdom of God or prevent the Messiah from reigning over his kingdom. The Gentiles would hear. "They will also hear." These are the last words of Paul recorded in Acts; they are the last words of the historian Luke of his life. In these words there is a note of triumph blending with a note of sadness; he regretted that his people would not hear the gospel and accept the Messiah and be saved; this brings sadness to him. He rejoiced that the Gentiles would hear and be saved. His preaching would not be in vain to them.

(29 Some of the best ancient manuscripts do not have this verse; hence, it is left out in the American Standard Revision. However, some ancient authorities insert it as follows: "And when he had said these words, the Jews departed, having much disputing among themselves." It describes accurately, doubtless, what actually took place. Some think that this verse was written on the margin to relieve the apparent abruptness of the narrative between verses 28 and 30, and has been inserted in the text of some manuscript by some transcriber who thought it had been accidentally omitted from the text of his copy.)

3. PAUL A PRISONER AT ROME TWO YEARS
28 : 30, 31

30 And he abode two whole years in his own hired dwelling, and received all that went in unto him, 31 preaching the kingdom of God, and teaching

---

30 **And he abode two whole years**—Paul has now changed his abiding place from some temporary abode to a more permanent one. Luke gives no account of these years. He had brought Paul to Rome; the gospel had now reached the center of the known world. This is what concerned Luke most. All this time Paul was a prisoner of state; the expenses incurred were probably defrayed by friends at Rome and in the provinces. Paul was, during the day, chained to a soldier, and probably in the night two soldiers watched him, according to the sentence of the Roman law. The New Testament contains four of Paul's epistles which were written while in prison at Rome—the epistles to the Ephesians, Colossians, and Philippians, and a short letter to Philemon. From these letters we learn that Luke, Timothy, Epaphras, Mark, Aristarchus, and Tychicus were among the friends who, during the whole or part of this time, were with Paul. During "two whole years" Paul dwelt in "his own hired dwelling"; the Greek "misthomati," from which we get "hired," means "hired for a price." We do not know anything further about Paul's hired "dwelling." We may be sure that Paul lived as economically as possible since he was dependent upon the gifts of Christians. (Phil. 4: 14, 15.) As a prisoner, he could not sustain himself as he did at Corinth and Ephesus. (Acts 18: 3; 20: 34; 2 Cor. 11: 9.) Paul was a prisoner two years at Caesarea before he came to Rome, and now he has been a prisoner two years in Rome. We do not know why his trial was delayed; his appeal would have to wait its turn. When his case came up for trial the records of it from Festus may have been lost in the shipwreck; hence, an order for an official copy would have to be sent for from Caesarea, and the hearing postponed until the copy of the record arrived. Hence, Paul's case would lose its place in the court calendar and there would be a longer delay in reaching it again. Paul's frequent references in his prison epistles as a prisoner confirms this view. (Eph. 6: 19, 20; Phil. 1: 1, 13; Col. 1: 1; 4: 3, 18; Phile. 1.)

the things concerning the Lord Jesus Christ with all boldness, none forbidding him.

---

31 preaching the kingdom of God,—Paul had great privileges as a prisoner; his friends could visit him and receive instruction from him; he had opportunity to write a number of letters to the churches. He preached "the kingdom of God" to all who came to him. "Preaching" is from the Greek "kerusson," and "teaching" comes from the Greek "didaskon." "Preaching" means "heralding," while "teaching" means "instructing." He was not hindered in this work. He was allowed complete freedom of speech, and he used his liberty to speak out boldly to all who came to him to hear the gospel. He tells us himself that other Christians who saw a bound prisoner speak so freely were encouraged by his example and the gospel was spread. (Phil. 1 : 12-14.)

none forbidding him.—Paul had now been a prisoner four years—two years were spent in Caesarea and two more years have been spent in the Roman prison. Perhaps he spent a longer time than the two years mentioned here. Paul continued faithfully, diligently, and boldly to proclaim salvation through Christ Jesus. Luke has now completed his first purpose; he wrote to assure Theophilus of the certainty of the facts concerning "all that Jesus began both to do and to teach, until the day in which he was received up, after that he had given commandment through the Holy Spirit unto the apostles whom he had chosen." (Acts 1: 1, 2; see Luke 1: 4.) He now closes his book. With Paul at Rome the gospel has spread and reached a climax; from Jerusalem it has won its way from city to city, province to province, over Jewish hatred and prejudice and Gentile idolatry to the metropolis of the world. Luke's record is a triumphal spread of Christianity until it has covered the civilized world; his closing words are a suitable conclusion for the book of Acts.

Although Paul was a prisoner in Rome for "two whole years," he was not idle. A portion of the New Testament scriptures were written while he was a prisoner. It is interesting to recount the many blessings and rich productions that have come from prison walls and chains. Savonarola wrote his Commentaries on Psalms 31 and 51 during his month of imprisonment before his execution; this shows that, though he had much spiritual conflict, neither his faith nor his comfort yielded to his persecution. Francis Baker composed the hymn, "Jerusalem, My Happy Home," while a prisoner in the tower; Walter Raleigh wrote his "History of the World" and some poems while a prisoner in the same tower. John Bunyan wrote his "Pilgrim's Progress" while he languished in Bedford jail. Paul, while imprisoned in Rome, wrote four epistles—Ephesians, Philippians, Colossians, and Philemon. Paul crowned his labors by the composition of these books of the New Testament as a prisoner for Christ Jesus; thus in prison Paul did some of the most important work of his life—work that has rendered him immortal in its usefulness. He did not spend his time in murmuring and complaining, but wrote from this prison to the Philippians to "rejoice in the Lord always: again I will say, Rejoice." (Phil. 4: 4.) Furthermore, it is interesting to note Paul's companions and visitors during his imprisonment. Rom. 16: 3-15 contains a list of salutations of Paul to Christians in Rome; this was written probably thirteen years before Paul reached Rome. In this list he mentions twenty-three men and eight women, of whom three are spoken of as his kinsmen and four in connection with their households. In addition to these, Paul mentions in his epistles as his special companions and friends the following: Timothy (Col. 1: 1); Epaphras, a fellow prisoner (Phile. 23); Onesimus, a slave (Phile. 10); Tychicus, a minister who delivered the epistles to the Ephesians and Colossians (Eph. 6: 21, 22; Col. 4: 7, 8); Aristarchus (Col. 4: 10); Mark, the writer of the gospel which bears his name (Col. 4: 10); Justus, who is also called "Jesus" (Col. 4: 11); Luke, the author of Luke and the Acts (Col. 4: 14); Demas (Phile. 24); Epaphroditus, who brought a gift to Paul from the Philippians and carried back Paul's letter to them (Phil. 2: 25; 4: 18); and some member of Caesar's household (Phil. 4: 22).

PAUL'S RELEASE, SECOND IMPRISONMENT, AND DEATH

Paul had made an appeal to Caesar; this brought him to Rome. He was retained a prisoner in Rome for at least two years, waiting for his trial. What was the outcome or final decision of this trial? The Acts closes before he had his trial. Some think that he continued in prison for a long time and finally died a martyr. Some good scholars doubt his release at this trial. They claim that since the New Testament is silent on the question, and that early profane history is uncertain as to the results, it cannot be determined with any degree of accuracy as to the final result. However, others are sure that Paul was released and preached the gospel for some years, and was finally imprisoned the second time in Rome and suffered martyrdom. Those who have so concluded base their conclusions on several important facts and inferences. In Paul's prison letters we learn that he expected to be released. (Phil. 1: 25; 2: 23, 24; Phile. 22.) We do not know whether Paul entertained this hope as a matter of judgment or whether he had special revelation by the Holy Spirit. It does not matter, since a fair conclusion from these scriptures warrants us in believing that he hoped to regain his liberty. Moreover, Clement, a disciple and companion of Paul, affirms that Paul, before his martyrdom, traveled "to the boundary of the West," which is an expression applied to the trans-Alpine country; some think that he even visited Spain. Eusebius, the father of church history, states the common belief of the early churches that Paul went forth to proclaim the gospel and afterwards came to Rome a second time and suffered martyrdom under Nero. It is thought that during his second imprisonment he wrote Second Timothy. The close of Paul's life is veiled from our eyes, but no cloud dims, or ever can dim, the splendor of the services of that life for God and for humanity. Coleridge has described that life as being "cultivated, refined, heroic, versatile, magnetic; a born interpreter of truth, a leader of men, a creator of life, and an epoch-making genius."

BIBLIOGRAPHY

Abbot, Lyman: Illustrated Commentary on the Acts.

Boles, H. Leo: Commentary on Matthew.

Boles, H. Leo: Elam's Notes on Uniform Lessons (1929-1931).

Boles, H. Leo: Adult Quarterly Uniform Lessons (1932-1940).

Bosworth, E. I.: Studies in the Acts and Epistles.

Clark, G. W.: Harmonic Arrangements of the Acts of the Apostles.

Clarke, Adam: Commentary (Volume 5).

Cowles, Henry: Acts of the Apostles with Notes.

Crawford, C. C.: Sermon Outlines on Acts.

Dick, John: Lectures on Acts of the Apostles.

Du Veil, C. M.: A Commentary on the Acts of the Apostles.

Gospel Advocate: Volume I to Volume LXXXI.

Hackett, H. B.: Commentary on Acts of the Apostles.

Harnack, Adolf: Date of the Acts and the Synoptic Gospels.

Henry, Matthew: Commentary (Volume 5).

Howson, J. S., and Spence, H. D. M.: The Acts of the Apostles.

Jacobus, M. W.: Notes, Critical and Explanatory, on Acts of the Apostles.

Jamison, Fausset, and Brown: Commentary on the Bible (Volume 3).

Jones, J. C.: Studies in the Acts of the Apostles.

Lindsay, T. M.: The Acts of the Apostles (two volumes).

Lipscomb, David: Commentary on Acts of the Apostles.

Luccock, H. E.: The Acts of the Apostles.

Lumby, J. R.: The Acts of the Apostles.

McGarvey, J. W.: New Commentary on Acts (two volumes).

Meyer, H. A. W: Critical and Exegetical Handbook to the Acts of the Apostles.

Morrison, Thomas: The Acts of the Apostles.

Overbeck, Franz: Introduction to the Acts of the Apostles (two volumes).

Peloubet, F. N.: Teachers' Commentary on the Acts.

Pendleton, J. M.: Brief Notes on Acts.

Pierson, A. T.: The New Acts of the Apostles.

Plumptre, E. H.: The Acts of the Apostles.

Rice, E. W.: Commentary on the Acts.

Ripley, H. J.: The Acts of the Apostles with Notes.

Robertson, A. T.: Word Pictures in the New Testament (Volume 3).

Schaff, Philip: The Acts of the Apostles.

Sitterly, C. F.: The Acts of the Apostles.

Stifler, J. M.: An Introduction to the Study of Acts of the Apostles.

Summers, T. O.: Commentary on the Acts of the Apostles.

Taylor, Malachi: Notes on Reading in the Book of the Acts.

Thomas, W. H. G: The Acts of the Apostles.

Trollope, W.: Commentary on Acts of the Apostles.

Vincent, M. R.: Word Studies in the New Testament (Volume I).

Whedon, D. D.: Commentary on the New Testament (Acts).

INDEX TO SUBJECTS